Art and

Architecture

of Viceregal

Latin America,

1521–1821

Other titles on Latin America available from the University of New Mexico Press:

Series advisory editor: Lyman L. Johnson,
University of North Carolina at Charlotte

Art and Architecture
of Viceregal Latin America,
1521–1821

Kelly Donahue-Wallace

UNIVERSITY OF NEW MEXICO PRESS ❈ ALBUQUERQUE

© 2008 by the University of New Mexico Press

All rights reserved. Published 2008

18 17 16 15 14   3 4 5 6 7

Printed in the United States of America

Library of Congress Cataloging-in-Publication Data

Donahue-Wallace, Kelly, 1968–

Art and architecture of viceregal Latin America : 1521–1821 / Kelly Donahue-Wallace.

— 1st ed.

p. cm. — (Diálogos)

Includes bibliographical references and index.

ISBN 978-0-8263-3459-6 (pbk. : alk. paper)

1. Art, Colonial—Latin America.

2. Art, Latin American.

I. Title.

N6502.2.D66 2008

709.8'09031—dc22

2007040603

Book design and type composition by Melissa Tandysh

Composed in 11.25/13.5 Fournier MT Std

Display type is Avenir

FOR RANDY, ANNIE, AND TAD

CONTENTS

Color plates follow page 132

ix

LIST OF FIGURES

COLOR PLATES

follow page 132

PREFACE

My interest in authoring a book on colonial Latin American art and architecture grew over several years of teaching the material to undergraduates. Even as colleges and universities added Latin America's viceregal period to their curricula, we nevertheless lacked adequate texts to accompany the course. The purpose of *Art and Architecture of Viceregal Latin America*, therefore, is to serve the college classroom, as well as the general reader looking for a broad survey of this fascinating and complicated era.

Like any text of its kind, *Art and Architecture of Viceregal Latin America* relies on a vast array of learned authorities from around the globe. My goal in writing has been to bring together their research, frequently presenting a variety of interpretations of the objects and monuments, to offer readers a summary of some, though definitely not all, of the scholarship on the topic. This book is particularly indebted to the foundational giants of colonial art history. These scholars are too many to mention here, but include George Kubler, Francisco de la Maza, Howard Wethey, Pal Keleman, Manuel Toussaint, Martin Soria, and Santiago Sebastián. The text also relies on the inspired writings of more recent scholars whose publications have enriched this still underresearched field of study. Among this group are Elisa Vargaslugo, José de Mesa, Teresa Gisbert, Clara Bargellini, Tom Cummins, Carolyn Dean, Susan Verdi Webster, Jaime Cuadriello, Elena Isabel Estrada de Gerlero, Donna Pierce, Marcus Burke, Gustavo Curiel, Luisa Elena Alcalá, Michael Schreffler, Ilona Katzew, Barbara Mundy, Dana Leibsohn, Sofia Sanabrais, and Guillermo Tovar de Teresa.

Since *Art and Architecture of Viceregal Latin America* began its life in my classroom, its organization and tone reflect my approach to teaching. The book maintains a chronological presentation because there are fundamental differences between the early and later colonial periods, particularly between the contact or evangelical era and those that followed. A less natural aspect of the book's organization is its presentation of the works by medium. This separation seems particularly awkward in the discussions of sixteenth-century art, with architecture and its sculpture in one chapter and mural painting in another, even though viewers experienced all three at once. In the writing process, however, it became clear that these issues needed to be considered separately so as not to gloss over

xv

aspects of production, function, and reception associated with each medium or to overwhelm the reader with an excessively long chapter.

Another aspect of the book that reflects my teaching style is the decision to include fewer objects and monuments than found in the typical broad survey, but to discuss these at greater length. Too often texts of this kind present laundry lists of objects and monuments, but say very little about them. Students come away with the impression that art history amounts to little more than memorization of titles, artists, and dates. This text, therefore, includes lengthy analyses of selected works, considering materials, labor, forms, iconography, function, and reception so that the reader may appreciate the work more profoundly and, hopefully, apply the information to similar objects and monuments. It likewise takes time to set the historical and social stage for the works, since colonial art, like all cultural products, participated in its society.

Art and Architecture of Viceregal Latin America has an uneasy relationship with period labels, both those borrowed from Europe for New World artistic production and ones created anew to describe local stylistic trends. There is ample reason to abandon these homogenizing labels. Terms like Renaissance, mannerism, and baroque were defined by past art historians using selected Italian examples, which consequently left all other art to appear to fall short of their aesthetic standards; this is particularly true in Latin America. Colonial art clearly illustrates the inherent problems of stylistic categories and the histories of art constructed around them. On the other hand, avoiding stylistic labels entirely means removing Latin American viceregal art from Western art history that, despite criticism, remains tied to stylistic chronologies. I therefore employ these labels, albeit sparingly, so that readers familiar with European art may appreciate the similarities and differences found in the Latin American forms. Each section offers brief summaries of formal characteristics but also points to problems inherent in the homogenizing labels. The book does not, however, spend time associating New Spanish or Peruvian artists with European schools, for example labeling painters in late sixteenth-century Mexico City as followers of Luis de Morales or Peruvian painters as students of Francisco de Zurbarán. Nor does it consider imported printed and painted models more than in passing. Too much attention has been dedicated to the imported prints or paintings that may have inspired colonial objects. The more significant information in my opinion is what role the building, painting, or sculpture played in its own context.

The text dedicates a great deal of time to the colonial environment. Each work is considered as a colonial product, participating in a viceregal society that was invariably informed in virtually every area by the fact of colonization. This approach may strike some as just as false as early attempts to demonstrate the exclusively European qualities of viceregal art and architecture or later nationalist writings that declared the uniquely American features of colonial objects. There are, of course, works that share form, iconography, and function with contemporary European examples, just as there are works that clearly reveal indigenous traditions; both examples may have been produced simultaneously and even for the very same patron. And this is precisely my point. This volume makes the basic assumption that the objects and monuments created in the Viceroyalties of New Spain, Peru, New Granada, and La Plata were the products of a colonial situation. They must be studied in light of that fact and for how they represent their makers' negotiation of the colonial circumstances, be it the indigenous painter recording his community's history, or the émigré academic sculpting an equestrian monument of the Spanish king.

Finally, the text addresses only the Spanish viceroyalties in the Americas; it does not consider Portugal's colony in Brazil. The decision to focus solely on the Spanish empire reflects the philosophies described above. While Brazilian objects and monuments share many formal, thematic, and functional characteristics with similar works from the Spanish viceroyalties, they are nevertheless products of a different colonial context. To present adequately the historical and cultural contexts of colonial Brazilian arts would require sacrificing aspects of the viceregal art of Spanish America. I therefore leave Brazilian colonial art and architecture to others. I retain, however, the descriptor Latin American despite ignoring much of what later came to be known as Latin America. Writing invariably involves making choices regarding appropriate words. Scholars employing the label "European" rarely address every nation within that continent; I am comfortable describing the scope of this book as Latin America without considering every part of the Americas. At the same time, while Latin America is a construct of later eras, I nevertheless consider it to be a useful term for its familiarity for North American readers.

I wrote this book with the assistance of a University of North Texas Faculty Research Grant. I would like to thank the following individuals for their assistance: Thomas A. Donahue, Randal W. Wallace, Michael Rivera, Nancy Brown, Catherine DiCesare, Michael Schreffler, Donna Pierce, Thomas B. F. Cummins, and Kris Lane. My editors Lyman Johnson and David Holtby offered invaluable advice and guidance; copyeditor Rosemary Carstens brilliantly polished the text. I am indebted to my colleagues, Susan Verdi Webster and Carolyn Dean, who generously shared their photographs. The photographers with whom I worked were wonderfully generous, especially James Brunker, who traversed the Andean highlands to take photographs for the book, and Jorge Pérez de Lara, whose beautiful photographs grace the early chapters. Ann Graham, Visual Resources Curator at the University of North Texas, prepared many of the images and again proved herself to be an invaluable asset to our art history program. Museums and private collections were similarly generous and I offer my warmest thanks to Marilynn Thoma, Donna Pierce, and all of the museum staff who aided my search for images.

NOTE ON TRANSLATIONS AND TERMS

The excerpted documents included in the call-out sidebars and the shorter quotes within chapters retain the flow, punctuation, and vocabulary of the original sources as much as possible.

INTRODUCTION

On August 13, 1521, Spanish conquistador Hernán Cortés took possession of Tenochtitlan, the capital of the Aztec empire and home to the Nahuatl-speaking Mexica people. Although helped by cooperative indigenous communities, European arms, and the imported diseases that ravaged Amerindian bodies, the conquest of the Aztecs had nevertheless been long and bloody. The military victory ended a two-year campaign for control of Mesoamerica, launched from Spain's Caribbean capital of Havana, Cuba. Cortés and the Spanish King Charles I for whom he worked understood that the land extended beyond the Aztec-controlled territories, but neither had any idea of the vastness of the continent or the numbers and diversity of its peoples. While Cortés and subsequent leaders had much work left to do to impose Spanish authority on the indigenous populations, the conquistador's 1521 victory marked the beginning of the colonial era, a period that lasted for the next three centuries. Tenochtitlan became México (Mexico City), capital of the Viceroyalty of New Spain, a political entity that stretched from Central America to an undefined northern border in today's United States. Its governance soon fell to the viceroy and a host of lesser bureaucrats who placed themselves atop existing indigenous local political structures. These viceregal officials began the task of establishing cities and outposts and exploring the unknown lands. At the same time, Europeans crossed the Atlantic to take up residence in the viceroyalty. Representatives of monastic orders arrived to convert native populations to Christianity and laymen of every stripe came to seek their fortunes.

Just over ten years later, Francisco Pizarro began the expedition into South America that finally encountered the powerful Inca empire. The empire was, in 1531, involved in a bloody struggle over royal succession. Pizarro took advantage of this political strife to defeat the Inca, first at Cajamarca and then at their capital of Cuzco in November 1533. Shortly afterward, Inca resistance in the city held Spaniards in a ten-month siege that was, according to European witnesses, only broken with the miraculous assistance of the Virgin Mary and the Apostle Saint James. In 1534, Pizarro claimed for Spain what would become the Viceroyalty of Peru. The colony's foundation did not end the warfare, however, as murderous internecine rivalries between Spaniards, and a vigorous Inca resistance, were not quelled for another forty years. The 1569 arrival of Viceroy Francisco de Toledo and the execution of the Inca rebel Tupac Amaru three years later imposed some order on the viceroyalty, which stretched from Panama to the Straits of Magellan.

For the diverse populations of indigenous Meso- and South America, life under colonial rule was difficult. Most communities experienced massive losses of life due to European diseases. Deaths from smallpox, influenza, and the other ailments for which Amerindians lacked resistance soared into the millions. The survivors became subjects of an unfamiliar and hostile empire that viewed them as inferior beings and imposed upon them new political, religious, and social orders. It is true that many Pre-Columbian Meso- and South Americans lived previously as subjects of Aztec or Inca overlords to whom they paid tribute and from whom they adopted state religions. The European culture, however, offered little that was familiar and the Spanish authorities disdained virtually every aspect of indigenous life; it would take a papal edict for the Europeans to accept even that Amerindians were fully human. The challenge for the Amerindians, therefore, was to find means of adapting themselves to the new circumstances.

While early writings on the colonial era emphasized the imposition of European ways on indigenous peoples, and later authors highlighted native resistance to foreign ideas and models, many scholars today see the Amerindian response to the colonial presence as a form of cultural negotiation. They understand that cultures are perpetually in flux, constantly evaluating new ideas, accepting those that make sense and that offer some advantage, and rejecting those that do not. Colonization accelerates the rate of change, but the colonized cultures nevertheless continue this process of evaluation, acceptance, and rejection. This negotiation allowed Meso- and South American Amerindians to retain their ancestral identities while simultaneously adapting as required by the context to the new circumstances. In the case of religion, for example, some indigenous communities accepted the Christian teachings, others incorporated the new beliefs into ancestral faiths, and still others rejected all but the faintest veneer of religious conversion. Similar negotiation occurred repeatedly throughout the Americas as each community found its way through the unfamiliar colonial landscape.

In colonial New Spain and Peru, however, cultural negotiation was not restricted to Amerindians. The Latin American viceroyalties were immensely diverse societies, and each population negotiated its place within the colonial context. Rather than merely establishing outposts from which to extract American resources, the Spanish crown founded permanent settlements, many of which soon grew to cities populated by peninsular Spaniards, locally born Spaniards known as *criollos*, free and enslaved Africans, and diverse Amerindian peoples; these groups furthermore intermixed to produce mixed-race peoples— *mestizos*, mulattoes, and others—who likewise populated the colonial cities. And while the viceregal social hierarchy placed peninsular-born Spaniards at the top and Africans and plebeian Amerindians at the bottom, each population nevertheless negotiated within this system to find its place and to assert its interests. Criollos, for example, developed distinct social customs and tastes that while

modeled after some peninsular practices, were nevertheless unique and promoted their sophistication in the face of European prejudices against anyone
born in the Americas.

Art and Architecture in the Colonial Context

Art and architecture played a significant role in the formation of Spain's Latin
American viceroyalties and the negotiations of Amerindian and Spanish populations. Their importance derived in part from their physical presence. In both
Amerindian and European traditions, objects and monuments stood in public
areas to embody the ideas associated with the state and its faith. Aztec pyramid
platforms climbed to the heavens just as the towers and domes of European
churches. Both simultaneously marked the religious fervor and the social and
political power of those who constructed them. Public sculptures of deities, rulers, and symbolic designs such as heraldry likewise filled cities on both sides of
the Atlantic to affirm religious and social values. On a smaller scale, important
religious and historical records were kept by Europeans and Amerindians alike
even if medieval and Renaissance manuscripts and printed books looked little
like Pre-Columbian Aztec codices or Inca knotted mnemonic devices called
quipus (or *khipus*). In all societies, specially trained clerics interpreted these
powerful documents.

It consequently comes as little surprise that the physical presence of
works of art and architectural monuments—or, better said, their creation and
destruction—was deployed in the formation of the colonial societies. As Cortés
entered Amerindian villages, for example, he cast indigenous sacred sculptures
from their pedestals and left in their place European images of the Virgin Mary.
Conquistadores entering Tenochtitlan and Cuzco moved into the palaces of the
indigenous elite, and colonists who came later from Spain were instructed by
viceregal authorities to construct their homes of stone. By the same token, missionaries engaged in the initial conversion of native peoples to Christianity tore
down Amerindian temples and erected Catholic churches from the discarded
stones and empty pyramid platforms. These and other acts of artistic imposition
were intended to communicate powerful symbolic messages to their Amerindian
viewers. Christian works physically took the place of indigenous objects and
monuments and Spanish domestic structures assumed permanent positions in
the former Amerindian cities to represent the new colonial religious and social
order. The Amerindian viewers undoubtedly understood these actions since
Aztec, Inca, and other powerful indigenous communities had done likewise.

The style of pictorial arts and architectural monuments created to serve both
the colonizer and the colonized likewise played an important role. In the history
of art, the formal characteristics and pictorial conventions artists of a particular
era practiced, particularly in urban settings, were generally determined by tradition and by the ideological underpinnings of the maker's society. Romanesque
artists in medieval Europe, for example, pursued an abstracted or unnatural

approach to images in part as a consequence of the period's overriding interest in spiritual rather than earthly matters. Renaissance painters, on the other hand, reflected the humanist philosophies of their day and employed linear perspective and chiaroscuro modeling to make their images function as windows onto the world. The baroque style of the European seventeenth-century courts reflected in part a pomp and grandeur appropriate for the celebration of the absolute monarch. These period styles communicated important messages and symbolized specific times and places for those who viewed them.

The artistic styles Amerindians practiced before the Spaniards arrived varied widely, but shared the fact that, as in Europe, style signified. Aztec sculptors, for example, practiced a style of art that merged monumental abstraction and sensitive realism unified by an underlying compositional balance and rounded geometry. This eclecticism was in part due to the Aztec practice of bringing regional artists with diverse traditions to serve the imperial court. The diversity of styles they practiced symbolized the power of the Aztec empire. Inca artists similarly employed formal qualities that viewers easily associated with Cuzco. Subjects of the Inca empire recognized patterned textiles, abstracted forms, and finely dressed masonry as signifying in part the imperial court and its authority.

As Amerindian and European cultures converged following the Spanish arrival, then, style carried great weight. A colonial object made more or less according to traditional Amerindian pictorial norms—an Aztec-style manuscript, such as the *Codex Telleriano-Remensis*, for example—made different meaning by the simple virtue of the artist's handling of line, color, and space, than one created to more closely resemble European stylistic conventions, such as the Florentine Codex. The manuscripts' two styles evoked distinct memories, embodied different cultural values, and declared affinity with different cultural values by virtue of their appearance even though both were produced by Amerindian artists. Even centuries into the colonial era, the choice of form or style carried immense weight, as evidenced by the development of the Cuzco School of painting and its stylized forms in the late seventeenth century, and the official promotion of neoclassical forms at the end of the eighteenth century. In short, style mattered in the colonial context.

It is important to note here, however, that nothing that could be called a colonial style existed in viceregal Latin America, even within a discrete historical period. The forms preferred in each region of Spain's American viceroyalties differed, sometimes dramatically. Although it is beyond the scope of this book to address more than the broadest regional variations, each urban center developed a unique stylistic vocabulary, sometimes strongly recalling European pictorial conventions or other viceregal preferences, and sometimes little if at all. The style of art and architecture produced in Puebla, for example, differed from that created in nearby Mexico City; Cuzco and Lima practiced quite different formal solutions. Likewise, the styles practiced in viceregal Latin America were distinct from those found in contemporary Europe. What scholars call baroque art made in seventeenth-century France, for example, had little in common with the baroque art of Quito. In fact, the art of viceregal Latin America exemplifies the problems inherent with stylistic period labels in general. Earlier generations of scholars, happy with period styles defined according to the principles of French or Italian art, viewed colonial art as derivative, folkish, or simply bad. Today however, as scholars question the value of period labels and their exclusion of non-European art (as well as of art created by women), the diversity of formal approaches is viewed as the hallmark of cultural negotiation and inherently valuable and interesting. In fact, the value of labeling period styles and regional variations is a question raised several times in this book.

Just as the style employed in works of art and architecture played a significant role in the formation of colonial culture, so too did the content or iconography of the objects and monuments. The colonial era had nothing that would recall the art-for-art's-sake of the twentieth century. And while early modern Latin Americans undoubtedly derived pleasure from viewing paintings, sculptures, and prints, these objects existed primarily to communicate the ideas found in their images. Carvings on church façades taught the stories of the faith to a population that was largely illiterate. Images of saints exemplified lives lived and lost in the service of God. Portraits told of status and visualized a family's right to its exalted social standing. In the colonial era, this didactic role was immensely important, as missionaries used images to teach Christianity to Amerindians and colonists deployed portraits and other images to embody the new social order of the colonial context. Fortunately for the colonizers, the colonized populations in Mesoamerica and South America came from cultures in which images similarly taught and signified social and religious values.

In short, the art and architecture produced in New Spain and Peru between 1521 and the 1820s participated in a constant and diverse cultural negotiation. From mission churches painted with indigenous pictographic signs to portraits of the heroes of early-nineteenth century independence movements, viceregal objects and monuments testified to their colonial contexts and the interests of their patrons and makers. Works of art operated as symbols of political and social authority, as tools of religious conversion, as opportunities to embody communal cultural identities, and, occasionally, as means of individual self-expression. Even when these objects shared formal and iconographic characteristics with contemporary European art, the fact of their colonial production inevitably distinguished them from their European peers. Simply put, our understanding of viceregal art must always and inevitably be informed by the colonial context.

Overview

This book considers the art and architecture of Spanish (as opposed to Portuguese) Latin America between 1521 and the 1820s. It privileges the viceregal capitals of Mexico City and Lima as well as the former Inca capital Cuzco, which remained a major center of artistic production throughout the viceregal period. In addition to these locations, the text discusses selected other cities and regions:

Quito and Bogotá in what became the Viceroyalty of New Granada in 1717, Potosí and the Andean highlands of today's Bolivia, Santiago de Chile in what became the Viceroyalty of La Plata in 1776, El Paraguay in the disputed jungle border between Spanish and Portuguese territories, the New Spanish cities of Tlaxcala and Puebla, and the mining communities of Zacatecas and Taxco, and New Mexico on the empire's far northern frontier. The art and architecture of these places offer a glimpse of the vastly diverse artistic production of colonial Latin America. Throughout the text, excerpts of primary documents reveal how contemporary colonists understood and discussed the objects and monuments that surrounded them.

Chapter 1 takes as its subject the architecture of evangelization constructed by missionaries and Amerindians between 1521 and the early seventeenth century. Using two exemplary mission complexes, San Miguel de Huejotzingo in New Spain and La Asunción de Chucuito in Peru, the chapter discusses at length the forms and functions common to these monuments. It likewise considers the social and political implications of mission building in the colonial context. While the mission complexes were in part based on European models, their architecture and sculptural ornamentation represent solutions adapted for the colonial setting. The chapter addresses Amerindian contribution to the construction and elaboration of the missions, and how friars accommodated native traditions to facilitate their conversion to Christianity. Excerpts from sixteenth-century documents, including a 1564 description of a New Spanish mission, an early seventeenth-century indigenous Andean's summary of Inca religious practices, and several mandates on mission building from a 1551 church council held in Lima offer the opportunity to understand the complexities of building in the evangelical era.

Chapter 2 addresses the two-dimensional pictorial arts of the contact era or early colonial period. The chapter begins with a description of the art schools at San José de los Naturales in Mexico City and San Andrés in Quito and examines the mendicant friars' use of images as teaching tools. It then addresses the mural paintings native artists and mendicant clergy used to decorate the mission churches and *conventos*. This section summarizes some of the principal themes found in monastic decorative programs and considers the meanings these images may have had for indigenous and clerical audiences. The next section considers the manuscript paintings produced primarily in New Spain during the early colonial period. These works drew upon indigenous and European traditions to communicate ideas and information from royal genealogies and religious practices to tribute records and town plans. And while most of the manuscripts discussed in Chapter 2 were painted by indigenous artists in the northern viceroyalty, two works from Peru illustrate Andean appropriation of the genre in the late sixteenth and seventeenth centuries. The chapter ends with a brief discussion of the fortunes of several Pre-Columbian media in the early colonial era: Meso-American feather mosaics and metalwork and Andean quero vessels and textiles. Documents excerpted in Chapter 2 include a missionary's description of Amerindian idolatry and indigenous artists, native author

Guaman Poma de Ayala's discussion of Andean Christian artists, and a New Spanish chronicler's account of what was perhaps the first manuscript painting of the colonial era.

Chapter 3 considers town planning and the civic and domestic architecture of early colonial Latin America. It begins with the Spanish laws developed for town building in the Americas. The typical characteristics of colonial urbanism including the municipal buildings, palaces, and central *plazas* found in most cities follow. The chapter then presents the unique histories of colonial cities and their monuments, including Mexico City, Cuzco, and Lima. Where local private homes from this era no longer survive, the chapter employs examples from other colonial cities. A significant theme running throughout the chapter is the significance of the city in the colonial context and the Spanish desire to use city building to convince native peoples of the new, imperial order under which they now lived. Excerpted documents in Chapter 3 include the Spanish laws of city planning, a 1636 inventory of an artist's urban home, and a chronicler's description of early colonial Lima.

Chapter 4 presents cathedrals, altarscreens, and churches constructed in New Spain and Peru circa 1600 to 1700. The chapter begins with a discussion of the Spanish sources of New World cathedrals. It then chronicles the building of these structures in several colonial cities, describing the architectural styles New Spanish and Peruvian builders employed. The chapter examines the function of the cathedrals in the colonial context and their place in the urban environment. Chapter 4 introduces the colonial guilds responsible for constructing churches and altarscreens, and examines their organization and regulations. Likewise, the chapter considers the special role played by the *maestro mayor* or chief architect in the development of local tastes. Following the discussion of the cathedrals, the chapter presents representative monastic churches and chapels built in Quito, Lima, Arequipa, and Puebla. This discussion gives special consideration to the regional formal and iconographic variations these structures exhibit, including the so-called Andean planiform or mestizo baroque. Finally, the chapter presents two seventeenth-century shrines constructed in New Spain and the Andean highlands of Peru to honor miraculous cult images. The primary documents excerpted in Chapter 4 are the 1599 ordinances of Mexico City's guild of masons and architects, a colonial scholar's definition of architecture, and an eyewitness account of Lima's devastating 1655 earthquake and its effect on the city's buildings and people.

Chapter 5 examines religious painting and sculpture produced in the viceroyalties of New Spain and Peru between 1600 and 1785. The chapter begins with the establishment of urban schools and guilds in Mexico City and Lima. This introductory material includes a description of the indigenous Cuzco painting school and the so-called mestizo baroque style of its art. Chapter 5 then surveys the religious themes popular for New Spanish and Peruvian painting and sculpture, beginning with Marian devotions to the Virgin of Guadalupe and the Virgin of Copacabana. The next section offers Christological themes such as the miraculous Christ of Santa Teresa and the Christ Child, followed by Latin

American saints including Rose of Lima and Philip of Jesus. The thematic survey ends with angels, allegories, and representations of religious processions such as the famous series depicting Cuzco's Corpus Christi celebration. The chapter considers how these themes were deployed by New Spanish and Peruvian patrons to promote their own interests. The chapter's excerpted documents come from the Mexico City painters' guild ordinances and the description of the 1614 installation of the Virgin of Copacabana in her Bolivian shrine.

Chapter 6 begins where Chapter 4 leaves off and surveys New Spanish and Peruvian architecture and altarscreens from 1700 to circa 1800. The chapter begins with the early eighteenth-century introduction of the *estípite* column to New Spanish architecture and altarscreen construction. The following section highlights the late colonial churches constructed by the Jesuit order before their 1767 expulsion from Spain and its territories. It then addresses churches built in the silver mining cities of Potosí, Zacatecas, and Taxco and considers their formal and iconographic relationships to architecture in the viceregal capitals. Like Chapter 4, Chapter 6 examines two shrines: the Sanctuary of the Manquirí built near Potosí and El Pocito constructed in the late eighteenth century at Tepeyac near Mexico City. The chapter then presents mission architecture of the late colonial era, with examples from South America and the US Southwest. The last section introduces two elite palaces, one in Lima and the other in Mexico City. Excerpts from nearly contemporary descriptions of Quito and Mexico City offer a glimpse of the splendor of late colonial urban settings; a late colonial architect's manual describes the creation of the so-called *retablo*-façades.

Chapter 7 examines secular themes in Latin American colonial painting between 1600 and 1800. It begins with official and society portraiture and considers the unique formal and iconographic characteristics colonists cultivated in their painted likenesses. This section addresses conventions for male, female, group, and ecclesiastic portraiture, including the images of *monjas coronadas* or crowned nuns. The next section discusses the *biombos* or painted screens popular in seventeenth- and eighteenth-century New Spain and Peru. Born of the trade with Asia, the screens present allegorical and historical images painted to enliven palace interiors. The biombo discussion presents several common themes, including the meeting of Hernán Cortés and Moctezuma, scenes of daily life, and emblematic imagery. The text examines the iconography of these unusual works, and considers their function within and beyond the colonial context. Finally, Chapter 7 examines the so-called *casta* paintings, representations of the miscegenation of colonial societies. After summarizing the typical characteristics of these works, the text makes a detailed examination of the iconography and considers the paintings' function in the formation of an American identity on both sides of the Atlantic. In order to understand how these secular works appeared in their original contexts, Chapter 7 includes an excerpt from the inventory of a wealthy woman's art collection. The other primary document is a letter describing a series of casta paintings sent from Peru to Spain.

Chapter 8 brings the colonial era to a close with the foundation of the Royal

Academy of San Carlos in Mexico City. The text examines the history of the art academy and the reasons for its foundation. A discussion of the neoclassical style and content taught by the European faculty follows. Several representative structures and objects illustrate academic production in Mexico City. The chapter also presents the New Spanish students and their work, and considers the academy's attempts to rid the colony of its baroque tastes. Chapter 8 then turns its attention to the neoclassical artists who worked in South America. It first addresses artists who accompanied the scientific expeditions that embodied Spain's participation in the international Enlightenment. The following section considers several European artists who traveled to the viceroyalties of New Granada, Peru, and La Plata and left behind examples of neoclassical painting and architecture. The chapter's excerpt is the statutes of the Royal Academy of San Carlos.

CHAPTER ONE

Architecture and Sculpture at the Missions

W hile today it is easy to reduce the colonization of New Spain and Peru to the events surrounding Hernán Cortés's battle for Tenochtitlan or Francisco Pizarro's defeat of the Inca at Cajamarca and Cuzco, the imposition of Spanish authority in the American colonies was neither sudden, spectacular, nor definitive. Colonization was instead a long process during which the new social and political order was introduced time and again to each individual community. Relatively few indigenous people, in fact, had direct contact with the battles chronicled in history books. For most Amerindians in the soon-to-be-designated viceroyalties, mendicant friars and the missions they constructed constituted their first sustained exposure to colonization. In manners as diverse as the peoples themselves, indigenous Americans interacted with the new religious representatives at the missions; some rejected the friars' presence while others folded Christianity and its human authorities into their spiritual lives. All negotiated their position within the new system and reconciled the foreign faith with the local.

Most of the earliest examples of Spanish colonial art and architecture came from the missions. The mendicant friars working in New Spain and Peru constructed missions to convert native peoples to Christianity. Many of these *conventos* remain today as the physical—and sometimes still active—remains of the evangelical era. During this period, which lasted from 1524 to circa 1580 in New Spain and 1532 to 1610 in Peru, the Franciscan, Dominican, Augustinian, Mercedarian, and, later, Jesuit monastic orders devoted themselves to persuading indigenous Americans to abandon pagan religions for Christianity. The Spanish Crown was likewise committed to the effort. From our vantage point centuries later, we can see that the success of this evangelical program varied widely, from communities that embraced Christianity to those that accepted little of the new teachings. At the time, of course, both church and crown declared its unequivocal success.

The spread of Christianity in the Americas suited the needs of both the Spanish crown and the mendicant orders. The Spanish monarchs Charles I (r. 1516–56) and his son Philip II (r. 1556–98) had both spiritual and earthly motives for converting native peoples. At their core was the firmly-held belief that Christianity was the only true faith; all other religions, therefore, were misguided and those who followed them put their souls at risk. By the early sixteenth century, Spain had experience in extirpating false religions from its territory, including the 1492 defeat of the last Moorish caliphate in Granada and the expulsion from the Iberian peninsula of all Jews and Muslims who refused to abandon their faiths. The kings furthermore interpreted their victory in Granada as proof of God's approval of Spain's spiritual cleansing. Upon discovering the peoples of Meso- and South America, the monarchs considered the conversion of Amerindians to Christianity to be God's will.

Spain's evangelical program functioned with the support of the Roman Catholic Church, which granted the crown expanded authority to implement the missionary effort. In 1508, Pope Julius II authored the bull *Universalis Ecclesiae*, giving the Spanish kings religious authority over the territories they received in the 1494 Treaty of Tordesillas.[1] This *Patronato Real*, as it was known, included the right to appoint bishops and archbishops, to collect tithes, to implement religious building programs, and generally to direct the spiritual life of the viceroyalties. In return for this unprecedented authority, the Spanish monarchs pledged to convert the native populations to Christianity, which they did by establishing missions in indigenous communities.

Converting indigenous peoples also had more earthly benefits for the crown. Aside from creating a population of Spanish citizens that made the empire the largest in the world—certainly bigger than Spain's rivals France and England— religious conversion represented a means to control territory. The Spaniards did not have the large standing armies needed to dominate by military force. They did have a spiritual militia of ready and willing clergy who forged into unconquered lands to transform pagan Amerindians into Christianized Spanish subjects. Spanish monarchs assumed that once converted, these Amerindians were less likely to rebel against colonial authority than un-Christianized natives. Hence the missions represented an inexpensive and efficient alternative to deploying soldiers across two vast continents.

The mendicant orders of the regular branch of the Roman Catholic Church, for their part, shared the crown's belief in the inherent fallacy of pagan religions and in the moral superiority of Christianity. The Franciscan, Dominican, and Augustinian friars furthermore believed that Christ's second coming, an event seen as impending since the turn of the millennium, was only possible when all people on earth were introduced to his teachings. This millenarianism drove the clerics to pursue urgent Christianizing efforts in the Americas so that the biblical prophecy might be realized. The mendicants furthermore saw these lands as an opportunity to construct anew a Christian society untainted by the corruptions plaguing the European church during the sixteenth century. They looked at the indigenous peoples as *tabulae rasae*, blank slates upon which to inscribe a pure form of the faith based on the values of early Christianity. The missionaries likened themselves to the apostles charged by Christ to spread his teachings, and set out to create Christian *repúblicas de indios*, communities of Amerindians.

The mendicant clergy were not always of the same mind as the crown, however, especially when it came to the Spaniards' mistreatment of natives. While the friars understood much of traditional Amerindian life as wrong and occasionally even demonic, they nevertheless defended Spanish America's indigenous peoples against abuses. Much of the problem lay in the *encomienda* system by which the Spanish Crown granted conquistadors and colonists the right to native tribute and labor within discrete regions; in return, the *encomenderos* agreed to provide religious instruction. This system placed Spaniards at the head of traditional tribute systems with little effective oversight by civil authorities. The encomienda system consequently was rife with abuses and the mendicant clergy regularly decried the abysmal working conditions and mistreatment of their native charges. At the root of the problem was the colonizers' perception of Amerindians as inherently inferior, even subhuman, beings. The 1542 New Laws of the Indies imposed new protections for native peoples and sought to phase out the encomienda system in favor of crown-administered drafts. Neither system pleased the clerics, although they, too, relied on labor corvées to construct their conventos.

The missionaries arrived in New Spain and Peru in ever greater numbers throughout the sixteenth century. The first friars to reach Mesoamerican shores were three Franciscans who began work in Mexico City in 1523; twelve more arrived in New Spain's viceregal capital the following year. The same number of Dominicans reached the city in 1526, followed seven years later by a group of Augustinian friars. In South America, the Dominican, Franciscan, and Mercedarian orders reached the Inca capital of Cuzco in 1534 and Lima, Peru's viceregal capital, in 1535; the Augustinians arrived in Lima in 1551. The newly founded Jesuit order was a late arrival in both viceroyalties, reaching Peru in 1568 and New Spain in 1571; their well-trained clergy and military-style order nevertheless made them indispensable despite their tardy entrance.

Upon arriving in Mexico City, Lima, Cuzco, Quito, and other larger colonial settlements, all of the orders constructed grand convents. Many of these would serve as the orders' principal monasteries and administrative centers—or mother houses—for the next three centuries. Most of the early urban foundations appear today in forms altered by construction programs that continued throughout the colonial era. The Convent of Santo Domingo in Cuzco, however, retains some of its early appearance, although most of the compound was reconstructed after the 1650 earthquake. In particular, the church's apse end (Figure 1) rests on the dressed masonry foundations of the Inca Coricancha, a temple dedicated to the sun and described by early observers as sheathed in gold. The Dominicans in Cuzco, like their colleagues elsewhere in Latin America, built upon this sacred site as a symbol of the new religious and social order. This strategy of physical appropriation and imposition had its roots in early Christian European practice and persisted throughout the colonial era. Although the Amerindian viewers undoubtedly understood the spirit of these acts, viewing remains of pagan temple foundations, pyramid platforms, and even sculpture incorporated into Christian churches may have evoked memories and religious sentiments distinct from what the friars tried to teach.

While the mother houses ministered to the indigenous populations and Spanish colonists living in the newly founded—or at least newly Hispanized—cities, they also sheltered the missionaries on their way to outlying Amerindian communities. Traveling in pairs, sometimes on foot and other times on donkeys, the missionaries founded *cabeceras* or main monasteries in larger towns. These were occupied by a handful of permanent clergy (or even just one), whereas the *visita* churches founded in smaller villages were visited on a regular schedule but not inhabited by resident friars. As the clerics entered the indigenous towns, they forged relationships with local leaders or *caciques*, whose assistance was essential in converting the population. Some of the villages were *reducciones*, newly created or coalesced native towns constructed to facilitate conversion, with the missions at their physical and spiritual center. Missionaries similarly claimed the core of existing villages, sometimes building on the ruins of temple platforms or pyramids as mentioned. As this process replayed throughout the sixteenth century, the mendicants constructed over four hundred missions across the New Spanish and Peruvian landscapes.

With their missions founded, at least symbolically while building got underway, the missionaries set to work teaching Amerindians about Christianity. Their methods for doing so, however, varied widely, and the experimental strategies

FIGURE 1.
Church of
Santo Domingo.
Reconstructed
after 1650.
Cuzco, Peru.
Photograph © Kelly
Donahue-Wallace.

FIGURE 2.
Fray Diego de Valadés,
Allegorical Atrium from
Rhetorica Christiana.
1579. Engraving.
photograph © Archivo
Fotográfico Manuel
Toussaint, IIE/UNAM.

the missionaries employed, including preaching in the native languages, were debated from the outset. The regular orders, like the Spanish crown, had unprecedented freedom in their conversion efforts. The papal bulls *Alias Felicis* (1521) and *Exponi Nobis Fecisti*, also known as the *Omnimoda* (1522), gave the mendicants authority to perform sacraments, a right usually reserved for the secular clergy; friars baptized native peoples, performed masses, officiated marriages, and heard confessions. This expanded authority did not sit well with the parish priests, bishops, and archbishops of Latin America's growing secular clergy. By the end of the sixteenth century, six church councils had been held in Mexico City and Lima to clarify ecclesiastical practices and the relationship of the missionaries to the episcopal hierarchy.

The 1579 engraving known as the *Allegorical Atrium* (Figure 2), referring to the open square preceding the church and monastery, pictures the missionaries' activities. The engraving, published in fray Diego de Valadés's *Rhetorica Christiana* (Perugia, 1579), emphasizes the mission's didactic role. No less than nine lessons take place within the atrium's walls, with friars teaching Christian doctrine, sometimes with the help of visual aids to illustrate abstract concepts for friars still learning native languages. Each lesson is attended by native neophytes identified by the *tilmas* (robes knotted at the shoulder) worn by the Aztecs of central New Spain. The devastating effect of European diseases on the Amerindians also appears in the print, as friars shelter the sick in the infirmary and perform funerals. In the center, New Spain's Franciscans, symbolically led by the order's founder, St. Francis of Assisi, bear on their shoulders the new church they created in the Americas.

Missions in the Viceroyalty of New Spain

Evangelical architecture in the Viceroyalty of New Spain began with the Convent of San Francisco in Mexico City and its chapel for Amerindians, San José de Belén de los Naturales. Built in the convent's atrium, San José de los Naturales may be considered the birthplace of Christianity in New Spain. Fray Pedro de Gante, a Flemish Franciscan whose 1523 voyage to Mexico City preceded the symbolic arrival of his twelve colleagues in 1524, founded the chapel to serve the capital's Aztec population. There he and his companions taught basic Christian principles to the masses to prepare them for baptism.

San José de los Naturales was more, however, than a religious institution; it was a school created to facilitate native integration into the new colonial system. There the sons of the indigenous elite received a higher education in Latin, grammar, and theology. The friars hoped that these young men would constitute an anticipated native clergy to be trained at the Colegio de la Santa Cruz in Tlatelolco, founded in 1536. Natives from humble families acquired professional training in a variety of crafts and professions. Gante taught these students to use metal tools and to construct the familiar forms of European architecture, including barrel and rib vaulting. Contemporary witnesses explain that the indigenous students, the heirs to long artistic traditions, learned these techniques quickly, and the masons, carpenters, painters, and sculptors trained at San José de los Naturales constructed and decorated many of the viceroyalty's Franciscan missions; a similar school sponsored by the Augustinian order at Tiripetío, Michoacán, did likewise after 1540.

Instruction at San José de los Naturales took place within the walled atrium and the chapel, the first of the so-called open chapels built in New Spain. Open chapels were, as the name suggests, religious structures that were not entirely enclosed. These structures varied in shape, but all had a consecrated altar for the mass, which all or most of the attending congregation witnessed while standing outside.

The open chapel of San José de los Naturales unfortunately succumbed to time and progress in the eighteenth century, but several witnesses described its appearance. Gante himself explained in 1532 that the structure began as a simple thatched shed. Scholars have interpreted this description to mean a long, single-aisled portico.[2] The chapel grew between 1532 and 1554 into a structure seven bays wide and deep, and accessed by two stairs. The façade opened onto an atrium containing a colossal wood cross; at least one tower also graced the structure by 1591, although its exact location remains unclear. The chapel's size is suggested by Gante's 1558 claim that the interior could accommodate 10,000 people and another 20,000 could observe from the atrium through the open façade.[3] The interior consisted of a forest of wood columns; decorative stone arches lined the central aisle. The chapel's wood roof reminded contemporary witnesses of the *Mudéjar* ceilings found in Spain.[4] These carved and polychromed wood ceilings inherited from Moorish architecture were popular in Spain, especially in the southern province of Andalucía. They were similarly common in New Spain and Peru for much of the colonial era.

San José's Moorish-influenced forms did not end with the roof; its plan appears to some scholars to resemble the Muslim hypostyle mosques constructed in Spain, the Middle East, and North Africa.[5] These structures similarly had open façades and colonnades added to accommodate growing congregations. It remains to be determined whether the resemblance to the mosque plan reflected a similar need for flexibility, a coincidence of architectural materials, or the friars' intentional appropriation of the mosque form for another infidel community. The Muslims were, after all, the Spanish crown's only experience with a large population of non-Christians, and Spaniards sometimes referred to un-Christianized Amerindians as Moors. Recent analysis suggests that sixteenth-century mendicants associated a specific mosque, Jerusalem's Al-Aqsa mosque, with the Old Testament King Solomon's temple, which may have inspired San José's construction.[6] Seen another way, however, San José's plan resembles an early Christian basilica built with evangelical zeal by missionaries who likened themselves to the apostles.[7]

San José de los Naturales's open chapel also apparently reflected the friars' desire to accommodate native religious traditions, using selected features of the old religion to familiarize Amerindians with the new faith. Indigenous Mesoamericans were accustomed to outdoor rituals held within a walled sacred precinct before a temple. Witnessing this practice, the mendicant friars constructed early chapels open to the atria of the soon-to-be-built convent complexes. In doing so, they undoubtedly hoped to facilitate native appreciation of Christian beliefs. The celebration of the mass at outdoor chapels and from balconies attached to churches was not unknown in Europe. Hence, like so much of the art and architecture of the evangelical period, the friars' solution of the open chapel reconciled different traditions and the unique demands of the new context.

San José's mosque-like plan was repeated at the Franciscan Capilla Real (Figure 3), the domed open chapel that remains today beside the Church of San Gabriel in Cholula. Constructed in 1570, the Capilla Real was actually built *after* the convent's church was completed, perhaps because the population of the *reducción* of Cholula was too large to fit inside the new temple.[8] A more clearly basilican version of San José de los Naturales's plan can be found at the open chapel of Santiago de Cuilapan in Oaxaca. Other open chapel plans reveal the period's experimental spirit. The 1550 open chapel at the Augustinian monastery of San Nicolás de Actópan (Figure 4) consists of a free-standing, single rectangular space covered by a tall barrel vault; a similar model was used at Yautepec and Epazoyucan. At several sites, including Acolman and Tepeji del Río, the single chamber model, albeit on a smaller scale, was integrated into the church façade.

FIGURE 3.
Royal Chapel,
Cholula, Mexico.
1570. Photograph
© Kelly Donahue-
Wallace.

FIGURE 4.
Open Chapel at
the Convent of San
Nicolás de Actopan,
Mexico. Mid-sixteenth
century. Photograph
© Jorge Pérez de Lara.

The circa 1560 open chapel at the Franciscan Convent and Church of San Luís Obispo de Tlalmanalco (Figure 5), on the other hand, consists of an arcaded bay before an apse. The hexagonal plan of the open chapel was similar to remaining examples at Coixtlahuaca and Teposcolula. The portico and apse, the latter accessed through a triumphal arch, were elevated above the surrounding atrium for maximum visual and iconographic effect. The carvings seen on the arches referred to sin and redemption, common themes in the decorative programs of open chapels and colonial missions, as discussed in the next chapter.

The New Spanish open chapels were, of course, part of larger mission complexes constructed throughout the viceroyalty in the sixteenth century. Although each New Spanish foundation displays unique characteristics, the Franciscan Convent and Church of San Miguel de Huejotzingo, near Puebla, exemplifies many of the missions' typical characteristics. It consequently offers an instructive example of these early religious foundations.

Franciscan friars began their conversion efforts at Huejotzingo in 1524 and built a provisional chapel in the middle of what has been described as an "impermanent camp" composed of several displaced indigenous communities.[9] In 1529, the resident friar, Juan de Alameda, moved this de facto reducción to its final location after deciding that the old site was unhealthy and unsuitable for evangelical activity.[10] Building at Huejotzingo's new location was underway between 1529 and 1539, although the work completed in that era is known only from documentary records and archeological excavations.

Huejotzingo's mission church was originally designed by fray Juan de Alameda as a three-aisled basilica with a façade open to the atrium.[11] In 1529, however, New Spain's governing council complained that the building was excessively large for the size of the lay and clerical population. Its enormous scale may have, in fact, inspired the so-called *Traza Moderada* attributed to New Spain's first viceroy, Antonio de Mendoza. Developed sometime between 1535 and 1550 in consultation with the Franciscans and Augustinians, the Traza Moderada encouraged the orders to build convents and churches commensurate with the size of the native communities they served; a 1563 royal decree confirmed this moderate approach. How precisely the new restraint affected the building at

FIGURE 5.
Open Chapel at the Convent of San Luis Obispo de Tlalmanalco, Mexico. Mid-sixteenth century. Photograph © Jorge Pérez de Lara.

Huejotzingo remains unknown, but it stands to reason that construction of the large, three-aisled church was halted and a smaller church begun. The extant Church and Convent of San Miguel de Huejotzingo, constructed between 1547 and 1571, likely reflects the guidelines of the Traza Moderada. (See Sidebar 1.)

Native encomienda laborers built the convento that Alameda designed based on his familiarity with European monastic compounds. The friar also relied on European architectural treatises including Leon Battista Alberti's *De re aedificatoria* (1485), Vitruvius's *De architectura* (1486), Sebastiano Serlio's *Regole generali di architettura* (1537, Spanish edition 1565), and Diego de Sagredo's *Medidas del romano* (1526). The variety of structural and formal solutions displayed at Huejotzingo and New Spain's other monastic compounds suggest, however, that treatises and European models were not the architects' only sources of inspiration. Constructing monuments for this new Christian *república de indios* meant deploying an array of forms to create an ideal mission setting.

The Convent of San Miguel de Huejotzingo constructed between 1547 and 1571 reflects the typical plan of New Spain's sixteenth-century missions (Figure 6). It features a walled atrium with corner chapels known as *posas*, a single-nave church with polygonal apse, an open chapel (now lost), and an adjoining convent. The entire complex supported the evangelical effort and deployed its architectural spaces, ornaments, and visual effects to achieve the friars' goals, beginning with the atrium.

Like other New Spanish missions, San Miguel de Huejotzingo rests on elevated ground; the atrium here occupies a platform constructed between 1544 and 1555. The sacred area of the mission atrium, which served as burial ground and a space for teaching and religious rituals, is distinguished from the adjoining town square by its crenellated wall and arched gates. Neither the crenellation nor the gates provided defensive protection, but symbolized the Heavenly Jerusalem and its protective walls, or perhaps even the Temple of Jerusalem, sometimes represented in Western art with a crenellated perimeter. One may question whether native viewers shared the Europeans' understanding of crenellations; they nevertheless undoubtedly grasped the walls' role since Pre-Columbian Mesoamerican sacred spaces frequently occupied walled precincts.

The atrium of San Miguel de

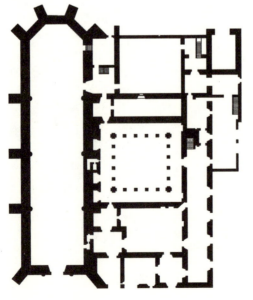

FIGURE 6.
Plan of the
Convent of
San Miguel de
Huejotzingo.
1547–71.
Huejotzingo,
Mexico. Drawing
© Virginia Green.

1564 Description of the Franciscan Church and Convent of San Miguel de Huejotzingo in Juan Gutiérrez de Bocanegra's Letter to Viceroy Luis de Velasco.

Your Excellency.

In compliance with your Excellency's order given to me by the provincial of the Franciscan Order, I came to look with my own eyes at the church and construction of the convent of the monastery of this city of Huejotzingo in order to better see and inform your Excellency of its state. And I brought with me a master stonemason who resides in the city of [Puebla of] the Angels . . . named Pedro de Vidania Viscaino to see what to this date has been done on the church and what has been done is little more than the first chapel [likely referring to the apse]. Its walls are as tall as they need to be and the other three chapels [the remaining bays of the nave] need walls to reach the same height necessary in this area. . . . [The church] has its two principal doors finished; the vault over the nave needs to be finished. There is cut stone for half of the vault of the first chapel. . . . There are some tools, but too few for the said work. The materials that are needed to finish the work are the lime that can be brought from the city [Puebla] of the Angels, which is about five leagues from here and the wood for the scaffolding and beams will be brought from Mount Calpa . . . about three leagues from this city. The stone for the masonry is available about two leagues from this city. It is hard work to quarry; it would be good to get it with oxen. To the common Indians I had them gather where they hear Mass and to listen to fray Diego de Valadés. . . . He told the common Indians that which your Excellency ordered. And [asked] if they wanted to agree to proceed with the building. . . . And everyone rose and said that they would be happy to go to said church because of the need they have for it. And I attempted to know and inquire if the Indians had any money saved in their town or elsewhere for the said work. They swore that they did not have any money. . . . [H]aving seen the state of said construction and that the common Indians by their will refuse to give said work two hundred Indians for your service and work eight months of the year without pay, [Pedro de Vidania] declared in God's name and in his conscience that it seemed to him that in three years with said people the church would be finished and that it would be necessary to spend ten thousand gold pesos more or less on the tools and the [guild] officials to finish the work.

—In Marcela Salas Cuesta, *La iglesia y el convento de Huejotzingo* (Mexico City: UNAM, 1982), 64–65. (Translation mine)

Huejotzingo features posas at each of its four corners (Figure 7) and a large stone atrial cross in its center. The posas, constructed by native laborers between 1550 and 1556, and used for outdoor services and rituals, are square structures, each with two arched openings and a pyramidal roof. A consecrated altar and fresco paintings of the chapel's titular saint originally occupied each interior. Relief sculpture on the exterior, likely also executed by indigenous artists, features angels grasping instruments of Christ's Passion flanking a Marian monogram, a cross, and an imperial crown. The angels are surrounded by the knotted cord of the Franciscan habit and surmounted by shields bearing the order's emblem: three nails and the five wounds on Christ's body. The iconographic program of posa chapels at the nearby Franciscan mission at Calpan similarly features passionary images.

The stone atrial cross, originally located in the center of the atrium but today found in the nearby town square, was carved to look like two roughly hewn tree trunks.[12] Remaining crosses from several other New Spanish mission complexes (Figure 8) feature relief sculpture of the instruments of the Passion,

FIGURE 7.
Posa Chapel from
the Convent of
San Miguel de
Huejotzingo. 1547–71.
Huejotzingo, Mexico.
Photograph
© Susan Webster.

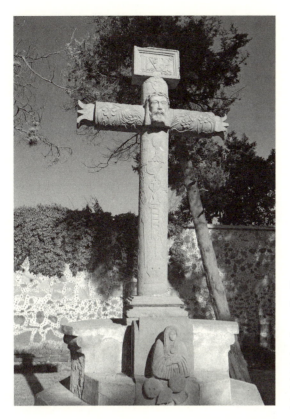

FIGURE 8.
Atrial Cross from the
Church of San Agustín
de Acolman. 1555–57.
Acolman, Mexico.
Photograph ©Tomás
Muñoz, Fotonautica,
photographersdirect.com.

Christ's face, flowers, and even occasional indigenous pictographs on the arm
and shaft of the cross. As deployed by the friars within the evangelical program,
these massive sculptures referenced Christ's death and helped teach the stories
of the Passion. The mendicants who designed them may have been inspired
by European prints bearing images of the cross surrounded by the symbols of
the Passion. The native artists and other indigenous viewers, at the same time,
may have additionally seen the crosses as symbols of the indigenous quincunx,
the five sacred directions (north, south, east, west, up and down) visualized in
a cross-like form. The cross may also have recalled the Tree of Paradise the
Aztecs planted before their temples.[13] Placed on the trunk and arms of the cross
without an apparent compositional strategy, the *arma Christi* may furthermore
have evoked the abstract native pictographs found in the Pre-Columbian codices. The friars who undoubtedly witnessed this iconographic conflation were
apparently not troubled by it. The quincunx and Tree of Life conveyed messages
that vaguely recalled Christian concepts and hence operated as familiar native
forms to facilitate conversion to Christianity; the abstracted organization of the
relief carvings disposed the native viewers to understand the power and significance of the images. But friars permitted accommodation to go only so far. The
crosses avoided representations of the crucified Christ since clerics feared that
the Savior's dead body would remind indigenous viewers of sacrificial rites.[14]

The relief sculpture found on the posa chapels and atrial crosses at Hue-jotzingo and elsewhere display what most scholars identify as an indigenous carving technique and style. The planiform figures with limited spatial exploration recall the geometric solidity and conceptual or symbolic (rather than illusionistic) approach of Aztec sculpture. In many examples, the forms also include indigenous pictographic signs executed in a similar style. At Huejotzingo, for example, the wounds of the Franciscan escutcheon resemble the Aztec sign for the *chalchíhuitl*, a precious stone used here to denote the precious blood of Christ.[15] This colonial carving style has been variously labeled *tequitquí*, Indo-Christian, and mestizo for appearing to reflect indigenous forms or preserve an Amerindian aesthetic while communicating Christian concepts.[16] Earlier generations of scholars believed that works executed in this style revealed native misunderstanding of European forms or demonstrated limited artistic training. Today this synthesized approach is generally thought to reveal both the friars' strategy of accommodation and the artists' cultural negotiation, as indigenous sculptors trained at San José de los Naturales and other monastic schools visualized Christian iconography in a form that referenced local pictorial traditions and therefore appealed to native viewers. It is important to note, however, that Amerindian artists did not work exclusively or necessarily in this Indo-Christian style. They instead produced images reflecting Mesoamerican and European practices in differing degrees depending upon the aesthetic criteria associated with each commission. Examples of Indo-Christian painting or sculpture should therefore be understood as occasions when artists and their patrons deployed style in the service of content and function.

To continue with our discussion of Huejotzingo, the convento's church (Figure 9) is likewise typical of New Spain's mission temples. The tall structure,

FIGURE 9.
Exterior view
of the Church
of San Miguel
de Huejotzingo.
1547–71.
Huejotzingo,
Mexico.
Photograph
© Susan Webster.

FIGURE 10.
Interior view of the
Church of San Miguel
de Huejotzingo. 1547–71.
Huejotzingo, Mexico.
Photograph © Archivo
Fotográfico Manuel
Toussaint, IIE/UNAM.

oriented on an east-west axis according to European practice, was built using the native technique of adobe brick and rammed earth walls faced with stonemasonry.[17] The single-nave plan lacks side chapels, a transept, or any other feature that would distract from the altar in the elevated polygonal apse. The nave is topped by four bays of European-style rib vaults with masonry webs (Figure 10); attached buttresses support the roofing system on the church's exterior.

Rib vaults, inherited from European Gothic architecture, were common in New Spanish churches, even though they were more costly and labor intensive than other roofing systems. In some examples, mostly Franciscan churches, the entire nave was rib vaulted; elsewhere barrel vaults covered the nave while the rib vaulting only sheltered the apse. It is important to note, moreover, that the ribs at Huejotzingo were not load bearing, but largely decorative additions in fired clay or plaster to domical stone vaults.[18] Why then did the mendicants here and elsewhere bother with rib vaults? The answer likely lies in the friars' Utopian vision of their efforts. Freed to create the ideal church for the república de indios, they selected from a variety of architectural vocabularies. Rib vaults likely evoked Europe's great Gothic churches and seemed to the friars a suitable roofing system for the church. What of the barrel vaults favored by the Augustinians? Here the associations may perhaps have been more modern, referencing the classicizing churches of the Renaissance humanists.

Finished in the 1570s, the church of San Miguel de Huejotzingo soon housed a huge European-style altarscreen with paintings and sculptures by émigré artists Simón Pereyns and Pedro de Requena. Virtually every New Spanish mission filled its apse and walls with altarscreens commissioned from urban locally and European-born artists. Like the others created in the late sixteenth and early seventeenth centuries, Huejotzingo's altarscreen employs a classicizing wood framework of ornate columns and niches occupied by Doctors of the Church, Franciscan saints, and martyrs. Its paintings and relief sculptures feature the life of Christ, the apostles, Saint Francis receiving the stigmata, and God the Father in the attic. Additional smaller altarscreens line the nave walls, covering a series of mural paintings illustrating local penitential processions. While teaching the stories of the faith, the grand altarscreens also provided a glimpse of celestial splendor to awe its indigenous and European viewers.

Visual effects and symbolism likewise shaped the exterior of San Miguel de Huejotzingo. The roof is lined with crenellations, which, along with the high walls, buttresses, and limited fenestration, cause the church, like most New Spanish mission churches, to look fortified. For the friars, this militaristic appearance undoubtedly symbolized their own role as the soldiers of God and the church's symbolic defense of Christianized natives against human and supernatural threats. Like the crenellated atrium wall, however, these rooftop battlements may not have held much meaning for the native viewer and were not used for real defense.

A lateral door, located on the north side of the church, is known as the *Porciúncula*. The door, found at most Franciscan foundations, refers to Saint Francis's original church and was used in annual religious festivities. Located beside the now lost open chapel, the door was closed for most of the year, but opened as a symbolic entrance into paradise.[19] Its lavish treatment is typical. At Huejotzingo, the door is decked with an arch flanked by ornate columns and topped by archivolts bearing pearls, floral motifs, and the chain of the European noble Order of the Golden Fleece. A rectangular frame bearing small rosettes surrounds the arch and the spandrels above it. This ornamental vocabulary recalled early modern visions of the Temple of Solomon, and perhaps symbolized the Franciscans' desire that Huejotzingo serve as an earthly Jerusalem in the New World.[20]

The façade at San Miguel de Huejotzingo similarly reflects the friars' evangelical agenda as well as the iconographic and formal experimentation characteristic of much sixteenth-century New Spanish mission architecture. Huejotzingo's ornamentation is massed around the door on a screen of dressed masonry laid atop the church walls. The door has an undulating ogee arch and is flanked by tall, thin columns topped by vegetal finials. These columns, like those of the Porciúncula, may have symbolized the Temple of Solomon.[21] A flat masonry field above the door bears seven medallions with low-relief monograms, which recent scholarship has compared to contemporary molds used for the Eucharistic host.[22] A Franciscan knotted cord, part of the order's habit, forms a low relief rectangle above the medallions; the arched choir loft window in the second story is framed by another Franciscan cord. The cord appears a third time surrounding twin Franciscan escutcheons to either side of the window.

San Miguel's façade displays a formal synthesis found in many of New Spain's sixteenth-century missions. The heraldic devices, like the medallions, exhibit the characteristic carving technique of the so-called Indo-Christian style; the stigmata remind some viewers of indigenous pictographs. At the same time, the rectangular frame around the door, composed of the columns and entablature, has been likened to the *alfiz*, an ornamental framing device employed in Spanish Mudéjar architecture. The ogee arch may likewise be derived from Moorish building practices. How do these Mudéjar forms contribute to the friars' vision of the ideal mission church? As with the mosque-like plan of San José de los Naturales, it is unclear whether the alfiz and ogee arch represented symbolic appropriations by friars who likened un-Christianized natives to Muslims. Perhaps the Mudéjar forms associated the New Spanish churches with the successful spiritual conquest of Spain or with the Temple of Solomon. The Mujédar elements, on the other hand, may simply have represented familiar and appreciated formal solutions for friars raised in Spain. They may have used them in the Americas without reference to political histories but instead as properly ornate adornments for the house of God.

The *portería*, an arcade to the right of the church, granted access to the convent at San Miguel de Huejotzingo. One arch is framed with an elongated chain molding, a motif also found on the posa chapel arches, and the other a pattern inspired by the collar worn by Spanish King Charles I and other members of the Order of the Golden Fleece. It seems likely that this form represents a symbolic reminder of the viceroyalty's new political order; the king did, after all, grant the Franciscans and other mendicant orders the duty of converting America's native populations to Christianity. At the same time, the sculpture on the portería has been described as reflecting Mudéjar tastes due to its linear low-relief patterns and rosettes.[23] Whatever the inspiration for its ornament, the portería at Huejotzingo, like at all New Spanish missions, served as more than an entryway; it, too, shared in the evangelical program. Missionaries employed this area for instructing natives, hearing confession, performing baptisms and marriages, and receiving neophytes into the convent proper; some porterías even doubled as open chapels.

Passing through the portería reveals a convent that housed and supported the resident clergy. The refectory, chapter room or *sala capitular*, kitchen, and the funerary *sala de profundis* were arrayed around the ground floor of the cloister. The friars' cells, a dormitory for visitors, and a library surrounded the cloister's upper story, according to European practices. But colonial conventos exceeded the function of their European counterparts, and served the indigenous community as well as the resident clerics. Early chroniclers agree that at least the children of the indigenous elite studied in classrooms within the convent walls.[24] The cloister likewise contained altars at the corners, providing even more opportunities for the celebration of the new faith. Virtually every wall within the convent, especially those surrounding the main cloister, were covered in mural paintings ranging from scenes of the life of Christ to ornate grotesque-filled friezes and scenes of local church history. As discussed in Chapter 2, these paintings both inspired the friars and facilitated native conversion.

As we have considered the Church and Convent of San Miguel de Huejotzingo as exemplary of New Spain's mendicant mission complexes, its variety of formal references have provided a glimpse of the stylistic variations of New Spain's sixteenth-century missions. In fact, mission designers and sculptors displayed an immense capacity for formal experimentation as the mendicants and the native communities explored different means of embodying their ideas about church ornamentation. Additional examples, the Augustinian Church of San Agustín de Acolman and the Dominican Church of La Natividad de Nuestra Señora de Tepoztlán, represent just two more solutions of the many employed at New Spain's mission churches.

San Agustín de Acolman, like Huejotzingo, was its order's principal convent in the region north of Mexico City. Founded in 1539 by fray Jorge de Avila, the mission complex visible today was constructed between 1555 and the late 1570s. The plan is similar to Huejotzingo's, and includes a walled atrium, barrel- and rib-vaulted church, rooftop crenellations, exterior buttressing, and an attached convent housing an unusually large clerical population of twenty-four friars. While posa chapels may have once occupied the atrium's corners, they no longer exist. The single-chamber open chapel remains embedded in the second story of the wall between the convent and church. The mission's atrial cross (Figure 8) is among the most beautiful produced in New Spain, with instruments of the Passion arrayed on the stem of the cross and Christ's face in the center. But while much of the complex reflects the general model, the 1560 façade has little in common with San Miguel de Huejotzingo and is, instead, among the most classicizing ornamental programs in sixteenth-century New Spanish monastic architecture.

The portal at San Agustín de Acolman (Figure 11) is organized as a triumphal arch. To either side of the door, a pair of ornate balustered columns flanks a niche. A sculpted Saint Peter rests in the niche on the left side, and Saint Paul in the niche on the right. Relief sculptures of the Annunciation occupy the spandrels above the door. The portal's archivolts bear images of different local and European fruits and relief sculptures of two friars appear on the jambs. The entablature features a frieze with reliefs of the Host, hippocampus, angels, and lions. A small pediment with three niches houses sculptures of Christ with two musician angels, a motif repeated at other Augustinian churches.[25] Semi-nude atlantids and small columnar pinnacles flank the pediment while an ornate choir loft window and Augustinian escutcheon appear above. The program presents the Augustinian apostolic mission, the triumph of Christianity, and a fitting offering of abundant fruits and music for the celebration of the faith. A similar program was employed at the nearby Augustinian mission of Meztitlán, and variations on the theme were found at Atotonilco el Grande, Actopan, Ixmiquilpan, and Yuriria.[26] The façade sculpture at Cuitzeo, signed by the indigenous artist Francisco Juan Metl, represents a distant relative of Acolman's program.

While stylistic labels derived from European traditions are only awkwardly applied in the colonial context, it is clear that the designer and sculptors responsible for Acolman's façade sought inspiration in contemporary European forms, not Mudéjar or the synthesized aesthetic of the Indo-Christian style. Acolman's ornate classicizing façade is frequently described as a New Spanish manifestation of the Spanish plateresque style, an approach characterized by its profuse ornamentation derived from Roman grotesques. The style and technique of the sculpture likewise are closely wedded to European practices, leading many scholars to attribute the carving to a European artist. Claudio de Arciniega, a Spanish émigré architect who later oversaw the church's masonry, may have designed the façade.[27] It stands to reason, however, that by the 1560s, indigenous artists interested in European forms had ample opportunity to learn Renaissance pictorial strategies. Whoever the artist, his vision of the ideal church was clearly different than that of Huejotzingo's designer. Acolman's artist instead viewed classical forms as the proper artistic vocabulary for the mission church.

The façade of the Church of La Natividad de Nuestra Señora de Tepoztlán, Morelos, reflects a different vision of the ideal mission church (Figure 12). This Dominican complex, founded in 1559, likewise shares the typical features of monastic plans: atrium, open chapel, single-nave church, posas, and an atrial cross adorned only with flowery terminations and a crown of thorns. The church façade, however, added after the church was completed in 1588, displays the

FIGURE 11.
Exterior view
of the Church of
San Agustín de
Acolman. 1555–57.
Acolman, Mexico.
Photograph © Jorge
Pérez de Lara.

FIGURE 12.
Exterior view of
the Church of La
Natividad de Nuestra
Señora de Tepoztlán.
1559–88. Tepoztlán,
Mexico. Photograph
© Jorge Pérez de Lara.

characteristics of Indo-Christian carving. The pediment over the door features relief sculptures of the Virgin and Child flanked by Saints Dominic of Guzman and Catherine of Siena. Marian and Dominican iconography continue in the spandrels above the door, with the Dominican escutcheon, sun, moon, stars, and the *canis domini* (dogs of God) a play on the order's name. Two large angels hold aloft a cartouche above the pediment. All of these figural sculptures display the planiform carving, limited spatial exploration, and linear decoration characteristic of the Indo-Christian approach. And while it is tempting to attribute the carvings to a native artist new to European figural techniques, it is more instructive to understand the sculpture as a conscious choice rather than an accidental effect. The ornamental program reflects a decision to articulate church teachings in the Indo-Christian style. In this case, the resident clergy and the artist chose to render the façade's sculpture in a style they likely understood to accommodate native tastes, communicating Christian ideas in a form familiar and attractive to the indigenous community.

The initial period of evangelical activity in New Spain ended in the late sixteenth century, and many missions were converted into parish churches ministered by secular clergy. It was, after all, only by special privilege and in the interest of conversion that the mendicant orders had the extraordinary powers they did in the sixteenth century. But the end of the evangelical period can also be attributed to the growing tension between the mendicants and New Spain's bishops and archbishops. During the 1560s, the secular clergy gained increasing numbers and power in the urban centers. A royal decree dated 1574, in accordance with the edicts of the Council of Trent, placed the missions under episcopal authority and gave bishops control over the colony's spiritual affairs.[28] The Tridentine reaffirmation that the word of God be delivered only in Latin likewise defeated the missionaries who had great success teaching Christianity in native languages.[29] At the same time, some mendicant friars looked more realistically at the success of their evangelical efforts and found disappointing results; indigenous rituals and beliefs still flourished and the practice of Christianity was inconsistent. As early as 1562, fray Jerónimo de Mendieta observed that some of his Franciscan colleagues had lost their missionary zeal. But even as the initial period of evangelization closed with the end of the sixteenth century, New Spain's missionary history was not finished. Apostolic fervor drove some mendicants and Jesuits to the fringes of the viceroyalty; these later missions are discussed in Chapter 6.

Missions in the Viceroyalty of Peru

The missions constructed in the Viceroyalty of Peru share many characteristics with those built in New Spain. Their purpose, after all, was the same: to convert the native population to Christianity, to serve as the physical representation of the new social and religious order, to embody the successful evangelization, and to hold territory for Spain. Hence we are not surprised to find scattered throughout the Andean highlands and coastal lowlands of colonial Peru sites with walled atria, posa chapels, single-nave churches, and convents organized around cloisters. Despite these similarities, the histories of the sixteenth- and early seventeenth-century South American missions and some of their forms and purposes differ from their North American counterparts.

The Dominican order led the evangelical effort in Peru. Francisco Pizarro's chaplain, in fact, was fray Vicente de Valverde, a Dominican who became the first Bishop of Cuzco. Histories of Pizarro's conquest of Peru include an episode at Cajamarca in which Valverde attempted to convert the Inca Atahuallpa to Christianity. Valverde explained the doctrine of the Trinity and of man's Fall and Redemption to the Inca, and encouraged him to become a Christian vassal of the Spanish king. Atahuallpa refused and Pizarro and his men turned their swords on the Amerindians and arrested their leader. Another Dominican in Pizarro's company, fray Tomás de San Martín, likewise introduced Christianity to the indigenous communities on the conquistador's path. San Martín established the first Peruvian missions in 1532, two years before the order's formal entry. The missions he founded at Chucuito, Juli, and Pomata soon offered some of the earliest examples of mission architecture in Peru.

San Martín established these first missions in the Andes mountains on the western shore of Lake Titicaca, near the border that today divides Peru and Bolivia. This region was known as El Collao, or the province of Chucuito, and was home to the Aymara-speaking Lupaqa people, subjects of the Inca empire. San Martín's desire to place the earliest missions in the Collao region reflected its Pre-Columbian religious significance. Lake Titicaca was sacred to the Inca and to the indigenous communities within their empire. According to the Inca foundation legend, the Sun god Inti sent his son, Manco Capac, and daughter, Mama Ocllo, to earth to bring order and civility, to teach the people to live off the land, and to introduce them to their father's worship. After arriving on an island in Lake Titicaca, this primordial couple traveled through the Andean highlands establishing towns, including Cuzco, the Inca capital that became the center of Tawantinsuyu, as the Inca called their empire.[30] The Inca established a temple to the sun on the island and all the peoples of the empire sent gold and other tribute goods to the shrine. Upon hearing of the Spaniards' taste for the precious metal, the shrine's caretakers threw the offerings into the water.[31] Since Andean religions celebrated holy sites or *huacas* without the need of temples or shrines, Lake Titicaca remained an important focus of devotion even after the introduction of Christianity and the construction of Christian churches. (See Sidebar 2.) Recognizing this type of worship, the mendicants eagerly sought the opportunity to impose the new faith on the holy lands of the old.

Missionary activity occurred throughout the viceroyalty, from the mountain and coastal regions between Cajamarca in the north and Potosí in the south, but the task of spreading the Gospel near Lake Titicaca initially fell to the Dominicans. Although provisional Christian temples dotted the landscape as early as the 1540s, the main period of evangelical construction in the area began in 1560, after Peru's civil conflicts and rebellions among the Spanish conquistadores finally ended. The evangelical period also coincided with the arrival of Viceroy Francisco de Toledo, who ordered the mendicants to step up their conversion efforts. To that end, Toledo turned ineffective Dominican missions in Collao over to the Jesuits in 1572. He also ordered the consolidation of the indigenous peoples of the Andean highlands into fifty-four reducciones, each with a church. (See Sidebar 3.) While some of these towns were located in existing native villages, many people were forced from their ancestral communities scattered in the mountains and valleys of the Andes. For the mendicant and Jesuit clergy who ministered to the reducciones, also known as *pueblos de indios* or *doctrinas*, a name that did not distinguish between the town and its church, the new sites offered the opportunity to distance the native populations from the lands they believed sacred and to facilitate the adoption of Christian practices. Many indigenous people, however, abandoned the reducciones and returned to their homes after the initial evangelical period.

At the center of the reducción villages was a square with the civic buildings and the mission complex all constructed with native labor. As in New Spain, encomienda laborers provided the construction; the encomendero in Collao was none other than the king of Spain, for whom Francisco Pizarro had reserved the

Excerpt from Garcilaso de la Vega, El Inca, *Royal Commentaries of the Incas and General History of Peru* (1612)

CHAPTER IV

Of many gods wrongly attributed to the Indians by the Spanish historians.

Returning to the idolatry of the Incas, we must enlarge upon the assertion already made that they had no other gods but the Sun, which they worshipped outwardly. They made temples to him, the walls of which were lined from top to bottom with gold plates. They sacrificed many things to him. They presented to him great gifts of much gold and all the things they held most precious, in gratitude for what he had given them . . . In addition to the Sun they worshipped Pachacámac . . . inwardly, as an unknown god. They held him in greater veneration than the Sun. They did not offer sacrifices to him or make temples for him . . . The Spanish attribute many other gods to the Incas because they are unable to distinguish the times and idolatries of the first age [before the Inca] from those of the second [under the Inca]. . . . [T]heir ignorance has led them to attribute to the Incas many or all of the gods the latter removed from the Indians they subjected to their empire, and these subjected peoples had many strange gods . . . A particular source of this error was that the Spaniards did not know the many diverse meanings of the word huaca. This, when the last syllable is pronounced from the top of the palate means, "an idol," such as Jupiter, Mars, or Venus. . . . It means "a sacred thing," such as all those in which the Devil spoke: idols, rocks, great stones, or trees which the enemy entered to make the people believe that he was a god. They also give the name huaca to things they have offered to the Sun, such as figures of men, birds, and animals made of gold, silver, or wood, and any other offering held sacred. . . . Huaca is applied to any temple, large or small, to the sepulchers set up in the fields, and to the corners on their houses where the Devil spoke to their priests. . . . The same name is given to other things of this same kind, such as a rose, an apple, or a pippin, or any other fruit that is better and more beautiful that the rest from the same tree. . . . On the other hand, they give the name huaca to ugly and monstrous things that inspire horror and alarm. . . . They also call huaca everything that is out of the usual course of nature, as a woman who gives birth to twins.

—Garcilaso de la Vega "El Inca," *Royal Commentaries of the Incas and General History of Peru*, trans. Harold V. Livermore (Austin: University of Texas Press, 1966), 75–77.

Excerpts from the First Provincial Council in Lima, 1551–52

Second Constitution—That churches shall be constructed in Indian towns, and the manner in which to do so.

Furthermore, because, for the goodness and mercy of God our Father, in most Indian towns and provinces there are many Christians, and each day there will be more; and for this reason there shall be temples and churches where God our Father will be honored, and they will celebrate the divine offices and administer the sacraments, and the Indians will attend to hear the preaching and doctrine: *Sancta Sínodo aprobante* we order that the priests in the Indian doctrinas in the Indian towns give and procure with diligence as in each *repartimiento*, in the principal town where the principal cacique lives . . . to make a church, according to the number of people in the town, in which shall be administered all the sacraments, except in cases of necessity. And said priest shall procure to adorn it with the art needed for the site's dignity and so that it is done, helping the people understand that that place is dedicated to God and to the faith and divine offices, and where we attend to ask God to forgive our sins, and in which are not to be done other illicit things, not to give a place for those things. And in the other small towns in which it is not possible to make a church, make a small house, like a hermitage, and put an altar in it adorned with an image or images, in the best manner possible. . . .

Third Constitution—That the huacas shall be torn down, and in their place, if it is decent, shall be made churches.

Furthermore, because [the priests] are not just to make houses and buildings where our Father shall be honored, but to tear down those that are made in honor of and devotion to the devil, for being counter to natural law, it [the indigenous temple] is a great prejudice and incentive for the Christianized [Indians] to return to ancient rites because they are together with infidel fathers and brothers, and to the same infidels it is a great obstacle to their Christianization: As such, *Sancta Sínodo aprobante* we order that all the idols and shrines that are in towns where there are Christian Indians be burned and torn down; and if the place is decent for them, that churches be built there, or at least put a cross there.

—From Rubén Vargas Ugarte, *Concilios limenses (1551–1772)*, vol. 1 (Lima: n.p., 1951), 8–9. (Translation mine)

region.[32] In Peru, the encomenderos and the friars modified the traditional *mita* labor system as they set to work constructing the new buildings. Under Inca rule, local communities paid tribute and provided labor to the state. Native Andeans consequently understood the Spanish labor demands, even if Spanish encomenderos were more brutal in their treatment of *mitayos* than their Inca predecessors. It has, in fact, been suggested that the large size of some of the Andean mission churches resulted from native laborers who preferred to occupy their time on local building projects rather than travel to distant mines where conditions were much less hospitable.[33]

Mita labor also coincidentally had provided much of the adult male population with a basic knowledge of traditional construction techniques, especially masonry and thatch roofing, which the friars put to good use.[34] Community elders undoubtedly also passed this knowledge on to youngsters. Indigenous builders additionally learned from the friars and Spanish craftsmen various European construction methods and materials, most notably arch construction, fired brick masonry with mortar, and clay roof tiles. Amerindians trained at several schools operated by the Jesuit order, including one established in 1577 at the Jesuit mission in Juli.[35] Native craftsmen also left their homes for apprenticeships with Spaniards in larger urban centers and brought these specialized building skills, especially carpentry, back to indigenous communities. As a result of these various educational opportunities, Andean builders acquired the requisite skills to construct the mission complexes. Chucuito masons became so talented, in fact, that they were called to build the new colonial city of La Paz; they also exercised their skills at home.[36]

The Church and Convent of La Asunción at Chucuito (Figure 13) exemplifies the convents built in the Collao region in the late sixteenth century. It is thought to be the most complete remaining complex from this era, even though its friars' residence no longer remains.[37] The structure visible today was constructed by the local Lupaqa peoples between 1581 and 1608. An earlier provisional church and convent were constructed around midcentury, the site undoubtedly selected for its nearby Pre-Columbian fertility shrine; a field of stone phalluses remains today near the town's other convent, Santo Domingo de Chucuito.[38]

The second church at the site, La Asunción, was one of the convents to

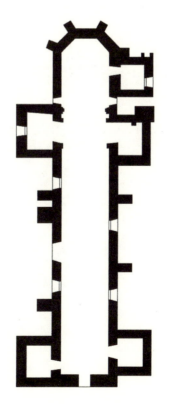

FIGURE 13.
Plan of the Church of La Asunción, Chucuito. 1581–1608. Chucuito, Peru. Drawing © Virginia Green.

benefit from a 1590 contract between the provincial governor Gabriel Montalvo y Peralta and three craftsmen: mason Juan Jiménez and carpenters Juan Gómez and Juan López. The trio, all residents of Chucuito, were contracted to construct sixteen churches in the region.[39] The structure may likewise reflect a Peruvian version of New Spain's *traza moderada*. Following Antonio de Mendoza's example, Peruvian Viceroy Luis de Velasco decreed in 1595 that missions be constructed of modest size and cost.[40] How this mandate affected church construction is unclear, but the lack of ostentatious structures, especially in Collao, may reveal its influence.

The atrium at La Asunción (Figure 14) recalls the atria of New Spanish missions. Located next to the main plaza, it is elevated above the surrounding town. Visitors had no trouble distinguishing this sacred space from the civic plaza as they ascended stairs to reach it. Elevated platforms were common in Andean mission churches, and some atria stand substantially higher than the neighboring square. At Chucuito, a low adobe wall topped by a stone arcade surrounds the atrium. As in New Spain, the Peruvian convent's wall is symbolic, not defensive, separating the *campo santo* or burial ground and the areas for outdoor worship from the secular world. Access to the atrium is granted through two tall stone arches that operate as symbolic gateways rather than physical barriers.

A large stone cross accompanied by two smaller figural sculptures occupied the middle of the atrium at La Asunción. The cross and figures, today located in the town square rather than the atrium, were created by local indigenous artists. The figures' stylized bodies and drapery reveal the hand of a sculptor with little interest in European pictorial practices. These figures of the Virgin Mary and

FIGURE 14. Atrium of the Church and Convent of La Asunción, Chucuito. 1581–1608. Chucuito, Peru. Photograph © James Brunker, photographersdirect.com.

Saint John the Evangelist are two of the few remaining examples of sixteenth-century Peruvian stone sculpture. Pre-Columbian Andean art did not have a tradition of figural stone sculpture—or at least not one that the mendicants recognized. Nor were Inca temples covered with figural relief sculpture. Lacking a handy workforce of stone sculptors or a population expecting to see figural carvings on holy buildings, the friars did not seek to outfit their churches with iconographic programs in a vernacular sculptural style as their counterparts in New Spain did. This is not to say that Andean artists could not have done so if asked. By the 1590s, indigenous artists interested in European forms learned Renaissance pictorial principles; indigenous sculptor Francisco Tito Yupanqui's 1582 wood sculpture of the *Virgin of Copacabana*, for example, is discussed in Chapter 5. Andean *doctrinas* nevertheless do not include developed programs of stone sculpture akin to New Spain's mission sculpture. The atrial cross figures at La Asunción are among the few known examples.

The atria of La Asunción in Chucuito and other Andean mission complexes functioned like their counterparts in New Spain. Contemporary chronicler José de Acosta's description of the convent in nearby Juli sheds light on Andean practices. "In the morning the Indians came to the large plaza in front of the church, and there, divided in groups of twelve . . . men separated from women, they said their prayers and recited the doctrine, with one serving as a teacher, and they pass the *quipus* or registers that they had . . . Afterward they all gathered again and Fray Barzana preached to them there, because there was not a church large enough to accommodate them . . . When the sermon was finished, they heard the sung Mass."[41] Acosta's description illustrates how Andean parishioners deployed traditional material culture to learn Christian doctrine. The reference to the quipu (or *khipu*), the knotted string mnemonic device employed by Andeans to keep records without an alphabetic or pictographic written language, is particularly significant. Passing the quipu around, the audience used its knots to recall Christian doctrine as they had previously done for local history. The reference to a sung mass is likewise important, since it reveals one of the accommodative strategies friars employed. Early clerics believed that the sung, rather than spoken, mass appealed to native traditions of religious rituals based on music and dance; friars in New Spain employed a similar practice. Hence even though the Andean atrium may have lacked some of the outward signs of synthesis of its New Spanish counterparts, it was nevertheless a site of significant cultural intersection, as both friars and Amerindians adjusted their traditions to negotiate the new situation.

La Asunción in Chucuito today reveals no sign of posas, an open chapel, or an Andean funerary chapel known as a Capilla de Miserere, but it may once have had at least two of these components. Acosta's chronicle demonstrates that the mendicant and Jesuit clergy who spread the Gospel in Collao accommodated the native tradition of outdoor worship. Other early histories likewise describe massive outdoor services preached to thousands of Amerindians. Documents from the early seventeenth century reveal that clerics employed open chapels for these exterior rituals.[42] However, this practice did not always translate into permanent structures, at least not in Collao. Mission churches in the area near Cuzco, like Andahuaylillas (discussed below), incorporated open chapels into the church façade. At Collao missions, on the other hand, early open chapels frequently rested in the atrium but, constructed of adobe walls and thatched roof, the structures soon succumbed to weather and time once friars and indigenous worshippers moved indoors.[43] Although regularly mentioned in documents, few of the open chapels survive today.

The open chapels at the Collao missions were likely inspired by the so-called Indian chapels at urban parish and monastic churches, where the clergy ministered to segregated congregations. These enclosed or mostly enclosed structures usually rested alongside a larger church intended for use by the city's Spanish population. The Indian chapels, on the other hand, were intended solely for the indoctrination of native peoples. Especially popular at Jesuit foundations, the Indian chapels were also known as *guayronas* from the Quechua word for wind, suggesting that they involved exterior worship. They continued to be used for ceremonies requiring outdoor celebrations into the seventeenth and eighteenth centuries.[44] Many of the urban Indian chapels exist today, though all are now totally enclosed; the most famous is the Indian chapel at the Jesuit Church of La Compañía in Cuzco, reconstructed after the devastating 1650 earthquake. Its sixteenth-century predecessor featured the eschatological paintings by the Italian Jesuit painter Bernardo Bitti discussed in Chapter 2.

La Asunción de Chucuito apparently never had posas, although other mission complexes in the region did. While today few posas remain among the missions of the Andean highlands, evidence suggests that many missions had them, including the posas at a church in nearby Pomata.[45] Interestingly, the posas at some Andean sites, including Tiquillaca, are located outside the atrium walls, suggesting that the processions and rituals that took place before them occurred in the civic space of the main square. This appears to be a feature unique to Peruvian sites.

Another Peruvian variation on the New Spanish mission complex plan was the Capilla de Miserere. Atria were, of course, cemeteries as well as contemplative spaces. For indigenous Andeans, celebration of the dead was integral to their religious life. This practice continued in the colonial era and soon led to the creation of a permanent structure for its celebration. These funerary chapels were known as Capillas de Miserere, named for the first psalm in the Old Testament, which is sung during the Catholic Office of the Dead. The structures look like posas chapels, but were generally located in the center of the atrium. Also like posas, Capillas de Miserere were built in the Andes through the eighteenth century.[46] Today La Asunción in Chucuito shows no sign of the Capilla de Miserere it likely once possessed.

The Church of La Asunción reveals the standard characteristics of similar structures in the region. The church consists of a single, long and narrow nave and a polygonal apse. A transept crosses the nave and provides space for two small chapels. The entrance on the long axis is covered by an elevated choir loft supported by stone sail vaults constructed in the eighteenth century; it is flanked by a heavy bell tower and a baptistery. This portal is not, however, the principal entrance into the church. As at other mission churches in Collao, the main portal at La Asunción is located midway down the nave, facing the main square and the larger of the two arched entrances to the atrium. La Asunción consequently runs parallel to the main square, a feature typical of missions in this region. Also like other Collao churches, La Asunción is constructed of adobe with a pitched wood beam roof; its tower, façade, and buttresses, however, are constructed of coursed and dressed masonry. The crenellation and heavy buttressing found at many New Spanish mission complexes is entirely lacking, and La Asunción and other Andean churches appear fortified only due to their immense size and stark walls. There was, however, nothing stark about the interior of La Asunción. As discussed in Chapter 2, Andean mission churches were profusely ornamented, with mural paintings covering virtually every surface from the dado to the wood beams. Although today La Asunción's walls are mostly bare, inventories demonstrate that it was once covered in painted canvases; whatever mural paintings it once sheltered were likely lost during the nineteenth century.[47]

The principal façade of the Church of La Asunción in Chucuito (Figure 15), unlike most in the region, is carved stone rather than the more common stuccoed brick. This may reflect the presence of the talented Chucuito stonemasons discussed above. The façade's classicizing ornamental vocabulary is typical of the Collao region, although it is among the more lavish of local examples. The portal features a triumphal arch motif, with a Doric pilaster and column to either side of the arched door. A triangular pediment crowns the group. The arched doorway is framed by a coffered archivolt and stylized rosettes occupy the spandrels. A small, empty niche in the pediment is echoed by four more niches beside the

FIGURE 15. Exterior view of the Church and Convent of La Asunción, Chucuito. 1581–1608. Chucuito, Peru. Photograph © James Brunker, photographersdirect.com.

door. The entablature frieze presents alternating rosettes and putti, with a lamb above the door. It should be noted that most mission church façades in the region feature less relief sculpture, and instead offer only the classicizing architectural elements. The portal located on the longitudinal axis at La Asunción is a simpler version of the main door and is more typical of the region.

Mission church façades in the Andean highlands display an apparent homogeneity of architectural solutions. Nearly every structure constructed for the mendicant and Jesuit clergy features a round-arched entrance surrounded by classicizing pilasters or attached columns, entablature, and pediment. A typical example is found on the Church of San Miguel in Ilave (Figure 16). Finished between 1601 and 1612, the façade is among the most severe found in the Americas. The round-arched doorway is flanked on either side by a pilaster and attached column. The entablature is devoid of ornamentation and the triangular pediment features only a tiny niche bearing a small sculpted figure. The only other articulation of the Ilave façade is a pair of roundels in the spandrels. Like other Collao churches, Ilave displays little of the formal experimentation that characterized the façades of New Spanish mission churches with their artistic and architectural vocabularies drawn from Mudéjar, Gothic, classical, and Indo-Christian vocabularies. Ilave's beauty derives instead from the clear expression of its classical architectural elements.

What explains the formal differences between the New Spanish and Peruvian mission church façades? As discussed above, local friars eschewed developed programs of relief sculpture, perhaps in light of Andean artistic traditions. Whether by coincidence or by design, these clerics may furthermore have had a relatively consistent vision of the ideal mission church. They preferred the classicizing architecture described in the architectural treatises of Alberti, Serlio, Vitruvius, and Sagredo to any alternative adopted from European or local traditions.[48] Another possibility is that the three craftsmen—Gómez, López, and Jiménez—who were contracted to oversee local mission church construction in the 1590s imposed the same classicizing model on each façade.[49] Finally, we should also keep the date in mind. New Spanish mendicants constructed their missions during the midcentury period of humanist zeal, and deployed a variety of solutions to accommodate the local indigenous populations. The Peruvian missions, on the other hand, were built circa 1600, after the Council of Trent and provincial councils held in Lima replaced humanist experimentation with a codified and conservative approach to evangelization.[50] The resulting architecture may have displayed classicizing façades to make an emphatic distinction between the Christian structures and pagan temples.[51]

That said, it is important to note that Andean mission churches as a whole, like their New Spanish counterparts, display a synthesis of different formal and architectural solutions, even if their façades did not. The structures themselves maintain Andean construction techniques, including masonry, wood framing, and adobe brick making. Inside the structures we can find Mudéjar-inspired brickwork and polychromed wood ceilings. Gothic rib vaults and pointed arches exist at some sites. Even at Ilave, an alfiz surrounds the entrance to the transept chapels.

FIGURE 16.
Exterior view of the
Church of San Miguel,
Ilave. 1601–12. Ilave,
Peru. Photograph
© James Brunker,
photographersdirect.com.

Careful observation of the classicizing mission church façades even reveals subtly different formal solutions.

Missionary activity in the Andean highlands was not restricted to the area around Lake Titicaca and its Aymara-speaking communities. Another significant focus of evangelical effort was concentrated in the region that extends north from the lake, past Cuzco, and down into the fertile valleys near the Inca capital. This region, of course, offered missionaries the opportunity to take the Christian message to the heart of the Inca empire and to extirpate its state and local religions among the Quechua-speaking peoples. The region surrounding Cuzco was particularly rife with huacas, sites sacred to the Inca and their subject communities.

The Jesuit Church of San Pedro in Andahuaylillas (Figure 17), an indigenous village near Cuzco, represents the architectural solutions favored by mission builders in this region. Located in one of the reducciones created in 1572 by Viceroy Toledo's order, the church features a single nave, a polygonal apse, a U-shaped elevated choir loft inside the door, and a heavy bell tower. Its foundations reveal Inca masonry techniques and some of the stones were clearly appropriated for symbolic and practical purposes from nearby Pre-Columbian structures. The buttresses are likewise constructed with finely dressed masonry undoubtedly learned from Inca practices; the remainder of the walls consists of whitewashed adobe. Located on an elevated platform beside the town's main square, the church is not contained within a walled atrium anymore, but documentary evidence suggests that the site once had both an atrium and posas.[52] A simple, two-story convent rests immediately to its right.

The interior of San Pedro de Andahuaylillas (Figure 18) features a *Mudéjar par y nudillo* type ceiling, meaning that the roof beams are placed in two ascending diagonals connected by flat beams, giving the structure the appearance of an inverted boat. Hexagonal forms close the roof at either end. All of the ceiling's surfaces are polychromed in a variety of vegetal and geometric designs. Although Mudéjar ceilings like this have sometimes been explained as expedient solutions, as secular and ecclesiastical builders sought quickly to cover their structures, this was probably not the case. Wood for long beams was in short supply in this part of the Andes and there was no tradition of woodworking among local communities to encourage the use of this roofing system. Andahuaylillas's ceiling therefore reflects significant expenditures of time and money.[53] It seems to participate yet again in the search for the forms of an ideal mission church. In this case, the Mudéjar form and technique were likely chosen because they were lavish, highly ornamental, and therefore seemed to the builder properly honorific for a house of God.

Andahuaylillas's church façade rests between two massive stone buttresses. It features a classicizing triumphal arch ornamental program, with two levels of niches between each pair of strongly projecting pilasters. The archivolts surrounding the door, like much of the façade, bear fresco paintings. The second story has a small door communicating the choir loft to an exterior balcony running the width of the façade and shaded by broad eaves. The walls of the balcony are likewise painted.

Although the enclosed atrium is now gone, the open chapel remains at Andahuaylillas where, as at other mission churches in the region, clerics delivered their sermons from the façade balcony. At some sites, an arcaded balcony

FIGURE 17.
Exterior view of the Church of San Pedro Andahuaylillas. ca. 1600. Andahuaylillas, Peru. Photograph © Neus Escandell-Tur and Alexandra Arrellano.

FIGURE 18. Interior view of the Church of San Pedro Andahuaylillas. ca. 1600. Andahuaylillas, Peru. Photograph © Neus Escandell-Tur and Alexandra Arrellano.

rested on arches standing in front of the classicizing portal; at others, like Andahuaylillas, the balcony was constructed of wood beams. Similar open chapels were found in the Chuquisaca region in today's Bolivia.[54] This model of elevated open chapels was, in fact, the most common type in colonial Peru. A variation on the model, also found in the Cuzco region, was the apsidal chapel located at the back, rather than the front, of the church. The most famous example of this second type may be the Church of Santo Domingo in Cuzco (Figure 1); others remain at Urubamba, Huarocondo, and Cai-Cai. A window in the apse and evidence of an attached platform at Andahuaylillas suggest that it too once had an apsidal chapel.[55] Open chapels of all types continued to be built and used in the Andes until well into the eighteenth century.

The evangelical period in Peru ended in 1610 when the monastic compounds in Collao were completed and many missionaries shifted their efforts from spreading the faith to extirpating idolatry.[56] At the same time, mendicants active throughout the viceroyalty, like their colleagues in New Spain, saw their evangelical role curtailed by the bishops and archbishops. While some missions remained in the hands of the orders, who claimed that the churches belonged to them rather than the episcopal hierarchy or the local indigenous community, others became parish churches administered by priests of the diocesan clergy. The missionaries' efforts nevertheless left indelible impressions throughout Peru and today's South American nations owe their Catholicism, albeit frequently combined with ancestral beliefs among highland indigenous populations, in no small part to these early mendicants.

Painting in Sixteenth-Century New Spain and Peru

The engraving known as the *Allegorical Atrium* (Figure 2, Chapter 1) in Diego de Valadés's 1579 *Rhetorica Christiana* visualizes how Latin American missionaries employed the atria of their convents as teaching spaces. It also pictures their pedagogical methods, with two friars using images to instruct their indigenous students. At the upper left, fray Pedro de Gante stands before a diagram labeled "Discunt Omnia," while his unidentified colleague in the upper right points to an image of God the Father in a lesson titled "Creatio mundi." Although the engraving elides the fact that most early colonial era images were not produced by the friars, but by native artists, it nevertheless illustrates the centrality of images in the missionary era.

This second chapter dedicated to the evangelical period (ca. 1524–1620) considers mural paintings, manuscripts, and other pictorial arts. Much of the work discussed here was produced by native artists trained at monastic schools, under indigenous masters, or both. The chapter begins with several mural paintings created at monastic compounds in the viceroyalties of New Spain and Peru. It introduces common themes and selected formal and iconographic strategies. The next section examines the production of painted manuscripts, both those produced in the service of or within the context of the missions, and those created for secular purposes. The chapter ends with reflection on how indigenous artists adapted traditional native arts to the new colonial context.

The mendicant and Jesuit missionaries who worked in the viceroyalties of New Spain and Peru, and the native communities they served, filled the churches and conventos with art. In doing so they perpetuated the Roman Catholic tradition of didactic imagery, from the early Christian catacomb paintings to Michelangelo's frescoes in the Sistine Chapel completed in the sixteenth century. The clerics and Christian Amerindians also embodied the soon-to-be-articulated tenets of the Council of Trent (1545–63) that promoted art that persuaded view-ers to piety; provincial councils held subsequently in Lima and Mexico City affirmed this and other Tridentine edicts to their New World parishioners.

The friars and their artists likewise drew upon indigenous traditions of sacred imagery. The Aztecs, for example, produced relief and full-round sculp-ture, mural paintings, and painted manuscripts bearing sacred figures. Inca art-ists similarly created weavings and metalwork that possessed religious value, and carved sculpted forms, which they placed at huacas, or sacred sites. (Huaca could also refer to the man-made objects found at sacred sites; see Sidebar 2 in Chapter 1.) Both Amerindian empires also employed religious art within their own colonizing practices. The Inca imposed their religion on subject peoples in part by constructing temples and locating huacas in the new territories. The Aztecs conversely brought the sacred art of conquered peoples back to Tenochtitlan, where the new deities entered the Aztec pantheon. Amerindians, therefore, likely had little difficulty understanding why the friars built churches on temple ruins and installed sculptures of the Virgin inside.

The mendicants' appreciation for art's efficacy in religious indoctrination did not translate into a respect for the objects of alien cultures. Many of the friars who entered native communities destroyed the sacred imagery they encountered. Among the most infamous instance was fray Diego de Landa's 1562 burning of Maya codices. Nor did time breed respect in most cases. In 1621, fray Pablo Joseph de Arriaga advised clerics working in the Andes to gather huacas and *mallquis* (mummified remains of venerated ancestors) and burn them; fray Pablo recalled seeing more than three hundred huacas, mallquis, cups, and silver figu-rines destroyed in one town's purging bonfire.[1] And while the destruction of native sacred objects continued for the next century, missionaries and their artists set to work creating images that reflected Christian teachings.

Mural Painting

The architectural reliefs and atrial crosses discussed in Chapter 1 functioned alongside mural painting at the New Spanish and Peruvian missions. As the *Allegorical Atrium* in Valadés's text illustrates, this imagery communicated con-cepts in visual form, which, the friars believed, facilitated native understanding of the faith; the images certainly bridged communication gaps while the clerics learned native languages. For the passage accompanying the illustration Valadés wrote, "Because the Indians lack letters, it was necessary to teach them by means of some illustrations; for this the preacher demonstrates the mysteries of our redemption with a pointer."[2] The New Spanish Franciscans claimed to have invented this method of teaching with images, specifically mural paintings; as Valadés explained, "We were the first to work zealously to adopt this new method of teaching."[3] Other orders in New Spain and Peru soon followed suit. In 1578, the Jesuit Provincial in Peru, Diego de Bracamonte, requested the services of Bernardo Bitti, an Italian Jesuit painter working in the southern viceroyalty.

Bracamonte declared that Andean peoples would learn well from "images that represent with majesty and beauty what they signify, because the people of this nation are lead by such things."[4] But whereas the New Spanish chroniclers spoke of exploiting native traditions of image-making to further their cause, Peruvian missionaries saw nothing so accommodating in the abstracted geometry of Pre-Columbian Andean art. Valadés confidently relied on Amerindian artists; Bracamonte believed that he needed the immediate assistance of the Italian painter, but other European artists were in short supply.

Faced with the urgent need to replace "idols" with Christian images, to create art that attracted the native peoples to the faith, and to fashion temples that paid

---

◯ SIDEBAR 4

Excerpts from fray Toribio de Benavente Motolinía's *History of the Indians of New Spain* (1536)

BOOK ONE. CHAPTER FOUR

It was then that the natives soon came and told the friars how the Indians were hiding the idols, how they were placing them at the foot of the crosses or beneath the stones of the altar-steps, pretending they were venerating the cross, whereas they were actually adoring the demon. In this way they sought to keep their idolatry alive. The idols, of which the Indians had very many, were set up in many places, in the temples of the demons, in the patios, and in conspicuous places, as in groves and on prominent hills and especially on the mountain passes and summits . . . Those who passed by drew blood from their ears or tongue or offered a little of the incense, called *copalli*, which is found in this land; others offered roses which they gathered on the road. . . . They had idols of stone, of wood and of terra cotta. They made them also of dough and of seed mixed with dough . . . some of them looked like bishops with miter and crosier; of these some were gilded and others made of various kinds of turquoise stone. Other idols resembled men; but these had on their head a mortar instead of a miter, and into this they poured wine because it was the god of wine . . . Others looked like women and were likewise in different forms. Others looked like wild beasts such as lions, tigers, dogs, stags, and whatever animals were found on the mountains and in the field.

Having finished destroying the public idols, the missionaries went after those that were hidden at the foot of the crosses, being in prison, as it were, because the devil could not be near the cross without suffering great torment. All of these were destroyed. Although there were some bad Indians who concealed the idols, there were also good and already converted Indians. To

proper homage to God, the mendicant and Jesuit clergy employed native artists trained at monastic schools. Franciscans in New Spain prepared indigenous artists at Gante's San José de los Naturales as of 1526. Fray Juan de Torquemada explained that Gante helped youngsters to "learn the trades and arts of the Spaniards, that their parents did not know, and to perfect those that they [the Amerindians] used before," including mural painting and feather mosaics.[5] These youngsters in turn educated others and traveled to outlying monasteries to produce ornamental programs. Gante's teaching was so respected by colonial authorities that in 1552 Viceroy Luis de Velasco required all native artists to certify their skills at San José de los Naturales before working for the public.[6] (See Sidebar 4.)

these the hiding of idols seemed wicked and offensive to God; wherefore they informed the friars of it, even though among these a friar was not wanting who tried to argue that this was not a good thing. Such activity was necessary, however, both to prevent offenses against God, lest the homage which belongs to Him be given to the idols, and also to protect many Indians against the cruel sacrifices, during which so many were killed either on the mountains or at night in the secret places.

BOOK THREE. CHAPTER THIRTEEN

In the mechanical arts the Indians have made great progress, both in those which they cultivated previously and in those which they learned from the Spaniards. After the arrival of the Flemish and Italian models and paintings which the Spaniards brought, excellent artists developed among the Indians. Some very valuable pieces of painting have come to this land. Everything comes to where there is gold and silver, and this helps especially the painters of Mexico, as anything of value that comes to this land ends up in this city. Formerly the Indians knew only how to paint a flower or a bird or design. If they painted a man or a man on horseback, the proportions were poorly done. But now they paint well. They learned also how to hammer gold thanks to a goldsmith who came to New Spain. He tried to hide his art from the Indians; but he was not able to do so. The Indians watched all the particulars of the goldsmith's art, counting the blows which he struck with the little hammer and noting how he set and reset the matrix. The result was that before a year passed the Indians produced hammered gold.

—From Motolinía's *History of the Indians of New Spain*, translated and annotated by Francis Borgia Steck, O.F.M. (Washington, DC: Academy of American Franciscan History, 1951), 107–9 and 299.

Monastic schools also operated in Peru; the most famous was located in the northern Andean city of Quito. Founded by Flemish Franciscan fray Jodoco Ricke (1498–1578) in 1536, the Colegio de San Andrés in Quito not only taught catechism, reading, and writing, but also sculpture, carpentry, and a host of other trades; Ricke's fellow Fleming, fray Pedro Gossael, taught painting. A contemporary document again emphasizes the European-style "perfection" students at San Andrés learned: "They say that fray Jodoco taught the Indians all types of trades . . . [producing] very perfect painters and sculptors, and scribes; their abilities and the perfection of the works by their hands are admirable."[7] In addition to the monastic schools, indigenous artists in the Andean highlands also trained with the working painters,[8] where they, likewise, were educated not in their own traditions but only in the new media. Native Andean arts, unlike Mesoamerican feather mosaics and mural painting, were too unfamiliar to the friars and European artists.[9] Hence Ricke's students at San Andrés did not learn to make the traditional knotted mnemonic devices known as quipus, nor the ceremonial cups known as queros. These arts did not disappear, however, and survived in indigenous communities.

More than simply making up for the lack of European artists, the indigenous painters and sculptors trained at San José de los Naturales, San Andrés, and the New Spanish Augustinian school at Tiripetío embodied, to the friars, the acculturation of native peoples into the new Utopian Christian kingdom. Teaching European arts and crafts was a means to indoctrinate. Spanish King Philip II wrote in 1562 that Ricke's Quito school taught the local native peoples "good customs and skills so that they can live in a Christian and orderly way."[10] The European-style illusionism students learned, which contemporary observers simply called "perfection," was furthermore, to the friars' thinking, evidence of both the native capacity for learning and of their successful acculturation; abandoning traditional styles supposedly meant rejecting the ideas they represented. According to colonial scholar Thomas B. F. Cummins, "[T]he re-training of native artists to create such images was interpreted as a sign of the success of the Spanish mission . . . The transformation of the makers of idols for idolatry into makers of images for Christian contemplation was an essential step in the transformative acculturation of native Americans."[11] Moving from the school to commissions throughout the viceroyalty permitted these apparently acculturated artists to model Christian conduct to their peers.

As the examples discussed here demonstrate, however, their paintings did more than illustrate Church teachings. They also offered the native artists an opportunity to communicate their own understanding of the world. Until recently, historians thought convento mural paintings generally reflected only the friars' interests; the indigenous artists' contributions were thought to be little more than physical. New scholarship suggests, however, that mural paintings were the result of more complex relationships between the friars and the artists. The paintings must consequently be understood to reflect the intellectual and artistic cooperation and negotiation of both parties, even when the forms and iconography appear overwhelmingly European. Furthermore, the images should not be considered distinct from Pre-Columbian artistic traditions. The mural paintings (and the manuscripts, feather mosaics, textiles, and quero cups discussed later in this chapter) instead represent the sometimes radical changes Amerindian artistic traditions underwent in the colonial era. As Bolivian art historian Teresa Gisbert and others have argued, indigenous culture persisted within the colonial context and artists pursued means to reconcile their traditional interests with the new Christian world.[12] They articulated their solutions on their church walls.

While Valadés's engraving shows friars teaching from portable canvases known as *sargas*, extant evangelical painting consists of mural paintings. Today dozens of mural cycles from the evangelical period remain scattered throughout the former viceroyalties of New Spain and Peru. Whereas most wall paintings executed in contemporary Europe employed the true or *buon fresco* technique of painting on wet plaster, Pre-Columbian Mesoamerican and Andean muralists used buon fresco, *fresco secco* (dry fresco), and tempera on dry plaster. These processes were used to paint symbolic motifs on temples, palaces, and cliff faces before the Spaniards' arrival, and continued to serve artists working at the early colonial missions. Mesoamerican and New Spanish muralists additionally burnished their murals with stones to achieve a glossy finish.

Scant documentation refers to the muralists' identities and working practices, and few of the paintings are signed. The only documented muralist in New Spain was Juan Gerson, an Amerindian.[13] Augustinian friar Andrés de Mata may have contributed to mural cycles at the churches he designed.[14] A handful of named artists from the Andean highlands, including the Italian Jesuit Bernardo Bitti and his follower Luis de Riaño, likewise suggests that both indigenous and non-indigenous artists painted church murals in Peru. Today's scholarly consensus holds that most colonial murals were made by teams of indigenous artists comprised of a master painter and his assistants.

Mural paintings are located throughout New Spanish and Peruvian monastic compounds and helped to transform the sites into teaching spaces and lavish settings for Christian rituals. Murals can be found in open chapels, posas, naves, rib and barrel vaulting, wood roofs, choir lofts, baptisteries, and sacristies, as well as in virtually every corner of the convents. Much of the mural painting is purely ornamental, consisting of simulated materials and coffering, classicizing friezes, and grotesques. Andean mural painters particularly delighted in articulating architectural spaces with painted pilasters, dados, and other fictive constructions.[15] Figural images presented a wide array of Christian subjects, with particular emphasis on the life of Christ, the Virgin Mary, the apostles, and the heroes, saints, and martyrs of the monastic orders.

In light of the mendicant millenarianism discussed in Chapter 1, it is not surprising that the theme of judgment appears in several New Spanish and Andean mural cycles. One of the most famous examples is found under the choir loft (Plate 1) at the Franciscan Church of San Francisco de Tecamachalco in central New Spain. The paintings, created in 1562 by local indigenous artist

Juan Gerson, were not painted directly on the wall, but rather on *papel de amate*, a paper made from the bark of the fig tree. Gerson painted twenty-eight narrative scenes within oval borders and glued them into the areas between the ribs of the choir loft vault. Painted in a palette of turquoise, white, and ochre, the images reveal Gerson's interest in European illusionism as well as his departures from optical reality. Figures, for example, are both modeled and outlined, and spaces are at once perspectival and conceptual.

Gerson's paintings tell stories from the Old and New Testaments. The chronology begins in the middle of the vault, with Cain's murder of Abel from the Book of Genesis. It continues through the Flood, the Tower of Babel, the Sacrifice of Isaac, the Dream of Jacob, and ends with Ezekiel's visions of the Heavenly Jerusalem and the Altar of the Holocaust. The outside ring of images depicts events from the Apocalypse (Book of Revelation), including the Four Horsemen, the Seven Seals, the Apocalyptic Woman, Christ enthroned with the twenty-four elders, the destruction of Babylon, and the Lamb of God. Four medallions bearing the images of the tetramorphs (Matthew, Mark, Luke, and John in symbolic form) complete the program. The artist's depictions of the scenes reveal his familiarity with European pictorial traditions learned from the printed woodcuts he employed as models.

The presence of this complicated iconographic program at the entrance of a mission church is significant. The images not only foretell the return of Christ, but also present a history of sin and punishment. Gerson and the resident friar undoubtedly expected native viewers to equate these events with their own lives. The Tower of Babel, for example, was to be compared to the Aztec pyramids that were similarly destroyed by God's will. God likewise stopped Abraham from sacrificing his son, not only to test the father's faith, but to condemn sacrifice itself. The allegorical references to the local context continue even in the apocalyptic events, as friars spoke of the plagues devastating native populations as evidence of Christ's imminent return.[16] We may consequently understand Gerson's choir loft paintings not merely as images of biblical stories, but as an allegorical representation of local history and an ominous prophecy of things to come.

A mural painting (Plate 2) in the church at Andahuaylillas near Cuzco likely played a similar role. The image, along with other murals within the church, is attributed to Luis de Riaño (1596–ca. 1643), who signed two of the temple's canvas paintings in 1626 and 1628. Riaño studied in Lima with Italian mannerist Angelino Medoro (1567–1631) before traveling to the Andean church. Scholars see stylistic affinities between the signed canvases and the mural paintings, which they date between 1618 and 1626.[17] The painting's iconographic program is attributed to the church's resident cleric, fray Juan Pérez de Bocanegra.

Riaño's painting is an allegory of good and bad conduct in two scenes painted to either side of the main door. To the right, a good Christian, naked before God, rejects the comforts of a rich table and an overflowing basket of fruit. He instead walks a spine-covered path to salvation; two other faithful precede him. At the end of this torturous path is the Heavenly Jerusalem, populated by the Trinity and the Christian pantheon of saints. Lines drawn from the good man's eyes, mind, and mouth to the Trinity symbolize his single-minded pursuit of salvation. Another line connects him to a demon that pulls in vain on this cord, his temptations insufficient to distract the virtuous man. This demon, however, already has an abundant harvest. Well-dressed figures on the painting's left side choose his easy path, symbolized by the flowers below their feet. But succumbing to temptation leads them to hell, a burning palace populated by demons and guarded by a fearsome beast. To avoid confusion, the painting includes identifying letters and explanatory texts taken from various biblical passages.

The message for viewers to live the good Christian life seems clear and was applicable to any audience. But the program's designer, Pérez de Bocanegra, undoubtedly considered Amerindian viewers when he selected the painting's European print source and its reference to Psalm 106. In this passage from the Old Testament, King David, perhaps shown at the painting's left, condemns the Israelites for worshipping false idols and performing sacrifices, among other sins.[18] Idolatry among the native populations was one of the main concerns of the Peruvian clergy in the early seventeenth century, even a half century after Viceroy Francisco de Toledo's 1574 ordinance prohibited homemade Andean idols. Interestingly, Toledo mentioned idolatrous images painted on doors of homes, perhaps explaining why Riaño located this painted allegory around the entrance of the church.[19] Murals located elsewhere in the church, however, seem more accommodating of Andean traditions. The Annunciation in the choir loft, for example, uses the light streaming through an oculus to symbolize the impregnation of the Mother of God, just as the sun god impregnated holy persons in the Andean lore.[20]

More explicitly eschatological imagery also appeared in Andean churches. Amerindian author Felipe Guaman Poma de Ayala, in his 1615 letter to King Philip III declared that every church needed a painting of the Last Judgment to educate its indigenous viewers. A famous painting of this subject by Italian Jesuit Bernardo Bitti filled the walls of the Indian chapel at the Church of La Compañía in Cuzco. Amerindian author Garcilaso de la Vega wrote in 1612 that many Andeans converted to Christianity after merely seeing Bitti's representation of the punishments awaiting them.[21] We may perhaps appreciate some of the impact of Bitti's lost painting at the New Spanish open chapels at Xoxoteco and Actopan, the latter perhaps also the work of Tecamachalco's painter, Juan Gerson. Mural paintings at both Augustinian convents employ Amerindian characters to picture God's punishment for traditional indigenous practices of polygamy and sacrifice. Good Christian natives, on the other hand, are rewarded for their conversion in both paintings.

Paintings of the Life of Christ, and especially the Passion, fill many of the missions in New Spain and Peru. Knowledge of Christ's life, death, and resurrection was, after all, considered essential for newly converted Amerindians. Meditation on Christ's Passion was furthermore part of the mendicants' daily prayers. Images of the subject were consequently common in *testerae* or niches located in convento cloisters.²² One example is the series of mural paintings in the cloister of the Church and Convent of San Andrés de Epazoyucan, an Augustinian mission constructed circa 1540 on the foundations of an indigenous temple platform. Paintings made in the 1550s by an anonymous artist(s) occupy each of the niches located in the upper and lower cloisters. The works illustrate the Last Supper, the Agony in the Garden, Christ as Ecce Homo, the Road to Calvary, the Crucifixion, the Descent from the Cross, the Transfiguration, and the Ascension. Like the other paintings in the cloister, the *Descent from the Cross* (Figure 19) reveals an artist interested in European pictorial conventions, with illusionistic forms and spaces described using chiaroscuro modeling and linear perspective. It is likely that these testeras not only served the friars' meditation, but also functioned as stages in religious processions held within the cloister. At the very least, they were seen by the indigenous students who attended classes within the cloister.

Like many New Spanish murals, the anonymous cloister paintings at Epazoyucan are almost entirely monochromatic. Color appears sparingly and was apparently painted on top of the dried grisaille, perhaps as late as the twentieth century.²³ The decorative friezes surrounding the narrative scenes are entirely monochromatic, with putti, vines, birds, grapes, and flowers in white and gray on a black background. The narrative paintings, with their passages of blue

FIGURE 19.
Descent from the Cross
from the Church
of San Andrés
de Epazoyucan.
Mural painting.
Epazoyucan, Mexico.
Photograph
© Gilles Mermet/
Art Resource,
New York.

FIGURE 20. *Immaculate Conception* from the Convent of San Miguel de Huejotzingo. 1547–71. Mural painting. Huejotzingo, Mexico. Photograph © Jorge Pérez de Lara.

and ochre, therefore stand out to the viewer passing through the cloister. The dominance of black and white imagery, common to much New Spanish mural painting, may have reflected the woodcuts and engravings that provided models for the indigenous artists. It may also evince the training method at the monastic schools. Art historian Samuel Edgerton has argued that Gante promoted painting in grisaille to make emphatic the distinction between Christian paintings and the colorful pagan murals and manuscripts of Mesoamerican tradition.[24] Monochromatic paintings also appeared in early Andean missions, although the Peruvian muralists soon opted for richer color palettes.

Like Christ, the Virgin Mary is well represented among the mural paintings of the evangelical period. The painting of the Immaculate Conception, at San Miguel de Huejotzingo (Figure 20) is executed in grisaille and rests in a cloister that was once entirely filled with narrative and decorative mural paintings; the church's nave included paintings of local penitential processions. The cloister mural features the Virgin Mary standing on the crescent moon below God the Father. Symbols of her purity, taken from the Psalms of King David and other Old Testament books float in the clouds beside her. To either side are the Dominican Saint Thomas Aquinas and the Franciscan Duns Scotus, who promoted devotion to Mary's Immaculate Conception. The Franciscan order, along with the Spanish monarchs, helped gain papal recognition of the feast of the Immaculate Conception in the seventeenth century. Images of this devotion likewise abounded in Andean churches; the late-sixteenth century mural painting at the Church of San Jerónimo in Cuzco is one of the oldest. While Marian imagery likely reminded Amerindian viewers in both viceroyalties of the female earth deities found in many indigenous faiths, neither mural makes direct reference to this syncretic role.

Mary is prominently featured in the murals at the Church of La Asunción in Juli as well. The Jesuit church, constructed in the late sixteenth century, is filled with anonymous mural paintings thought to be the oldest in the Collao region.[25] In addition to Marian paintings in both transept chapels and probably in the nave (now lost), the apse murals (Figure 21) offered several scenes from Mary's life. The right sidewall features a badly damaged scene of the Holy Family with the Holy Spirit and God the Father. Images of an unidentified male saint and an angel appear to the left in simulated frames; female martyrs Isabel of Hungary

FIGURE 21. Apse paintings. Church of La Asunción, Juli. ca. 1600. Mural painting. Juli, Peru. Photograph © Daniel Giannoni. Reproduced from *Pintura mural en el sur andino* (Banco de Crédito, Peru).

and Martha appear in the intrados of the apse arch, also known as the triumphal arch. The left apse wall, not seen here, shows Mary's death and, just above, Christ welcoming her soul into heaven.

Although Marian themes were popular throughout Europe and the Americas, the paintings at Juli may reveal her special regard in Andean Peru. As they reconciled Christianity with traditional religions, Andeans came to associate the Virgin Mary with Pachamama, an earth deity ascribed maternal characteristics and generative powers. The evangelical period saw the development of several syncretic cults to the Virgin, the most explicit being the Virgin of Potosí, a miracle-working intercessor whose seventeenth- and eighteenth-century images show her body conflated with the Cerro Rico de Potosí (Rich Hill of Potosí).[26] Although the Juli mural paintings offer no visible syncretism—visually syncretic images were uncommon in Peru before the mid-seventeenth century—the paintings' themes undoubtedly reminded Amerindian viewers of the association of the Virgin Mary and Pachamama. The Jesuit priests who staffed the church likely encouraged this kind of syncretism when it facilitated the appreciation of Christian teaching.

Like many Andean colonial murals, the anonymous narrative and iconic paintings at La Asunción in Juli share the walls with ornate simulated architecture. Painted Corinthian columns flank the altar and short pilasters appear to support the painting of the Holy Family. Decorative dados and friezes articulate the lower and upper zones of the wall, and floral borders suggest archivolts over the triumphal arch. Simulated curtains to either side of the apse entrance are pulled back to reveal the mystery of the altar. Like the figural paintings, the ornamental elements reveal an artist familiar with and interested in European pictorial principles and illusionistic devices, including foreshortening and modeling. Naturalistically rendered grapes in the upper frieze, for example, are modeled to suggest a single light source. These colorful decorative motifs deploy a classicizing architectural and ornamental vocabulary to deny the church's humble materials and create the illusion of an earthly paradise.

Andean muralists also simulated other sculptural and architectural forms in their quest to create lavish settings for Christian rituals. At the Church of Oropesa near Cuzco, anonymous artists lined the walls of the nave with painted altarscreens. The circa 1570 example seen here (Figure 22) has two stories and a triangular attic supported by Corinthian columns. The lower level features full-length figures of Saint Catherine of Siena and Mary Magdalene to either side of a niche that once presumably housed a sculpture. In the upper story, Saints Francis of Assisi and Dominic of Guzman flank a narrative of the Visitation of Mary and Elizabeth, the mother of John the Baptist. God the Father occupies the attic accompanied by two reclining angels.

Oropesa's fictive altarscreen occupies a sparse painted landscape also inhabited by a kneeling donor. This identifiably indigenous figure represents one of the few direct references to the contemporary context found in Andean mission murals. It was more common in New Spain, as examples to be discussed

FIGURE 22.
Nave paintings.
Church of Oropesa.
ca. 1570. Mural
painting. Oropesa,
Peru. Photograph
© Daniel Giannoni.
Reproduced from
*Pintura mural en
el sur andino* (Banco
de Crédito, Peru).

demonstrate, to include local figures, both missionaries and Amerindians, in the early paintings; Peruvian artists would not do so regularly until much later. Allegorical references to the local context may have abounded, however, as the Andahuaylillas and Juli paintings discussed above reveal. Another simulated altarscreen in the Oropesa nave includes a painting of Saint James the Moor Killer, which Amerindian viewers associated with the saint's intervention against the Inca in Cuzco.

Another common type of painted ornamentation in indigenous Andean churches is found in Checacupe de Carangas. This late sixteenth-century structure, built on the site of a pre-Hispanic huaca, features one of the most lavish painted ceilings (Figure 23) found in Spanish America. The sloping wood beams of the apse ceiling feature illusionistic paintings of the apostles on the outside register. Each figure occupies a fantastic architectural niche and carries his attribute. The next frieze contains the monograms of Christ and Mary, as well as grotesque masks inscribed within ornate strapwork frames. The flat central portion of this *par y nudillo* roof is entirely decorative and includes classicizing elements as well as floral and geometric motifs recalling Mudéjar architectural ornament. Careful observation reveals roses, grapes, and pomegranates, giving the paintings Christian, not just ornamental, value. The polygonal area over the triumphal arch contains a painting of the Annunciation revealed by simulated curtains.

Scholars have questioned what inspiration indigenous Andeans found in

Mudéjar forms. Some conclude that the abstract geometry and linear motifs of the imported forms appealed to local viewers for their similarity to Andean designs. Colonial art historian Pablo Macera argues, "The . . . [Mudéjar] style imposed by European colonization was received and appropriated by the colonized peoples and they converted it into a means of conserving their own tradition."[27] Others suggest that the lush vegetal and floral ornamentation at Checacupe may have evoked a vision of a fecund earthly paradise. Even before the introduction of Christianity, Andeans believed in the promise of an afterlife paradise known in Quechua as Hanacpacha. This garden was filled with birds and the souls of the good.[28] Missionaries exploited the similarities between Hanacpacha and the Christian paradise to facilitate native understanding of the immortality of the soul. They described the Christian paradise as a lush garden inhabited by the saints and available to good Christians. Some sixteenth-century theologians in fact argued that paradise was located in the Americas; author Antonio León Pinelo even placed the heavenly garden in the Amazon jungle in the eastern Inca territories.[29] The ceiling paintings at Checacupe may have evoked this paradise.

The cloister murals at the Church and Convent of San Salvador de Malinalco in New Spain similarly took the vision of a flowery paradise as their principal theme. Located in the lower cloister of the 1540 Augustinian convento, the mural paintings (Figure 24) were executed by a team of indigenous artists circa 1571. These artists painted a Christian paradise filled with abundant vegetation and

FIGURE 23.
Painted ceiling.
Church of Checacupe.
ca. 1570. Mural
painting. Checacupe
de Carangas, Peru.
Photograph
© Daniel Giannoni.
Reproduced from
*Pintura mural en
el sur andino* (Banco
de Crédito, Peru).

FIGURE 24.
Cloister paintings.
Convent of
San Salvador de
Malinalco. ca. 1571.
Mural painting.
Malinalco, Mexico.
Photograph
© Jorge Pérez
de Lara.

animal life. Plants and animals, along with the monograms of Christ, Mary, and the Augustinian order, fill the cloister walls and cover the vault above. Some of the elements derive from European artistic traditions (and geography) and others are local; several, such as the snake and the owl, are common to Spanish and Andean traditions. The painting style is also polyfacetic, in places illusionistic and elsewhere more abstracted, revealing several hands with varying familiarity with or interest in European conventions. Indigenous pictorial practices are well represented at Malinalco, from the pictographic signs—scrolls signifying speech emerging from the mouths of animals, for example—to outlines, flat areas of color, and profile views common to local pre-Hispanic painting.

Malinalco's formal and iconographic synthesis extends to the meaning of the paintings. Many of the symbols have unambiguously Christian value, such as the pomegranate and the rose. Others derive solely from Pre-Columbian indigenous culture, including the cacao that was used as a unit of currency and a beverage reserved for the Amerindian elite;[30] other plants were used in local religious rituals. Still other elements, such as the ominous owl, held coincidentally similar associations in both traditions. Finally, a number of plants and animals had different associations for indigenous and European viewers. The sinful snake in European traditions was a god in Mesoamerican lore; one community's over-sexed monkey was the other's playful and creative inventor of the arts.[31] On a broader level, both the Christian and the indigenous religions shared the notion of a garden paradise. While the Garden of Eden was lost to Christians, Heavenly Jerusalem was gained by Christ's death. In local indigenous tradition, a flowery paradise known as the House of the Sun awaited deceased Aztec warriors, women who died giving birth, and those sacrificed to the gods.[32]

The presence of overt indigenous symbolism within a Christian convent may seem unusual today, but is entirely consistent with mendicant humanism. The Augustinians were the most liberal of the missionary orders operating in the Americas; they were well known for adopting accommodational strategies to facilitate native understanding of and participation in the faith.[33] According to Saint Augustine, all pagans descended from the biblical tribes of Israel and therefore retained long-suppressed and altered Judeo-Christian values. The Augustinians working in New Spain and Peru consequently attempted to convert the Amerindians to Christianity by exploiting these latent memories.[34] Pre-Columbian forms therefore possessed, to the Augustinians, some Christian value and could be exploited for evangelical purposes. Some scholars conversely believe that the friars did not understand the signs indigenous artists painted into the murals.[35] Most, however, agree that the friars at Malinalco appreciated the native artists' translation of the Christian concept of a paradisiacal afterlife into a formal and iconographic vocabulary and a conceptual framework that put the notion of Christian salvation in familiar terms.

The same spirit may explain the mural paintings in the Augustinian Church of San Miguel Arcángel de Ixmiquilpan (Plate 3). Arrayed in friezes running along the nave dado and vault springing, as well as between the ribs of the apse vault, choir loft, and side chapels, the murals at Ixmiquilpan are disturbing and fascinating. The theme appears, on first glance, an unlikely choice to decorate a Christian church. Warriors and fantastic beasts battle among vines, grasping defeated foes by the hair and wearing their severed heads on their belts. In some areas the human warriors, some dressed in the costumes of Aztec knightly classes (eagles and jaguars), battle each other with arrows and obsidian-blade swords known as *macanas*. In other places, humans struggle against beasts that seem inspired by Greco-Roman mythology, including centaur-like creatures and dragons. What Christian message could viewers possibly take from these violent images? As it turns out, the paintings communicate fundamental principles of the faith.

In one reading of the images, the local Christianized Otomí peoples, formerly subjects of the Aztec empire, battle the nomadic and heathen Chichimec Indians. The Chichimecs were currently plaguing the area near Ixmiquilpan, attacking Spaniards and indigenous peoples traveling to the newly discovered mines in northeastern New Spain. Colonial scholars Donna Pierce and Elena Isabel Estrada de Gerlero have argued that the indigenous painters at Ixmiquilpan ornamented their church with allegorical scenes of their own defense of Christianity against their real foes. They battle the uncivilized Chichimecs and the fantastic beasts that have represented irrationality and incivility in Western art since antiquity. Another interpretation holds that the murals represent the same flowery paradise seen at Malinalco, populated here by the deceased warriors and sacrificial victims who earned eternal grace.[36] This reading is bolstered by the parallels between the church's titular saint, the Archangel Michael, and the Pre-Columbian deity Tezcatlipoca, the Aztec patron of warriors. Whatever their exact meaning, the paintings celebrate the virtues of a devout life and the eternal battle between temptation and righteousness, a theme known in Christian traditions as the psychomachia.

As at Malinalco, Ixmiquilpan's murals display both formal and iconographic synthesis. The figures reveal European pictorial conventions in their natural proportions, but are painted with flat washes of color within firm outlines, as in pre-Hispanic paintings. Likewise, the vegetal scrolls are based on classical acanthus leaves and other European decorative motifs, but appear alongside speech scrolls, four-petaled flowers (known as the *ollin*, the Mesoamerican glyph for movement and one of the Aztec celestial bodies), and victorious warriors grasping the hair of their defeated enemies just as they had in pre-Hispanic paintings.

Before leaving the murals, we must consider one last category. Most convents include mural paintings that reference the monastic order, its saints and martyrs, and its own missionary activities. Several New Spanish sites, for example, include images of Tebaid, the Egyptian birthplace of Christian monasticism. More contemporary references appear in the Huejotzingo mural of the twelve Franciscans who traveled to New Spain in 1524. Another cycle at Coyoacán pictures local Franciscans martyred in Japan in 1597.

The mural cycle in the cloister staircase at San Nicolás de Actopan in New Spain (Figure 25) is among the most developed examples of this genre of monastic self-consciousness. The elaborate program, painted circa 1575, is composed in up to five stories and covers the staircase walls. Each level features an ornate classicizing arcade filled with the Doctors of the Church whose writings shaped Catholic practices, and the saints, theologians, and humanists of the Augustinian order. These intellectual ancestors of the New Spanish missionaries sit at their desks and compose the texts that regulated Augustinian beliefs. The painter employed intuitive linear perspective to allow the figures to share the viewer's space, although their largely monochromatic portraits taken from European prints distance them from the real world. At the bottom of the staircase, however, the convent's prior fray Martín de Acevedo kneels with two indigenous parishioners, Juan Atocpa and Pedro Izcuicuitlapico, bringing this Augustinian family tree into the present for friar and Amerindian alike; this group may also represent the murals' designer and painters.[37]

The Actopan staircase murals undoubtedly inspired the clerics who studied at the convento, one of three centers of higher education for New Spanish Augustinians. Mounting the staircase surrounded by the heroes of their order, the mendicants at once recalled their teachings and understood their call to action.[38] At the same time, however, the native painters and the mendicant designer may have

FIGURE 25.
Cloister stairway
murals. Convent
of San Nicolás de
Actopan. ca. 1575.
Mural painting.
Actopan, Mexico.
Photograph
© Jorge Pérez
de Lara.

wanted to communicate with indigenous audiences. Historian Serge Gruzinski argues that the artists composed the cycle with Aztec painted genealogies in mind. These works, painted in manuscript codices like those discussed below, both recorded past rulers and their deeds, and also defined communal identities. The Actopan staircase murals may therefore have presented an opportunity to inspire the mendicant audience and to frame Augustinian religious authority in terms familiar to the local population.[39]

Manuscript painting

Painted manuscripts were among the earliest examples of colonial art and some, like the mural paintings, assisted the evangelical effort. At least thirty-five books known as Testerian codices survive, most painted in New Spain. They are named for the Flemish friar Jacobo de Testera who employed painted articles of the faith to teach his native charges.[40] But while their ends may have been similar, these manuscripts' formal qualities differ dramatically from the mural paintings. Instead of Renaissance pictorial principles or synthesized combinations of Pre-Columbian and European conventions, these catechisms employ abstracted pictographs. They likewise do not offer stories of the life of Christ or the Virgin

Mary, but instead include catechetical teachings such as the Creed, the Sign of the Cross, and the Hail Mary. Their purpose was to translate Christian teachings into forms presumably understood by indigenous viewers.

The painted catechism that once belonged to fray Pedro de Gante (Figure 26) is typical of the Testerian codices. Over its eighty-two pages, the manuscript represents Christian doctrine in highly abstracted pictographs and symbols drawn in ink and sparingly painted with tempera. The page seen here represents the Sign of the Cross and part of the Lord's Prayer. Read across both folios, the painted figures and symbols stand rebus-like for the words and phrases to be recited. Some of the forms are conventional Pre-Columbian pictographs but most present a new repertoire of signs developed to communicate Christian ideas. The new pictographs are mainly ideographic (standing for larger ideas), such as the Spanish soldier who stands for the phrase "our enemies" in the Sign of the Cross, the haloed head at the beginning of the second line representing God, and, on the next line, the dove of the Holy Spirit; others signs are phonetic (combining representational and ideographic signs to produce spoken sounds). But unlike the murals, there is reason to believe that these images were painted by friars, not native artists.[41] The friars who painted the Testerian codices nevertheless similarly took advantage of a well-established native artistic tradition to facilitate Amerindian conversion to Christianity. Before examining other colonial manuscripts, let us briefly consider indigenous painted texts.

Before the Spaniards arrived, Mesoamerican Maya, Mixtec, and Aztec peoples painted pictorial manuscripts or codices to record and preserve calendrical, genealogical, historical, ritual, geographical, and divinatory knowledge. Painters known as *tlacuilos* in the Aztec Nahuatl language employed conventionalized

FIGURE 26.
Catechism of Fray Pedro de Gante. 1524. Tempera on paper. Photograph © Biblioteca Nacional, Madrid, Spain.

writing systems to communicate their information. (See Sidebar 5.) While Maya painters employed hieroglyphic signs, Mixtec and Aztec painters used pictographs that were representational, ideographic, or phonetic. The tlacuilos painted their works on sheets of cloth or, more commonly, on screenfolds made of bark paper or animal skins. These codices were read by *tlamatinime*, the keepers of communal knowledge who, like the painters, were trained at schools known to the Aztecs as *calmecacs*.[42]

The style of Mesoamerican manuscript painting varied by region, but all stressed concept and convention over illusionism. In Mixtec manuscripts, which have survived in the greatest numbers, the pictographic figures and objects are bound within firm contour lines and painted with flat colors.[43] Human figures occupying undefined spaces appear in profile, with large heads and hands, and attributes to aid identification. Their poses and gestures are conventionalized symbols that support the narrative. Numbers, such as dates, are rendered in combinations of dots, bars, and other forms. The earliest colonial manuscripts displayed many of the same characteristics, and scholars still debate the pre- or postconquest provenance of some codices. Spanish reaction to Pre-Columbian manuscripts was mixed. Unlike their bewilderment at the knotted string quipus Andean peoples used to record and recall information, the Spaniards recognized Mesoamerican pictographic writing systems as a mode of communication similar to European book illustration. The colonizers found the information the paintings communicated, however, at once abhorrent and useful. As evidence of pagan practices, of course, many religious manuscripts were burned; no Aztec manuscripts and only one Maya codex survived these purging flames. Some sacred Mixtec codices, however, were sent to Spain as examples of the curious New World peoples. Other manuscripts, especially histories and genealogies, remained in New Spain where they continued to serve native communities. A handful of friars even collected the paintings, recognizing the destruction of traditional native ways. Colonial authorities likewise employed the paintings to understand and administer the region they occupied. Pre-Columbian codices even served as legitimate visual evidence in Spanish courts, since early modern Europeans implicitly trusted this kind of visual record. In 1531, for example, Amerindians from Huejotzingo testified with the help of manuscript paintings as part of a land dispute involving encomendero Hernán Cortés.[44]

Mesoamerican indigenous manuscript painting did not end with the Spaniards' arrival but, like mural painting, it experienced profound changes. As the Gante catechism illustrates, pictographic communication remained a valuable tool not just for recalling old ways, but also for negotiating the new context. Amerindian artists continued to paint manuscripts for their communities under colonial rule, adapting their images as their situation demanded. Fray Toribio de Motolinía explained how native peoples recorded current events in pictorial form. Speaking of the Christians at his convent, Motolinía wrote, "I told them I could hear confession of only those who would bring their sins written down in figures, because writing in figures is a thing they know and understand . . .

**Excerpts from fray Diego Durán's *The History of the Indies
of New Spain* (1581) on Aztec painting.**

After hearing of the Spaniard's arrival, the Aztec emperor Moctezuma looked
to local divinatory codices to learn about the strangers. Durán's description
of the event, compiled with the help of native informants and Pre-Columbian
manuscript paintings, highlights Amerindian use of painted codices. The
painting Moctezuma (also sometimes spelled Motecuhzoma) ordered made
of the Spaniard may perhaps be considered the first example of colonial art.
It has not survived.

> Tlillancalqui answered that he would be happy to comply with the king's
> wishes and have the painting made, whereupon he ordered that the best
> artist in the country, an old man, be brought. Motecuhzoma warned this
> man that he must not reveal anything that might happen, under pain of
> death. The painter was cowed but exclaimed that he was not a man to
> uncover secrets of such a great and mighty lord. His paints were brought
> to him and Tlillancalqui began to describe to him what he should depict.
> The artist drew a picture of the ship the way it had been seen, showing
> the Spaniards with their long beards and white faces. He painted their
> clothing in different colors, their hats and caps upon their heads and their
> swords in their belts. When Motecuhzoma saw this, he marveled and gazed
> upon the painting for a long time. Finally he asked Tlillancalqui, "Were
> those things like the ones that have been painted here?" And the answer
> was "Yes, O lord, they are exactly so. They are identical." Moctezuma
> paid the artist for his work and said, "Brother, I beg you to answer this

[I]mmediately they began to bring so many writings with their sins that I could
not attend to all of them."[45] In addition to their usefulness in the missionary
endeavor, the pictorial manuscripts of early colonial New Spain served secular
purposes as well.

The *Tira de Tepechpán* (Figure 27), for example, was produced in its native
community by and for native viewers. This screenfold of twenty-three papel de
amate leaves chronicles the history of Tepechpán, a town of Acolhua peoples,
and the nearby Aztec capital, Tenochtitlan. Beginning with the mythic migration
from Aztlán in 1298, the *Tira* records the political and military histories of the
two communities along a linear chronology of circular date glyphs read left to
right. Tepechpán's events appear above the dates and Aztec Tenochtitlan's below.
Some years include no historical information, while others present several events

question: by any chance do you know anything about what you have painted? Did your ancestors leave you a painting or a description of those men who were to arrive in this land?" The painter answered, "Powerful lord, I shall not lie to you, tell you an untruth, or deceive you, for you are the image of the god. Therefore I shall tell you that I and my ancestors never were dedicated to any arts save those of painting pictures and other symbols. My forebears were merely the artists of past kings and they depicted what they were ordered. Thus, I know nothing of that which you ask. If I said I did my answer would be a lie."

. . .

Motecuhzoma summoned all the oldest painters of books from Malinalco, those from a region that is the Marquesado or Hot Lands, and those from Claco . . . [H]e begged them to tell him if they knew anything about strangers who were to arrive in the land . . . He also wished to know if the ancestors of the painters had left information regarding these things or painted manuscripts or images. When all this had been asked of them, the Malinalcas brought a picture and showed it to him. It portrayed men with a single eye in their foreheads like Cyclops. . . . The painters from the Marquesado displayed a drawing in which men appeared who were fish from the waist down, explaining to Motecuhzoma that they were to come to this land. Others showed the king creatures who were half men, half snake. But in the end, none was able to present anything that looked like a painting that would clarify Motecuhzoma's doubts.

—From Diego Durán, *The History of the Indies of New Spain*, translated and annotated by Doris Heyden (Norman: University of Oklahoma Press, 1994), 503–4.

connected by lines to their corresponding dates. Changes in ruler are marked by the colors of the date glyphs.[46] The history includes seventy-five years of Spanish colonial rule and ends in 1596. An anonymous tlacuilo painted much of the manuscript at an unknown date, perhaps relying on a Pre-Columbian codex for older events. A second painter continued the chronology where the first left off in the 1550s.[47] Both artists maintained their source's conservative style and pictographic vocabulary, but adjusted their repertoire of pictographs to account for the foreign presence.

The fragment of the *Tira de Tepechpán* illustrated here spans the years 1344–59. The figures seen above the line of date signs are believed to be Aztecs, thanks to their clothing and hairstyles. They have apparently emigrated to Tepechpán, sacrificed animals, and made offerings at the local temple found to their right.[48] The Aztecs' decision to relocate to Tepechpán was caused by the events seen below the date signs. These images refer to the Aztecs' expulsion from Chapultepec, a site they inhabited before arriving at Tenochtitlan. An Aztec warrior battles an enemy from Chapultepec and a burning temple between them signifies the Aztec defeat. Footprints leading away from the burning temple illustrate the Aztec flight to Colhuacan. The Aztec ruler Huehuehuitzilihuitzin, with a black band painted over his eyes, appears at the end of the path of feet, while another path leads to the Aztec figure Ténoch making an offering to the Colhua

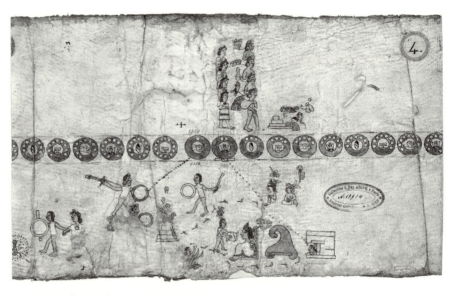

FIGURE 27.
Tira de Tepechpán.
Detail. Finished
1596. Tempera
and ink on
papel de amate.
Photograph ©
Bibliotheque
National,
Paris, France.

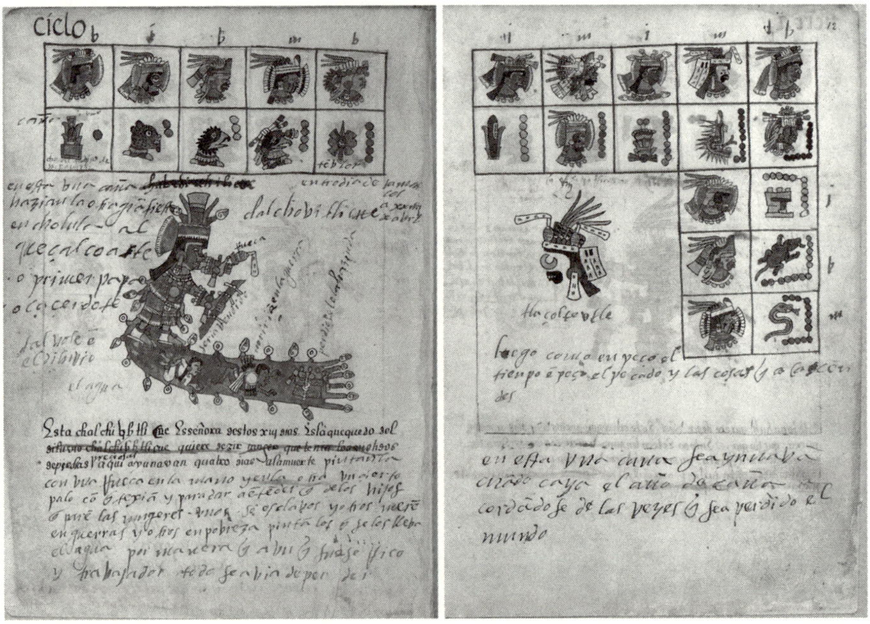

FIGURE 28.
*Codex Telleriano-
Remensis.* Detail of
fols. 11 verso and
12 recto. 1562–63.
Tempera and ink on
paper. Photograph
© Bibliotheque
Nationale,
Paris, France.

leader, Cocox. Legend explains that the offering contained the relics of the Aztec god Huitzilopochtli.⁴⁹ The Aztecs would leave Colhuacan to found Tenochtitlan within a decade.

At the same time that the *Tira de Tepechpán's* anonymous artists and other tlacuilos deployed manuscript painting to chronicle their own changing histories, Spaniards looked to the painted records to understand the Amerindian world. An indigenous tlacuilo painted the *Codex Telleriano-Remensis* (Figure 28) for Spanish patrons in 1562–63. While the circumstances of the commission are unknown, the patron likely responded to the viceregal government's desire to employ native manuscripts to study New Spain's Amerindians. It appears that the anonymous painter copied several Pre-Columbian manuscripts (now lost) to compile a kind of cultural encyclopedia for his European audience.⁵⁰ One of his or her sources was, like the *Tira*, a pictographic history of the Aztecs. Another was an eighteen-month calendar, each month bearing an image of its reigning god.

The *Telleriano-Remensis* page seen here was inspired by a third manuscript type, a 260-day divinatory calendar known as a *tonalamatl*. This type of almanac, used to determine significant ritual dates or to predict the future of a newborn child, was also known as a *veintena* for its division of time into twenty segments of thirteen days.⁵¹ Each veintena falls under the influence of two deities, one with great power over the events and the other less influential. In this example, the veintena is governed by Chalchiuhtlicue, an Aztec fertility goddess identified by her butterfly nose ornament, weaving spindle, and the water that flows from her blue costume.⁵² The second deity is Tlazolteotl, the goddess of filth, represented only by her costume worn in religious rituals. The squares above the two deities are the dates with their numbers and pictographic names.

The *Codex Telleriano-Remensis*, like the *Tira de Tepechpan*, is a combination of Mesoamerican and European forms, materials, and purposes. The anonymous painter retained the conservative style of his Pre-Columbian sources, and the paintings reflect the formal characteristics of Aztec art. The profile figures, for example, all appear bound within outlines, with color applied in flat washes. Chalchiuhtlicue occupies an undefined space without setting or other contextual information. The pictographs, including the shells that identify water, maintain traditional shapes and proportions. The artist nevertheless employed European paper and composed his or her efforts into a Western-style book rather than a screenfold. His patron was not an Amerindian holy person, but a curious foreigner. This unidentified Spaniard and others added explanatory notes or glosses over the years in Nahuatl and Spanish to help European viewers understand the images.

The colonial tlacuilos' biggest non-Amerindian clients were the mendicant friars. Some of these ecclesiastics commissioned painted books of indigenous traditions to aid the extirpation of idolatry; others wanted to record traditions undergoing rapid changes. Franciscan friar Bernardino de Sahagún (1499–1590) was one of the latter. In 1557, the Franciscan provincial asked Sahagún to compose a text in Nahuatl of Christian doctrine and other information useful for missionaries.[53] For the next three decades, Sahagún learned about the Aztec peoples, helped by his native students at the Colegio de la Santa Cruz at Tlatelolco, a school of higher learning founded in 1536. Sahagún and his assistants, who may have contributed to the murals at Malinalco,[54] relied on Pre-Columbian and early colonial manuscripts, as well as the memories of local peoples. From these sources, the Franciscan and the students produced the manuscripts known as the *Primeros memoriales* (1558–60) and the *General History of the Things of New Spain* (1575–80), better known as the *Florentine Codex*. Both manuscripts were profusely illustrated by native tlacuilos. As art historian Eloise Quiñones Keber explains, the friar's goal was "to gather and record information about the life, language, culture, and beliefs of the people among whom he labored."[55] Throughout the endeavor, Sahagún faced an array of challenges including a 1572 royal decree prohibiting colonists from recording the Amerindians' "superstitions and way of life."[56] The Franciscan scholar thankfully persevered.

The *Florentine Codex* is a monumental encyclopedia consisting of three volumes totaling more than twelve hundred pages. The manuscript is organized into twelve books on topics from the Aztec gods and the history of Tenochtitlan, to events of everyday life and the natural history of the region. Two columns of text tell the lengthy story in Spanish and Nahuatl accompanied by over 1,800 illustrations. Most illustrated pages feature a single drawing; some have three.

The *Florentine Codex* page seen here (Figure 29) comes from Book Two, Part Three. The unpainted drawing features the conquistador Hernán Cortés and the Aztec emperor Moctezuma. Between this pair stands doña Marina, known in Mexican lore as La Malinche, the translator who assisted Cortés in his passage into central Mexico; she may also have been his mistress. Although she would become a symbol of Mexico's *mestizaje* as the first indigenous woman to bear a Spaniard's child, this polemic is not referenced in Sahagún's manuscript. Instead, here she mediates as the two powerful figures speak to each other. The speech scrolls emerging from their mouths reveal that the two are deeply involved in conversation, which Marina/Malinche translates in her central position. The structure in the background represents the Aztec ruler's palace and is adopted from the glyphic sign for such buildings.

Like the drawings in other manuscripts, the Sahagún illustrations are synthetic products of the colonial context. Although their artists were clearly interested in European pictorial illusionism, such as the chiaroscuro modeling of the figures and the representation of three-dimensional forms and space, the images preserved some ancestral traditions. Their use of native pictographic speech scrolls or the stereotypical renderings of costuming, for example, reveal that the artists were willing to draw upon two repertoires of formal and symbolic visual languages to communicate their story.

The Spanish desire to learn about indigenous cultures was not solely for curiosity's sake, religious efficacy, or scholarly pursuits. Royal officials, who had imposed their authority atop the existing indigenous political system, looked to pictorial manuscripts for information useful in governing the territory. In

FIGURE 29.
Fray Bernardino de
Sahagún, *Florentine
Codex*: Book Two,
Part Three, fol. 68.
1575–80. Tempera
and ink on paper.
Biblioteca Medicea-
Laurenziana,
Florence, Italy.
Photograph
© The Bridgeman
Art Library.

1530, for example, King Charles I ordered New Spanish administrators to look
to Pre-Columbian manuscripts for information about Aztec tribute systems.[57]
Colonizers also consulted maps and histories to understand Amerindian life.
In 1541, Viceroy Antonio de Mendoza commissioned a painted manuscript that
has come to be known as the *Codex Mendoza* (Plate 4). The book, created for
King Charles I, includes more than seventy illustrated pages recording the Aztec
history from the foundation of Tenochtitlan to the reign of Moctezuma. It also
provides an account of religious and political practices, as well as social customs
associated with marriage and childrearing.

The tribute record in the *Codex Mendoza*, known as the *matrícula de tributos*,
identifies the goods sent by subject tribes to Moctezuma, and was undoubtedly
copied from a lost Pre-Columbian manuscript. The page seen here (Plate 4),
shows the tribute paid by Tepequacuilco and thirteen other communities identified by their place glyphs lining the left side and bottom of the page. The offerings
are impressive. The bundles in the first and second rows represent 3,600 cloaks,
skirts, and tunics. The next two registers record one feathered costume, one jag-
uar costume, and twenty ordinary feathered costumes created for Aztec military
regiments; each outfit includes a shield. Elsewhere on the page are one hundred

copper axes, five necklaces of a precious green stone known as *chalchihuitl*, two hundred jars of honey, twelve hundred varnished bowls, and bins of corn, beans, and amaranth.[58]

The last part of the *Codex Mendoza*, the so-called ethnographic section, is titled "Daily Life Year to Year." It was likely created without the assistance of an existing manuscript, since indigenous people had no reason to record how they raised children, got married, entered professions, or participated in Aztec society. The section was hence newly created for Mendoza. This likely explains the conspicuous absence of religious rituals, since the viceroy had little interest in viewing these pagan acts.[59] Instead, civil themes dominate this part of the manuscript, including the governance of Moctezuma. In Figure 30, the emperor, identified by his crown, sits in the private quarters of his palace; the stone lintel and circular disks mark this as an important building according to the Mesoamerican pictographic language.[60] On the lower floor, beyond the courtyard, members of the governing council sit on *petate* mats. Speech scrolls emerging from their mouths reveal that they converse, perhaps discussing the litigants outside the palace. The female figures, identified by their hairstyles, dresses, and kneeling posture, point in a gesture that may indicate their accusations against the men

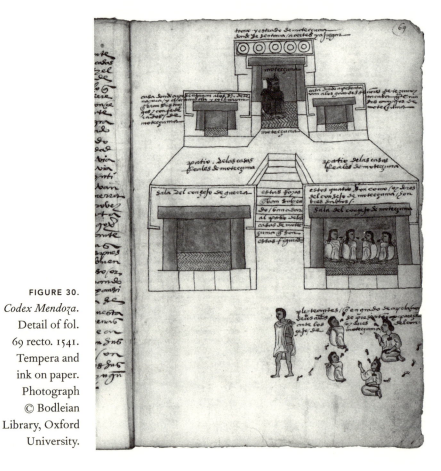

FIGURE 30.
Codex Mendoza.
Detail of fol.
69 recto. 1541.
Tempera and
ink on paper.
Photograph
© Bodleian
Library, Oxford
University.

they face.[61] Footprints, symbolizing travel, suggest that the men and women have come from elsewhere; a third man walks away, perhaps after his own appearance before the council.

Although the *Codex Mendoza's* anonymous tlacuilo retained many conventions of Pre-Columbian Aztec art even in paintings that were not based on an existing source, his art also reveals an interest in selected Western conventions. Visualizing Moctezuma's palace, for example, reflects an interest in narrative staging not found in Pre-Columbian Mesoamerican art. The palace's intuitive perspectival rendering is likewise born from an interest in European illusionism. The figures in "Daily Life" are noticeably more naturalistic in their proportions than the figures in the tonalámatl, copied from a Pre-Columbian source. At the same time, the painter maintained the pictographic vocabulary, outlines, and flat colors of local painting traditions. The *Codex Mendoza* consequently offers a vivid example of visual and conceptual synthesis present in much colonial art.

The maps of the *Relaciones geográficas* also offer a glimpse of the variety of representational strategies operating in early colonial manuscript painting. They similarly reveal the usefulness colonial authorities found in a traditional Mesoamerican art that was, coincidentally, common to Europe as well. In 1577–78, King Philip II sent a questionnaire to royal officials throughout the Spanish empire requesting information about the territories they governed. With questions on local geography, trade, and transportation, the king hoped better to understand and administer the diverse lands. Three of the questions asked for drawn maps of the local town plans, regions, and coastlines. These maps would ultimately contribute to a vast album mapping the entire Spanish empire. Disappointed with the governors' lackluster response, Philip sent the questionnaire again in 1584.

The king and his royal cosmographers were unprepared for the array of maps the European, criollo, and Amerindian respondents offered. While colonial bureaucrats in the viceroyalty of Peru returned five maps drawn in the European style, New Spanish authorities offered the king sixty-nine maps, forty-five of which were likely made by native tlacuilos who employed traditional Mesoamerican mapping strategies.[62] The 1580 *Map of Amoltepec* (Figure 31), an indigenous town near Oaxaca, undoubtedly baffled the Spaniards accustomed to maps that employed linear perspective and geometric projections to record topography, and town plans based on physical spatial relationships. The Amoltepec map, on the other hand, defines territory conceptually. Amoltepec, identified by its glyph, a hill with soap plants, occupies the center of the page. Two figures sitting nearby represent the indigenous ruler's palace while the church signifies the local monastery, a feature shared by many colonial maps.[63] A ring of place glyphs identifies local towns, but their location on the map bears no relationship to their physical distance from Amoltepec.[64] The map is not topographic, but communicentric—that is, the map located Amoltepec conceptually at the center of a territory defined by historical relationships rather than mountain ranges and roads.[65] The river, identified by its shell water glyphs, cuts diagonally across the right side to signify its role in defining the relationships between the towns. But while the king and his cosmographers may not have appreciated this and other similar maps, viceregal courts did. Indigenous communities employed maps like this to establish town boundaries in court cases throughout the colonial era.

The present discussion of early colonial codices has exclusively considered works created in New Spain, but New Spanish administrators and Amerindians were not the only ones to deploy painted manuscripts for their own purposes. Andeans may have recorded their histories on knotted quipus rather than pictographic codices, but they nevertheless soon appropriated the manuscript medium to negotiate within the colonial system. Although much fewer in number, the Andean manuscript paintings nevertheless have important lessons to offer about colonial art. The *Arms of the Descendents of the Inca Tupa Yupanqui* (Plate 5) is a case in point.

Spanish colonial authorities granted privileges to indigenous nobles in New Spain and Peru, including the right to avoid taxation and tribute. Ruling elites therefore pursued recognition of their nobility before the Spanish government. In 1545, Felipe Tupa Yupanqui and his brother Gonzalo Uchu Hualpa, heirs of the royal Inca dynasty, received official recognition of their position in the form of a coat of arms granted by King Charles I.[66] The anonymous painting

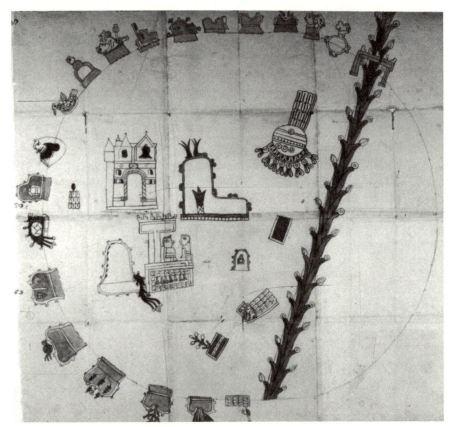

FIGURE 31.
Map of Amoltepec.
1580. Ink and
watercolor on
paper. Photograph
© Nettie Lee Benson
Latin American
Collection,
University of
Texas, Austin.

seen here, which references that event, combines Andean and European symbols to visualize the family's status. Painted in the late sixteenth or early seventeenth century, the painting's left side features the brothers standing behind their ancestor, identified as "The Great Topa Inca Yupanqui." The Great Inca wears the insignia of his nobility, including the *maskha paycha* headdress and red *llakota* cape; his *uncu* tunic displays the traditional checkerboard design Andeans employed to signify social status. At the same time, the Great Inca possesses signs of European power, including the scepter, a pike bearing the new heraldic device, and the European crown resting nearby. The coat of arms on the right side features emblems referencing the family's Inca heritage including the bird (perhaps a condor) flanked by jaguars under a rainbow, and crowned serpents. This painting demonstrates how elite Andeans learned to negotiate within the colonial circumstances, employing the colonizer's art for their own ends, as the native Andean family turned to manuscript painting to maintain its privileged status.

The most famous Andean manuscript is Felipe Guaman Poma de Ayala's 1613–15 *Nueva corónica i buen gobierno* (*New Chronicle and Good Government*). Like the anonymous painter of the Tupa Yupanqui arms, Guaman Poma appropriated the manuscript medium to serve his own needs. In this case, the elite indigenous author told Spanish King Philip III of his frustration with the conditions of colonial Peru using a form the foreign ruler would understand. Guaman Poma furthermore composed his manuscript expecting to see it published in typographic print, which the astute Andean understood as an efficacious medium for communicating to a wide audience, and one Europeans considered even more trustworthy than drawings.

Over 1,189 pages bearing 389 line drawings, Guaman Poma chronicled the history of the Andean world from Adam and Eve and the indigenous primordial couple through the conquest and the early colonial period. His text and illustrations include the abuses native peoples suffered at Spanish and mestizo hands, and the good conduct of Andean Christians. Rather than the knotted quipus of his ancestors, which he included in several drawings, Guaman Poma employed words and drawings to weave his story. His doing so not only embodied the widespread appropriation of figural narrative art by Andean colonial artists, but also permitted the king to witness the events for himself and understand the truth of the author's claims.[67] But even within this European framework of written text and figural illustrations, Guaman Poma preserved Andean artistic conventions.

In the first illustration seen here (Figure 32), Guaman Poma visualizes his offering to the king. The inscription at the top reads, "The kings asks and the author responds. King Philip III King and Monarch of the World." The illustration accompanies a section of the text in which Guaman Poma holds an imaginary discussion with the king, who asks him about Peru and how the author would remedy its ills. The drawing of this fictitious meeting features Guaman Poma, wearing European clothes but a stereotypical Andean haircut, kneeling before the monarch. He reads from the open book, his right hand raised in a gesture of

FIGURE 32.
Felipe Guaman
Poma de Ayala.
*The Author with King
Philip III* from *Nueva
corónica i buen gobierno.*
1615. Ink on paper.
Photograph © Det
Kongelige Bibliotek,
Copenhagen, Denmark.

oration. The king, represented as an idealized type rather than a specific portrait, listens from his throne. He wears the same symbols of royal power seen in the Tupa Yupanqui painting—crown, scepter, and cloak—and sits on a raised dais under a broad canopy to mark his superior status. But alongside these European pictorial devices that identify the king's power, Guaman Poma employed a traditional Andean compositional strategy to communicate the nature of this relationship. The author located the two figures on a diagonal that runs from upper right to lower left (seen reversed in the drawing so that it would be correct in print). Andean artistic conventions used this spatial arrangement to symbolize the superior status of the figure on the upper right.[68] Guaman Poma deploys this strategy throughout the text to inform knowledgeable viewers about the nature of the scene. Most significantly, he reverses the arrangement to denote the poor government of Spaniards or others whose superior status was not deserved, illustrating, as Guaman Poma–scholar Rolena Adorno has described it, the "chaos of colonial life."[69]

Despite his complaints about the abuses Spanish viceregal officials, parish priests, and colonists committed, and his disgust at the misbehaviors of the viceroyalty's African, mulatto, and mestizo populations, Guaman Poma did not advocate Peru's separation from Spain. He instead argued for the creation of a Christian Andean nation that would be part of the Spanish empire, but governed by native peoples.[70] The Peruvian people, Guaman Poma informed the king, were devout Christians. To illustrate their good behavior, the author included illustrations such as Figure 33, in which Christian Amerindians work reverently on a sculpted Crucifixion. (See Sidebar 6.) The drawing not only illustrates the significant role native Andeans played in the ornamentation of local churches, but also evidences the application of European pictorial practices. The pictured sculpture is illusionistic and based on newly introduced notions of verism. The drawing itself evinces an artist interested in linear perspective and chiaroscuro, albeit to a limited extent, to create the illusion of three dimensions on a two-dimensional surface. Recalling the friars' belief that abandoning Pre-Columbian pictorial systems in favor of Western illusionism symbolized true conversion and adoption of Spanish ways, Guaman Poma embodied the

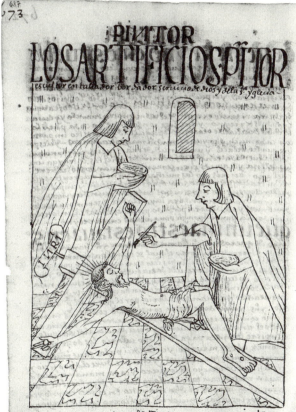

FIGURE 33.
Felipe Guaman Poma de Ayala. *Amerindian Artists* from *Nueva corónica i buen gobierno.* 1615. Ink on paper. Photograph © Det Kongelige Bibliotek, Copenhagen, Denmark.

Excerpt from Felipe Guaman Poma de Ayala,
Nueva corónica i buen gobierno (1615).

Painter, sculptor, embroiderer, artisans in the service of Our God in this Territory: The Christians dedicate themselves to the creation and emulation of God. All the world attends to this for the service of God and of his Majesty and for the good of their souls and the health of their bodies. Since seeing the holy objects, we accede to the service of God. Kings, princes, dukes, counts, marquises, gentlemen of the world learn this art. And in the churches and temples of God there should be ornamentation and many paintings of saints. And in each church there should be a painted [Last] Judgment. These show the return of the Savior, heaven, the world and the punishment of hell, so that the Christian sinner may see it. And in that way shall be paid to the said [church] official alms for the construction or the alms . . . for the goods within the church. And [good Christians] shall serve him and give him food and the *caciques* will not involve him in their drunkenness.

    If he is a drunk or lecher, the said painter will not receive a license for the said work, even if he is a good artist do not allow him this. And he shall be punished by justice because being drunk he does not (*sic*) commit heresies with the holy images because he should be Christian, although a sinner. A drunk, even if he is Spanish, is an idolater. Even if he is not drunk he is not in his right mind, which the demons control.

—From Felipe Guaman Poma de Ayala,
Nueva corónica i buen gobierno (1615), fol. 688.

successful evangelization of the Americas. It is just as true, however, that this author's manuscript demonstrated that native peoples were not *tabulae rasae* upon which to inscribe new information, and were instead savvy intellects who used all of the tools at their disposal to negotiate the new context.

Traditional Arts in the Colonial Context

Feather mosaics, woven textiles, and quero cups were items produced in Mesoamerica and the Andes before the Spaniards arrived. They were deployed in ways that supported the state and displayed the typical artistic characteristics of their respective cultures. All three media continued under Spanish colonial rule in altered forms, but to different ends. The final portion of this chapter considers a New Spanish feather mosaic, and an Andean quero cup and tunic, and examines the fates of these traditional arts in the viceregal context. Comparing the *Christ at*

FIGURE 34.

Mystic Mass of Saint Gregory. 1539. Feather mosaic. Photograph © Musee des Jacobins d'Auch, France.

the Age of Twelve (Plate 6), the *Mystic Mass of St. Gregory* (Figure 34), the Quero Cup (Figure 35), and the Uncu (Plate 7) completes this introduction to the arts of the so-called evangelical era.

Feather mosaic, known as *amantecayotl*, was a highly prized art in Pre-Columbian Mesoamerica. Aztec emperor Moctezuma kept an aviary at his palace to supply his *amantecas* with their colorful and precious materials. These specialist artists painstakingly applied individual feather barbs to drawings on paper made from the maguey plant to fashion objects from cloaks and fans to warrior costumes and shields. As the *Codex Mendoza* demonstrates, tribes subject to the Aztecs also produced feather mosaics and offered them as tribute to the lords in Tenochtitlan. The medium consequently operated as a visual reminder of the hierarchy of Mesoamerican society and as a symbol of the relationship between the Aztecs and subject communities. The iridescent feather work, which changed color as it moved through the light, may have additionally possessed religious value, reminding viewers of the god Quetzalcoatl; scholars believe that those who wore the shimmering works became god-like.[71] The Spaniards who saw the feather mosaics were amazed by the shifting colors and complicated designs. Cortés mentioned the works in a 1520 letter to King Charles I and included 117 feather mosaics in a 1522 shipment to European dignitaries.[72]

The mendicant friars promoted feather mosaics in the early colonial era.

Amantecayotl was one of the arts taught at Gante's school of San José de los Naturales. Mission communities in Michoacán, organized in a Utopian plan that assigned each native village a marketable craft, also produced feather mosaics. With no experience in the medium themselves, friars employed older amantecas to teach the youngsters. These indigenous artists no long made warrior costumes, but instead produced an array of new objects for the colonial context. Writing at the end of the sixteenth century, fray Jerónimo de Mendieta explained that amantecas made "birds, animals, figures of men, capes and mantles to cover oneself, and vestments for the priests in the churches, crowns or miters, shields, fly swatters, and other things that they like."[73]

Indigenous artist Juan Bautista made the feather mosaic *Christ at the Age of Twelve* (Plate 6) in Michoacán, the site of the Augustinian school of Tiripetío. The image features the bust of a youthful Christ inscribed within an oval frame. The frame includes an inscription from the Gospel of Luke referring to the story of Christ's three-day debate with the doctors of the Temple of Jerusalem. This event from Christ's youth is one of the Seven Sorrows of the Virgin Mary and the feather mosaic has a companion image of the sorrowing Virgin also signed by an artist, Juan Cuiris, who may be Juan Bautista.[74] Both images are based on European engravings and evince an artist interested in the illusionistic potential of his medium, as he employed chiaroscuro to suggest the volume of his figures.

Another well-known New Spanish feather mosaic is the 1539 *Mystic Mass of St. Gregory*. The mosaic (Figure 34) features Christ and the Instruments of the Passion, also known as the Eucharistic Ecce Homo, appearing during a mass conducted by the sixth-century Pope Gregory the Great. The Instruments or *arma christi* were presented in sixteenth-century New Spanish art as the objects by which Christ defeated the devil and appeared regularly on atrial crosses. At the same time, the mosaic may reference Pope Gregory's championing of images as tools for instructing people without letters. The work, created by indigenous Christian hands in an indigenous medium, would seem to embody the truth of Gregory's message and justify the image-based teaching methods employed by New Spain's mendicants.

The inscription on the feather mosaic, however, provides

FIGURE 35.
Quero cup. Late sixteenth century. Oil on wood. Museum Expedition 1942, Frank L. Babbott Fund. Photograph © Brooklyn Museum, New York.

still more information about the commission: "Fashioned for Pope Paul III in the great city of Mexico of the Indies by the governor don Diego under the care of fray Pedro de Gante of the Minorites, A.D. 1539."[75] It is believed that the mosaic's patron was Diego de Alvarado Huanitzin, the indigenous governor of the community of San Juan Tenochtitlan. The gift may have celebrated Paul III's 1537 bull *Sublimis Deus*, in which the pope declared the full humanity of New World Amerindians and freed them from enslavement.[76] Like Guaman Poma, then, don Diego and his indigenous artists deployed narrative images rendered in an illusionistic style to communicate their ideas to a European audience. At the same time, for the missionaries, the feather mosaic demonstrated the acculturation of native peoples and illustrated the truth of Paul III's estimation of Amerindians as capable of acquiring Christianity and European-style civility. The *Christ at Age Twelve* and the dozens of other feather mosaics on liturgical goods and wall hangings produced in the next two centuries similarly confirmed the efficacy of this unique art as proof of the success of the evangelical effort.

Andean quero cups (Figure 35) were likewise produced by specialist artists before and after the Spaniards' arrival. Quero cups are small wood vessels with flared openings used for *chicha*, an alcoholic beverage used in religious rituals. Artists known as *querocamayoc* carved and ornamented the cups with incised registers of geometric designs, including concentric shapes and highly abstracted figures. Common throughout the Andes, the queros display different regional formal characteristics; the Inca examples, for example, were identifiable by their particular type of abstraction.[77]

But the meaning communicated by Pre-Columbian quero cups was less in their ornamental vocabulary than in their context. Andean leaders gave queros and *uncus* (tunics) jointly as offerings to allies. Together the cup and tunic functioned as mnemonic devices recalling the circumstances of the alliance through the Amerindian notion of reciprocity.[78] The woven uncus bore *tocapu* designs, registers of squares with geometric patterns that are thought to communicate social status; tocapus may also have referenced specific historical events, such as the battles that resulted in the alliances the offerings commemorated. Communities displayed the queros and uncus during significant rituals, and interpreted their historical and political significance through accompanying songs and dances. The queros could only have meaning, therefore, within the appropriate context of cup, uncu, and performative ritual. Needless to say, this signifying system made little sense to the Spanish colonists, who nevertheless feared it.

The rituals that allowed the queros to communicate to Andean viewers were consequently prohibited as paganism. In a 1582 manual on the extirpation of Andean idolatry, Cristóbal de Albornoz advised priests to confiscate any queros they encountered, since the cups were used in rituals of ancestor worship and helped native peoples to evoke memories of the Pre-Columbian past.[79] A text on idolatrous practices written six years later explained, "They adore lizards big and small, snakes big and small, [and] butterflies; and all these creatures were made into figures, and they are painted on the vessels in which they drink . . .

[I]n all this they had superstition, which they keep even until today because these animals are omens. They consult these omens and dreams, and they fear them and on seeing them they presume bad luck."[80] Finally, in a general edict warning of idolatry, Viceroy Francisco de Toledo likewise warned of sacred animals and birds painted on quero cups.[81]

Toledo's edict and the 1588 text demonstrate that quero painting, even though it was not an art taught at the monastic schools, had independently undergone an iconographic transformation by midcentury. Instead of the concentric geometric shapes and highly abstracted human faces found on Pre-Columbian examples, late sixteenth-century queros featured animal images; they also soon included tocapu designs. Art historian Thomas B. F. Cummins believes that as the rituals involving the quero and uncu could no longer be celebrated, queros accepted the tunics' tocapu patterns in order to retain the signifying power of the paired objects.[82] The quero also compensated for the lost oral information with narrative and iconic representations. By the end of the century, queros like the example seen here were dominated by figural representations, many of them apparently enacting the rituals that Andeans were no longer able to celebrate.[83] Hence, even away from official circles, indigenous arts experienced profound change in the new colonial context. And although the sacred vessels of Christian ritual might have offered the opportunity for missionaries to incorporate queros into Christian rituals as a form of accommodation, they did not. Unlike the Mesoamerican feather mosaics, queros were not embraced by the missionaries or appropriated for use in the church. Their abstract designs and their associated non-visual communication were simply too strange and unfamiliar for the friars. The art form nevertheless survived and flourished away from official circles, adapting at each turn to the circumstances it faced.

But what of the tunics known as *uncus* bearing abstracted tocapu patterns and colors to communicate social status? Extant examples reveal that uncu production continued in the colonial context. Early Spanish observers praised Andean textile production; Viceroy Francisco de Toledo went so far in 1572 as to say that the cloth represented Andean intelligence.[84] Hence Andean artists continued to weave their beautiful cloth under Spanish rule. More than mere examples of skilled craftsmanship, however, the tunics remained a visible sign of social position both for Andean and Spanish viewers. These garments, like the Aztec knotted wrap or *tilma* in New Spain, even assumed the burden of symbolizing a generic Inca male identity in European and colonial paintings and prints made throughout the colonial era. This is not to say, however, that the uncu survived the colonial experience either unchanged or unproblematically.

A seventeenth-century uncu (Plate 7) reveals a shift in material as well as form. The garment is woven from the traditional dyed camelid yarn, but additionally uses metallic thread and silk. The latter materials, introduced by Europeans, undoubtedly appear in the object for their inherent beauty. They additionally symbolize the wealth of the uncu's Andean owner, as he, like his Spanish and European contemporaries, viewed silk and silver thread as luxury goods appropriate to their elevated station. The tocapu patterns along the edges of the garment recall traditional patterns. The embroidered designs just above these, some of which may have been added after the uncu was finished, conflate European and Andean forms. This decoration includes repeated scenes of Inca rulers receiving tribute, musicians, animals, vegetal and floral ornaments, and tocapu designs. The most vivid example of cultural change in the ornamentation is the double-headed Hapsburg eagle that appears next to tocapu designs at the neck opening. As colonial textile specialist Elena J. Phipps has noted regarding this work, "The juxtaposition of these European heraldic devices with their native equivalent—the tocapu—strongly suggests that this was a garment intended to reinforce elite status."[85]

While the production of uncus and other Amerindian Andean garments continued under colonial rule, viceregal authorities were not always comfortable with their display. Texts and paintings reveal that the Andean elite wore these objects in public ceremonies. Uncus and other garments appeared in portraits as markers of elite status. (See Chapter 7.) Even images created by and for non-Amerindians pictured native peoples in modified versions of traditional dress to embody the Amerindian acceptance of the colonial status quo. Over time, however, colonial authorities came to fear this display of non-European identity. Following the 1780–81 rebellion of the Amerindian Tupac Amaru II, the Spanish crown outlawed as subversive uncus and other examples of indigenous noble clothing.[86]

Hence, like feather mosaics and quero cups, uncus survived colonization but saw their forms and uses change. To these examples of native arts could be added manuscripts, metalwork, ceramics, and stone sculpture, all of which underwent radical change with the Spaniards' arrival. Those that easily fit the colonizers' ends thrived publicly, others existed beyond church and state control, and still others functioned somewhere between the two. All illustrate the political, social and religious importance of art in the viceregal Americas and the complexity of artistic production and consumption within the colonial context.

CHAPTER THREE

Colonial Cities

When the Spaniards arrived in the Americas, they encountered large urban centers and small villages. They left some of these as native communities, adding only the mission complexes discussed in Chapter 1; others they transformed into colonial cities. The early colonists founded still more settlements in previously uninhabited locations, both the reducciones described earlier in this book and communities created for the colonizers. Colonial cities and towns sheltered their Spanish, native, and mixed-race residents and served as administrative centers and sites for economic exchange. Beyond mere practicality, however, town planning and urban development in the colonial context carried significant political and social messages. In particular, the decisions regarding where and how to build reflected the colonizers' desire to create visually impressive, well organized, and emphatically permanent Spanish settlements in the new territories.

This chapter examines the urban development of colonial Spanish America. It begins with the Spanish laws, ideologies, and sources for town planning, then considers the civic and domestic architecture associated with the new cities. The chapter also compares the planning strategies applied in two viceregal cities for their efficacy according to the goals articulated by Spanish authorities. In all sections, the chapter addresses urban spaces as representatives of complex social relationships and political hierarchies. It furthermore considers the impact urbanism and civic ritual were intended to have on native and mixed-race viewers, and offers a reading of this audience's appropriation of the city for its own ends.

Spanish Laws for Town Planning

Philip II wrote the *Ordenanzas sobre descubrimiento nuevo y población* (Ordinances on the Discovery and Population of Towns) in 1573, well after viceregal authorities founded many of the most important settlements of colonial Latin America. The recreation of Tenochtitlan as the capital Mexico City, for example, began in 1521; its central district was virtually complete by the time Philip put pen to paper. Lima, the capital of the Viceroyalty of Peru, was founded in 1535 and likewise well settled—with room left for growth—by 1573. The king's laws consequently did not guide the construction of these cities, but instead summarized a multiplicity of previous royal and viceregal orders, and articulated what had been until then general practice. They also aided later town planners through the end of the colonial era. It is instructive, therefore, to review the ordinances to understand what town planners had in mind as they created (or recreated) the towns and cities discussed below. (See Sidebar 7.)

Although it was not always possible or practical, the king's ordinances urged city founders to choose elevated sites for their settlements, since high ground was more defensible and less prone to flooding. The laws also required reliable accessibility by land for travel, trade, and, if necessary, escape from native attack. The surrounding environment needed fertile land for farming, a handy supply of timber, and a clean water source. Likewise, the town should be located near an established native community to supply labor for farms and ranches. The local indigenous population could also help with construction projects.

The new town was to be based upon a plan and not grow haphazardly. Philip II and the colonial urban planners hoped to avoid the chaotic maps of contemporary European cities, most of which had grown by accretion since antiquity. By the mid-sixteenth century, Spanish authorities saw Toledo and Sevilla as mazes of narrow, twisted streets that lacked visual order, abetted thieves and ne'er-do-wells, and offered generally unhealthy living conditions. The newly founded American cities presented the opportunity to create salubrious, ordered, and impressive urban centers designed to provide comfortable spaces for the colonists and room for future planned growth. As such, the king believed that the cities would represent the civility and order of the Spanish government and life under its care.

Before a single stone was laid, therefore, the king's ordinances demanded that the town founders locate and plan the main square, principal streets, and building plots using measuring instruments and string. They were to locate the rectangular *plaza mayor*, with its corners pointed to the cardinal directions, at the heart of the plan. With a width-to-length ratio of 1:1.5, the plaza would be suited for the movement of horses and horse-drawn vehicles during festivals, but the square's specific measurements depended upon the size of the population. Eight streets were to meet at the square, each straight and wide enough for the movement of horses and soldiers in case of attack. All subsequent streets would meet these at right angles, so that the city might grow with measured order according to this grid plan, with space left at regular intervals for additional plazas. Any structures that violated the plan and interfered with movement could be (and were on occasion) torn down in the interest of uniformity and defense.

With the main square and its streets mapped, building could begin on the principal civic and religious structures. Space on the main square was highly

Excerpts from King Philip II's 1573 *Royal Ordinances Concerning the Laying Out of New Cities, Towns or Villages.*

110. ... On arriving at the locality where the new settlement is to be founded (which according to our will and ordinance must be one which is vacant and can be occupied without doing harm to the Indians and natives or with their free consent) the plan of the place, with its squares, streets and building lots is to be outlined by means of measuring by cord and ruler, beginning with the main square from which streets are to run to the gates and principal roads and leaving sufficient open space so that even if the town grows it can always spread in a symmetrical manner ...

111. The chosen site shall be on an elevation; healthful; with means of fortification; fertile and with plenty of land for farming and pasturage; fuel and timber; fresh water, a native population, commodiousness; resources of convenient access and egress ...

112. In the case of a seacoast town, the main plaza, which is to be the starting point for the building of the town, is to be situated near the landing place of the port. In inland towns the main plaza should be in the centre of the town and of an oblong shape, its length being equal to at least one and a half times its width, as this proportion is the best for festivals in which horses are used and any other celebrations which have to be held.

113. The size of the plaza shall be in proportion to the number of residents, heed being given to the fact that towns of Indians, being new are bound to grow ... [The plaza] shall not be smaller than two hundred feet wide and three hundred feet long nor larger than eight hundred feet long and three hundred feet wide ...

115. The whole plaza and the four main streets diverging from it shall have arcades, for these are a great convenience for those who resort thither to trade ...

regulated, and those buildings permitted on the plaza mayor represented the twin powers of the colonial system: church and state. The king's ordinances dictated that one side of the square be given over entirely to the main parish or mission church. The church itself should be located on elevated ground set back from the square for maximum visual effect. The remaining three sides of the square were to be occupied by the Viceregal Palace, Cabildo or Town Council Building, Customs House, and military garrison; these structures were similarly constructed with an eye toward impressive display. The third force within the colonial system, the economy, made its appearance in the arcades located on the ground floor of the

118. At certain distances in the town, smaller, well-proportioned plazas are to be laid out on which the main church, the parish church or monastery shall be built so that the teaching of religious doctrine may be evenly distributed. . . .

120. After the plaza and streets have been laid out building lots are to be designated, in the first place, for the erection of the main church, the parish church or monastery and these are to occupy respectively an entire block so that no other structure can be built next to them . . .

121. Immediately afterward the place and site are to be assigned for the Royal and Town Council House, the Custom House, and Arsenal which is to be close to the church and port so that in case of necessity one can protect the other . . .

136. If the natives should wish to oppose the establishment of a settlement they are to be given to understand that the settlers desire to build a town there not in order to deprive them of their property but for the purpose of being on friendly terms with them; of teaching them to live in a civilized way; of teaching to know God and His Law by means of which they shall be saved . . .

137. While the new town is being built the settlers, as far as possible, shall try to avoid communication and intercourse with the Indians . . . Nor are the Indians to enter the circuit of the settlement until the latter is complete and in condition for defense and the houses built, so that when the Indians see them they will be filled with wonder and will realize that the Spaniards are settling there permanently . . . They will consequently fear the Spaniards so much that they will not dare to offend them and will respect them and desire their friendship.

—From "Royal Ordinances Concerning the Laying Out of New Cities, Towns or Villages," translated by Zelia Nuttall, *The Hispanic American Historical Review* 5, no. 2 (May 1922): 249–54.

civic structures, built to provide covered access to merchants' shops. Although the king's ordinances did not address the topic, textual and visual evidence demonstrates that mercantile activity took place in the middle of the square as well and represented the coincidence of native and European traditions of squares as marketplaces (or *tianguis* in the Mexica language). Cristóbal de Villalpando's 1695 painting (Figure 36) shows Mexico City's main square, known as the Zócalo, occupied by merchants and the market building called the Parián, which occupied the plaza until the nineteenth century. A similar painting, by an anonymous Peruvian artist, shows Lima's plaza in 1680 bustling with mercantile activity (Plate 8). While presenting idealized visions and eliding the race and class distinctions that regulated colonial existence, both paintings nevertheless illustrate the main square's importance to the colonial cities' economic, political, and social lives.

The king's ordinances did not permit private homes on the main square, though examples discussed below illustrate that the practice was not unknown. Home plots outside the plaza were distributed by lottery to worthy Spanish candidates. The king required that colonists' homes be constructed of permanent materials on solid foundations, to convince native viewers of the permanence of the Spanish presence. The façades were to be uniform in their architectural style to present the most beautiful aspect. In case the aesthetic and material qualities were not enough to convince indigenous audiences of Spanish authority, the homes were to be placed close together and organized around interior courtyards to provide protection and defense for man and beast in the event of an attack.

Throughout the ordinances, Philip repeatedly referred to the effect of Spanish urbanism on the native population. Broad streets, plazas proportioned for equine movement, and solid buildings revealed his intention that architecture and urban design embody the colonial system and its orderliness for the good of Spaniard and native alike; he also hoped that they illustrated the futility of rebellion. The laws nevertheless required that town planners seek the approval of local native populations before building, although indigenous resistance was not to preclude settlement. Until the new town was completed, the colonists were to keep indigenous people away, so that when they finally entered the city the native viewers would be overwhelmed and awed into submission. While Philip's description of

FIGURE 36.
Cristóbal de Villalpando. *View of the Zócalo.* 1695. Oil on canvas. Metheun Collection. © Corsham Court, Wiltshire/The Bridgeman Art Library Corsham Court, England.

the psychological effect that the town would have upon the native population seems overly optimistic and the idea that native people could be kept out of the city while it was under construction is naive, these ideas represent the potency viceregal authorities ascribed to urbanism and helps to illuminate the intentions that lay behind the cities and civic architecture discussed below.

The sources of the colonizers' city planning, specifically the grid plan, also contributed to the potency of urban design. The rectilinear plan organized around a main square with streets meeting at right angles traced its lineage to ancient Roman military encampments and the imperial outposts they became. Similar urbanistic ideas were articulated by the Roman architect Vitruvius, whose *Ten Books on Architecture* received renewed attention during the fifteenth century. In 1491 Spanish authorities appealed to antiquity as a model of civility and order when they constructed the military encampment of Santa Fe de Granada before the final reconquest of Spain from the Moorish occupiers. That victory, which was understood as confirmation of God's approval of Spanish policies, likely also justified the continued use of the grid plan. Similarly, town planners had access to Italian Renaissance theorist Leon Battista Alberti's *On Architecture*, an annotated 1512 edition of which belonged to Antonio de Mendoza, the first viceroy of New Spain and son of the humanist diplomat whose ideas may have inspired the plan of Santa Fe de Granada.[1] Alberti's stamp on Latin American town planning is likely revealed in the ideal proportions of the main square and the aesthetic uniformity prescribed by Philip II. Recent scholarship has furthermore determined that colonial town planners, and even the king's ordinances, based their designs on the Heavenly Jerusalem described in Ezekiel's prophetic vision.[2]

Even this brief review of Philip's ordinances reveals the significance the Spanish crown and its colonial representatives attributed to urban design. The city embodied Spanish culture and civility by an appeal to ancient and Renaissance authority; it likewise symbolized divine sanction of the colonial effort and operated as the physical manifestation of the new social hierarchy. By the specter of military forces moving through its streets and defenders lying in wait behind its solid façades, the city discouraged native rebellion, while its uniform civic and domestic buildings hopefully precluded altogether such rebellious thoughts. Seemingly placed by God's hand, the city and its buildings summarized the colonial effort and may have evoked visions of heaven itself. But the king's laws did not take into account the actual circumstances colonists faced as they transformed native centers and new sites into Spanish cities. A detailed look at selected viceregal urban centers offers a more complete understanding of colonial urbanism and its outcomes.

Tenochtitlan Becomes Mexico City and Soldiers Become *Señores*

The Aztec capital of Tenochtitlan was an ordered urban center well before the Spaniards arrived. The Sacred Precinct, located in the heart of the city, was a colossal, walled square measuring approximately 1,300 feet on each side. Its orientation, like many Pre-Columbian sites, referred to the cardinal directions and the movement of heavenly bodies. A number of structures surrounded the paved plaza including schools, a ceremonial ball court, and the Great Pyramid dedicated to the gods Huitzilopochtli and Tlaloc; the emperor's six-acre palace complex sat nearby. Aztec builders, much like Philip II, understood the administrative efficacy of a well-ordered city. Four neighborhoods radiated out from the plaza and were organized along straight streets and canals that met at right angles. Man-made causeways connected the lake city to the shore and an aqueduct brought fresh water from Chapultepec Hill to the city center.

The first Spaniards to see the beauty and order of Tenochtitlan were uniformly awed by the city, but Hernán Cortés and his soldiers nevertheless demolished much of it during the final campaign of 1521. Their actions should be considered both practical and symbolic. Cortés wrote to Spanish King Charles I that it pained him to destroy the magnificent city, but he did so to humiliate his enemies. Then, demonstrating the potency of urbanism in the Spanish mind, Cortés decided to locate the colonial capital on the ruins of Tenochtitlan instead of other geographically more suitable sites, such as Coyoacán or Texcoco. Cortés needed his city to occupy the seat of Aztec authority and demanded that it be reconstructed in a way that would show the native people that the Spaniards were "strong and secure and well in charge."[3] It should be noted that a different strategy informed the founding of Puebla de los Angeles, built in 1531 among—but not on top of—native communities and intended solely for Spanish inhabitants.

Alonso García Bravo redesigned Tenochtitlan's center, drawing on the existing palaces, roads, and canals as points of departure for the new *Traza*, as his 1523–24 plan came to be called. Amerindian laborers executed the central district, which was reserved for Spaniards and their institutions; the four surrounding *barrios* housed an indigenous population numbering up to 100,000. A description of native workers written a few decades later likely provides a glimpse of the rebuilding efforts.

> [T]he crowds of laborers were so thick that one could hardly move in the wide street and causeways. Many died from being crushed by beams, or falling from high places, or in tearing down old buildings for new ones . . . The laborers carry everything on their backs; they drag great stones and beams with ropes; and in the absence of skill but abundance of hands, four hundred men are used to move the stone or beam for which only one hundred are necessary. It is their custom, when moving materials, that the crowds sing and shout, and these voices continued by night and day, with the great fervor of building the city in the early years.[4]

And just as this description narrates a horrific abuse of native labor, it also raises important questions about the efficacy of Cortés's agenda. While the forced rebuilding undoubtedly humiliated the city's former masters at one level, at another we may wonder how much the native laborers identified with the visible infrastructure of the former Aztec capital and the structures they erected by their own hands with the stones of their own temples and palaces. By the same token, it stands to reason that the sculpted images of Aztec deities buried under the square—some intentionally and some in the wreckage of the initial destruction—permitted the site to retain sacred associations for New Spain's native population.

Around the main square, which occupied a mere quarter of Tenochtitlan's sacred precinct, the native laborers set to work constructing the buildings of Spanish secular and religious administration. Cortés first occupied Moctezuma's reconstructed palace (also known as Axayácatl's palace) on the west side of the square, since this building befit his royal appointment as governor and captain general of the new territory. Covering an entire city block, the palace employed a standard domestic plan, with multipurpose rooms organized around central courtyards lined with arcades or colonnades. As late as 1554, Cortés's Casas Viejas, as the sprawling complex was known, still housed the viceroy, members of the Audiencia, an arsenal, workshops, and kitchens. The massive structure also contained dozens of shops on its south, west, and north sides.

Although the Casas Viejas no longer stand, the 1563 drawing of Mexico City (Figure 37) provides a glimpse of the architecture and a telling statement about

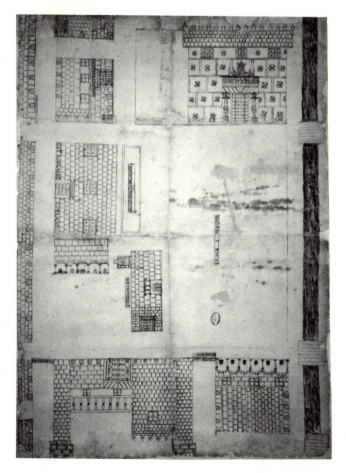

FIGURE 37.
View of Mexico City.
1563. Ink on paper.
Photograph © Archivo
General de Indias.
Sevilla, Spain.

contact-era architectural strategies. The massive stone structure presents two competing images. The heavy walls and crenellated towers at either end of the building suggest defense and strength, much like the so-called fortress monasteries discussed in Chapter 1 and with the same questionable effect on native viewers unfamiliar with European medieval architecture. Cortes constructed an open loggia between the towers, visible in the 1563 drawing as a colonnade and in a 1596 view (Figure 38) as an arcade, not on the ground level as the king's ordinances recommended, but elevated above the street. From this balcony, the conquering Cortés could address his people and survey his lands. Contradicting the defensive aspect—and likely defeating its protective potential as well—the loggia referred to the palaces built by the nobility in sixteenth-century Europe. Cortés's more immediate source was perhaps the 1510 Admiral's Palace in Santo Domingo built by Christopher Columbus's son, Diego, which similarly combined the aesthetics of strength and Renaissance gentility.

When King Charles I dashed Cortés's aspirations to permanent leadership of New Spain and awarded him only a noble title and lands south of the capital, the conquistador employed the same dual personality for his palace in Cuernavaca (Figure 39). It is interesting to note that the loggia became the *leitmotif* of civic authority for both Spanish and native communities. Viceregal town council buildings, known as cabildos or *ayuntamientos*, constructed throughout the colonial era employed this element. Likewise structures designed for native self-administration, called *tecpanes*, appropriated the arcaded loggia by the mid-sixteenth century. Cortés's model endured even into the late eighteenth century, when wealthy Mexicans placed small towers separated by arcaded loggias atop their grandiose homes (see, for example, the Palace of the Marqués de Jaral de Berrio discussed in Chapter 6).

Across from Cortés's Casas Viejas on Mexico City's main square, Martín de Sepulveda, a mason from Spain, directed the reconstruction of Moctezuma's other palace on the plaza's east side. The conquistador occupied this structure, soon to be called Cortés's Casas Nuevas, in 1531; it was sold to the Crown in 1562 by the conquistador's son, and became the Palacio Virreinal (Viceregal Palace). It stands today in a much modified form as the Mexican National Palace, having been nearly destroyed in the 1692 riots and remodeled several times over the next three centuries.

Like the monastic compounds discussed in Chapter 1, the Casas Nuevas seen in early drawings and paintings defies European stylistic labels. The 1563 view presents a combination of Gothic crenellations and plateresque architectural ornaments. These forms referred simultaneously to the military strength, ostentatious wealth, and cultured civility colonizers attributed to themselves. Although not visible in the drawing, the building's internal disposition was organized around three courtyards. Modifications begun with the 1562 sale added a fourth patio and a new character to the façade. As seen in the 1596 view, the palace now assumed a more severe and classicizing appearance. The changes likely speak to the associations viceregal authorities (or the artist responsible for

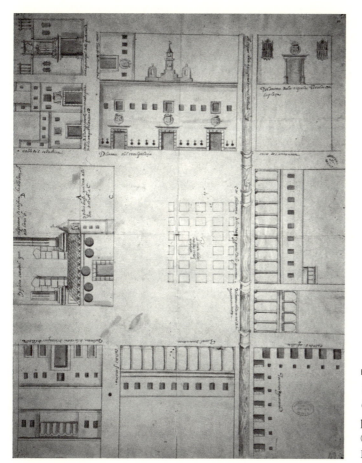

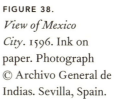

FIGURE 38.
*View of Mexico
City*. 1596. Ink on
paper. Photograph
© Archivo General de
Indias. Sevilla, Spain.

FIGURE 39. Palace of Cortés. Mid-sixteenth century. Cuernavaca, Mexico. Photograph
© Kelly Donahue-Wallace.

the drawing) hoped to make, employing classical restraint to evoke an image of studied humanism and unostentatious power, perhaps following the model of Philip II's monastery and palace, San Lorenzo del Escorial. A similar architectural vocabulary appears on most buildings shown in the 1596 drawing, suggesting that perhaps renovations to other structures similarly followed this trend. The Casas Nuevas's cultured image was tempered, however, by the ominous cannon holes lining the lower story. The openings faced into the square and accompanied the central fountain and a planned *rollo* or public gallows to remind residents of the crown's magnanimous and punitive aspects.

The city's cathedral sat on the north side of the square, nearly atop the buried ruins of the Aztec Templo Mayor. Construction began with the 1524 arrival of Mexico City's first bishop, fray Juan de Zumárraga, and finished in 1534. Contemporary descriptions of the three-aisled structure are nearly unanimous in their disapproval. One author, who was otherwise quite enamored of the capital city, lamented that the cathedral seemed "so small, so humble, and so lacking in adornment."[5] Despite this criticism, the cathedral's construction as a provisional representative of the Catholic Church's role in the foundation and administration of the colony was a significant act. For Cortés, Zumárraga, and the first viceroy, Antonio de Mendoza, the church's presence on the site was more important than its physical appearance, as Spanish authorities employed the sacred structure to represent the new religious order as much as the new viceregal palace represented the civic one. Philip II's ordinances echoed this sentiment. Once again, however, the message of Catholic dominion may have been clouded for native viewers, if not actually subverted, by the use of stones from the Aztec temples. Some of the early cathedral's columns are believed to have been recycled from the serpentine wall surrounding the sacred precinct.[6] Even if this was an accommodating act by church authorities seeking to facilitate native conversion, rather than merely a symbolic act of possession, it stands to reason that there was certainly room for multiple readings. Plans for a new, more suitable cathedral began almost as soon as the older building was finished, and construction was underway by the 1570s. The new cathedral, which would take over two hundred years to complete, still sits on the north side of the square and is the subject of Chapter 4.

A wide canal bordered the southern edge of Mexico City's main square and passed in front of the Ayuntamiento building and its colonnaded *portal* for merchants. This structure reflected the multipurpose dwelling type employed for most secular public and private buildings. Begun in 1527 and organized around colonnaded courtyards, the Ayuntamiento building housed the mayor or *corregidor* and his family, the town council chambers, the jail, the mint, a granary, the municipal meat market, and the silver assay office. The structure gradually expanded over the course of the sixteenth century and underwent a major renovation by Claudio de Arciniega (1520–93) in 1574. It also faced the Parián, the market building, first constructed of wood and later of stone, located in the middle of the square next to the canal that brought goods into the city. Together the Ayuntamiento building and Parián represented the civic and economic aspects of the new colonial system.

Other public and private structures grew up around the main square over the course of the sixteenth century. The Viceregal Palace by 1600 was surrounded by the archbishop's palace, a hospital, a new Royal Mint, the Royal and Pontifical University, and neighborhoods of artisans grouped by trade. The Convent of Saint Francis, with its open chapel and the school for indigenous artists known as San José de los Naturales (discussed in Chapter 1), sat to the west of the plaza; the Dominican and Augustinian convents were found to the north and south of the square respectively. The Jesuit Convent of Saint Ignatius, known as La Profesa, was underway behind Cortés's Casas Viejas.

The homes and palaces of Spanish colonists also surrounded the square, including Pedro de Alvarado's home resting opposite Cortés's Casas Nuevas. Few of these structures, which sheltered up to 1700 Spaniards by 1570, remain today in their original state. The so-called Casa de la Imprenta likely represents the typical home in the central portion of the Traza. Built in 1524 for conquistador Jerónimo de Aguilar, the structure reflects the urban *domus* plan inherited by Spain from the Romans. The home is organized around interior patios, which provide light and access via staircases and walkways to the rooms that surround them. It is unclear precisely how large the structure may have been, since like most sixteenth-century buildings, it was subdivided into smaller spaces for homes and businesses. The remaining structure with its single patio may only represent a fraction of the home's original size.

Nor do any extant sixteenth-century homes in Mexico City reveal their original ornamental programs. Fortunately, several palaces built outside the capital during the early colonial era may afford a glimpse of their decoration. The façade sculpture of the 1549 Casa de Montejo in Mérida, for example, presents a striking image of Spanish authority. Built directly on the Yucatan city's main square by Francisco de Montejo, who finally brought the region under Spanish control, the palace reflects a contemporary formal and iconographic language adapted from European architectural treatises, memories of peninsular buildings, the owner's imagination, or some combination of these.

The façade ornamentation at the Casa de Montejo (Figure 40) employs a visual language reminiscent of the Spanish plateresque style, displaying a similar profusion of decorative elements derived from Gothic and classical architecture. The main door is flanked by Corinthian columns and a Latin inscription reading, "Love of God Triumphs." Fluted pilasters supporting an entablature and a small pediment surround the balcony. The family arms appear above the balcony door; two lions flanking an inscription naming Francisco de Montejo fill the pediment. Rosettes, putti, acanthus leaves, griffins, circular pearl-like elements, and an interlacing vine relief called a rinceau pattern enliven most surfaces. Human figures also appear throughout the program, including the stooped figure supporting the trapezoidal balcony on his back. Two armed soldiers in armor stand on grotesque heads to either side of the heraldic device on the second story. Smaller wild men, identifiable by their wooly fur and rustic clubs, appear next to the pilaster bases and stand on pedestals bearing fearsome faces and halberds. Eight other

FIGURE 40.
Casa de
Montejo. 1549.
Mérida, Mexico.
Photograph
© Jorge Pérez
de Lara.

heads project in high relief at different locations on the façade; the individualized features of several heads suggest that these are portraits of the Montejo family. Similarly, a bearded figure, presumably Francisco de Montejo himself, crowns the pediment. The Renaissance vocabulary continues on the frieze that wraps around the home and in the pedimented windows flanked by herms.

The Casa de Montejo's façade program is an affirmation of the colonial order recently imposed on the region, with the most obvious symbols of Spanish domination being the oversized armed soldiers. But more than military might, Montejo projected an image of reasoned civility triumphing over irrational beastliness. To the sixteenth-century European viewer, wild men and grotesque heads represented uncivilized, subhuman beings. Considering the context of the sculpture on a conquistador's home, it stands to reason that these figures more specifically represented the recently defeated indigenous peoples. Certainly the stooped figure Montejo would stand upon when he surveyed his city from the balcony would seem to support this reading. That Montejo chose European mythical characters rather than actual images of defeated natives suggests that he sought to project an image of studied intellectualism rather than brute strength. In other words, translating the conquest of the region into a vocabulary of Renaissance mythical beings—alongside the more obvious conquering figures—spoke to Montejo's participation in the general intellectual climate of contemporary Europe.

Complicating such an interpretation, however, is the question of the artist's identity. Early colonial authorities lamented the lack of European skilled laborers in the viceroyalty. While this situation changed as more people crossed the Atlantic in the later sixteenth century, early builders employed skilled indigenous laborers trained within their native communities, at San José de los Naturales or other monastic contexts, or some combination of the two. If the sculptors working on the Casa de Montejo were, as some suggest, local Maní Indians familiar with European pictorial strategies,[7] one may wonder about their thoughts as they executed this politicized iconographic program. While the native artist may have been unaware of the associations of wild men with Amerindians in the European imagination, he could not have escaped the meaning of the outsized, armed conquistadores flanking Montejo's balcony.

Native artists likely also executed the paintings inside another urban palace. The Casa del Dean in Puebla, like the Montejo façade, provides a glimpse of how the palaces of Mexico City—in this case the home of a clergyman rather than a conqueror—may have looked in the sixteenth century. Puebla de los Ángeles was the second city of New Spain in 1580 when Tomás de la Plaza, dean of the Puebla Cathedral, built his urban palace. The relatively austere classicizing façade hides a richly ornamented interior that although denuded of its original

FIGURE 41.
European and Persian Sibyls.
Casa del Deán, Puebla. ca. 1600.
Mural painting.
Puebla, Mexico.
Photograph
© Gilles Mermet/
Art Resource,
New York.

furnishings still contains beautiful and complex fresco cycles. (See Sidebar 8 for an inventory of a slightly later home.) The paintings project a cultivated image of sophistication, luxury, and witty intellectuality; the cleric Plaza had no reason to refer to military feats or prowess and, after all, the age of the conquerors was becoming that of the colonists.

The paintings in the second story great room of the Casa del Deán illustrate the *Triumphs* by fourteenth-century Italian poet Petrarch. Allegorical carts representing the triumphs of Death (Plate 9), Time, Chastity, Love, and Fame process around the room in a broad frieze trimmed with ornamental registers. Each wheeled vehicle, pulled by different animals, contains personifications of those whom each triumphant figure might reward or punish. For example, the wheeled cart bearing Death rolls over clerics, children, kings, and commoners,

---

⟋ SIDEBAR 8 ———————————————————————

Excerpt of an Inventory of the Contents of an Artist's Home (1646)

Although today none of the early homes and palaces built in early colonial Spanish America contains its original furnishings, the 1646 inventory of painter Luis Juárez's Mexico City home provides a glimpse of the unique goods well-to-do colonists possessed.

2. A platter, a paint brush, four candlesticks, one silver cup, two censers . . . , one simple silver spoon . . .
3. One silver chocolate jar, one round silver serving tray, one silver salt cellar from Mendoza (Argentina), two small silver spoons . . .
4. Some gold and pearl earrings that belong to Mariana de Esquivel . . .
5. Some pearl bracelets . . .
6. A Moorish rug measuring 3.5 *varas* long [one vara equals roughly 33 inches] and 2.5 wide.
7. An ebony writing case inlaid with tortoise shell and ivory.
8. Eight pillows of embroidered Chinese velvet, four blue and four multicolored, stuffed with wool.
9. Half a bed of *tapincerán* (a tropical wood) garnished in gilded bronze.
10. Four old stools of painted cowhide with yellow silk embroidery . . .
12. An empty Mexican desk, one third vara high and three quarters wide, with silver hardware. . . .
14. Another empty Mexican desk, one vara long and one third vara wide, lined with black cowhide.

since no one escapes the reaper's scythe. Two smaller registers containing animals, vines, satyrs, and grotesques frame the large frieze, and recall the mural paintings found in contemporary New Spanish convents.

The adjoining dining room at the Casa del Deán is surrounded by a frieze of female figures riding horses through a lush countryside. Nine of these are pagan prophetesses known as sibyls (Figure 41); the tenth figure personifies the Jewish Old Testament. Each woman is identified by her inscribed name, an emblematic banner, and a circular inset painting bearing her prophecy; the blindfolded personification of Judaism carries the tablets of Mosaic Law on a broken staff. Two decorative registers defined by rope borders and filled with flowering vines, centaurs, monkeys, and putti appear above and below the sibyls; speech scrolls emerge from the mouths of several animals. A third row of painted

15. A small, old, empty trunk, lined with velvet.

16. Two [polychromed wood] boxes from Michoacán, one smaller and the other midsized, both empty and old. . . .

19. A cloth of Rouen linen, embroidered with blue silk and stitching of gold and blue silk, used.

20. Two pillows and two pincushions of Rouen linen embroidered in blue silk, with gold buttons and silk borders, somewhat used. . . .

23. Five engraved coconuts [as cups for chocolate, usually with attached silver stands].

24. One gold ring with white stones in the shape of a heart . . .

25. Two [painted buffalo hide] table cloths from New Mexico, one new and one old.

26. Two paintings, one of the Ecce Homo and the other of Saint Francis kneeling, one vara long, with gold frames, damaged.

27. One painted landscape of one vara and a quarter long, in its frame, old.

28. Another landscape, unframed, old.

29. Another landscape two varas long, unframed, showing two men on horseback.

30. Another landscape, one vara and a half long, in tempera, old.

31. A small box made of tortoise shell and in it a rosary made of date pit.

32. A portrait of said Luis Juárez, two varas long and one wide.

—From Manuel Toussaint, *Pintura Colonial en México*, 3rd edition (Mexico City: UNAM, 1990), 228–29. (Translation mine.)

arches bearing plants and knights rests at the bottom of the wall, while Tomás de la Plaza's heraldic device is painted over the entrance.

The content and style of the Casa del Deán's decorative program permit multiple readings. The frescoes reflect Christian principles; the pagan sibyls who look forward to Christ's birth may refer to the imposition of Catholicism on the indigenous population and the triumphant carriages to local evangelical success.[8] At the same time, however, there is an unmistakable message of secular sophistication, as Tomás de la Plaza surrounded himself and his guests in contemporary European Renaissance themes; the selection of Petrarch, who frequently wrote love poems, may refer to de la Plaza's own amorous adventures. Likewise, the images are painted according to Renaissance pictorial strategies. Naturalistically proportioned figures ride horses defined by chiaroscuro modeling within a perspectival landscape; selected passages of drapery reflect studies of light and shadow on folded cloth. Although the artist's identity remains unknown, his stylistic affinities with contemporary mission murals by indigenous painters would seem to suggest native heritage. Thus the viewer is left once again to marvel at a truly colonial effort, as the conflation of cultures is so thorough as to be inextricable. What is clear, furthermore, is that the paintings permit a glimpse of the sophisticated (and complicated) culture of late sixteenth-century New Spain, as the art of the conquistador gave way to urbane programs reflecting the courtly sophistication of urban viceregal life, and executed by an indigenous artist who easily met its needs.

Cuzco and Lima: A Comparison of Urbanistic Strategies

Much like the experience in New Spain, town planning in the Viceroyalty of Peru was informed by preexisting indigenous towns, practical concerns, and potent symbolism. The South American cities' foundations generally followed Mexico City's model: planners defined main squares, built provisional churches that became cathedrals, and began constructing colonial cities. Private individuals and the institutions of church and state then took their places according to rank within more or less regular trazas, some built on the foundations of indigenous communities and others newly founded. Like the New Spanish capital and other North American towns, the building practices in the southern viceroyalty would similarly coalesce into Philip II's 1573 ordinances. But a comparison of two of these cities, the former Inca capital of Cuzco and Lima, the new viceregal capital known as the City of the Kings, offers a fascinating study of the motives and effects of urbanism in diverse and complex colonial contexts.[9]

As Francisco Pizarro entered the Andean Inca capital of Cuzco in 1533, he found a city constructed around a huge open plaza, with palaces and temples of finely dressed masonry and a fortress of colossal cut stone looming above on a nearby mountain. The city of roughly 200,000 occupants was saturated with sacred power as the religious and political capital of the Inca empire; even the sand of the main square was holy.[10]

Spanish observers marveled at the order and regularity of the city plan and the beauty of its buildings. Pizarro's secretary wrote, "The city of Cuzco . . . is so beautiful and has so many buildings that it would be worthy of admiration even in Spain, and it is made up entirely of the houses of Lords, because no poor people live here . . . The majority of these houses are of stone . . . and they are well ordered, the streets are set at right angles to one another, all quite straight, and all are paved, and down the middle of each runs a stone-lined water conduit."[11] They were particularly awed by the wealth of materials, especially the gold sheathing on the Coricancha or Temple of the Sun. It therefore comes as no surprise that Pizarro and the early colonists, like Cortés a decade earlier, opted to occupy and remake the Inca city in a symbolic appropriation of power from the old order to the new.

The strategy employed to transform Inca Cuzco into a colonial city was in many ways, however, less radical than that of Mexico City. While Pizarro and his men occupied some Inca structures, others were left in the hands of their native owners, even within the city center. The first Spanish construction in Cuzco was the *picota* or rollo placed in the middle of the Inca main square days before Pizarro's March 1534 foundation ritual. But even this gallows structure may have agreed with native practices: the conquistador's picota is believed to have occupied the site of the Inca *usnu*, a stone pillar in the center of the square used for meting out punishment.[12] The town plan of Inca Cuzco was similarly permitted to remain largely unchanged despite its departures from the ideal grid plan; its only major alteration occurred in the late sixteenth century when colonial authorities reorganized the large Inca main square as three separate plazas. The scale of the original square can be appreciated in an anonymous painting (Figure 42)

FIGURE 42.
Ex-Voto Painting with View of Cuzco. 1650. Oil on canvas. Cuzco Cathedral, Cuzco, Peru. Photograph © Paul Maeyaert/ The Bridgeman Art Library.

commissioned shortly after an earthquake devastated the city in 1650. Other Inca structures likewise housed colonial institutions, the most famous example being the Convent of Santo Domingo begun in 1534 (Figure 1, Chapter 1), which rests on the tall masonry foundations of the Coricancha. Cuzco's Jesuit church, unusually located directly on the main square, also employed the foundation of an Inca palace acquired from the descendents of a conquistador.

As in Mexico City, Cuzco's first Catholic church occupied a site sacred to the indigenous population, in this case the palace of the Inca Viracocha on the northeast side of the square. Plans to build a permanent church on the site, which became a cathedral a few decades later, first circulated in 1538. When construction began in 1560, sand from the square provided the church's foundations and stones quarried from the mountaintop Saqsayhuaman fortress, the site from which a force of native rebels attacked in 1536, became its walls. Contemporary accounts reveal that these materials were selected not only for their convenience, but also as a statement of Spanish authority.

At the same time, early colonists renovated their Inca palaces located around the plaza to suit European tastes. They outfitted homes of stone, adobe, or fired brick on the Inca masonry foundations with carved stone portals and red tile roofs. Some of the two-story structures gained colonnades or arcades for mercantile activities on the lower level and elaborate wooden balconies called *miradores* projected from the walls above. Their interior plans reflected the common domestic organization employed throughout Spanish America, with rooms arranged around open courtyards. The Casa del Almirante (Figure 43), named for its seventeenth-century owner Admiral Gabriel de Castilla y Mendoza, is one of the early palaces still extant in Cuzco. Two levels of colonnades surround the inner courtyard; a stone staircase, located in one corner, provides access to the upper story. According to European Renaissance practices, a reception hall occupied the second-story space over the main entrance. A two-light window, unusually located on the building's corner, is divided by a stone herm, male on one side and female on the other, that overlooks the street and the plaza mayor below. This entrance is flanked by classicizing architectural elements carved of stone and a lintel above the door bears an oversized heraldic device.

The so-called Casa de los Cuatro Bustos or House of the Four Busts (Figure 44) is another early *cuzqueño* palace. Built in the latter part of the sixteenth century, the stone portal employs an architectural vocabulary not unlike that found at the Casa de Montejo in Mérida and the Casa del Almirante. A pair of fluted engaged columns flanks the door, squat in their proportions but otherwise classicizing. The columns appear next to pilasters bearing large and small rosettes and supporting a heavy entablature. The frieze running across the portal includes two grotesque heads facing outwards at the corners and four portrait busts over the door. The relief busts appear to be specific enough to represent individual members of the family whose arms appear atop the ensemble. Their technical execution and formal qualities suggest an artist with limited interest in European pictorial strategies.

No complete examples of early domestic mural painting remain in Cuzco,

FIGURE 43.
Casa del Almirante.
ca. 1600. Cuzco, Peru.
Photograph © Kelly
Donahue-Wallace.

FIGURE 44.
Casa de los Cuatro
Bustos. ca. 1600.
Cuzco, Peru.
Photograph © Kelly
Donahue-Wallace.

but the Casa del Fundador in Tunja, Colombia, offers a glimpse of how conquistadors in the Viceroyalty of Peru decked out their new palaces. On the ceilings of two chambers in the late sixteenth-century palace of Captain Gonzalo Suárez de Rendón, mural paintings offer sophisticated moralizing lessons. Instead of the triumphal carts found in the Casa del Deán, the Tunja paintings deploy arcades populated by animals and plants. Each of these elements derives from contemporary emblem books, and stood for a different moral virtue. To one side of the main salon, for example, appear an apple tree, ox, palm tree, horse, and elephant; to the opposite side are a pomegranate tree, deer, cypress, laurel tree, and rhinoceros, to name just a few. Some of the items, such as the pomegranate tree and the cypress, represent Christian symbols. Others, such as the date tree, reference European emblematic literature and literary symbolism; the date tree took years to give fruit and therefore stood for patient diligence.[13] The family's coats of arms anchored the program and made clear their associations with the house's occupants.

The ornamental strategies employed at the Casa de Cuatro Bustos, the Casa del Almirante, and the Tunja Casa del Fundador therefore seem to reflect the same ideas informing palace ornamentation in contemporary New Spain. Owners deployed the heraldic devices, portrait busts, mural painting, and classicizing architectural elements to speak of their status within the larger Spanish imperial system as well as their participation in the tastes and trends of the contemporary Western world. Seen alongside structures constructed in the unornamented masonry techniques of pre-Conquest Inca builders, the façades in particular would have stood out for their emphatic colonial character. But it seems appropriate to question precisely how these ornamental and architectural vocabularies were understood by their viewers. Fellow Spanish colonists likely understood the associations the homeowners wished to make, and indigenous viewers, even if they were not familiar with European heraldry and classical architecture, would undoubtedly see the forms as non-indigenous, and, therefore, representative of the new colonial order. At the same time, however, the stones borrowed from Inca structures, the visible indigenous foundations, and even the carving technique employed on the portals may have presented a very different message to native viewers.

To modern eyes, the urbanistic strategy employed in colonial Cuzco seems naive. Scholars today question the effect the symbolic imposition of Spanish authority on the highly visible foundations of Inca civilization may have had on native viewers, particularly since Inca religion celebrated the holiness of materials and locations.[14] While Pizarro and the Spanish colonists probably looked to the model of Mexico City's reconstruction, they failed to take into account the powerful effect of the initial destruction of Tenochtitlan's center and the heterogeneity of Amerindian religious practices. Sixteenth-century Spaniards further seemed unable or unwilling to examine their efforts with such subtle self-awareness. Their actions were instead big and brash. As one recent author explains,

> It was expedient [for the Spaniards] to skate over the existence of large
> Indian towns full of civilized Indians, it was expedient to skirt round the

Spanish appropriation of such towns, and it was expedient to appropriate them because not only did they provide temporary accommodation and a supply of Indian labor to hand, together with ready-made foundations for the new colonial buildings and a large, leveled central plaza, but also because once appropriated by the Spaniards they of course no longer existed as Indian towns.[15]

Another modern author notes that to contemporary European witnesses, the mere ceremony of foundation was enough to translate Inca Cuzco into a Spanish, Christian city.[16] But it stands to reason the native residents would not have seen the matter the same way. In fact, for this and other reasons, Cuzco retained a strong Amerindian identity throughout the colonial era.

Lima, the future viceregal capital, did not present anything resembling Cuzco's splendor in the early days of colonization. Instead of a backdrop of stone palaces and gold-clad temples, Francisco Pizarro's 1535 foundation ceremony took place on a plain occupied by small native villages. The architecture in the region consisted of adobe walls and *quincha* or plaster-coated reed roofs. The site nevertheless attracted the conquistador for possessing features Cuzco did not: a more hospitable elevation, plentiful farmland, a dependable water supply from the río Rimac, and coastal access. Further, the area did not have Cuzco's historical baggage. Consequently Lima's urbanism did not require the reinvention of a powerful native space as a colonial center, with the potentially subversive associations made by native inhabitants. As colonial art historian Tom Cummins has explained, "The newness of Lima afforded a historical clarity, whereas the ancientness of Cuzco produced a historical ambiguity."[17] In other words, a new site provided the opportunity to build a viceregal capital that conformed more closely to conquistadors' vision of a colonial city and was comparatively free of the ghosts of Inca ancestors.

Contemporary descriptions suggest that by the time Pizarro held the January 1535 foundation ceremony for Lima, the City of the Kings, the traza was already drawn with a picota or rollo erected in the middle of its newly defined plaza mayor. Thus the conquistador established Spanish authority not only by inhabiting the homes of defeated enemies, but by erecting a symbol of Spain's punitive strength and order. Pizarro immediately began work—with his own labor, if the sources are to be believed—on the adobe town church, perhaps employing the platform of an indigenous pyramid for its foundation. Then, following the drawn traza that marked off several hundred home plots, he marked the locations of civic buildings on the square and distributed plots along the grid to the Spanish colonists.

While Pizarro's plan may not have departed much from the preexisting native town and its adobe buildings, Lima's colonial authorities went to great lengths to ensure that colonists respected the order and regularity of the traza. Government officials measured streets for their width and straightness; they even ordered torn down houses that violated the grid plan. Only wealthy and powerful monastic orders and select individuals flouted the rules. Otherwise, *limeño* authorities closely guarded their ideal city plan, a plan which did not allow room for Amerindian inhabitants. By midcentury, after they took advantage of native labor, city officials pushed indigenous residents out of the central district, which was reserved for Spaniards. In 1571, most Amerindians lived in the planned, walled reducción known as the *Cercado* or Enclosure located across the river, on the east side of the city. This planned area designed to contain native populations alongside the Spanish city was, in fact, the earliest of Viceroy Francisco de Toledo's reducciones.[18]

Like Cortés in Mexico City and himself in Cuzco, Pizarro appropriated Lima's principal native structure as his own palace. The home sat on the main square atop an elevated adobe platform facing the provisional church. In 1549 stonemason Diego de Torres redesigned Pizarro's palace to reflect its new function as the Cabildo building. He did so according to the model of Spanish and Mexican municipal structures with an arcaded loggia dividing the second story. The structure was built of adobe with brick accents and wood supports, probably on the plaza façade. By 1573, stone pillars replaced these as the merchants' arcade was made more permanent. The ubiquitous Peruvian miradores likely hung from the upper story windows. The 1680 painting of Lima's main square (Plate 8) reveals that the structure conformed to the standard multiuse secular plan employed throughout the Americas, with offices, apartments, and workshops organized around internal courtyards. The council meeting hall occupied a large space on the upper story with the jail, chapel, and scribes offices below.[19]

Another residence begun by Francisco Pizarro became the viceregal palace after his death and rested beside the new cathedral on the plaza's northern perimeter. The two-story structure had a massive stone sculptural entrance—perhaps exaggerated in the 1680 painting—executed in a classicizing architectural vocabulary during the tenure of Viceroy Luis de Velasco. A central balcony rested above the door and was used by viceroys to address the colonists. The upper story exterior likewise included projecting wooden grated balconies. While these provided light, air, and privacy to the palace's privileged occupants and hid the large, arched windows, market stalls erected along the lower level of the building offered a variety of products to shoppers of all races and classes (the painting's inscription notes Lima's good bananas). The palace also housed the offices of the royal council, a law court, an armory, and a large chapel. By 1639, the structure was organized around two internal courtyards and sheltered a large garden.

Most homes in viceregal Lima were constructed of adobe, a fact that troubled early chroniclers and city authorities who saw the poor materials as inappropriate to the aspect of permanence colonial structures were supposed to offer. Stone and wood were in short supply in the coastal valley and had to be shipped from Central America or carried overland from as far away as Chile. Therefore, stone sculpture around the entrances of wealthy homes made clear statements of status and wealth. Likewise, the projecting balconies, inherited from Moorish models in southern Spain, with their fine wood latticework spoke as much about the owner's wealth as the modesty of his wife and daughters. It has also been suggested that the new, imported materials contained nothing of the Amerindian past—at least not to the local population—so were therefore appropriate for this new city.[20]

But if some of their materials were different, the limeño palace plans were the same as those of contemporary homes in New Spain, with rooms organized around open courtyards. (See Sidebar 9.) The circa 1600 Casa de Pilatos (Figure 45),

---

⌒ SIDEBAR 9 ─────────────────────────────────────

Excerpts from Padre Bernabé Cobo, *First Book on the Foundation of Lima* (1639).

Chapter IX: On the form and grandeur this city possesses today, the number of families and houses, and review of building materials.

The first homes were built to shelter the settlers; their construction was poor and humble. Using the materials at hand, the houses only occupied the two blocks surrounding the square, since there were few residents then. The rest of the site was planned for those who would come and there were plots to distribute in this way for many years. The settlers built their rooms with earthen walls; the same kind of walls also surrounded the plots and homes of the Indians and Blacks . . . I have seen so many houses built that today there is not a single plot available within the city that is not filled with Spanish buildings . . . In their plan and form these houses [today] have great style and art; most were built according to plans and drawings and there are excellent artisans to design and plan them. There is not a single principal house that does not have a showy portal of stone or brick; making one of these costs 3,000 or 4,000 pesos. The homes have covered entries and courtyards with upper and lower passageways bearing stone or brick columns. The columns come from Panama and each one costs more than 100 pesos. The rooms are very large . . . The chapels are well adorned with rich images and ornaments; in a short time the devotion and religious fervor in these parts has grown so much that there are more than two hundred private chapels. Further, the houses have so many rooms and bedrooms that they are easily shared, allowing two or three residents [and their families] to live together comfortably (as many do), with ample room for masters and servants. The owners go to great lengths to construct large and elaborate wood balconies, and many homes have them. Some are very expensive and all are great recreation, especially those on corners; since the streets are so straight it is possible to see from each corner all the way to the edge of the city.

—From Bernabé Cobo, *Obras del P. Bernabé Cobo*, Biblioteca de Autores Españoles (Madrid: Ediciones Atlas, 1956), 305–7. (Translation mine.)

FIGURE 45.
Casa de Pilatos.
ca. 1600.
Lima, Peru.
Photograph © Kelly
Donahue-Wallace.

built by Diego de Esquivel y Xaraba and located northeast of Lima's main square is one of the few early palaces to retain its original character. Its façade presents a strikingly classicizing character, with a stone entrance of rusticated masonry, one broken and one rounded pediment, and other classical ornaments including dentils, corbels, finials, and carved acanthus leaves. The nearby Casa del Oidor, constructed on the site of a local native governor's home, occupied a privileged location next to the main square. The Casa Osambela, west of the plaza, also dates from this period, and presents a similar, though more elaborate, plan and façade. As elsewhere in the world, these palaces were exceptional, and most homes in Lima were simple, single-story adobe structures with red tile roofs.

On the surface, at least, it would seem that the urbanistic strategy employed in Lima was just as effective, if not more so, than that employed in Cuzco. Certainly for European observers the ordered central traza and the lack of visible indigenous forms permitted Lima to be a Spanish city. No doubt this contributed somewhat to Lima's creole character as the more European of the two Peruvian cities. The presence of the viceregal court and the constant arrival of peninsular bureaucrats and other European colonists were factors, of course, just as decisive in determining Lima's nature.

The Power and Spectacle of Spanish Colonial Cities

Cities are, of course, more than streets and buildings; they are places where people interact with each other and with the structures and spaces of the urban setting. To conclude this examination of early colonial urbanism, it is therefore important to consider how colonists used their cities.

The importance of colonial cities cannot be underestimated. Spanish imperial power was meted out through the viceregal courts in Mexico City and Lima, as well as the sites of regional judicial districts or *audiencias* such as Quito and Guadalajara. Elite colonists who lived in these and other cities dominated colonial society economically, politically, and socially, frequently controlling whole trades as well as encomiendas, repartimientos, mines, or *haciendas* from city residences. The cities' ability to shape colonial life was furthermore aided by the presence of the printing press. First established in Mexico City in 1539 and in Lima three decades later, print shops permitted church and state officials to disseminate standardized religious and political tracts throughout the viceroyalties. In fact, the first press in the Americas, founded by the firm of Jacob Cromberger under the local direction of Juan Pablos (Giovanni Paoli), operated thanks to a royal monopoly and the efforts of Mexico City's archbishop and viceroy. The small towns and villages that existed throughout the American viceroyalties received government representatives and printed missives, traded with urban merchants, and consequently lived in the shadow of and at the mercy of these powerful centers and their residents.

Viceregal cities were also sites of impressive performances that reinforced the authority of Spanish rule and the significance of the colonial city. Processions, executions, celebrations, bullfights, fireworks displays, and other public events said as much about the city and its residents as did the buildings and plazas. These messages generally repeated the positions of church and state articulated in the stones and mortar of temples and palaces. The two views of Mexico City (Figure 36) and Lima (Plate 8) discussed in this chapter, for example, paint pictures of strong governments, robust economies, racial harmony, and deep piety. Despite the damage to the viceregal palace visible in Villalpando's image of Mexico City, which was caused by the riots of 1692, the city is the intersection of colonial life, a "flourishing *civitas*, peaceful and prosperous," as historian Richard Kagan described it, with colonists behaving according to their station within an ideal viceregal social hierarchy.[21] The anonymous limeño artist likewise constructed a scene of urban good will, as residents of all races and classes come together to enjoy the region's natural and man-made bounty. Even the ex-voto painting of Cuzco after the 1650 earthquake (Figure 42) illustrates a community identity promoted by colonial authorities, with colonists on bended knee before the upraised sculpture of a single, Christian deity: the Christ of the Earthquakes. Rather than picture economic and political health, the plaza in this image is the location of the supposed homogeneity of cuzqueño faith after a century of effective evangelization.

Similarly the processions held to mark the entrances of new viceroys, university graduations, and Inquisitorial *autos de fe*, most unfortunately recorded in textual rather than visual forms, restated the colonial order as they marched through the streets and squares of the city. Common working people may not have participated much in planning these celebrations, but they could not have missed their clearly stated political, social, and ethnic order. And the people's presence at and participation in these events constituted, at least for colonial authorities, an affirmation of the status quo.[22]

The social function of colonial processions is clearly illustrated in Melchor Pérez Holguín's 1718 *Entrance into Potosí of the Viceroy Archbishop Morcillo* (Plate 10). The Villa Rica e Imperial de Potosí in the Viceroyalty of Peru owed its existence to the nearby mines of the Cerro Rico, the mountain that appears in the upper right corner of the painting. According to legend, silver was discovered on the Cerro Rico in 1545 by an Aymara-speaking Amerindian named Diego Gualpa (or Huallpa). The llama herder chased his escaped animals up a hill that local native people considered a huaca or holy place associated with the earth deity Pachamama. Gualpa found a vein of silver when, after corralling his llamas, he either dislodged a bush while steadying himself or burned the underbrush with his campfire. He informed his master of the find, and the region's silver mining frenzy began.

In 1572, Viceroy Francisco de Toledo officially founded the Rich and Imperial City of Potosí, which was already a bustling center. By 1600, this city at the foot of the Cerro Rico housed between 60,000 and 85,000 residents.[23] Despite not being a viceregal capital, Potosí grew to be one of the largest cities in colonial Spanish America and its fabulous wealth helped to sustain Spain's imperial power. Potosí's riches were so great, in fact, that Europeans and Americans came to describe immense wealth as being "as rich as Potosí." But the city's good times did not extend to the entire population. Extracting the silver was dangerous work, and forced mita labor and harsh conditions cost thousands of native workers their lives.

Pérez Holguín's painting pictures the viceroy's entry into this important city. Morcillo appears under a canopy, having just passed through a triumphal arch. These ephemeral constructions were common in colonial civic celebrations and usually displayed an iconography that simultaneously celebrated the visiting official and promoted the city's unique identity and interests. Potosí is additionally adorned in the image by paintings and colorful banners hung from homes and the parish church of San Martín; inset images above show similar decorations on private and government buildings surrounding the city's main square, called the Regocijo. Residents of colonial cities were ordered to display these items for civic and religious celebrations, thereby transforming the urban space in recognition of the event. The city consequently operated as a changeable stage set for the performance of the colonial social order.

The city's constructions and ephemeral decorations in the painting share the stage with Potosí's complex, multiethnic population. Careful examination of the image reveals *potosinos* of different ages and ethnicities, from the stereotypically dressed Amerindians, mestizos, and Africans observing from atop the buildings, to the elegantly garbed and ethnically diverse soldiers and courtiers passing below. The two inset images likewise depict Potosí society; representatives of different religious orders, guild officials, and town council members appear on the left while miners dressed as figures from Spanish history entertain elite colonists on the right. In sum, these characters may be understood to construct an ideal image of colonial social order. Each person's presence in this display embodies his/her tacit approval of and participation in the city's ethnic and economic hierarchy that is performed just as much by the architectural spaces the potosinos occupy as by the dress and behavior they exhibit. The painting also evidences, however, what has been described as a criollo anxiety over the disdain they initially felt toward the region's indigenous past and their exploitation of the Amerindian cultural ancestry in criollo self-promotion.[24] This complex aspect of colonialism is discussed further in Chapter 7.

Religious Architecture
and Altarscreens circa 1600–1700

Antonio Ramírez's 1678 painting, *The Construction of the Cathedral of Santiago de los Caballeros de Guatemala in Antigua*, renders in detail the massive building's unfinished walls, vaults, dome, and façade. More than a portrait of the cathedral, however, Ramírez's painting depicts the human activity that swirls around the structure. Animals and men carry materials, women cook and sell food, and clerics observe the building's progress. A handful of wealthy colonists and bureaucrats pass by in elegant coaches or watch from a nearby balcony. The builder, local architect José de Porras, takes measurements on the drum of the unfinished dome.[1] Rendering people and architecture together, Ramírez captured the centrality of cathedrals in urban viceregal life.

By the latter years of the sixteenth century, the colonial cities discussed in Chapter 3 enjoyed growth and prosperity. In the Viceroyalty of New Spain, Mexico City and Puebla became robust urban societies, regional cities grew in areas of rich mining and ranching, and exploration pushed the Spanish presence into today's US Southwest. In the Viceroyalty of Peru, Lima's 25,000 multiethnic residents enjoyed the presence of the viceregal court. The city's religious processions and pious ceremonies no doubt bolstered the fervent spirituality of Isabel de Herrera, better known as Saint Rose of Lima, the first saint from the New World, canonized in 1671. Cuzco retained a strong Amerindian character, helped in large part by its majority indigenous population who resided in neighborhoods organized by ethnicity. Immigrants from Europe continued to travel to both viceroyalties hoping to find fortune. The mendicant orders, which had been granted broad powers to evangelize among the Amerindian populations, turned many of their convents over to secular priests and these missions henceforth became parish churches. While some displaced monks opted for missionary activity on the fringes of the empire, many returned to urban convents in Mexico City, Lima, and other cities.

This chapter examines urban religious construction between circa 1600 and 1700, as secular and regular clergy constructed fabulous cathedrals and convents that testified to their faith. It begins with cathedral construction in the viceregal capitals and Cuzco, before considering representative monasteries and convents in Quito, Lima, Arequipa, and Mexico City. The chapter ends with two shrines constructed to shelter cult images of the Virgin Mary. For each structure type, the discussion considers the style of architectural ornamentation appropriate to the region and period, although a comprehensive stylistic survey is beyond the scope of this book. The chapter instead focuses on exemplary models, emphasizing their organization and function, so that readers may apply the information to the many regional variations in colonial religious architecture.

Cathedrals and Their Altarscreens

Most colonial cities quickly outgrew the provisional churches erected on their plazas mayores. Colonists and viceregal authorities soon criticized the small, rustic structures erected during the initial colonization. As early as 1543, for example, Peruvian Captain General Cristóbal Vaca de Castro reported that Lima's main church was old and too small for the city's growing population. A 1555 observer of the first Mexico City cathedral similarly complained that the structure was "small, humble, and poorly ornamented."[2] Consequently, over the next two and a half centuries, many urban centers saw the perpetual construction, renovation, and restoration of the bishops' churches as earthquakes, construction delays, and changing tastes shaped and reshaped the colonial cathedrals.

New Spanish and Peruvian cathedrals were not simply large churches and the seats of bishops and archbishops; they were colossal symbols of the colonial order. They occupied town squares as symbols of Catholic dominion, frequently resting atop the ruins of indigenous temples, as discussed in Chapter 3. The cathedrals that replaced the provisional churches maintained this position to recall evangelical triumphs. This location also meant that the buildings occupied the space opposite the government palaces and symbolized one of the twin powers of church and state that governed colonial life. And as they rose above the surrounding city, displaying their sophisticated architecture and fashionable ornamentation, the cathedrals embodied the faith of the community and the centrality of Catholic ritual to the social fabric.

Colonial cathedrals were commonly based on sixteenth-century Spanish models; the cathedrals at Valladolid (1585) and Jaén (1546) were particularly influential. Most colonial cathedrals repeated their three aisles and side chapels. They also copied the Spanish structures' rectangular plans with their inscribed crosses composed of nave and transept. Many of the Spanish American structures also employed Valladolid's domed crossing and corner towers; some featured the small projecting apse adopted from Sevilla's cathedral (finished 1519).

Although the cathedrals discussed here are sometimes called "mannerist" for employing classical architectural orders and elements, the structures' stylistic characteristics are varied. The buildings generally display no single period style (as defined by European conventions). For example a colonial cathedral with a mannerist plan may also contain Gothic rib vaults, Mudéjar polychrome wood ceilings, Renaissance barrel and groin vaults, baroque altarscreens and façades, and even a neoclassical dome. Cathedral builders, like the mission architects, were supple in their use of forms and turned to different solutions for a variety of aesthetic, symbolic, and practical reasons. Lengthy construction histories like-wise contributed to the stylistic diversity. Consequently, as with most colonial art, applying stylistic labels derived from European traditions is imprecise. It is nevertheless safe to say that many New Spanish and Peruvian cathedrals share a generally classicizing style that reflected the refined sensibilities of the urban merchants and courtiers who succeeded the conquistadores as the viceregal elite. How individual colonial architects deployed the classical architectural elements and ornaments, however, varied greatly.

Cathedral builders, generically known as *alarifes*, generally came from the ranks of masons or stone carvers, but clerics also contributed to some structures. These architects were responsible for designing the building's plan, walls, and roofing system; most also assumed responsibility for the ornament found on the structure. Their designs reflected the influence of local tastes, European models, and imported architectural manuals, including the treatises of Sebastiano Serlio (1475–1554) and the Roman architect Marcus Vitruvius (b. late first century BC). The architect in charge of a cathedral's construction was the *maestro mayor*. The title was usually granted by the viceroy to the most senior and respected architect working in the city.[3] And while the maestro mayor necessarily had to follow existing plans, depending upon the state of the cathedral's construction, many managed to inject their own personality into the building by updating the style of the ornament or architecture. In fact, the formal solutions introduced by a new maestro mayor might change the tastes of a city. New Spanish architect Cristóbal de Medina Vargas, for example, single-handedly altered the course of Mexican architecture while maestro mayor of several churches in the New Spanish capital; the builder of Cuzco's Jesuit church (1651–68) likewise influ-enced subsequent builders.

The maestro mayor did not work alone on the cathedral. As the Guatemalan painting illustrates, cathedral construction sites were busy places. *Canteros* or stonemasons cut thousands of stones for the massive walls. *Albañileros* or brick-layers placed the stones and the bricks in the walls and vaults. Carpenters made confessionals, pulpits, choir boxes, doors, window frames, and the scaffolding essential for the lofty constructions. *Ensambladores* assembled the altarscreens that gilders, sculptors, and painters outfitted. The ornate façades of colonial cathedrals were designed by architects, ensambladores, or canteros, but the carv-ing inevitably fell to the latter. Cathedrals were also constructed on the backs of thousands of anonymous manual laborers, many of them Amerindians from the city or nearby towns and villages. The diversity of native laborers meant that translators were on the cathedral payroll. Beyond this first tier of workers who were directly employed at the building site, the structure's economic impact extended to a second rung of merchants, restaurateurs, tavern owners, prostitutes, and others who benefited from their presence. It is no exaggeration to say, therefore, that the cathedral was in many ways an industry for a colonial city.

Most of the workers at the cathedral building sites belonged to professional organizations known as guilds. The guilds took charge of training and regulating the practices of each profession; they also certified their members' skills and protected the trade from uncertified competition. Some guilds also excluded indigenous, African, or mixed-race members. Many were in fact founded by European and criollo craftsmen seeking to keep Amerindian workers from lucrative jobs. In all trades, youngsters began as apprentices and spent several years working under a master. At the end of this term, the apprentice took an exam to become an *oficial* or journeyman, which meant that he could seek employment with a master. He took another exam to attain the status of master and open his own shop. Guilds also had associated religious confraternities devoted to specific patron saints. These lay brotherhoods cared for deceased members and sponsored a chapel in the patron saint's honor at a local church. The most powerful guild associated with cathedral construction was the Guild of Masons and Architects; selected passages from the New Spanish guild's 1599 ordinances appear in Sidebar 10.

The Cathedral of Our Lady of the Assumption in Mexico City (Figure 46) began under the direction of Archbishop Alonso de Montúfar with a plan drawn in 1562 by Spanish émigré maestro mayor Claudio de Arciniega (ca. 1520–93). Although earlier plans repeated Jaen's flat apse and Seville's five aisles flanked by chapels, Arciniega's design featured a polygonal apse, three aisles, side chapels, and four corner towers. The city's watery site required that builders construct a platform for the structure, which was built with stone and wood pylons on the ruins of Tenochtitlan's Aztec temples. With royal approval for the plan and the platform complete, the cathedral's construction began by 1573. Although Arciniega's design called for Mudéjar wood ceilings and explicitly prohibited a dome, maestros mayores Juan Miguel de Agüero and Alonso Martínez López, working between 1600 and 1626, constructed stone vaults.[4] In 1635, maestro mayor Juan Gómez de Trasmonte (d. 1647) discarded the original hall church elevation in favor

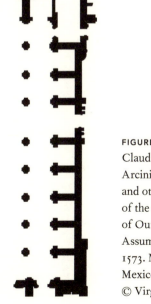

FIGURE 46. Claudio de Arciniega and others. Plan of the Cathedral of Our Lady of the Assumption. Begun 1573. Mexico City, Mexico. Drawing © Virginia Green.

Excerpts from the ordinances of the Mexico City Guild of Masons and Architects, 1599.

ARTICLE 1.

First, at the beginning of each year . . . all the examined masters in said profession will gather before the scribe of the City and the Council to elect overseers. . . . All examined masters will gather for this election, *so pena*, he who does not come, having been called, of ten gold pesos. . . .

ARTICLE 2.

Furthermore, it is ordered that no person of any quality or condition may practice said trade without being examined and having a letter of examination and title from this City. . . . He who was examined in a capital city in Castilla [Spain] . . . may be considered examined, so long as he first presents in this city his letter of Examination. . . .

ARTICLE 3.

Furthermore, he who is not examined in said trade, nor possesses a letter of examination in the described form, cannot participate in any work of said trade nor commit himself nor contract any work, . . . in light of the danger that can happen when one who does not understand takes charge of a work . . .

ARTICLE 4.

Furthermore, it is ordered and decreed that if a poor and unexamined official comes from Castilla [Spain] the examiners are obliged to examine him at no cost and not discriminate against him due to his great poverty; and if he lacks clothing or anything else impeding his work, said governors and

of a basilican profile and adopted sail and barrel vaults in place of rib vaults.[5] He also recommended the addition of a dome, but its construction did not begin until 1656 during the tenure of his son, Luis Gómez de Trasmonte (d. 1684), who was named maestro mayor of the cathedral circa 1640. By 1666 the nave vaults were closed, the first dome was finished, and most of the building was complete. The façade and two front towers would nevertheless take more than a century to finish; the towers planned for the rear of the structure were never built.

The Mexico City Cathedral, built of local chiluca and tezontle stone and oriented on a north-south axis, conforms to the typical rectangular plan of Spanish American colonial cathedrals, with three-aisles, side chapels, a broad transept,

examiners will ask the rest of the examined masters to help him with the requisite wardrobe.

ARTICLE 5.

Furthermore, this trade of masonry consists of many types of constructions such as deep foundations, royal buildings and temples, monasteries, castles, excavations, houses, communal rivers and irrigation ditches, plans of cities; and the masters who practice and teach it must be examined in all or part of these, such as constructing the abovementioned, constructing a house with all its components, arcades of round arches, . . . pointed arches, [and] segmental arches . . . and know the buttressing that each needs, and which are appropriate, and from what each arch derives, know the width and depth of walls according to why they are raised, French and Castilian chimneys, . . . know the types of chapel vaulting such as rib or barrel vaulting, chapels with groin vaulting, chapels with domical vaults. . . . The measurements and proportions that portals are to maintain according to the characteristics of the site, and where to build for sanitation; and in all this are to be examined those who will [practice the trade] due to the great inconvenience and danger that occurs for not being examined and knowledgeable in them . . .

ARTICLE 11.

Furthermore, it is ordered and decreed that no one who is not an examined master with title can have or teach apprentices, they should not engage him, because not being master, he should not have them for the danger that results for the republic.

—From Martha Fernández, *Arquitectura y gobierno virreinal. Los maestros mayores de la Ciudad de México siglo XVII* (Mexico City: UNAM / Instituto de Investigaciones Estéticas [IIE], 1985), 287–90. (Translation mine.)

and a polygonal apse. The nave and transept (Figure 47) sport tall compound Doric order piers supporting barrel vaults with lunettes. Shallow saucer domes rest on pendentives throughout the rest of the building, although rib vaults top the earliest chapels and the sacristy. After initially constructing these roofing systems in the gray chiluca stone, builders turned to red volcanic tezontle, which better withstood earthquakes.

The interior of Mexico City's cathedral was lavishly outfitted with more than one dozen altarscreens (*retablos* in Spanish) located behind the main altar and in the side chapels along the nave. These wood structures, sponsored by confraternities and wealthy families, employed an architectural framework to

FIGURE 47.
Claudio de Arciniega
and others. Interior
of the Cathedral
of Our Lady of
the Assumption.
Begun 1573. Mexico
City, Mexico.
Photograph © Kelly
Donahue-Wallace.

house religious paintings and sculptures organized hieratically, from the predella to the attic. Developed in the Middle Ages to aid those who could not read the holy books or understand the Latin mass, the altarscreens of the early Modern era coupled the didactic function with the desire to create properly ornate and stylish settings for the faith. The architectural and ornamental vocabulary of each retablo reflected prevailing tastes of the day, and, as fashions changed, parishioners and lay organizations paid to update the cathedral's altarscreens.

The *Altarscreen of Our Lady of Solitude* (Figure 48) is one of the earliest retablos remaining in the Mexico City Cathedral. Constructed between 1670 and 1680 by an anonymous ensamblador, the altarscreen consists of a predella, two stories, and an attic. An anonymous painting of Our Lady of Solitude appears on the lower level and Pedro Ramírez's paintings of Christ's Passion occupy the wings. Ramírez's *God the Father* appears in the attic story above the 1811 *Last Supper* painted by José María Vázquez and added later. While this seventeenth-century altarscreen is filled with paintings, other contemporary examples in New Spain privileged sculpture. Most nevertheless shared the Solomonic columns seen here. These twisting columns were inspired by the Puebla Cathedral's 1646 *Altarscreen of the Kings* designed by Spanish sculptor Juan Martínez Montañés or émigrés Lucas Méndez or Sebastián López de Arteaga. The columns' presence on the Mexico City altarscreen reveals how quickly this new form entered the local architectural repertoire. Colonists appreciated its powerful symbolism, referring both to the Temple of Solomon, a structure designed by God, and to Gianlorenzo Bernini's grandiose baldachin (1624–33) at Saint Peter's in Rome. Within a few years, Solomonic columns were found on altarscreens throughout New Spain. They also graced the so-called retablo-façades of local churches.

The façade of the Mexico City Cathedral (Figure 49) was executed in the latter part of the seventeenth century, although the upper portion was not finished until circa 1800. Maestro mayor Luis Gómez de Trasmonte and architect Rodrigo Díaz de Aguilera designed and built the classicizing architectural elements surrounding the central portal between 1672 and 1678.[6] Like the two flanking doors to either side of the massive external buttresses, the central door features a Doric order triumphal arch on the first story; sculptures of Saints Peter and Paul occupy shell niches between the columns. The upper story, constructed between 1684 and 1689 by Cristóbal de Medina Vargas (1635–99), has a relief sculpture of Mary's Assumption in white *tecali* stone in an eared frame. This image, like the

FIGURE 48.
Altarscreen of Our Lady of Solitude.
Cathedral of Our Lady of the Assumption.
1670–80. Mexico City, Mexico. Photograph © Archivo Fotográfico Manuel Toussaint, IIE/UNAM.

saints below, is attributed to sculptor Miguel Sánchez.[7] The flanking paired Ionic columns are separated by tecali sculptures of two apostles in shell niches, with decorative diamond relief panels above.

Between 1684 and 1686, Medina Vargas constructed the aisle portals flanking Gómez de Trasmonte's central door. Their two-story retablo-façades repeat the center door's triumphal motif at the ground level, but include the new Solomonic columns. Medina Vargas's design soon inspired other architects, and Solomonic retablo-façades appeared on Mexico City's Augustinian, Dominican, and Jesuit

FIGURE 49. Luis Gómez de Trasmonte, Rodrigo Díaz de Aguilera, and Cristóbal de Medina Vargas. Façade of the Cathedral of Our Lady of the Assumption. 1672–78 and 1684–89. Mexico City, Mexico. Photograph © Kelly Donahue-Wallace.

FIGURE 50. Diego Arias de la Cerda and Francisco Domínguez de Chávez y Arellano. Façade of the Cathedral of Our Lady of the Assumption. 1583–1654. Cuzco, Peru. Photograph © Kelly Donahue-Wallace.

churches and virtually every other church built over the next century by New Spanish architects such as Diego de la Sierra, José Durán, and Pedro de Arrieta. In Peru, as we shall see, the new column first appeared on façades around 1700 and remained a popular architectural element throughout the colonial era.

The Cathedral of Our Lady of the Assumption in Cuzco (Figure 50) was begun in 1560, but, as in Mexico City, construction proceeded slowly throughout the sixteenth century. The site chosen for the Cuzco Cathedral held immense significance for both the indigenous and criollo populations. The planned structure covered the ruins of the Inca Suntur Huasi, an imperial armory. The cathedral was built next to the Triunfo Chapel, where the miraculous assistance of Saint James the Moor Killer and the Virgin Mary helped Francisco Pizarro break the 1536 Inca siege. The new structure was also located on the site of the provisional church, torn down in 1538, and shared the old building's foundation stones, originally taken from the massive Saqsaywaman fortress above the city.

The plan of Cuzco's cathedral is attributed to architect Francisco Becerra (ca. 1540–1605), who had recently designed the Puebla Cathedral in New Spain. Becerra redesigned a plan by Juan Manuel de Veramendi and Juan Correa.[8] Becerra's design, dated 1583–85, features three aisles, side chapels, a flat apse, and groin vaults. Although originally intended as a basilican church, the plan changed when maestro mayor Miguel Gutiérrez Sencio (d. 1649) constructed brick rib vaults of equal height in the nave and aisles, giving the structure its hall church elevation; the side chapels, however, have slightly lower sail vaults. The cathedral, located on a north-south axis, was virtually completed when the devastating 1650 earthquake caused substantial damage. Reconstruction progressed quickly, however, and the cathedral was finished in 1654.

The Cuzco Cathedral features an elaborate retablo-façade around the central door and more modestly ornamented portals to either side. The façade was designed by Diego Arias de la Cerda and Francisco Domínguez de Chávez y Arellano in 1649 and carved by indigenous stonemasons. The retablo-façade is organized in three levels. The lower story features the Puerta del Perdón flanked to each side by paired and single columns, with a niche in the middle. Unlike the engaged columns that make the Mexico City Cathedral's façade appear relatively flat, the Cuzco Cathedral's columns project from the wall in striking relief. The entablature on the lower level does not cross horizontally above the arched doorway to divide the first level from the second. It instead intersects the arch just before the height of the keystone. Its cornice rises into the second story and opens upward in the center to become a rounded, broken pediment. This treatment of the central portion of the façade became characteristic of Peruvian baroque architecture. The second story repeats the lower level's organization, but adds broken pediments between each column pair. The top register, which is only as wide as the door, features two columns, a rounded broken pediment, and a cartouche with the royal arms. The repeated violation of discrete levels gives the Cuzco Cathedral's retablo-façade a visual verticality, and emphasizes the central area over the main portal. The aisle doors offer more sedate ornamentation, with simple rounded arches of rusticated masonry surmounted by mixtilinear pediments and pinnacles. The façade is anchored to either side by two heavy, low towers topped by small domes and lined, like the façade, with pinnacles. The short towers, a concession to the region's persistent seismic activity, give the building an emphatic horizontality and heaviness that contradict the retablo-façade's delicate fantasy. The Cuzco Cathedral's formal solutions nevertheless exerted great influence on later colonial architecture in Peru, helped in large part by the movement of its artists and craftsmen to other projects within the vice-royalty.[9] Its impulse to verticality and its imaginative use of classical architecture became the leitmotifs of Peruvian altarscreens and retablo-façades.

The Cathedral of Our Lady of the Assumption in Lima is the product of multiple renovations. When limeños found the provisional cathedral built between 1549 and 1551 lacking, viceregal authorities planned a grand structure, with five aisles plus side chapels like the Sevilla Cathedral. Between 1582 and 1594, architect Francisco Becerra, who was concurrently engaged with the cathedral in Cuzco, reduced the size of the immense structure to three aisles and lateral chapels (Figure 51). Becerra's plan included groin vaults, a flat apse, and a hall church elevation, with aisles and nave of the same height as had been used earlier in Hispaniola (Santo Domingo) and Mérida. An earthquake in 1609 damaged some of the vaults of the half-built church, leading architect Juan Martínez de Arrona to cover the structure with rib vaults and exchange the hall church elevation for a basilican profile. The cathedral, located on the eastern side of the plaza mayor, was largely finished in 1622, although the towers took another two years to complete. When another earthquake damaged the towers and vaults in 1687, maestro mayor fray Diego Maroto (1617–96) replaced the damaged stone vaults with wood (Figure 52); over time, many of Lima's public and private structures did likewise. The catastrophic earthquake of 1746 led the re-builders to replace all of the nave and aisle vaults with wood and plaster. The fallen towers and the façade were rebuilt by 1800, preserving the baroque style of the façade, but employing a neoclassical vocabulary for the towers.

The retablo-façade of the Lima Cathedral (Figure 53) was designed in 1628 by Martínez de Arrona and finished in 1645 under the direction of Spanish architect Pedro de Noguera (1592–ca. 1655). The façade offers a triumphal arch

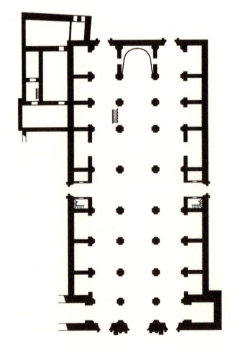

FIGURE 51.
Francisco Becerra and others. Plan of the Cathedral of Our Lady of the Assumption. Begun 1583–85. Lima, Peru. Drawing © Virginia Green.

FIGURE 52.
Francisco Becerra and others. Interior of the Cathedral of Our Lady of the Assumption. Begun 1582. Lima, Peru. Photograph © Reidar Husmo.

FIGURE 53.
Juan Martínez de Arrona and Pedro de Noguera. Façade of the Cathedral of Our Lady of the Assumption. 1628–45. Lima, Peru. Photograph © Kelly Donahue-Wallace.

motif around all three doors, but the Peruvian architects exercised expressive license with the classical architectural vocabulary. For example, the aisle portals feature two levels of columns around each arched door. The central portal, contained between two large buttresses, remains more closely tied to classical traditions, with paired columns flanking sculpture-filled niches and supporting an entablature. The retablo-façade in Lima nevertheless shares the Cuzco Cathedral's transgression of discrete stories. The cornice of the first tier rises in the center, opening to either side of a niche sculpture and projecting into the second story. The upper level repeats the same organization as below, but substitutes thick pilasters for columns; here, too, the central niche projects into the attic level. The façade is topped by a rounded pediment and balustrade. In its verticality and its free exploration of classical elements, the Lima Cathedral retablo-façade exemplifies Peruvian baroque architecture.

The *Altarscreen of the Virgin of the Immaculate Conception* in the Lima Cathedral (Figure 54) likewise summarizes the character of limeño retablos in this era. It remains today as one of the few survivors from the twenty altarscreens that filled the church by 1821. Ensamblador Asensio de Salas and sculptor Bernardo de

FIGURE 54.
Pedro de Noguera,
Asensio de Salas, and
Bernardo de Robles.
*Altarscreen of the Virgin
of the Immaculate
Conception*. 1654.
Cathedral of Our Lady
of the Assumption.
Lima, Peru. Photograph
© Reidar Husmo.

Robles constructed the altarscreen in 1654 following a design by maestro mayor Pedro de Noguera.[10] The architect's plan again employs a classical vocabulary with great artistic freedom. A contemporary description of the altarscreen noted that the twelve columns of the lower tier and the four columns above were covered in seraphim and vegetal ornamentation.[11] While many later altarscreens in Lima were not gilded and instead displayed the rich darkness of its Central American cedar, *La Concepción*, like other seventeenth-century altarscreens, was covered in gold leaf (it was subsequently painted). The altarscreen fills the chapel with strongly projecting wings and a deeply recessed central zone. A later sculpture of the Virgin and Child stands in the middle under a trilobed shell niche. Another larger shell projects over the central area from the upper level. The altarscreen and its spatial manipulation consequently enveloped the faithful within a gilded vision and provided Lima's cathedral, like the others, with a spectacularly ornate site for religious worship.

Monasteries, Convents, and Parish Churches

Colonial cities were filled with monasteries and convents belonging to the regular clergy. Monasteries for the mendicant orders that conducted the initial evangelization were built as soon as city sites were chosen, their plots being among the first granted by town planners. Franciscan, Dominican, Augustinian, and Mercedarian monasteries can consequently be found within a stone's throw of every city's cathedral; when the Jesuits arrived in 1568–72, they too founded monasteries in the city center. Few of the early mother houses remain today in their sixteenth-century condition. The Church and Convent of Santo Domingo in Cuzco discussed in Chapter 1 was built on the ruins of the Coricancha (Temple of the Sun) and is remarkable for retaining so much of its early appearance.

The monasteries, particularly those in the viceregal capitals, experienced a building boom in the late sixteenth and seventeenth centuries. By 1700, for example, Mexico City had twenty-nine monasteries and twenty-two convents. Orders and pious colonists throughout Latin America spent huge sums transforming these houses and their churches into spectacles of power and wealth. In fact, the Franciscans in Lima grew concerned that their monastery's opulence violated the order's vow of poverty. A papal bull from Clement X reminded the friars that the materials of their convent belonged to the Holy See, not to the monks; its splendor was consequently Christ's not theirs.[12]

The colonial monasteries were centers of local communities, as well as cities unto themselves. The larger complexes included a hospital, a seminary, or both; many offered a school for local boys. The Convent of Santo Domingo in Lima, for example, contained a hospice, a carpentry shop, a jail, stables, a bell foundry, a hen house, and an infirmary for the local African population.[13] Not surprisingly, these urban houses required large staffs. A census conducted in Lima in 1700, revealed that 16 percent of the city's population lived in convents and monasteries, most as servants to the nuns and monks.[14] Although the institutions varied by size, style, organization, and function depending upon such factors as date, order, and region, two institutions in the Viceroyalty of Peru exemplify their architecture. The Church and Convent of San Francisco in Quito retains the early character of its architectural design, while the Franciscan convent in Lima presents a slightly later aspect.

Founded as a Spanish city in 1534, Quito had been the stronghold of the rebel Inca Atahualpa, whose bid for control of the empire just before the Spaniards arrived probably facilitated the conquest. In 1563, Quito became the seat of the Audiencia de Quito, a regional administrative center within the Viceroyalty of Peru. Thanks to its elevated location, good climate, and abundant natural resources, Quito soon supported a large population of Amerindians, mestizos, criollos, and immigrant Europeans. Among the new arrivals were members of the mendicant orders. The Franciscan order was the first to enter the city and found its monastery for male clergy in 1535 on land granted by the town council.

The Church and Convent of San Francisco (Figure 55) rests today on a tall

FIGURE 55.
Façade of the Church of San Francisco. Begun 1535. Quito, Ecuador. Photograph © Hernán L. Navarrete.

platform overlooking a large square two blocks from Quito's plaza mayor. The Flemish friar Jodoco Ricke began the structure in 1535 on the ruins of the palace of the Inca Huina Capac, either with his own design or one provided by an émigré architect. By 1575 the church was complete and soon the monastery boasted two cloisters and accompanying cells and chambers. By the end of the colonial era, the complex had a church, two chapels, and thirteen patios, including the main cloister with its two-story Tuscan Doric colonnade. The site also housed the school of San Andrés Ricke founded for the training of indigenous craftsmen and artists. (See Chapter 2.)

Scholars have noted that the façade of the Church of San Francisco in Quito seems to reflect conquistador Francisco Pizarro's wish that the structure dominate the city, inspire awe in those who saw it, and discourage native attack.[15] Even its elevated position, which requires the faithful to access the structure by a circular staircase, communicates authority and permanence. The façade's ornamental elements and organization reveal a designer interested in classical architecture; research has demonstrated his particular indebtedness to Sebastiano Serlio's treatise.[16] The two-story mannerist façade recalls the severe classicism of the Spanish monastery and palace of El Escorial. The lower level employs a triumphal arch in the center. Widely spaced engaged columns flank windows in the tower bases. These outer areas are covered in bands of heavy rustication that even wrap around the column shafts. A thick entablature with a strongly projecting cornice caps the lower level, sealing its Doric columns, rusticated stones, corbels, and triangular spandrels in an austere and beautiful geometry. The central portal's upper story duplicates this organization, with a window instead of an arched door in the center. This area is more ornate, with Ionic columns, smaller rustication patterns, sculptures to either side of the window, and pyramidal pinnacles around the perimeter. Here the rusticated bands are less pronounced. The towers visible today reflect changes made after the colonial era, but the façade's rounded pediment and its sculpture of Christ are original.

Entering San Francisco's principal entrance reveals a three-aisle, cruciform church with a rounded apse; its basilican elevation permits an ample clerestory. This plan was popular for urban monastic churches throughout the colonial era, while parish churches employed a simpler single-aisle cruciform design. What surprises the visitor who has just witnessed San Francisco's exterior geometry and restrained classicism, however, is the fantastic interior ornament. The church has a gilded and polychromed wood ceiling (Figure 56); small masonry domes top the aisles. Although the original wood roof over the nave was destroyed in the late eighteenth century, the choir and crossing retain their original Mudéjar ceilings. The area over the crossing is particularly ornate, with a multifaceted wood dome on an octagonal base. In addition to the typical geometric and vegetal designs inherited from Moorish art, the ceiling at San Francisco includes relief sculpture of holy figures. The walls are similarly covered in ornate gilded stucco patterns.

While the exterior and the interior ornamental programs at the Church of San Francisco in Quito appear incongruous, it bears recalling that colonists

FIGURE 56. Interior of the Church of San Francisco. Begun 1535. Quito, Ecuador. Photograph © Andrew Holt/Alamy.

commonly employed Mudéjar ceilings for all types of buildings. Early scholars believed that Spanish American colonists looked to the Moorish-style wood roofing as a convenient, temporary solution in a land with many trees and skilled carpenters. More recent writings argue that Mudéjar ceilings may have represented an intentional strategy of cultural hegemony. Having used the ornate roofing system to acculturate conquered Muslims in southern Spain after 1492, the Spanish Crown brought this tool to the Americas to facilitate the conversion of Amerindians at various secular and sacred institutions.[17] As discussed in Chapter 1, sixteenth-century mission churches in both viceroyalties employed Mudéjar forms. While we may never know exactly why colonists employed Mudéjar ceilings in the Americas, their popularity and continued use throughout the viceregal era suggest that Spanish Americans liked the gilded and polychromed wood, geometric patterns, and vegetal designs. They considered these to be elegant and beautiful forms worthy of gracing the ceilings of churches and palaces. In fact, an eighteenth-century description of Quito declared San Francisco's special beauty and compared it to the best works in Spain.[18] Likewise, chronicler Bernabé Cobo's description of similar ceilings in early seventeenth-century Lima invariably describes them as costly and beautiful; he was particularly fond of the wood ceilings at the city's Franciscan monastery.[19]

The Church and Convent of San Francisco in Lima exemplifies later seventeenth-century male monastic sites, even though its history began simultaneously with the Franciscan house in Quito. Soon after Lima's 1535 foundation, the Franciscan order received a large plot northwest of the plaza mayor and next to the río Rímac. The order increased its allotted space in 1557 with a grant of additional land from Viceroy Hurtado de Mendoza; it acquired land twice more in the seventeenth century to eventually become the largest monastic compound in the Americas. The land was necessitated by an increasing population. Two hundred monks plus a greater number of support staff lived at San Francisco in 1629.[20] These men were served by a colossal complex of buildings. By 1674, the monastery's plan was organized around ten to twelve cloisters and patios; like most colonial cloisters, these were square or rectangular, although round cloisters could be found at the Dominican College of Santo Tomás in Lima and the Capuchin Convent of San Miguel in Antigua, Guatemala. San Francisco's monastery and church suffered heavy damage in the 1656 earthquake (described in Sidebar 11), but were soon rebuilt. Most of the structures visible today were erected between 1657 and 1678 and serve as spectacular examples of colonial monastic architecture.

The present complex of San Francisco was designed by the émigré Portuguese architect Constantino de Vasconcelos and finished by the criollo Manuel de Escobar. Like other monasteries, San Francisco included a chapter room for administrative meetings, a library, a refectory, an infirmary, and a sala de profundis. Its most impressive area is the two-story main cloister (Figure 57) with its elliptical openings in the second-story arcade. This and other parts of the complex are topped with carved wood roofs, some gilded and others polychromed; a Mudéjar wood dome soars over the cloister stairs. Fortunately, this and other areas within the complex retain their lavish ornamentation from the colonial era.

FIGURE 57.
Constantino de Vasconcelos and Manuel de Escobar. Main cloister of the Monastery of San Francisco. 1557–1678. Lima, Peru. Photograph © Kelly Donahue-Wallace.

Excerpts from Josephe de Mugaburu's Description of the 1655
Earthquake in Lima

This chapter has mentioned the devastating effects of Spanish America's
seismic instability on its architecture. The following is an account of the
1655 Lima earthquake and its aftermath, written by a soldier named Josephe
de Mugaburu.

> Saturday, the 13th of November of the year 1655, at three in the afternoon
> there was the greatest earthquake so far felt in the major part of Lima. It
> occurred while I, Sergeant Josephe de Mugaburu, was standing guard on
> the *Santiago*, royal consort ship of this sea . . . The ship made such a noise
> that it seemed it wanted to throw off the bulkhead brackets and burst into
> pieces. I saw a large section of the island in the bay [San Lorenzo Island]
> break loose and fall into the ocean. The dust clouds formed were so thick
> that the island could not be seen for quite a while. Returning later to the
> town of Callao [Lima's port], I saw the chapel and dome of the Jesuit
> church of that port caved in. Many houses also collapsed, whereupon all
> the inhabitants moved into the plazas and the streets to sleep.
>
> It caused great damage to all the houses in Lima. Only a married
> woman . . . and a Negro were killed. But the houses were uninhabitable
> for many days, so that all the people went out into the plazas and streets,
> the large patios and gardens, and the *chácaras* [farms]. In the space of
> three dates there were more than a hundred tremors, and everyone
> trembled [with fear] at what had never been perceived in this city. For
> a period of fifteen days the churches were open day and night with the
> Holy Sacrament uncovered. In the main plaza there were three pulpits
> where the predicators preached without stopping, in competition; as one

The cloister is lined with frescoed paintings of the life of Saint Francis, later hidden by canvases of the same subject. Elsewhere in the monastery are paintings by
Spanish artist Francisco de Zurbarán and his followers, the Italian émigré painter
Angelino Medoro, and various named and anonymous limeño and cuzqueño artists. A dado of polychrome tiles imported from Spain lines the monastery walls.
Donated by the daughter of an indigenous cacique, the tiles feature vegetal and
geometric designs, as well as figural representations of saints, martyrs, and even
mythological characters.[21]

The Church of San Francisco in Lima (Figure 58) was erected after the
devastating 1656 earthquake reduced the original temple to rubble. Like many

descended another went up. In the main plaza alone twenty sermons were preached in one day, and there were [services] in the other small plazas and churches. It was something that cannot be imagined.

Three [processions] started out from the cathedral with all the religious orders, Viceroy Count of Alba de Liste and his audiencia, and Archbishop Don Pedro de Villagómez with his canons. Many penitents took part. Another procession went forth at midnight with the religious of the Franciscan order performing great acts of penance. All the religious were without cowls, barefoot, and their bodies covered with ashes. Another procession then set forth with the miraculous statue of Our Lady of Copacabana, traveling from the church of San Lázaro to the cathedral where there were many penances. On Friday, the 26th of the month, another procession with all the merchants went from the Mercedarian monastery to the cathedral, bringing forth the [image of the] Mother of God, [Our Lady] of Mercy, which had never been taken out of the church . . . There were eight hundred persons participating and doing great penances . . . All the Augustinian priests went barefoot, giving what food they had for themselves to the poor in the prisons. And so it was for two days . . .

In the afternoon of . . . Saturday the 27th . . . , a procession set out from the cathedral proceeding around the plaza where there were seven altars of devotion. The [image of the] Visitation of Saint Elizabeth was brought out, and more than a thousand persons of all classes did penance: men, women, and children, Indian men and women, Negroes and Negresses, and mulatto men and women.

—From *Chronicle of Colonial Lima: The Diary of Josephe and Francisco Mugaburu, 1640–1697*, trans. and ed. Robert Ryal Miller, 36–37 (Norman: University of Oklahoma Press, 1975).

monastic churches, San Francisco has a cruciform plan, a wide nave, narrow side aisles, and deep chapels. An elevated choir loft sits over the entrance with its ornate choir box and large music stand. The crossing is also typical, housing a broad dome resting on pendentives. Although the church originally had an ornate gilded-wood roof, quincha barrel vaults were erected after 1656 to withstand the frequent seismic activity. These vaults sport stucco relief in geometric designs painted today in contrasting colors. The door to the sacristy is a spectacular example of limeño late baroque carving. Executed in 1730 by Lucas Meléndez and fray Nicolás del Pozo, the doorway features a virtual explosion of architectural ornament deployed for maximum expressive effect. Vaulted crypts

FIGURE 58.
Constantino de
Vasconcelos and
Manuel de Escobar.
Façade of the Church
of San Francisco.
1656–78. Lima, Peru.
Photograph © Kelly
Donahue-Wallace.

or catacombs containing the bones of donors, friars, and confraternity members rest underneath the church floor.

As at most New Spanish and Peruvian churches, many of San Francisco's side chapels were owned and outfitted by wealthy Lima families; others belonged to local confraternities. The confraternity of Our Lady of the Immaculate Conception of the guild of Amerindian and mestizo tailors operated a chapel; so did the Basque émigré confraternity of Our Lady of Aránzazu. The confraternity of the West African Mandingo peoples cared for the church's chapel of Saint Benedict of Palermo.[22] The cost these groups shouldered to outfit the chapels was substantial. For example, to replace the altarscreen of Our Lady of the Light in the late eighteenth century, the confraternity of immigrants from Corsica paid 11,909 pesos for its ornately carved Central American cedar and its sculpture by the renowned sculptors of Quito.[23]

The opulence of the interior of the Church of San Francisco mirrors its ornate exterior. The tall and narrow retablo-façade features three stories and, like most colonial monastic façades of its era, employs a classicizing vocabulary treated with great freedom. The first level takes the triumphal arch motif as a point of departure, with paired columns resting on tall pedestals to either side of an arched doorway. Behind these columns are four smaller columns, creating the dynamic rhythm and rich chiaroscural effects typical of Peruvian baroque architecture. The cornice of the first story rises around the arched door to form a broken pediment, entering the second story and opening to either side of a marble sculpture of Our Lady of the Immaculate Conception. The papal arms and other decorative motifs occupy the tympanum-like area over the door. The second story, which includes kneeling figures of Saints Francis and Dominic adoring the Virgin, features stacked pilasters and columns that project with increasing energy toward the central figures. Here, too, the distinction between stories is transgressed, as the entablature rises into the attic story. The upper level is a conglomeration of arched elements, scrolls, and a profusion of architectural ornamentation that climbs up to a final rounded cornice over the elliptical choir loft window. The corner towers with their broad profile and domes are typical of Peruvian monasteries. The entire façade of the church is dressed in rusticated ashlar masonry that creates an emphatic and ordered geometry that balances the fanciful curvilinearity of the retablo-façade. The expressive effect of this impressive façade must have been quite different in the colonial era, however, when a cemetery occupied the space in front to remind viewers of their mortality.

Although the Quito and Lima Franciscan complexes represent the general characteristic of Spanish American monastic architecture between 1585 and 1700, each monastery reflects the specific tastes of its local community. The Jesuit Church and Convent of La Compañía in Arequipa, Peru (Figure 59) displays a different regional approach to monastic architecture, or at least its ornamentation. Constructed between 1590 and 1660 of the local *sillar* stone, the church has suffered many catastrophic earthquakes. The structure employs the standard three-aisle cruciform plan with a dome over the crossing and an elevated choir loft above the entrance. A heavy tower anchors the front corner and supports the barrel and sail vaults found inside. The convent attached to the church, built in 1738, follows the general organization shared by Spanish American monastic compounds, although little of the original architecture survives today. What remains is the elaborate architectural ornamentation on the church façade, which embodies the local *arequipeño* architecture of the late seventeenth century.

The retablo-façade of La Compañía displays many of the typical characteristics of the planiform style (also called Andean or mestizo baroque) popular in the Andean region from Arequipa to Potosí from the late seventeenth to the late eighteenth century. Carved ornamentation appears tapestry-like and covers the surface of the building. The flatness of the carving and the white sillar stone provide a brittle and lacy appearance that negates the structural vocabulary of its classical orders. Typical of the planiform style, the ornamentation at Arequipa's Jesuit church is primarily vegetal, with vines, rosettes, pomegranates, grapes, and urns of flowers. The façade is also populated by an army of faces, profile heads with tails, birds (including the bicephalic Hapsburg eagle), and pumas. While some of the iconography presents clearly Christian content, such as the grapes, the pomegranates, and the Christ Child on the third level, other elements, like the puma, may have referenced indigenous religious traditions. The presentation of a flowery setting populated by birds, angels, and other animals likely recalled the Andean sacred paradise known as Hanacpacha (discussed in Chapter 2), deployed here as a promised reward for those who enter the church. Colonial author Antonio León Pinelo even suggested the Peruvian pomegranate (granadilla) as the fruit of the Tree of Knowledge of Good and Evil in the Garden of Eden he located in the Amazon.[24] The granadilla's flower was thought to bear the symbols of Christ's Passion.

This iconographic polyvalence and the flat, non-illusionistic carving style have led scholars to conclude that the style reflected indigenous tastes and meaning. Early art historians argued that the planiform style was a synthesis of European and Pre-Columbian Andean form and symbolism. Recent analysis suggests that rather than reviving pre-Hispanic—and even pre-Inca—forms, the Aymara-speaking artists of Arequipa re-invented a local indigenous style.[25] In other words, the planiform style may not have been an old style, but an entirely new one created according to the tastes of the living indigenous population. It should be noted, furthermore, that this new style was not found only within indigenous contexts. Arequipa had a large population of criollos and European émigrés, including many of the Jesuits who lived in La Compañía; in fact, local lore claims that the city was known as the White City both for its white stone

FIGURE 59.
Façade of the
Church of
La Compañía.
1590–1660.
Arequipa, Peru.
Photograph © Kelly
Donahue-Wallace.

buildings and for its high percentage of European residents. It seems likely that arequipeños of every race appreciated the planiform style; they certainly kept the indigenous carvers busy. Arequipa's Church of Santo Domingo built in the late seventeenth century, to name just one local example, displays many of the same characteristics. Elsewhere in the Central Andes, the Cathedral of Puno and the Church of San Francisco in La Paz, both dating to the eighteenth century, likewise exemplify the broad appeal of the planiform or mestizo baroque style.

Regional variations of architectural ornamentation also proliferated in New Spain. In many areas of the northern viceroyalty, colonists covered their churches and other holy sites with stucco relief decoration. Two of the most spectacular examples of this art form, inherited from Spain's Moorish occupiers, are the Rosary Chapels attached to the Dominican monasteries in Puebla and Oaxaca. The rosary was a special devotion of the Dominican Order, owing to the Virgin Mary's thirteenth-century appearance to the order's founder, Saint Dominic of Guzman. Sculptures and paintings of Our Lady of the Rosary are common in Dominican churches; the New Spanish Rosary Chapels were constructed to house sculptures of this devotion.

The Rosary Chapel at the Church of Santo Domingo in Puebla (Plate 11) is a small, cruciform structure opening off of the main nave of the seventeenth-century Dominican monastic church. The chapel was constructed and ornamented between 1632 and 1690. The small space overwhelms the viewer with its gilded and polychromed ornamentation. Stucco vines and Renaissance strapwork climb up the walls and through the vaults, parting to reveal sculptures of saints, martyrs, apostles, and other holy persons. On the walls below, a dado of local *poblano* tiles is topped by large paintings surrounded by more relief strapwork. The octagonal crossing dome features the dove surrounded by the gifts of the Holy Spirit; female martyrs rest on pedestals within the drum. Supporting the entire grouping are the four pendentives bearing images of the archangels. Beyond these figures, hundreds of putti, angels, and other holy characters occupy the gilded vines and straps surrounding a central baldachin sheltering the sculpture of Our Lady of the Rosary. An equally brilliant example of gilded *horror vacui* is found in Oaxaca at the rosary chapel attached to the local Dominican church. Both sites employ gilding, polychromy, and sacred imagery to lift the spectator out of the mundane world and offer him a glimpse of Heaven.

Like the planiform carving in Arequipa, decorative stucco relief became a popular regional solution for New Spain's churches and monasteries. Colonists likened the intricate and colorful carvings to Mudéjar woodwork in Spain; the denial of architecture under a dense network of ornamental elements reminded them of the peninsular woodcarving.[26] The work at the Rosary Chapel in Puebla was sponsored by the confraternity of the pearl diver's guild and has been attributed variously to artists Francisco Pinto, Pedro García Durán, and Juan Bautista de Alarcón.[27] It has also been suggested that anonymous craftsmen from Sevilla carved the designs. And while scholars have searched for indigenous features in the angels' faces and have attempted to parse the Spanish, Amerindian, and

Moorish genealogy of the forms, it is just as productive to acknowledge that colonists and friars viewed the ornate decoration as attractive, appropriate to its context, and reflective of their faith. The dense stucco strapwork and vegetal patterns appealed to their senses and spirits and effectively transported their souls in a lavish and expressive exercise in baroque rhetoric.

The period between 1585 and 1700 also experienced a surge in the construction of convents; the first institutions for women were constructed in Mexico City and Lima in 1550 and 1558 respectively. In fact, convents outnumbered monasteries in some colonial cities; add the *recogimientos* and *beaterios*—convent-like institutions for laywomen who entered either voluntarily or involuntarily—and the numbers grow. Several social factors promoted convent construction. First among these was the fact that colonial spirituality embraced an isolated, cloistered existence dedicated to prayer and meditation as the ideal of Christian womanhood. Second, communities viewed the proliferation of convents as proof of their wealth and spirituality. Rich patrons enthusiastically supported new institutions and paid large dowries to place their daughters in the best houses. Third, even secular women lived cloistered lives, at least temporarily. Parents placed young girls in convents to educate them and keep them free from scandal. Upon completing a largely domestic education in their early teens, the young girls either remained in the convent or were married to older, well-off gentlemen. Many widows likewise entered convents after the deaths of their husbands.

For these and more reasons, convent populations swelled during the seventeenth century. In 1633, the Convent of the Encarnación in Lima housed over four hundred nuns plus even more servants, girls, and laywomen. Seventy years later the neighboring Convent of the Purísima Concepción sheltered over one thousand residents. The convents were so large by 1681, in fact, that critics decried the lack of order and Spanish King Charles II ordered a reduction of convent populations with little effect.[28]

Convent life in some orders seemed rather secular. Depending upon the order and the family's wealth, a nun might live quite well. Even some of the more austere orders allowed nuns to have at least one servant. The convents were likewise ornamented according to the order's character. Many convents contained extensive collections of paintings, sculpture, and textiles, many of the latter made by the women. Thanks to income generated from donations and dowries from pious colonists, cottage industries of food and crafts sold to customers beyond the convent walls, and rents collected from tenants—religious orders were the largest landlords in the viceroyalties—the convents and their churches were frequently lavishly appointed.

The Dominican Convent of Santa Catalina in Arequipa, Peru, exemplifies colonial convent architecture. Founded in response to the growing number of women wishing to serve God, the convent was subsidized by local widow María Álvarez de Carmona y Guzmán.[29] Over time the complex grew to cover two blocks in the city center, having begun with the purchase of two private homes in 1568.[30] Despite several earthquakes that reduced the convent virtually to rubble, the nuns living in Santa Catalina occupied a veritable city by the mid-eighteenth century, with several cloisters and dozens of patios and streets. An account in 1750 noted that at least 325 women lived in the convent, including nuns, novices, the girls placed in the convent to be educated by the nuns, *beatas* (laywomen seeking respite from the secular world), and servants.[31] The occupants were housed by rank, with cloisters for nuns separate from areas reserved for novices and laywomen.

Like many convents, Santa Catalina grew haphazardly over the centuries. As new nuns entered the order they constructed cells, many of them more like multi-room townhouses than the austere chamber of the popular imagination. A typical cell at Santa Catalina (Figure 60) consisted of a sitting room, a kitchen, a bedroom for the nun, and a sleeping area for her servant(s). Seismic activity in Arequipa kept the cells to a single story, but two-story cells were also common throughout Spanish America. The cells belonged to the nuns' families and were bought, sold, and rented by them as part of the complicated convent economy of land rents, money lending, cottage industries, and internal trade between nuns; Santa Catalina had a patio named for its weekly trading sessions, when nuns exchanged their needlework. Santa Catalina also had common dormitories, today visible in the two intersecting galleries that comprise the museum. According to local lore, the dormitories were constructed in the late colonial era, when the city's bishop ordered the nuns to embrace a communal life to which many objected. In stricter orders, such as the Discalced Carmelites and the Capuchins, communal dormitories and refectories were common.

FIGURE 60.
Interior of a nun's cell in the Convent of Santa Catalina. Begun 1568. Arequipa, Peru. Photograph © Kelly Donahue-Wallace.

Several features distinguish Santa Catalina and other female convents from the complexes built for male clergy. The Church of Santa Catalina attached to the convent, for example, was a nuns' church, an architectural type consisting of a single nave without side chapels or a projecting transept. It did, however, have a dome over the area in front of the main altar. Nuns' churches also typically had a single tower and a narrow atrium, although modern streets have claimed Santa Catalina's patio. Overall, nuns' institutions offered less showy exteriors to the public as a sign of female humility and the sisters' distance from the outside world.

Most of the differences between monasteries and convents like Arequipa's Santa Catalina, however, reflect the need to keep nuns physically, not just symbolically, away from the public. For example, each convent possessed a *locutorio* located near its main entrance. In these chambers nuns spoke to outsiders through a barrier. The locutorio at Santa Catalina is a long gallery near the church, with several openings covered by metal grills. Nuns communicating with family sat on the low bench that lined the wall. Other convents had larger locutorios that resembled salons divided by bars. Since most nuns rarely left their convents, the locutorio was their only point of contact with the outside world.

The need to keep cloistered nuns separated from outsiders presented a special challenge when it came to church architecture, since the nuns' churches also served the spiritual needs of the surrounding community. The Church of Santa Catalina even served as Arequipa's cathedral for a period in the seventeenth century. The plan of this nuns' church reveals a common solution that allowed lay and cloistered populations to share the structure. The single nave church is open to the public only in the two thirds closest to the altar. The back third of the church is reserved for the nuns' choir, which allowed the cloistered women to attend mass shielded from public view by a metal grill. Nuns' choirs were typically two stories, with an elevated loft for singing and a lower choir used for meetings and other official functions. The abbess of the convent witnessed the mass from an elevated balcony that also kept her shielded from view. The balcony at Santa Catalina is, like most, located high on the contiguous wall between the convent and the church. A confessional cut into the lower part of the same wall near the choir allowed nuns to confess without entering the main part of the church.

With the back third of the church closed to the public, nuns' churches had their entrances along the long sidewall. The side façade of Arequipa's convent Church of Santa Catalina exemplifies the type, with two simple doors cut into the church's thick walls. The New Spanish Convent of Santa Teresa la Antigua, the name popularly given the Discalced Carmelite Convent of San José de Santa Teresa de Jesús (Figure 61), however, offers a more ornate example. The New Spanish nuns' church portals were constructed between 1678 and 1684 by Cristóbal de Medina Vargas, the architect responsible for popularizing the Solomonic column in local architecture. Funds for the structure were donated by Esteban de Molina Mosquera and his wife Manuela de la Barreda.[32] For their

FIGURE 61. Cristóbal de Medina Vargas. Façade of the Church of Santa Teresa la Antigua. 1678–84. Mexico City, Mexico. Photograph © Kelly Donahue-Wallace.

donations totaling 750,000 pesos, Molina and his wife asked only to be remembered in the nuns' prayers.[33]

Like the retablo-façades of contemporary cathedrals and monastic churches, the portal ornamentation at Santa Teresa la Antigua reflected the interior retablo of the main altar (no longer in situ), also completed in 1684 by Medina Vargas. The paired doors, separated by an exterior buttress, each feature a triumphal arch motif on the lower level. Two engaged Solomonic columns with ornamental strapwork on their lower thirds rest to either side of each door. The spandrels and frieze are decked with decorative vegetal motifs. The upper story contains a window in a rusticated eared frame bearing the monograms of Joseph, Mary, Joachim, and Anne. Single Solomonic columns flank the windows and support broken triangular pediments and small sculptures of the Christ Child. The columns on both levels rest atop pilasters, which provide a certain tenuous baroque dynamism and spatial manipulation. While the twin portals at Santa Teresa la Antigua reflect the tastes of late seventeenth-century Mexico City, it should be kept in mind that other convent façades corresponded to the styles popular in their eras and regions.

Colonial Shrines

In addition to cathedrals and monastery and convent churches, colonists satisfied their spiritual needs at local shrines. These structures were constructed to house sacred images with local or regional followings. Some shrines are freestanding, while others are attached to churches; the Rosary Chapels in Oaxaca and Puebla are examples of the latter, and were constructed to house sculptures of Our Lady of the Rosary. Most shrines are small, but a few boast buildings comparable in size to local cathedrals. The Basilica of Guadalupe near Mexico City (Figure 62) is a spectacular example of colonial shrine architecture. Constructed by architect Pedro de Arrieta (ac. 1691–1738), the large shrine was built between 1695 and 1709 to offer the sacred painting of Our Lady of Guadalupe a worthy home and to accommodate the growing numbers of pilgrims who came to pray before it.

According to the well-known legend, Juan Diego, a native man from Tepeyac, experienced three visions of the Virgin Mary in 1531. During the first two, Mary told Juan Diego to ask Bishop Juan de Zumárraga to erect a shrine on the site of a Pre-Columbian temple dedicated to the mother deity Tonantzín. The bishop rebuffed Juan Diego and asked for a sign that the story was true. Juan Diego returned carrying in his tilma the roses the Virgin Mary provided as evidence. But when he opened the cloak, the flowers had become the image of a dark-skinned Virgin Mary dressed in a cloak of stars and surrounded by the rays of the sun. A convinced Zumárraga began constructing her shrine. By Mary's request, the image came to be known as the Virgin of Guadalupe, named for the dark-skinned Madonna enshrined in Extremadura, Spain. Initial interest in her cult was localized and generally restricted to indigenous populations. By the seventeenth century, however, devotion to the Virgin of Guadalupe grew and spread across the social spectrum, helped by the miracles attributed to this acheiropoietic image. The Guadalupana's cause was also promoted by New Spanish clerics who attempted to turn her into a criollo cult, most notably with the 1648 publication of Miguel Sánchez's *Imagen de la Virgen María Madre de Dios de Guadalupe.*

When Pedro de Arrieta began the present Basilica of Guadalupe, two other shrines already occupied the holy site at Tepeyac. By 1568 a church rested at the bottom of the hill; an English traveler observed at the time that every person who passed the structure stopped to pray.[34] The second shrine was erected with the assistance of pious donors whose giving conformed with the Catholic mandate of good works to ensure salvation. In 1615, for example, Flemish émigré print-maker Samuel Stradanus (ac. 1592–1622) engraved a print bearing images of the Guadalupana's miracles and requesting donations for a new temple in her honor. This structure, completed in 1622, was larger than the earlier shrine and featured an ornate polychrome wood ceiling and a life-sized silver sculpture of the Virgin Mary donated by a wealthy New Spanish miner.[35] The third shrine, Arrieta's building, was by far the grandest, and was funded in large part by donations from wealthy local criollos. Their desire to promote the faith and status of the colony within the larger Spanish empire and beyond is known as criollo patriotism and will be considered in Chapters 7 and 8.

The Basilica of Guadalupe was originally designed by architect José Durán, who planned three aisles, an octagonal dome over the crossing, and a basilican elevation. It has been suggested that Durán's plan reflected the central plan of the Heavenly Jerusalem as described in the Book of Revelation.[36] Durán also designed octagonal towers on the façade and a combination of rib vaults and sail vaults for the interior. Arrieta maintained much of Durán's design, adding two doors flanking the central portal, groin vaults in the nave, and octagonal towers on the backside of the church.

The façade of the Basilica of Guadalupe reflects many of the characteristics of local New Spanish architecture circa 1700, most notably its emphatic geometry and use of contrasting color. Arrieta deployed polygonal shapes dynamically throughout the façade. The octagonal towers, their shape emphasized by gray quoins, project from the surface. All three doors are topped by semi-octagonal arches, again made emphatic by the contrast between the gray chiluca and red tezontle stone. The ornamentation surrounding the central portal stands out from the building and is inscribed within a rectangle. Its surface is articulated by projecting and receding paired columns on pedestals. The second story of the portal offers a relief sculpture of the miraculous apparition inscribed within an eared frame. Although the attic level has been renovated since 1705, its mixtilinear parapet supports the geometric appearance of the rest of the façade.

The taste for geometry in Mexico City may reflect local history, specifically the 1637 creation of a professorship in mathematics and astronomy at the Royal and Pontifical University. The first professor in the position became highly involved in the city's architectural and engineering projects, and viewed architecture as the application of geometry.[37] At roughly the same time, Carmelite friar Andrés de San Miguel (1577–1644) composed in Mexico City a treatise on a wide range of mathematical, astronomical, and architectural topics, including perspective and its application in local buildings and engineering projects. (See Sidebar 12.)

FIGURE 62.
Pedro de Arrieta. Basilica of Guadalupe. 1695–1709. Mexico City, Mexico. Photograph © Kelly Donahue-Wallace.

Excerpts from fray Andrés de San Miguel's circa 1630 treatise, "What is Architecture?"

Architecture is a science that includes many disciplines and different forms of erudition, which considers and employs all other arts. This science is born and sustained by practice and reason. The practice requires continuous and well-understood reasoning, since continuous use perfects the hands, in material appropriate to the constructed object; reason is that which explains the objects composed with proportion. The architect who without letters draws and designs engages only in manual work [and] does not give authority to his works, and he who engages only in reason and letters, which are just speculative, achieves only the shadow and not the truth of this science; but those who learn both perfectly reach the apex of the art because all things, especially Architecture, possess both, which are the signifier and what is signified. The signified is a proposed structure, while what signifies is the proposal, explained with reason that shows and teaches, so that we infer that to be an architect one must know one and the other; thus it serves to have natural genius and a facility for learning the science, because neither science without genius, nor genius without science, makes for a good builder.

It is necessary that the architect be skilled and knowledgeable in design and drawing, and that he understand geometry and does not ignore perspective and know arithmetic, because without design and drawing he cannot make the proposal nor explain what is to be done on the work. According to Vitruvius, the good architect should be versed in History, Philosophy, Music, Medicine, and Astronomy. It is not difficult for the intelligent and studious man to understand each of these and its necessity, especially if he begins at a young age.

—From *Obras de fray Andrés de San Miguel*, introduction, notes, and paleographic version by Eduardo Báez Macías (Mexico City: UNAM/IIE, 1969), 105. (Translation mine.)

It stands to reason that the geometric forms and architectural elements that appeared in local buildings were therefore more than merely decorative. Colonial viewers from the educated elite likely associated them with the divine geometry that thinkers since the Renaissance claimed ordered the world. Hence the octagons, squares, circles, and other shapes popular in New Spanish façades and stucco decoration provided an additional layer of religious significance to the more obvious iconography of the paintings and sculptures. By the same token, the Basilica's central plan placed the Virgin of Guadalupe at the center of a sacred geometry—the perfect shapes of circle and square that ordered the universe—and made her home a kind of *axis mundi*.[38] In fact, the 1709 sermon dedicating the structure noted the architect's use of Vitruvian principles and their humanistic proportions.[39] The building thus made a potent statement about the significance of this American devotion and its colonial context.

The South American devotion that comes closest to the Guadalupe's popularity is the Virgin of Copacabana. Her shrine, constructed during the seventeenth century, is located on the shores of Lake Titicaca where Peru and Bolivia meet today. As discussed in Chapter 1, the lake and its islands of the sun and moon were sites of indigenous devotion before the Spaniards arrived. The holy site of Copacabana was founded by Tupac Inca Yupanqui, and the town functioned as a rest stop for pilgrims traveling through the sacred region.[40] With such potent pagan roots, it comes as no surprise that Lake Titicaca attracted Dominican missionaries as early as 1532 and, like Tepeyac, was soon home to a miraculous Christian cult image.

According to legend, indigenous artist Francisco Tito Yupanqui set out in 1576 to make a sculpted Virgin Mary out of maguey for the small church on the town square in Copacabana. After consulting Marian images in La Paz and Potosí, he based his work on a Virgin of the Rosary in Potosí's Dominican convent. When a local governor decided to sell the new sculpture to resolve a dispute among indigenous communities, the image began emitting rays of light. This miracle convinced authorities to install the Yupanqui's sculpture (discussed in Chapter 5) in Copacabana in 1583.[41] The sculpture soon developed a fervent following, necessitating a grand shrine in honor of the Virgin of Copacabana (Figure 63).

Work began in 1610 on Spanish architect Francisco Jiménez de Sigüenza's design for the structure.[42] The shrine's dedication on April 6, 1614, was attended

FIGURE 63.
Francisco Jiménez de Sigüenza. Sanctuary of Copacabana. Begun 1610. Copacabana, Bolivia. Photograph © James Brunker, photographersdirect.com.

by the region's civic and ecclesiastical dignitaries and local faithful, including dancers and indigenous nobility.[43] By 1640, the compound consisted of a single-nave cruciform church topped by rib vaults and a crossing dome, and a walled atrium with four posa chapels and a Miserere chapel for funerary services. Like other South American churches, the shrine at Copacabana features a simple portal on the nave axis and a more elaborate lateral entrance. The structure has experienced many renovations since the seventeenth century, but retains much of its original appearance. A tall open chapel rests to the west of the church, next to the axial façade. Each of these chapels features a tile-covered circular or elliptical dome over its masonry supports. A convent for the resident Augustinian friars sits opposite the atrium on the other side of the church. The interior of the shrine remains lavishly outfitted with altarscreens from the seventeenth to nineteenth centuries. The altarscreen of the Virgin of Copacabana was finished in 1618 and displayed the cult image within the gilded construction.

The sculpture of the Virgin of Copacabana is today displayed in a lavish gilded silver altarscreen built in 1684, and the shrine continues to attract pilgrims from throughout South America. The Andean temple, like the recently restored Basilica of Guadalupe at Tepeyac, embodies the powerful role cult images play in Spanish American Catholicism. Although the New Spanish cult image gained a new home in the twentieth century, which allows pilgrims to view the Virgin of Guadalupe from a moving walkway, Arrieta's building and the shrine at Copacabana remain today as enduring testaments to the power of these popular devotions in the hearts of the faithful.

PLATE 1.
Juan Gerson. Choir loft paintings. Church
of San Francisco de Tecamachalco. 1562.
Tempera on *papel de amate*. Tecamachalco,
Mexico. Photograph © Gilles Mermet/Art
Resource, New York.

PLATE 2.
Luís de Riaño. *Two Paths*. Church of San Pedro,
Andahuaylillas. 1618–26. Mural painting.
Andahuaylillas, Peru. Photograph © Neus
Escandell-Tur and Alexandra Arrellano.

PLATE 3.
Nave paintings. Church of San Miguel
Arcángel de Ixmiquilpan. ca. 1570.
Mural painting. Ixmiquilpan, Mexico.
Photograph © Gilles Mermet/Art
Resource, New York.

PLATE 4.
Codex Mendoza. Detail of fol. 37 recto. 1541.
Tempera and ink on paper. Photograph
© Bodleian Library, Oxford University.

PLATE 5.
Arms of the Descendents of Inca Tupa
Yupanqui. 1600–1630. Tempera and
ink on paper. Photograph © Archivo
General de Indias.

PLATE 6.

Juan Bautista. *Christ at the Age of Twelve*.
1590–1600. Feather mosaic. Photograph
© Kunsthistoriches Museum, Vienna, Austria.

PLATE 7.
Uncu. Seventeenth century. Wool,
silk, and metallic thread. Gift of the
Ernest Erickson Foundation, Inc.,
86.224.51. Photograph © Brooklyn
Museum, New York.

PLATE 8.

View of Lima. 1680. Oil on canvas. Location unknown. Photograph © Oronoz.

PLATE 9.
Triumph of Death. Late sixteenth
century. Mural painting. Casa del
Deán. Puebla, Mexico. Photograph
© Jorge Pérez de Lara.

PLATE 10.
Melchor Pérez Holguín. *Entrance
into Potosí of the Viceroy Archbishop
Morcillo*. 1718. Oil on canvas.
Photograph © Museo de América.

PLATE 11.
Rosary Chapel of the Church of Santo
Domingo. 1632–90. Puebla, Mexico.
Photograph © José Vicente Recino,
photographersdirect.com.

PLATE 12.

Cuzco School. *Virgin and Child*.
ca. 1700. Oil on canvas. Photograph
© Museo de Arte, Lima, Peru/
The Bridgeman Art Library.

PLATE 13.
Juan Correa. *Virgin of Guadalupe*.
1704. Oil on canvas. Parroquia de
San Nicolás y Santa María la Blanca,
Sevilla, Spain. Photograph
© Archivo Fotográfico Arenas.

PLATE 14.

Our Lady of Cocharcas. ca. 1700. Oil on
canvas. © Brooklyn Museum of Art, New
York/Bequest of Mary T. Cockcroft/The
Bridgeman Art Library.

PLATE 15.
Formerly attributed to Melchor Pérez Holguín.
The Young Virgin with a Distaff. 1699. Oil on canvas.
Photograph © Museo de Arte Hispanoamericano
Isaac Fernández Blanco, Buenos Aires, Argentina.

PLATE 16.
Diego Quispe Tito. *Virgin of the*
Immaculate Conception with Litanies.
ca. 1650. Oil on canvas. Photograph
© Denver Art Museum, Denver, Colorado.

PLATE 17.
Nicolás Rodríguez Juárez. *The Christ
Child*. Late seventeenth century. Oil
on canvas. Photograph © Museo Franz
Mayer, Mexico City, Mexico.

PLATE 18.
Gregorio Vásquez de Arce y Ceballos.
Holy Family of Nazareth. 1685. Oil on
canvas. Photograph © Museo de Arte
Colonial, Bogotá, Colombia.

PLATE 19.
Trifacial Trinity. Eighteenth century.
Oil on canvas. Photograph © Wadsworth
Atheneum, Hartford, Connecticut.

PLATE 20.
Cuzco School. *Santiago at the Battle of Clavijo.*
1653. Collection of Marilynn and Carl Thoma.
Photograph © Thoma Collection.

PLATE 21.

Cristóbal de Villalpando. *Mystic Marriage
of Saint Rose of Lima.* 1690. Oil on canvas.
Photograph © University Art Museum,
University of California, Santa Barbara.

PLATE 22.
Master of Calamarca (La Paz School).
Angel with Arquebus, Asiel Timor Dei.
1660–80. Oil on canvas. Photograph
© Museo Nacional de Arte, La Paz, Bolivia/
Paul Maeyaert/The Bridgeman Art Library.

PLATE 23.
Cuzco School. *Finale of the Corpus Christi Procession*. 1674–80. Oil on canvas. Museo de Arte Religioso, Cuzco, Peru. Photograph © Carolyn Dean.

PLATE 24.
Higinio Chávez and Miguel Cabrera. Interior
of the Church of San Francisco Xavier and
altarscreens. 1753. Tepotzotlán, Mexico.
Photograph © Kelly Donahue-Wallace.

PLATE 25.
Altarscreen of the Torre Tagle Palace.
1733–38. Lima, Peru. Photograph
© Adriana Orozco/Foto Latino,
photographersdirect.com.

PLATE 26.
Miguel de Herrera. *Portrait of a Lady*.
1782. Oil on canvas. Photograph © Museo
Franz Mayer. Mexico City, Mexico.

PLATE 27.

*The del Valle Family at the Feet of the Virgin of
Loreto.* ca. 1751–52. Oil on canvas. Photograph
© Museo Soumaya. Mexico City, Mexico.

PLATE 28.
José de Alcíbar. *María Ignacia de la Sangre de Cristo*. ca. 1777. Oil on canvas. Photograph © Museo Nacional de Historia. Mexico City, Mexico.

PLATE 29.

Emblems from Vaenius. Eighteenth
century. Oil on canvas. Photograph
© Dallas Museum of Art, Dallas, Texas.

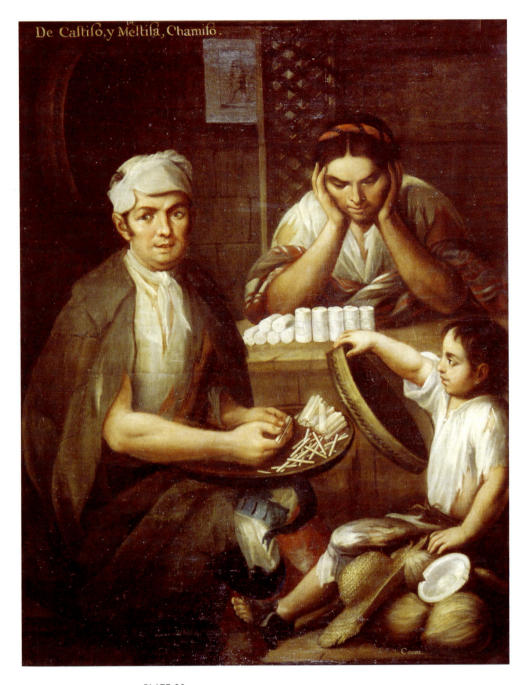

PLATE 30.
Miguel Cabrera. *Castas: Castizo y Mestiza: Chamizo*. 1763. Oil on canvas. Photograph © Museo de América, Madrid, Spain.

PLATE 31.
Ignacio María Barreda. *Castas*. Late
eighteenth century. Real Academia.
Madrid, Spain. Photograph © Oronoz.

PLATE 32.
Rafael Ximeno y Planes. *The Miracle of the Well*. 1809. Oil on canvas. Photograph © Museo Nacional de Arte, Mexico City, Mexico.

Religious Art 1600–1785

Religious themes dominated viceregal art between 1600 and 1785, but a comparison of two nearly contemporary paintings illustrates the genre's immense diversity in the colonial context. Baltazar de Echave Rioja (1632–82) painted *The Triumph of the Church and of the Eucharist* (Figure 64) in 1675 for the sacristy of the Puebla Cathedral in New Spain. The painting is an allegory of the Catholic Counter Reformation's affirmation of the holiness of the Eucharist that the figure in the papal tiara holds aloft. Its criollo maker was the great-grandson of Baltazar de Echave Orio (1548–1620), a Spanish painter who emigrated to New Spain in the late sixteenth century and founded an artistic dynasty. The painting shows the younger Echave's familiarity with the Western repertoire of symbols, emblems, and personifications; it also reveals his interest in the European exuberant baroque style. His elite clerical audience undoubtedly admired the triumphalist theme, which celebrated both the Catholic victory over Protestantism and their own evangelical achievements. They likely also approved of the painter's skill in translating into paint the engraving designed by the Flemish master Peter Paul Rubens, and viewed the style as appropriate for their courtly context.

The anonymous *Virgin and Child* (Plate 12) painted in Cuzco a few decades later differs in its appearance and history. An indigenous Andean artist created the image during a period that saw indigenous and mestizo artists look beyond urban criollo and European forms. Its appearance has much less to do with contemporary European tastes than Echave's; instead, the stereotyped figures, truncated space, and flowery setting are characteristic of the so-called Andean mestizo baroque style. And while this artist, too, may have come from an artistic family, his anonymity represents his community's concept of "artist," one that celebrated his prolific work for God and community more than his individual achievements.

Comparing the two works begs the question of which painting best represents

FIGURE 64.
Baltazar de Echave
Rioja. *The Triumph
of the Church and the
Eucharist.* 1675. Oil
on canvas. Puebla
Cathedral. Photograph
© Archivo Fotográfico
Manuel Toussaint,
IIE/UNAM.

the religious art of its era. The fact that both artists undoubtedly responded to their patrons' tastes hints at how the study of viceregal religious (and secular) art is complicated by the colonial circumstances. To understand New Spanish and Peruvian viceregal art, we cannot simply follow the careers of guild-trained artists working for elite criollo and indigenous patrons at the viceregal courts in Mexico City and Lima. This approach would ignore many significant examples of colonial cultural production. Nor can we look solely at native artists reconciling the newly introduced religious and pictorial systems with ancestral traditions, new social circumstances, and contemporary indigenous tastes. This method would deny the achievements of the urban schools.

The answer to the question, therefore, must be "both." The two paintings are equally representative of colonial religious art and the complexity of art created for diverse populations, in diverse regions, for diverse purposes. And yet despite their differences, both works equally reflect the powerful and pervasive faith that governed the colonists' lives and transcended ethnicity and class, even if the precise forms and interpretations differed by artist, viewer, and context.

The present chapter examines religious pictorial arts produced by New Spanish and Peruvian artists between 1600 and 1785. The chapter privileges themes over forms, but does not attempt a complete survey of popular subjects. The Catholic colonists adorned their homes and churches with the standard early modern repertoire of images of the Virgin Mary, Christ, and the saints. Taking those common themes for granted, this chapter considers the religious subjects that held particular appeal for viceregal artists and their patrons, or point to local devotional practices. Furthermore, while objects and monuments are described using standard art historical period labels, the chapter leaves the study of stylistic chronologies to monographs and texts with narrower geographic and chronological focus.

Like the European builders who erected the early viceregal churches and palaces, visual artists also crossed the Atlantic to ply their trades in the new urban centers; many came from Spain, but others arrived from Flanders and Italy. By the 1580s, artists' communities in Mexico City, Lima, and other cities filled newly constructed churches and homes with sacred paintings and sculptures. Their efforts were frequently displayed alongside art imported from Europe, creating an opulent environment for the celebration of the faith.

The flow of art and artists across the Atlantic reached its height in the early seventeenth century, when Italians Bernardo Bitti (1548–1610), Mateo Pérez de Alesio (ca. 1547–1616), and Angelino Medoro (1567–1631) worked in the Viceroyalty of Peru, while Spaniards Andrés de Concha (ac. 1575–1611), Luis Juárez (ac. 1600–1639), and Baltazar de Echave Orio (1548–1620) led the painting profession in New Spain. Their mannerist painting styles profoundly impacted the local schools they founded. Bitti's *Agony in the Garden* (Figure 65) illustrates the formal approach the Italian Jesuit brought to South American

FIGURE 65.
Bernardo Bitti. *Agony in the Garden*. ca. 1600. Oil on canvas. Photograph © Museo de Arte, Lima, Peru.

shores in 1575. His elongated and graceful Christ and angel are wrapped in pastel-colored draperies that respond more to pattern and the artist's whim than to gravity or the bodies they clothe. Medoro's later mannerist approach reveals itself in *Christ at the Column*, 1619, in which the Italian painter, who worked throughout the Viceroyalty of Peru, displays a naturalistic approach to the figure and an incipient chiaroscuro. Like Bitti and Medoro in South America, Andrés de Concha (d. 1612) brought an elegant mannerist style to New Spain upon his 1568 arrival, embodied by paintings like *Saint Cecilia* circa 1590 (Figure 66). Concha's elongated figures and blonde, androgynous angels with delicate features exerted strong influence on his followers. Basque émigré Baltazar de Echave Orio (ca. 1558–ca. 1623) painted the *Agony in the Garden* (Figure 67) for the main altarscreen in the Jesuit church in Mexico City. The painting combines late mannerist elongated figures and metallic draperies with a baroque naturalism and dramatic chiaroscuro.

From this formative group, local urban painting schools in Mexico City, Lima, Cuzco, and elsewhere developed styles that appealed to their elite patrons. And while the forms practiced by the criollo, mestizo, and indigenous artists

FIGURE 66.
Andrés de Concha. *Saint Cecilia*. ca. 1590. Oil on canvas. Photograph © Museo Nacional de Arte.

FIGURE 67.
Baltazar de Echave Orio.
Agony in the Garden. 1610–20.
Oil on canvas. Photograph
© Archivo Fotográfico
Manuel Toussaint, INBA,
Mexico City, Mexico.

sometimes incorporated trends from Europe when these appealed to the artists and their patrons, they nevertheless developed distinct visual languages and formal qualities that differed from city to city. Too, foreign artists continued to arrive throughout the colonial era, but adapted their own approaches to please their local patrons.

Artists and ecclesiastical authorities alike worried about the decorum of religious art in the viceroyalties. Questions arose almost immediately after the conquest about the quality of religious art. Colonial authorities were troubled by the appearance of religious art, since the works were executed and seen by persons from decidedly different artistic and religious traditions. Many urban artists and ecclesiastics trained in European pictorial traditions viewed the hybridized holy images by native artists discussed in Chapter 2 as inappropriate for the celebration of the faith. Clerics feared that these "ugly" images or those reflecting native pictorial traditions might mislead or confuse indigenous parishioners. Émigré and criollo artists decried what they considered the inferior works by native artists, out of both a sense of decorum and a fear of competition.

Responsibility for policing the decency of viceregal religious art fell to church authorities and the artists' guilds. At the 1555 First Provincial Council held in Mexico City, for example, ecclesiastics declared that neither Spanish nor indigenous artists could paint holy images or construct altarscreens without being examined first by church officials. Following the Council of Trent, provincial councils held in Mexico City and Lima required artists to consult treatises on the decorum of religious imagery. Clergy throughout Latin America were charged with removing indecent art from their churches and towns; egregious offenses were turned over to the Holy Office of the Inquisition.

Artists' guilds likewise assumed responsibility for the decorum of religious art as they administered their professions. The New Spanish painters were the first to formalize their rules. (See Sidebar 13.) Their 1557 ordinances demanded skill in European painting techniques and Renaissance pictorial traditions, including

---

ᖚ SIDEBAR 13

Excerpts from the Ordinances of the Painters' and Gilders' Guild (Mexico City, 1557 and 1686)

FROM THE 1557 ORDINANCES:

[N]o painter, imagemaker, nor gilder, nor painter of wood panel or fresco, nor makers of [religious canvases known as] sargas, either those who now live in the city or those who would come here, nor any other person may open a shop in said trades . . . without first being examined by the official overseers of said trade . . . because some painters in said art have opened and continue to open shops, and practice said trades without being examined, not being skilled or good enough to do so, such that there has been and there continues to be danger to the common good of this City and Republic . . .

Image-makers wishing to open shops in this City of Mexico . . . may not do so without first being examined by the governors, overseers, and two other officials of the appropriate profession to be named; they are to be examined in the principle of composition and the principles that are necessary for the execution of the work, and also in working with the panel and give a good demonstration of drawing, and that those who would be examined be . . . very skilled in drawing and that they know how to do so to good account, as in drawing and in preparing the colors, and that they know how to work with the drawing and to show their skill in drawing a nude male, and clothing and drapery necessary for [representing] clothing and can make faces and hair very well so that the person who would be examined in said trade of imagemaker, should know how to make a perfect image and to make good account, as much in practice as in the actual work, to the said examiners . . .

the rendering of naturalistic nudes and drapery, and convincing linear perspective. Painters in Lima and Cuzco apparently did not feel the same urgency to articulate their practices and did not publish their ordinances until 1647 and 1649 respectively, that is, nearly a century after establishing vigorous painting schools comprised of foreign, criollo, mestizo, and native artists. Sculptors in New Spain and Peru also organized into guilds that demanded skill in rendering the human figure, both nude and clothed. New Spanish sculptors published their first ordinances in 1568. Interestingly, documents reveal no evidence of a guild for the most famous sculpture school in viceregal Latin America, the renowned Quito sculptors, until 1742.[1]

Guild ordinances also regulated entrance into and work within the profession. Interested youngsters entered contractual apprenticeships with local artists,

[N]o person may sell in the plaza or the public market any image or altarscreen because it is a great insult to Our Father . . .

[N]o merchant may purchase an image on panel or canvas to re-sell . . .

[N]o examined official with a public shop may order an Indian or other painter to make a painted or gilded altarscreen to sell unless he is examined, since being examined he will know how to draw and compose them without any error.

FROM THE 1686 ORDINANCES:

[N]o Indian may make a painting or other image of the saints, if he has not learned the trade to perfection and been examined without which he has no rights, and this is because the paintings and images they make are so irreverent that they have to be removed; but if they do not make paintings of saints, they are permitted, without being examined, to paint landscapes on panel, flowers, fruits, animals, and birds and grotesques and other things, so long as they are not images of saints . . .

[A]s it is written in one of the ordinances, the third, of the [guild of] altarscreen assemblers, sculptors and carpenters, that they not receive or accept any work of painting or gilding . . . painters and gilders shall not accept work in wood appropriate to those trades . . .

[F]rom the date of publication of these Ordinances, and forward no master painter may take on or agree to teach any apprentice who is not Spanish.
—From Manuel Toussaint, *Pintura colonial en México*,
3rd edition, ed. Xavier Moyssén, 221, passim
(Mexico City: UNAM, 1990). (Translation mine.)

living and learning within the master's home for between two and six years. In a 1678 apprenticeship contract, potosino painter Melchor Pérez Holguín (see Plate 10) promised to teach all he knew about painting, not hiding any professional secrets, in preparation for his apprentice's guild examination; for his part, the student agreed to complete all work the master assigned to him.[2] Tasks included copying prints and assisting with paintings; some students also studied Spanish art treatises by Francisco Pacheco, Vicente Carducho, and Antonio Palomino. Apprenticeship experiences helped artists to learn accepted formal and thematic solutions for common religious and secular themes, which also bred the stylistic and thematic conservatism that characterizes much colonial religious art. The apprentice became an official upon completing the guild examination; this granted him access to paid positions with a master's studio. Promotion from official to master, with the lucrative incentive of opening his own shop and accepting commissions directly from the public, followed a second examination.

Guild ordinances frequently restricted membership by ethnicity. The New Spanish sculptors' guild, for example, prohibited Black artists in 1568, but allowed Amerindians; local painters initially permitted examined Amerindians, but prohibited indigenous apprentices in 1686. The 1649 Lima painters' ordinances allowed Amerindian members, but stipulated that guild administrators be of Spanish descent; members were also prohibited from accepting Black and mixed-race students.[3] But despite the guild restrictions, the sculpture and painting professions were apparently quite diverse. Two of Mexico's greatest painters were the mulatto Juan Correa and the mestizo or mulatto Miguel Cabrera. Lima's painters included Blacks and at least one woman.[4]

The Cuzco painters' guild was similarly diverse until 1688, when its indigenous artists tired of the shabby treatment they received from their Spanish and criollo colleagues. The guild divided then along racial lines; the Spaniards joined the sculptors' guild, while the indigenous painters worked alone. The break represented more than a professional rupture; it led to the creation of the renowned Cuzco school of painting. The cuzqueño artists rejected the academic approach and employed more stylized forms, truncated spaces, and the flora seen in the *Virgin and Child* (Plate 12); the paintings regularly also included the gilded decoration known as *brocateado* that covers the two figures' garments. Scholars have attributed the style to a desire to marry indigenous and European artistic traditions in forms that appealed to indigenous viewers. Andean artists' communities in Collao and elsewhere employed similar forms and iconography. This style, generically known as the mestizo baroque, was not confined to provincial parishes or indigenous audiences. Andean mestizo baroque paintings are found throughout South America and even Europe. And while early scholars condemned the factory-like production required to meet patrons' demands, the Cuzco school and other Andean painters were in high demand and apparently held broad appeal among the array of colonists, even if their working practices did not agree with historians' paradigm of artistic creativity based on the myth of the European singular artist-genius.

The Virgin Mary was one of the most popular themes for artists working between 1600 and 1785 in New Spain and Peru. Spaniards brought their fervent devotion to the Mother of God to American shores and her cult grew throughout the colonial era. Like all Catholics, the colonists embraced Mary's role as intercessor, relying on her kind nature to bring them closer to God. They also venerated her as the Queen of Heaven, whose role in Christ's miraculous birth earned her a place in the celestial hierarchy second only to the Trinity. She and her images operated as role models for all women as she accepted the word of God and assumed her domestic responsibilities.

Most Marian imagery produced in colonial Latin America reflected the themes popular in contemporary European art, such as the Cuzco school *Virgin and Christ Child* of a lactating Mary. Altarscreens in both viceroyalties abounded with her likeness accompanying Christ from his miraculous birth to his death and resurrection. She also appeared in scenes of her own life, bringing joy to the barren Anne in a 1610 copper painting by Luís Juárez, meeting and marrying Joseph in Cristóbal de Villalpando's circa 1690 canvas, and assuming her role as Queen of Heaven in Bernardo Bitti's work for the Mercedarians in Lima. Mary also appeared in paintings of the saints who saw her in miraculous visions. In all images, she is the picture of ideal womanhood, the beautiful and patient mother who guided her son and comforted believers.

Images of the Virgin Mary also played a role in the colonization. Conquistador Hernán Cortés carried a banner of the Immaculate Conception on his journey to Tenochtitlan. One of his companions bore a small Marian sculpture on his horse's halter; the image, known as the Virgin of los Remedios, subsequently developed a popular following. In 1536, a sculpture of the Immaculate Conception rose to the roof of Cuzco's burning Sunturhuasi tower, extinguishing the flames and saving the Spaniards sheltered inside during the lengthy Inca siege; a chapel built on the site is still known as El Triunfo or The Triumph. The miraculous sculpture nevertheless ended up in Lima.[5]

The Catholic Church in Latin America promoted this kind of localized devotion to miraculous images of the Virgin Mary, a practice inherited from Spain. Stories of Mary's appearances on American soil soon circulated in the viceroyalties. Many of the legends involved painted or sculpted images, either of miraculous manufacture (or acheiropoietic) or made by human hands and subsequently touched by divine powers. Shrines built to house the holy images quickly followed in urban centers and native villages. Devotion to these local Marian cults grew as native parishioners accepted the Virgin into their belief systems, and Spaniards and criollos embraced familiar traditions. Belief in powerful images was, in fact, a point of religious overlap between some native and Spanish belief systems, and New World ecclesiastics consequently used the American legends and images, particularly those involving newly Christianized natives, to promote evangelical successes. More specifically, clerics may have attempted to substitute Mary for the Pre-Columbian earth deities Pachamama in the Andes and Tonantzin in Central Mexico. Whatever the reasons, Latin American Catholics embraced Marian devotions and the landscape quickly filled with shrines in her honor.

The most famous viceregal cult image remains the Virgin of Guadalupe. The legend involving her miraculous 1531 apparition to Amerindian witness Juan Diego was discussed in Chapter 4. Devotion to this New Spanish cult figure grew throughout the sixteenth and seventeenth centuries, helped by the miracles attributed to the image. When the painting helped to end a deadly plague in 1737, her fame was clinched and she soon became patroness of New Spain. In 1751, New Spanish ecclesiastics convened a panel of respected painters to establish the image's divine or human provenance, since early doubters attributed the image to Amerindian painter Marcos Cipac. Painters Miguel Cabrera, José de Ibarra, Juan Patricio Morlete Ruiz, Francisco Antonio Vallejo, José de Alcíbar, and Manuel Osorio found that the tilma image had techniques and materials (oil, gilding, gouache, and tempera) that human artists never used in combination. Cabrera published the group's findings in *Maravilla Americana y conjunto de raras maravillas* in 1756, stating that the painting was of divine origin.

Paintings of the Virgin of Guadalupe, like Juan Correa's 1704 work seen here (Plate 13), abound in colonial figural arts. Reproductions were engraved and printed, embroidered, inlaid with shell and mother-of-pearl, and painted on copper panel, wood, and canvas. Like all reproductions, Correa's painting carefully copies the original image, showing the dark-skinned, crowned Mary standing on a crescent moon; a small angel holds up the hems of her cloak and gown. Her mantle is covered in stars and she is surrounded by a mandorla of 129 golden rays of sunlight. Correa's image may in fact have been based on a tracing he made of the miraculous likeness, which reflects the iconography the Apocalyptic Woman described in the Book of Revelation. Correa also maintained the miraculous image's barely modeled figure and angular drapery, which early writers said resembled Pre-Columbian drawings and proved that God and the Virgin Mary addressed this miracle to the indigenous people of central New Spain.[6] Like most colonial painters, however, Correa exercised artistic license for the narrative scenes and framing elements, and surrounded the figure with flowers and blonde and brunette (and dark-skinned) cherubs who hold aloft floral-framed roundels describing the four apparitions. The inscription at the bottom testifies to the painting's cultic value and reads, "This painting was touched to the Holy Image on 10 April 1704." Hence Correa's painting was at once a likeness and a relic, which transferred something of the New Spanish Virgin's powers to the new painting.

But more than a religious figure, the image of the Virgin of Guadalupe was a national symbol. Her miraculous appearance identified God's approval of the new nation, of the friars' apostolic missions, and of the deep piety of the colonists. Hence reproductions of the miraculous image frequently included the Latin motto "Non fecit taliter omni nationi" (It was not done thus to all nations), taken from Psalm 147.[7] Her associations with criollo national pride, also known as criollo patriotism, led Miguel de Hidalgo to carry a standard bearing her image in 1810 as he fought for independence from Spain.

The most famous Marian image in colonial South America was the 1582 sculpture known as the *Virgin of Copacabana*; a reproduction of the sculpture also found at the Copacabana shrine is seen in Figure 68. The legends associated with this cult reveal that unlike the Virgin of Guadalupe, the Bolivian sculpture was made by human hands. As discussed in the last chapter, indigenous sculptor Francisco Tito Yupanqui set out to make a sculpted Virgin Mary for his community on the shores of Lake Titicaca, where an ancestral devotion to Pachamama remained strong.[8] In 1560, in fact, Augustinian friars discovered a blue stone carving of the deity and heaved it into the lake, and substituted the Virgin Mary for the indigenous god.[9] Tito Yupanqui's new sculpture was created to celebrate this new devotion.

Yupanqui modeled his work after a sculpture of the Virgin in Potosí. Its miraculous history began when the image gave off a mysterious light.[10] This miracle led to the sculpture's placement in the Copacabana shrine, across the lake from the Islands of the Sun and Moon. (See Sidebar 14.) Like the temple at

FIGURE 68.
Reproduction of Francisco Tito Yupanqui. *Our Lady of Copacabana*. 1582. Maguey. Santuario de Copacabana, Bolivia. Photograph © Anders Ryman/Alamy.

Tepeyac, the shrine's location was the site of Pre-Columbian devotion, in this case to Manco Capac and Mama Occlo, mythic founders of Cuzco and the Inca empire. From this location the image subsequently performed other miracles involving indigenous Christians, including ending a drought.

Tito Yupanqui's sculpture, like the reproduction seen here, is a columnar figure of the Virgin Mary. One hand holds the Christ Child and the other a candle, symbol of the Virgin's purity. But while Yupanqui's sculpture generally reflects the artist's adherence to Renaissance pictorial practices, and resembles Spanish early sixteenth-century sculpture, the artist's first attempt was rejected by church authorities and criollo artists, some of whom declared that Amerindians could not make images of the Virgin.[11] Unlike the Virgin of Guadalupe, whose supposedly native pictorial style was acceptable as God's attempt to reach out to indigenous peoples, the Virgin of Copacabana's human manufacture required the application of a European-based approach to image-making. Consequently, the cult's legend invariably begins with the indigenous artist's effort to learn European formal strategies, including his apprenticeship

---

☜ SIDEBAR 14

Excerpts from Alonso Ramos Gavilán's history of the Virgen of Copacabana (1621)

CHAPTER XLI

A Short Account of the Festival Held for the Installation of the Holy Image of Our Lady in her Chapel.

On April 6, 1614, the very Reverend Miguel Gutiérrez, being Provincial of our Holy Order, and the Prior of this Holy Convent of Our Lady of Copacabana, Father Fray Juan Vizcayno . . . having finished the main chapel of the Church, which is vaulted with a triumphal arch, and that is 35 feet wide and 50 feet long, to be able to place in it the Holy Image, took her from the old altar where she was . . . to put her in her Tabernacle in the main altar of the said chapel. They put her on her litter in the sacristy where she remained in veneration for two or three days, without anyone seeing her but he who cared for the Holy Relic. The church was decked with hangings and on the altars of the main and side chapels were placed large and costly ornaments adorned with many decorations; the dome of the vault . . . had thirteen lamps, which made an agreeable sight. They put in the nave of the church and at the sides of the main altar thirty ten-pound candles . . . From the surrounding territories and other parts, attended the priests, ecclesiastics, *Corregidores* [civil administrators],

with Spanish sculptor Diego Ortiz. Tito Yupanqui's struggle to acquire these skills may therefore be understood as an allegory of the church's attempts to suppress idolatry and the native community's desire to negotiate the new social system.[12] The robust sculpture school Yupanqui founded in the Lake Titicaca area confirmed, at least to Peruvian ecclesiastics, the efficacy of the religious, artistic, and social conversion.

The *Virgin of Copacabana* is entirely carved from the trunk of a maguey plant and painted in lifelike polychrome. The sculpture is furthermore treated as an *imagen de vestir*, or dressed image. The practice of dressing sculpture came from Spain, where medieval seated sculptures of the Virgin Mary with the Christ Child were refashioned according to the Renaissance preference for standing Madonnas. To cover the saw cuts and to update the Virgin's clothing, Spanish parishioners dressed the sculptures, frequently in campaniform (bell-shaped) gowns. The practice appealed to the Spanish taste for realism, as the Virgin appears almost human in her contemporary fashion, and by the eighteenth century, sculptures were regularly made specifically to be dressed. Sometimes this

the Governor of Chucuito, and more than 180 other important people, and more than 2,000 Indians from out of town, and there was music from Juli, which, accompanied by the music from the Convent, sounded very good . . . That night there were one million lanterns, pipes, trumpets, bells ringing, and fireworks . . . The next day Sunday, an infinite number of dancers attended, and the Inca made a show at the beginning of the procession, dressed very well with great pomp and with their weapons, harquebuses, pikes, whips, saddles, arrows, drums, and piper; and all of the people gathered for the procession, and they took on the rich litter the Holy Virgin with a white mantle, all embroidered with much detail, and all sewn with very valuable jewels and pearls, and the Holy child with the same, and their gold crowns with many stones; four outfitted ecclesiastics carried her, and hence they left the sacristy at the same time that they took from the tabernacle the Holy Sacrament, and under the pallium they took it to the main door of the church . . . and there began the procession with many litters bearing Saints and standards . . . and in this way they returned to the main chapel, and to one side they left the Holy Image on her litter. They began the holy offices and the aforementioned Father Provincial said the Mass.

—From Alonso Ramos Gavilán, *Historia del Santuario de Nuestra Señora de Copacabana*, ed. and notes by Ignacio Prado Pastor, 415–16 (Lima: Ediciones Ignacio Prado, 1988). (Translation mine.)

meant only sculpting heads and hands; an armature covered in canvas replaced the rest of the body. This not only saved money, but made the sculpture lighter for carrying in religious processions.

Sebastián Quimichi, a pilgrim who experienced the miraculous powers of the small sculpture of the Virgin of Copacabana, helped spread her fame and spawn a new cult. After suffering a wound, Quimichi made a pilgrimage to Copacabana in 1598; the cult image rewarded his journey by healing his wound. The event inspired Quimichi to acquire from Francisco Tito Yupanqui a reproduction of the holy image for his community of Cocharcas. He installed the reproduction in a newly constructed shrine, from which the Virgin of Cocharcas performed miracles and attracted her own pilgrims. Like the Virgin of Copacabana, the Cocharcas cult included miracles involving native peoples, which again offered church authorities the opportunity to demonstrate the benefits of indigenous conversion.

The sculpted Virgin and Child at Cocharcas soon became a locus of fervent Marian devotion and a popular pilgrimage site. The quantity of painted reproductions of her image testifies to her popularity. The busy Andean mestizo baroque *Virgin of Cocharcas* (Plate 14) features the sculpted image on a canopied altar. She holds the Christ Child in one hand and a bouquet and a bent candle in the other. Both figures wear rich, lace-trimmed clothes; the Virgin's gown is embroidered with flowers and adorned with precious stones and ribbons. Flower-bearing urns, ubiquitous in this type of painting, rest on the corners. The Cocharcas painting also illustrates the pilgrimages Spanish Americans made to visit her shrine. Pilgrims walk from the painting's upper left corner to the town and church of Cocharcas, found in the upper right corner. The multitude encounters dangers along the way including falls from steep paths, demonic possessions, and perilous water crossings; they are saved only by the Virgin of Cocharcas's miraculous powers. It is important to note that the pilgrims represent the broad colonial society and include clergy, criollo men and women, and Amerindians. They are also accompanied by the flowers, birds, and angels characteristic of Andean mestizo baroque painting. The lush setting may furthermore recall the Pre-Columbian paradise known as Hanacpacha, which early missionaries compared to the Christian Garden of Eden, as discussed in Chapter 2.

Paintings reproducing miraculous sculptures have come to be known as "statue paintings," or *trampantojos*.[13] These works, which usually reconstruct the cult image in its altarscreen, entered the Andean pictorial repertoire in 1600.[14] Like the representations of the Virgin of Guadalupe, statue paintings (and prints) identified the cult, reproducing the specific attributes associated with the devotional sculpture or painting. The attributes sometimes included geographic references. The most extreme example of this type of geographic marker is the Virgin of the Hill of Potosí, in which Mary is grafted upon the mining hill (an indigenous huaca) known as the Cerro Rico. Virgin of Cocharcas and other cult images sometimes also presented scenes of miraculous interventions. Basilio Santa Cruz Pumacallao's *Virgin of Bethlehem* in the Cuzco Cathedral is a particularly informative example, with several developed narratives and a donor portrait surrounding the cult figure.[15]

Beyond specific Marian cults, themes from Mary's life appealed to colonial artists and their patrons. Her youth was particularly popular with Andean artists. The 1699 *The Young Virgin with a Distaff* (Plate 15) reflects a popular theme for *potosino* and *cuzqueño* painters.[16] The painting features a young Mary, sitting in an ornate chair holding a distaff (or spindle) with wool yarn. She wears a decorated gown, an *illicla* cloak covered in *brocateado*, and silver earrings. In typical Andean fashion, she is surrounded by flowers painted in pastel colors; flowers appear on her cloak and headband as well. These may have been painted by an artist who specialized in flowers, since Andean paintings were routinely created by multiple hands. The painting, formerly attributed to Melchor Pérez Holguín (ca. 1660–1733), a mestizo painter who dominated painting in Potosí between 1680 and 1730, exhibits typical Andean baroque characteristics, with limited spatial exploration, an idealized figure, and a profusion of brightly colored flowers.[17]

The Young Virgin with a Distaff and other similar works reflect an Andean vision of Christianity that was loving and approachable, but it may also reveal the coincidence of ancient Andean and Christian practices. Apocryphal stories from Spain told of the Virgin Mary learning to weave from Saint Anne and spinning a veil for the Temple in Jerusalem. This humanized vision of Mary and other holy figures resonated with Spanish and criollo colonists. Indigenous viewers undoubtedly appreciated the story for the same reason, but Mary's weaving may have held additional meaning for Andean audiences. Inca royalty wore vicuña clothes bearing tocapu designs woven by *acyllakuna*. These seamstresses, also known as the Chosen Women or Virgins of the Sun, were selected as children to serve the divinely chosen Inca ruler. They spent their lives isolated from secular society in a home near the Coricancha palace in Cuzco.[18] It stands to reason that indigenous Andean artists embraced the theme of Mary as seamstress both for her role in Christian redemption and for her similarity to ancestral beliefs. Dressing her in clothes combining European garb and the wardrobe of an Inca *ñusta* or princess, including the headdress and hairstyle that may recall the Inca royal headdress, leaves room for multiple readings.[19]

Like their colleagues throughout the Spanish empire, viceregal artists regularly represented the Virgin of the Immaculate Conception. The Immaculatist doctrine—the belief that Mary was born without sin like her son—was promoted by the Franciscans and the Spanish Hapsburg monarchs. Although it did not become dogma until 1854, the celebration of the feast of the Immaculate Conception of Mary was sanctioned in 1661 when Pope Alexander VII declared Mary's birth free from the stain of original sin. It comes as no surprise, therefore, that New Spanish and Peruvian artists painted her image regularly.

The renowned Cuzco school painter Diego Quispe Tito (ca. 1611–80) painted the *Virgin of the Immaculate Conception with Litanies* (Plate 16) circa

1650. The beautiful and youthful Mary dominates the composition in her red gown and blue mantle covered in brocateado. Tiny figures of Saints Francis of Assisi and Anthony of Padua kneel on clouds beside the Virgin, while Christ, God the Father, and the dove of the Holy Spirit occupy the top of the painting. Mary wears a crown with a halo of twelve stars and angels above her head. With clasped hands and bowed head, she humbly rests on the crescent moon held aloft by angels. Six additional angels hold the symbols of her purity as described in the Old Testament. This Immaculatist iconography was outdated by 1650, however, when most painters in Spain and the Americas followed Francisco Pacheco's proscription. The Spanish theorist required artists to paint Mary hovering aloft in a golden mandorla, wearing a white dress and blue robe, crowned with a halo of twelve stars, and standing on a down-turned crescent moon; the symbols were to be painted into the landscape. Quispe Tito's iconography blends Immaculatist signs with those common to her medieval precursor, the Virgin Tota Pulchra. The painting nevertheless embodies the pervasive devotion to the cult in Spain and its colonies.

Christological Images in Viceregal Art

Images of Christ, not surprisingly, abounded in colonial churches, chapels, homes, and even streets. Many altarscreens, regardless of period style, represented his life from the Annunciation through the Resurrection. Latin American artists working in the period following the Council of Trent, like their colleagues in Europe, privileged the drama of Christ's Passion, and allegories of his triumph over sin and death dominated every pictorial medium. The artists also embraced new post-Tridentine devotions, including the representation of Christ's youth. To a greater degree than the sixteenth-century mural paintings discussed in Chapter 2, seventeenth- and eighteenth-century Christological images were as inspirational and theatrical as they were didactic. Spanish theorist Francisco Pacheco embodied this post-Tridentine spirit when he declared that someone who did not experience heightened devotion or a knot in the stomach upon viewing images of Christ's Passion was made of stone or bronze.[20] Colonial artists, like their peers in Spain, deployed both form and material to heighten their objects' dramatic impact. This suited the church's needs as ecclesiastics exploited images of Christ, like those of the Virgin Mary, to inspire devotion and promote their evangelical enterprise.

Colonists believed that Christ, like his mother, performed miracles through images, resulting in regional cults that appealed to parishioners and ecclesiastics alike. The *Christ of the Earthquakes*, discussed in Chapter 3, earned its miraculous status in 1650 by ending the temblor destroying Cuzco. The New Spanish *Christ of Chalma* appeared on the site of an indigenous cult in 1539, transforming a barren landscape into an earthly paradise. Other Latin American Christological cult images include the *Black Christ of Esquipulas* in Guatemala, the *Christ of Guápulo* in Ecuador, and the *Christ of Sacromonte* near Mexico City. And while these cult images were disseminated in statue paintings similar to those described above, they saw even wider distribution in prints.

The anonymous eighteenth-century engraving of the *Holy Christ of Santa Teresa* (Figure 69) from the Convent of the Discalced Carmelites in Mexico City, exemplifies colonial devotional prints of cult images. It features the 1545 sculpted Crucifixion made of corn paste for a chapel in Ixmiquilpan. The image was in poor condition by 1615 when the sculpture, alternately known as the *Christ of Ixmiquilpan*, miraculously repaired itself.[21] The renovated sculpture appears in the print on its altar in the Discalced Carmelite Convent of San José de Santa Teresa de Jesús (popularly known as Santa Teresa la Antigua), where it was taken shortly after the miracle. As in the statue paintings of the same cult image by New Spanish artists José de Mora and José de Ibarra, the sculpture in the engraving wears the lacy loincloth favored in Latin America and is accompanied by ornate silver urns. The inscription at the bottom of the print reads, "True portrait of the most beautiful image of the miraculously renovated Christ Crucified venerated in the Old Convent of the Discalced Carmelites in Mexico. The most eminent don Luis Antonio Archbishop of Toledo concedes one hundred days of

FIGURE 69.
Holy Christ of Santa Teresa/Ixmiquilpan. Eighteenth century. Engraving. Nettie Lee Benson Latin American Collection, Austin, Texas. Photograph © Kelly Donahue-Wallace.

indulgence to all those who recite one Lord's Prayer, Credo, or complete another Act of Faith in front of this print, praying to God for peace." The image hence offers a reward to its owner for his or her pious behavior.

Like most engravings made during the colonial era, the *Holy Christ of Santa Teresa* is unsigned and represents the bustling but largely unstudied printmaking industries in both viceroyalties. Printing and printmakers arrived in New Spain and Peru in the mid-sixteenth century. The first printing press, under the care of Juan Pablos, operated in Mexico City by 1539; the first South American press arrived several decades later. As the presses required illustrations for their imprints, local printmakers began practicing their art. Some of these artists emigrated from Spain and elsewhere in Europe; others were local. The artists produced illustrations and single leaf prints for publishers and private patrons, first in woodcut, and later in copperplate engraving. After a period of rapid expansion in the seventeenth century, robust printmaking industries operated in Lima, Mexico City, Puebla, and other colonial cities; in 1767, Mexico City alone had at least a dozen print shops.[22] These artists did not belong to a guild and competition may have been fierce. Some artists drew clients by inscribing their addresses at the foot of their prints or by advertising in local gazettes.

The customers who purchased the *Holy Christ of Santa Teresa* and other prints came from all sectors of colonial society; the paper images were found in the homes of elite bureaucrats and rural peasants alike. Colonists purchased religious prints in huge numbers; they tacked them to the walls of their homes, framed them, glued prints into books, and carried them on their bodies. Shrines associated with cult images, and others interested in exploiting popular devotion to the miraculous figures, commissioned prints to sell to these pious colonists. The prints commonly included indulgence statements like the one found on this engraving of the *Holy Christ of Santa Teresa*. Some indulgences were legitimately granted by church officials and others were invented by the printmaker or his patron to boost sales. In this case, the grant was probably true, since the move from Ixmiquilpan to Mexico City was in part done to raise funds for the Carmelite convent.[23] Calling the image a *verdadero retrato* or true portrait promised purchasers that their prayers would not be misdirected; similar messages appeared regularly on paintings as well as prints.

While inscriptions promising a true printed or painted portrait put the devout viewer's mind at ease, realistic images of Christ's suffering disturbed his soul. In the Spanish world, artists persuaded viewers to piety with sculpted Passion figures vividly illustrating Christ's suffering. Christ's flagellation in Pilate's house, his walk to Calvary, the Crucifixion, and a host of other subjects offered opportunities to communicate Christ's human pain. These expressive representations of a bloodied Christ likely appealed to colonists for a variety of reasons. For Amerindian viewers, they may have evoked memories of indigenous blood sacrifice, whereas criollos recalled Spanish religious and artistic practices. For all colonists, the images furthermore reflected the post-Tridentine celebration of Christ's humanity.

The eighteenth-century *Christ Recumbent* (Figure 70) by the quiteño indigenous sculptor Manuel Chili, known as Capiscara (ca. 1723–96), presents many of the features common to colonial Passion imagery. Removed from the cross, Christ's expired body is bruised and bloodied. Likely created for placement in a gilded sarcophagus, the image's material and technique of execution heighten its expressive realism. After sculpting the naturalistic wood figure, Capiscara likely gave the work to a painter, since the guild of painters took official responsibility for painting sculptures.[24] The unnamed painter employed a polychrome technique known as *encarnación*, an appropriate name for a process that seems to make flesh of the inanimate material. Introduced from Spain, encarnación consisted of applying gesso to the sculpture, sanding it, painting flesh tones, varnishing, and repeating these steps until the painter achieved a life-like glow of natural skin. But the realism did not end with flesh tones. Capiscara's painter added blue, black, red, and brown pigments to simulate bruises, blood, and dark hair; some of the wounds may even be modeled from plaster applied on top of the wood. Though not employed in this example, Passion figures regularly included human- or horse-hair wigs and eyelashes, glass eyes, and ivory teeth and fingernails. Clear or colored crystal became realistic tears or glistening drops of blood. Even bits of cork were added to molded gesso wounds to make ripped flesh and spilling blood real to the viewer. And if this static realism was not enough, many large sculpted images of Christ included articulated joints, allowing the figure to be variously posed throughout the liturgical calendar; the joints likewise made the sculptures appear to move during processions. Even without movement, Capiscara's figure is hauntingly and pathetically lifelike.

In fact, Capiscara and other South American sculptors were famous throughout the Americas for precisely this reason. Their work shared the realistic style and lifelike materials preferred in Spain, no doubt helped by the fact that works by such famous Sevilla sculptors as Juan Martínez Montañés and Pedro de

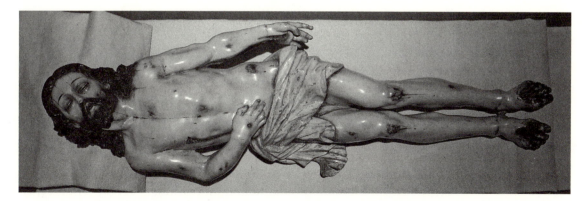

FIGURE 70. Capiscara (Manuel Chili). *Christ Recumbent*. Eighteenth century. Wood and pigment. Photograph © Museo del Banco Central de Ecuador, Quito, Ecuador.

Mena shared space in colonial churches with local products. By the eighteenth century, South American sculptors, like their New Spanish colleagues, added dynamic movement to their lifelike style and high-keyed emotion, and sometimes employed gesso-stiffened cloth to create billowing draperies. Capiscara in particular, part of the quiteño school of sculptors founded in the sixteenth century by fray Jodocus Ricke (see Chapter 2), was renowned for his full round sculptures of theatrical tableaux of religious stories; *Christ Recumbent* may have been at one time surrounded by mourning figures. Even alone, the image undoubtedly evoked a deep pity and religious fervor from its colonial audience.

Images of Christ's childhood similarly tugged at colonists' heartstrings and inspired their piety. The popularity of these works, like those of the young Virgin Mary, reflected the softer, more human version of Catholicism preferred in the colonies in the later seventeenth and eighteenth centuries. In most of the scenes, an infant or prepubescent Christ meditates on his death as he examines the crown of thorns or other instruments of the Passion; in some cases, he sleeps on the cross. The images, therefore, present dual messages of innocence and wisdom, pain and triumph.

New Spanish artist Nicolas Rodríguez Juárez (1667–1734), a member of the criollo painting dynasty founded by his great-grandfather Luís Juárez, painted *The Christ Child* (Plate 17) in the late seventeenth century. The work displays the typical characteristics of the artist's baroque style. The Christ Child appears within an oval framing device accompanied by the instruments of his Passion, including the column on which he sits. Having just pricked his finger on the crown of thorns resting in his lap, he displays his bleeding finger and gazes sadly at the viewer. The idealized figure and landscape, and genre-like treatment of the instruments gathered into a basket belie the painting's solemn message. The work communicates profound piety in a sweet, late baroque style with its pastel blue sky, pink-cheeked figure, and soft, airy brushstrokes.

Viceregal Christological images regularly placed Christ within the earthly hierarchy of his family and the heavenly hierarchy of the Trinity. The Holy Family, a popular theme in post-Tridentine Europe, resonated with New Spanish and Peruvian clerical patrons. Mary, Joseph, and the Christ Child appeared in period literature and art as the model nuclear family working together for mutual benefit and for God. The *Holy Family of Nazareth* (Plate 18) by Colombian criollo painter Gregorio Vásquez de Arce y Ceballos (1638–1711), represents one approach to the subject. Inspired by a late sixteenth-century European engraving, the painting nevertheless reveals a skilled draftsman known for his regular use of preparatory drawings. Vásquez is in fact one of the few seventeenth-century Latin American artists whose drawings have survived to the present.[25] Whether executed completely by Vásquez or with the assistance of his large studio, the painting's pleasant atmosphere, soft palette, and vaporous brushwork demonstrate an academic approach akin to the contemporary work of Spanish painter Bartolomé Esteban Murillo.

Vásquez's painting features the Holy Family at home in Nazareth. The Virgin

Mary, performing her motherly domestic duties, stirs a pot at the fire and turns to look sadly at her son. The kindling held by the angel behind her represents the sorrows that will pierce her holy breast. The Christ Child sweeps the family home, piling the waste beside a pile of wood reminiscent of the wood that will soon make his cross. Joseph labors outside the house at his carpentry, his hammer and plane reminding the viewer of the tools used to prepare Christ's cross. The local bird resting in the window reveals the artist's familiarity with contemporary Andean trends, despite the painting's close formal and iconographic ties to its Flemish print source and Spanish late baroque painting.

It should come as little surprise that the Holy Family appeared regularly in colonial art. Not only did the church promote family values and gender norms to criollo audiences like their colleagues across the Atlantic, but ecclesiastics also contended with native family structures, polygamy, cohabitation, and divorce, all of which they considered to be abominations.[26] They consequently offered the Holy Family as the model for colonial families of all races: a well-ordered unit headed by a loving, industrious, and faithful father who acted as the family's spiritual guide and in turn submitted to the will of God. Like others of its genre, Vázquez's painting demonstrates how each Holy Family member behaved according to proscribed gender and social roles: Mary complied with her domestic responsibilities, Joseph worked outside the home, and the Christ Child humbled himself before his parents. It has been suggested, however, that in addition to church-sanctioned meanings, indigenous Andeans may have associated Joseph and Mary with Manco Capac and Mama Ocllo, the Inca primordial couple.[27] Consequently, this painting of a subject promoted to the breadth of viceregal society, likely held different meanings for its diverse viewers.

The Holy Trinity enjoyed great popularity in the Americas, and images of the three aspects of God—an elderly God the Father, a youthful Christ, and a dove for the Holy Spirit—appeared in paintings in both viceroyalties. But Latin American artists sometimes responded to unique American concerns in their Trinitarian images. Faced with native polytheism and animal deities, early ecclesiastics stressed the tripartite nature of the single Christian God. This translated into images of the Trinity as three identical human figures distinguished only by the sun, lamb, and dove emblazoned on their robes. This representation of the Trinity did not comply, however, with the church guidelines. Clerics at the Council of Trent demanded that artists represent God the Father, the youthful Christ, and the dove of the Holy Spirit; Pope Benedict XIV again prohibited representations of the identical Trinity in 1778. In 1790, however, the Holy Office of the Inquisition in Mexico City agreed to ignore this order. They determined that enforcing Benedict XIV's prohibition might have been appropriate in Europe, but not in New Spain. After 270 years, native viewers had seen thousands of images of the Trinity as three identical figures.[28] Altering the iconography at this late date would confuse the Amerindian populations.

Not even the New Spanish clerics, however, could abide the heterodox iconography of the anonymous *Trifacial Trinity* (Plate 19). Rather than three identical figures, the New Spanish artist pictured the Trinity as one figure with three faces. While graphically reinforcing the notion of a single deity with three aspects, the painting certainly violated religious decorum. The fact that many images like this came from New Spanish and Peruvian studios, however, illustrates the limits of Inquisition authority and enforcement.

Saints in Viceregal Art

The pantheon of Christian saints popular in colonial Latin America generally mirrored that found in Spain. Franciscan, Dominican, Augustinian, and Jesuit saints were highly favored, reflecting the orders' local prominence. Female saints associated with conventual life were also popular, as was the repentant Mary Magdalene. Holy figures who shaped Christian doctrine and history, including John the Baptist, the Doctors of the Church, Thomas Aquinas, and the vast array of mystics and martyrs likewise found appeal among colonists. Their images occupied altarscreens, hung in homes, and rested in domestic shrines or *oratorios*. But as with Marian and Christological themes, selected saints found particular favor in the colonies and reflected the colonial context.

Images of Saint Joseph are closely related to those of the Holy Family. And while images of the latter promoted the ideal family structure in the post-Tridentine, New World context, Joseph's images specifically addressed early modern concerns about fathers and their roles within the family. By extension, the images of Joseph in the Americas addressed spiritual and real fatherhood. Mendicant clergy, for example, sought solace in Joseph and his demonstrated virtues of chastity, poverty, and obedience.[29] Joseph was furthermore considered the special protector of Amerindian populations, for whom legend has it he performed many miracles.[30] His early promotion among newly converted people is evidenced by Mexico City's first chapel for Amerindians, San José de los Naturales (Saint Joseph of the Indians). Colonial authorities did not understand Joseph as a solely native devotion, however, and the 1555 New Spanish First Provincial Council named him patron of New Spain. And although Joseph was eventually displaced as New Spain's patron by his holy wife, Joseph's appeal did not wane and the faithful continued to honor him in works of art and architecture throughout the colonial era.

The anonymous New Spanish *Saint Joseph and the Christ Child* (Figure 71) typifies the saint's treatment in viceregal art. Joseph stands with his young son and offers a loving gaze, while the Child looks back towards his surrogate father. Joseph's mature age reflects Francisco Pacheco's demand that he appear as a man in his early thirties, mature yet youthful enough to provide for his family's safety and well being.[31] Joseph holds the flowering staff that, according to the Golden Legend, identified him as God's selection for Mary's bridegroom. The Child holds a globe to symbolize his dominion over the earth, while in similar works he holds a heart to symbolize his love of humanity or the apple Joseph gave him on the trip to Egypt and symbolizing his defeat of sin.

FIGURE 71.
*Saint Joseph and
the Christ Child.*
Eighteenth century.
Oil and mother-
of-pearl on panel.
Photograph
© Museo de
América,
Madrid, Spain.

The painting of *Saint Joseph and the Christ Child* is an example of the New Spanish technique known as *enconchado*. This process combined oil painting and inlaid mother-of-pearl, and may have been inspired by goods imported from Asia.[32] The process became popular in New Spain in the late seventeenth and early eighteenth centuries and was used for a variety of religious and secular themes. Although the pearlescent shell could be used anywhere within the painting, New Spanish artists almost invariably took advantage of the material to represent fine clothing. In this case, Joseph's and the Christ Child's garments seem to radiate on the surface of the canvas.

Most viceregal saints' images consisted of iconic paintings or sculptures featuring the saint and his or her attributes. Painters and sculptors frequently created these iconic images in groups, intending them to be seen together within an altarscreen or architectural setting. Other series offered biographical narratives in highly detailed pictorial compositions chronicling the saint's life from birth to death. These paintings commonly lined the walls of convents, cloisters, schools, and other religious organizations, replacing the frescoes painted in early convents, and promoting the order's heroes. Illustrating visions and miracles, the series not only demonstrated ideal Christian lives, but also divine rewards for spiritual perfection. The series, therefore, both educated and inspired the clerical and lay viewers who passed beneath them. They also demonstrated the divine favor (and wealth) enjoyed by the institutions responsible for their execution and display.

Miguel Mateo Maldonado y Cabrera (1695–1768) painted *Life of Ignatius of Loyola* in 1750–55 for Pedro de Arrieta's Church of Saint Ignatius, better known as La Profesa, in Mexico City. The thirty-two canvases begin with the saint's birth and youth. Following his 1521 near-fatal injury in battle, Iñigo López, as he was known, experienced a life-altering vision of the Virgin Mary and dedicated his life to God. He wrote his *Spiritual Exercises* in 1541, a year after he founded the religious order known as the Society of Jesus or the Jesuit Order.

Cabrera's series mirrors an earlier set of twenty-eight canvases painted in 1710 by Cristóbal de Villalpando for the cloister at San Francisco Xavier in Tepotzotlán and Cabrera's own series painted for the Church of Saint Ignatius in Querétaro. These and other paintings symbolize the power of the Jesuit order in the Americas. As elsewhere in the Catholic world, Jesuit colleges and seminaries were the intellectual heart of viceregal society. The eighteenth century has been described as the century of Jesuit triumph and their pedagogical, spiritual, and financial success in New Spain was embodied in the renovation of the seminary at San Francisco Xavier in Tepotzotlán and Cabrera's painted series.[33]

Cabrera's painting of the *Birth of Saint Ignatius* for La Profesa series recalls contemporary paintings of the birth of the Virgin Mary, and the reference was likely as much symbolic as practical. Placing the saint's mother sitting up in her bed, with servants engaging the young Iñigo—just as contemporary artists represented Mary and her mother, Anne—established the saint's holy credentials even if his religious life was not to begin for several decades. Unlike the Virgin Mary's humble surroundings, however, Ignatius's family home is elegant and filled with luxury goods, from clocks to a canopied bed. The onlookers include two clergy, Abbott Joachim and the Venerable Angela, who prophesied the saint's birth.[34] Like other paintings created for specific architectural settings, the work's odd shape reflects the shape of La Profesa's cloister vaults.

Saint James the Greater (better known in the Spanish-speaking world as Santiago) is another saint regularly represented in viceregal art. Santiago was one of Christ's disciples who followed his teacher's charge at the Pentecost and worked to spread the Gospel. This evangelical effort and the fact that his body is said to be buried in Santiago de Compostela, earned him the title of patron saint of Spain. But the miracles he performed on Spanish and Latin American battlefields secured his place in colonial painting and sculpture.

In 834, Santiago appeared miraculously at the battle of Clavijo, helping the Spanish soldiers defeat the Moors. The appearance also earned the saint his gruesome nickname, Santiago Matamoros (Saint James the Moor killer). He consequently became the patron saint of soldiers, who cried "Santiago and close Spain" and "Santiago and at them" in battle. In light of his guest starring role in Spanish military endeavors, particularly the Reconquest of Spain from the Moors, it comes as no surprise that Santiago appeared on behalf of the conquistadores in the Americas. His most famous intervention came during the 1536 Inca siege at the Sunturhuasi in Cuzco, when the Marian sculpture likewise miraculously responded to the Spaniards' plight. According to the legend, Santiago appeared from the sky, riding a white horse and brandishing a sword that reflected light and looked to the Inca warriors like a bolt of lightning. This miracle and other similar events in which he intervened on the Spanish behalf earned the saint a new nickname: Santiago Mataindios (the Indian killer).

New Spanish and Peruvian images of Santiago are found in all pictorial media and feature both his Spanish and American miracles. The anonymous Andean *Santiago at the Battle of Clavijo* (Plate 20), like all colonial images, presents the apostle riding his white horse and brandishing his sword. He wears a pilgrim's hat, signifying his tomb's popular pilgrimage, and a billowing cape. His rearing horse leads the Spanish army in the 834 battle against the Moors; Spanish King Ramiro I appears just behind the saint. Santiago and the king appear again in the background, with the saint knocking the Moorish caliph from his horse in this continuous narrative.[35] In other colonial paintings and sculptures, Santiago appears alone trampling the bodies of defeated enemies—Moors or even Amerindian warriors—under the hooves of his horse. Since Spaniards regularly called un-Christianized native peoples Moors, the North Africans and Andeans symbolized Spanish triumph over non-Christian peoples.

Santiago's popularity among Amerindian populations, and especially the Andean peoples whose ancestors are trampled in some of the saint's images, may seem difficult to understand. Cuzco school artists routinely represented this conquering saint. How could native peoples celebrate a hero of their defeat, the same figure who Spaniards invoked to represent their military and social superiority in the Americas? Santiago's devotion in the Americas, however, has been described as simultaneously reinforcing Spanish hegemony and offering opportunities for resistance.[36] At the very least the images have multiple meanings depending upon the audience. Scholars believe Andean Amerindians identified Santiago with lightning, one of the natural phenomena worshipped in local religions before the Spaniards' arrival. In the Andean region, missionaries facilitated conversion by drawing parallels between Santiago and Illapa, the god of thunder and lightning, even calling the apostle Son of Thunder.[37] Native Andeans persisted in celebrating the cult of Illapa through the Christian feast of Santiago well into the eighteenth century. Hence the miraculous appearance in the paintings confirmed the continuity of traditional beliefs under the new Spanish order. It likewise confirmed the city of Cuzco as a still-potent site of supernatural attention for indigenous audiences.[38]

While Santiago and other saints assumed new roles in Latin America, new saints were born locally and became important additions to the colonial artists' pictorial repertoire. Criolla *limeña* Isabel de Flores y del Olívar (1586–1617), better known as Saint Rose of Lima, was the first canonized American, selected in 1671 for her extreme piety and mystical relationship with God. When Isabel/ Rose was a young girl, there was no Dominican female convent in Lima. The pious child consequently lived a self-imposed cloistered existence within her own home. There, like many nuns, she fasted and practiced brutal acts of penance to cleanse her body of impurity, to embody her chastity, and to demonstrate her love of God. To reward his faithful servant, God granted Rose visions of the Christ Child.

New Spanish artist Cristóbal de Villalpando's circa 1690 *Mystic Marriage of Saint Rose of Lima* (Plate 21) represents one of the miraculous visions. According to her legend, Rose prayed at the nearby Dominican church one day when Christ appeared, offered her a rose, and said, "Rose of my heart, I take you as my wife." Villalpando (1645–1714) painted the young, beautiful Rose kneeling in her habit before the Christ Child who rests on his mother's lap. He extends the flower and Rose reaches to accept it. The Virgin Mary offers a string of rosary beads, symbolizing the Dominican Rosary Chapel where the miracle occurred; the garden setting seen in the painting refers to Christ's gift to Rose and operates as an allegory of her spiritual fecundity. Dominic of Guzman, the founder of the Dominican order, witnesses the scene from the shadows. Typical of New Spanish painters in this era, Villalpando surrounded his figure group with animated angels and cherubs, and filled the background with a brilliant glimpse of heaven.

Saint Rose of Lima's canonization just fifty-four years after her death and her subsequent devotion reflected the colonial social and political context. Her rapid rise to sainthood has been attributed to Spanish desire to confirm the faithful legitimacy of the New World program, the power of the Dominican Order, and the Latin American wish to show divine sanction of their faith.[39] Colonists throughout the Americas offered her devotion, but criollos in New Spain were particularly attracted to her cult and promoted her as an example of criollo faith. Villalpando's painting privileges this function as American icon. The inscription in the lower cartouche reads in part "Saint Rose *Indiana*" (from the Indies), emphatically stating her criollo identity. Rose's American-ness was made more emphatic in selected later paintings that added an indigenous figure among the witnesses.

New Spain also produced its own saint. While Felipe de las Casas (1572–97), better known as Philip of Jesus, was not canonized until 1862, his 1627 beatification was sufficient justification for painted, printed, and sculpted likenesses. Philip was a young criollo merchant who traveled on the Manila galleon from his home in Mexico City to the Spanish settlements on the Philippine Islands. Seeking his fortune, Philip found religion instead and joined the Franciscan order. On his return trip three years later, his ship was damaged in a storm and took harbor in Japan. After a few weeks on Japanese shores, Philips and twenty-five others were martyred.

The anonymous seventeenth-century New Spanish sculpture of *Philip of Jesus* (Figure 72) represents his martyrdom. Crucified, burned, and stuck through with lances, Philip lifts his head in agony; his pallid face makes his dark, unfocused eyes and the blood oozing from his mouth and ears stand in relief. Two of the three lances travel through his torso and emerge from his shoulders; the third is suggested by the wound in his chest. Although the cross is absent, Philip's pose and the bloody ligature marks on his wrists imply its presence.

FIGURE 72. *Saint Philip of Jesus.* Seventeenth century. Wood, pigment, and gold. Mexico City Cathedral, Mexico City, Mexico. Photograph © Archivo Fotográfico Manuel Toussaint, IIE/UNAM.

A tour-de-force example of expressionism and encarnación painting, the life-size and lifelike sculpture still evokes the pathos of those who view it in the Mexico City Cathedral.

Philip's brocaded robe relieves the sculpture's graphic physical and emotional suffering. As a member of a Franciscan discalced order, Philip probably wore a rough habit to his execution. The New Spanish patron who commissioned the work, like many of the artists who painted Philip's image, found rough clothes inappropriate for this national hero. Hence he chose the *estofado* painting technique for the gilded robe, although he left the Franciscan cord appropriately unadorned. Like the encarnación flesh tones, the estofado was executed by a painter. The unnamed painter or gilder (*dorador*) covered the sculpture's clothed areas in gold leaf and a layer of brown paint. He then scratched through the paint to create a golden pattern simulating brocade fabrics. This technique, brought from Spain, made sculpted figures both lifelike and ornate. Resting on a gilded altarscreen, *Philip of Jesus* consequently made for a shimmering vision of personal sacrifice for faith.

New Spanish criollos had little trouble deploying Philip's image to reflect their own piety. In 1629, the Cabildo of Mexico City declared him "Glorious Proto-martyr of the Indies" and the cathedral opened a chapel in his honor seven years later. Paintings, sculptures, and prints—including José María Montes de Oca's 1805 book of etchings of the saint's life—operated as symbols of New Spanish pride. Philip was also promoted as a symbol of God's approval of Franciscan efforts in New Spain.

Other Religious Themes in Viceregal Pictorial Arts

Angels are ubiquitous in Latin American colonial art. These androgynous figures identified God's approval of the depicted religious events and added baroque splendor to altarscreens, retablo-façades, sculptures, paintings, and prints. Viceregal artists created a virtual army of angelic types from chubby cherubs cascading from the heavens to tall winged figures introduced by sixteenth-century European mannerists and retained in paintings made two centuries later. New Spanish artists even painted and sculpted angels with varying skin tones and facial features, imagining a heavenly hierarchy with a diversity recalling viceregal society itself.[40] The most famous angels in Latin American colonial art, however, came from the Viceroyalty of Peru in today's Bolivia.

The Master of Calamarca's (José López de los Ríos?) *Angel with Arquebus, Asiel Timor Dei* (Plate 22), circa 1660–80, is one of Bolivia's famous *ángeles arcabuceros* or harquebus-carrying angels. This painting genre may even have originated in the Collao region near Lake Titicaca where the work was made. Although found alone today, it was likely part of a series that also included an angelic drummer, bugler, standard bearer, and angels holding lances and swords. The painting features the beautiful, androgynous angel wearing military garb and the gold embroidered fabric and lace favored by the local indigenous elite. The feathers emerging from behind his broad-brimmed hat similarly communicate the angel's American identity, albeit in a more generic fashion. Aiming his gun, the figure seems to embody the accompanying Latin inscription "Asiel Timor Dei," meaning "Asiel Fear of God." But while his weapon is fearsome, his figure is anything but; its elongated proportions and graceful, dance-like pose reflect the persisting taste for mannerist elegance in the late seventeenth century, a feature of painting from both viceroyalties. The painting's so-called Andean mestizo baroque style seems particularly appropriate for its otherworldly theme.

Scholars believe that this painting and similar series were based on Flemish engravings and Spanish paintings. These European works drew upon a variety of sacred writings and introduced new named archangels to the three identified in the Bible (Raphael, Gabriel, and Michael).[41] Church authorities condemned the apocryphal archangels, but Latin American artists did not desist. Andean artists furthermore armed these angels in what appears to be a regional contribution to the iconography.

Andean *ángeles arcabuceros* may reflect the persistence of a familiar missionary strategy. During the evangelical era, as discussed in Chapter 2, missionaries redirected indigenous veneration of huacas and other sacred beings and forces into acceptable Christian substitutes. In place of celestial phenomena, such as stars, rain, hail, and comets, friars offered the Christian cult of angels derived from the apocryphal Book of Enoch.[42] In fact, Peruvian author Fernando de Valverde claimed the angels acted as the emissaries of the Virgin Mary and expelled the celestial deities from Lake Titicaca in his 1641 poem, *El Santuario de Nuestra Señora de Copacabana del Perú*.[43] The ángeles arcabuceros may consequently have referred to the militant church assuming spiritual control of the region. It undoubtedly also reflected the Catholic Counter Reformation militaristic rhetoric, which promoted the church as an army and heavenly beings as its soldiers. Seen in this light, Asiel's gun protected Christians;[44] his clothing made this protection available to a specifically American and indigenous audience.

Indigenous iconography also appeared in paintings celebrating Cuzco's feast of Corpus Christi, or specifically its processions (Plate 23). Latin American painters represented religious and secular processions of every stripe, from small parties carrying miraculous images to end disastrous natural events, to lavish entrances of viceroys and other citywide religious and social festivals. One famous example discussed in Chapter 3 (Plate 10) illustrates a procession conducted in 1650 to end the earthquakes destroying Cuzco; the resulting miracle earned the Christ of the Earthquakes its name. Another well-known painting chronicles the miracles that occurred as the Virgin of Guadalupe was carried to her shrine at Tepeyac. And while processions were similarly popular in Europe, the colonial representations, like the events they chronicled, frequently addressed local concerns.

As discussed in Chapter 3, processions brought the colonial context into high relief. The authorities representing the twin powers of church and state walked or rode through the city streets to embody the social and political order. They were followed by representatives from the social institutions and organizations, from Spanish knights and professional guilds to Amerindian nobles and native confraternities. Viewers likewise participated—consciously or unconsciously—simply by attending this public display of the social order. And while the processions reaffirmed imperial hegemony, they also offered local populations the opportunity to voice their own interests. The most famous examples are the triumphal arches designed by poetess Sor Juana Inés de la Cruz and criollo intellectual Carlos de Sigüenza y Góngora for the Marqués de la Laguna's 1680 entrance into Mexico City. Both employed complex allegories to celebrate the entering viceroy and the intellect and civility of the New Spanish people: hers with characters from Greco-Roman mythology and his with the figures of Aztec legend. While most processions were not recorded visually for posterity, the Cuzco school's Corpus Christi paintings offer pictorial representatives of this type of social ritual.

The Catholic feast of Corpus Christi celebrates the Eucharist. The event gained additional significance during the Catholic Counter Reformation as church officials celebrated the Eucharist's triumph over the Protestant heresy that denounced the truth of Transubstantiation, the miraculous transformation of the wafer into Christ's body during the mass. Processions held for the feast featured the Host prominently displayed in a monstrance. During the early modern period, these processions wound their way through highly decorated streets and passed beneath the triumphal arches derived from imperial Roman processions to embody the victory. In Spain the Host passed by personifications of Moorish heresies, while in the Americas indigenous participants represented Spanish Christian triumph and the Amerindian celebration of their conversion to the new faith.

Finale of the Corpus Christi Procession (Plate 23) belongs to a series of six-teen images painted for the Amerindian Church of Santa Ana in Cuzco. This last painting in the sequence visualizes the end of a procession. It was painted circa 1674–80 by an anonymous indigenous artist, perhaps a follower of Cuzco painter Basilio de Santa Cruz Pumacallao (ac. 1661–1700), working in the so-called mestizo baroque style.[45] All of the city's venerated sculptures have finished their march through the streets and wait at the cathedral door for the arrival of the consecrated Host. Each is accompanied by members of its indigenous parish, identified by its standard. The company of viceregal and ecclesiastic authori-ties arrives with the Host held by the bishop under the baldachin. The bishop's military guard, composed of Cañaris and Chachapoya peoples, stands to the left side, firing their guns into the air.[46]

While *Finale of the Corpus Christi Procession* likely made a potent statement of Spanish imperial authority for Spanish and criollo viewers, new scholarship suggests that the painting requires a more nuanced reading that takes viewership into account. One recent analysis claims that for Andean viewers, the paintings and the processions they visualized recalled Pre-Columbian Inca ancestor wor-ship ceremonies in which processions of mummies passed through the sacred streets of Cuzco.[47] Considering the regularity with which colonial ecclesiastics substituted Christian devotions for indigenous ones, it stands to reason that the sculpted saints in the painting might bring to mind Inca mummies. Another aspect of the painting that demands consideration is its representation of Cuzco's multiethnic indigenous population. Representing the diverse indigenous peoples in traditional costuming reaffirmed discrete communal identities, but, as art his-torian Carolyn Dean notes, "not as nostalgic references to an irretrievable past, but as a means of constructing new selves" within the colonial context.[48] In the face of viceregal authorities who homogenized native peoples as an indistin-guishable mass of *indios*, Cuzco's distinct Amerindian communities used the painting to state their presence in a social ritual Spaniards easily understood.

All of which brings us back to Baltazar de Echave Rioja's 1675 allegori-cal procession, *The Triumph of the Church and of the Eucharist* (Figure 64). The range of allegories in Latin American painting and sculpture is vast and touches on nearly every aspect of Christian belief, from Christ's blood to mendicant successes to death and salvation. In this case, the allegory shares its triumphant theme—the exaltation of the Eucharist—and the processional composition with the Cuzco Corpus Christi painting. Nearly identical paintings by New Spanish painter Cristóbal de Villalpando and an anonymous South American for the Monasterio de Santa Teresa in Arequipa do likewise.

Echave's painting, however, celebrates the Eucharist from a different per-spective and for a different audience than the anonymous Corpus Christi painter. The result was not merely a different style, as Echave captured the formal quali-ties of Rubens's exuberant baroque painting and print, but a different meaning. Is it less colonial? Not at all. Echave's painting testifies to the spread of European forms to Latin America. It occupies a space within a cathedral that rested on

Puebla's town square as a symbol of evangelical successes, just as the nearby government buildings represented the triumph of the Spanish political system. The painting shows the triumphant spirit shared by the clerics who saw their work in the Americas as a grand success. And Echave's audience is every bit as representative of the colonial context as the native viewers in the Church of Santa Ana in Cuzco. Puebla's criollo elite represented the creation of a new system of nobility and authority that would eventually fight to remove Spanish authority alongside indigenous and mestizo colonists. And their faith was just as profound and complicated as that practiced by their indigenous neighbors. Though there was probably little that could be called syncretic in the way Echave's audience celebrated its faith, they did recognize the uniqueness of American religion, promoting the Virgin of Guadalupe (a much later reproduction of which is coincidentally also seen in this photograph) and other forms of popular religion and, as evidenced by the discussion of the orthodoxy of the identical Trinity, practicing Christianity through the filter of their own specifically American interests, ideas, and experiences.

CHAPTER SIX

Architecture and Altarscreens circa 1700–1800

The eighteenth century began with a change of Spain's ruling dynasty. In 1700, the last Hapsburg king, the sickly Charles II (r. 1665–1700), died and the French Bourbon Philip of Anjou, grandson of French King Louis XIV, ascended to the Spanish throne as King Philip V (r. 1700–46). The new king and his successors Ferdinand VI (r. 1746–59) and Charles III (r. 1759–88) introduced French tastes and customs to the Spanish empire. More importantly, the kings also instituted political, economic, and social changes collectively known as the Bourbon reforms. A central goal of these so-called enlightened despots consisted of improving colonial administration so as to better exploit the economic resources of the viceroyalties. To this end, the Bourbon kings established royal monopolies and factories producing goods from cigarettes to coins. They also promoted education and reason for the sake of improved industry, founding academies that eventually supplanted the guilds. The Bourbons furthermore centralized power in themselves and their courts, stripping authority from local councils and civic authorities and placing it in the hands of peninsular bureaucrats. Finally, Bourbon reforms also changed political boundaries. In 1739, the portion of the Viceroyalty of Peru that is today Colombia, Ecuador, and Venezuela became the Viceroyalty of New Granada, with Santa Fe de Bogotá as its capital. Its creation, like that of the Viceroyalty of Rio de la Plata carved in 1776 from the southern regions of Peru, was intended to improve administration in this vast territory.

This chapter addresses a broad array of monuments and altarscreens constructed in eighteenth-century viceregal America. It begins with New Spain's so-called churrigueresque architecture, including the famous Sagrario Metropolitano in Mexico City. The next section considers the architecture of the Society of Jesus, the monastic order that enjoyed immense power and influence in the viceroyalties until the Spanish king took spectacular action against it in

1767. Following this, the chapter looks at three churches constructed in regional mining centers and addresses how local architects expressed their communities' unique tastes. The next sections examine late colonial missions in South America and the US Southwest, and two pilgrimage shrines associated with popular religious cults. The chapter ends with grand palaces constructed for wealthy colonists in Lima and Mexico City.

Eighteenth-century viceregal architecture continued to appropriate forms introduced from Europe and to adapt them for local use. The rocailles, shells, and lambrequins found in the colonial architecture of this era, for example, reflect the French rococo tastes of the new Bourbon monarchs. A classicizing restraint in some examples of later eighteenth-century viceregal architecture, the *neóstilo* of New Spain and the *barroco germánico* or *bárbaro* of South America, likewise shared qualities with contemporary European tastes. But while local architects adopted new forms that appealed to them and their patrons, they did not always appreciate the foreign architects who introduced them, as local architectural schools developed a firm sense of identity discrete from the schools on the peninsula. Architecture was the visible manifestation of local pride, and chroniclers celebrated a city's appearance as proof of the wealth, sophistication, and virtues of its residents. Some architects consequently jealously guarded the practice of their profession, especially in New Spain.

Architects and builders still belonged to guilds for most of the eighteenth century, but they pursued greater social recognition than they had previously enjoyed. Additions to the New Spanish architects' guild ordinances in 1746, for example, illustrate some of the shifts in the discipline's self-image. The first was the change of the guild's name, from masons and architects to solely architects. Guild masters were furthermore now required to demonstrate their good character, and architects working in outlying areas had to complete examinations in the capital. The guild additionally barred persons of mixed race, since they were not considered qualified to interact with their elite clientele. The proposed ordinances permitted Amerindian membership so long as they belonged to noble families and displayed good manners.[1] The addition of racial criteria to the guild's ordinances was subsequently amended by the viceregal government to permit all natives, mestizos, and castizos (persons of mestizo and Spanish parents), but permitted the exclusion of "mulattoes, lobos, and others of equal nature and quality."[2] These additions to the ordinances reveal a desire to maintain a high level of professional decorum, as architects sought to affirm their social standing among the secular and ecclesiastical bureaucrats who ran the cities. They also reflect persisting racism and its institutionalization through the ethnic hierarchy known as the caste system.

A New Style for Mexico City

The arrival of Spanish émigré sculptor Jerónimo de Balbás (ca. 1650–1748) single-handedly altered the appearance of Mexico City's churches and altarscreens for the next half century. Trained in the circle of Spanish ensamblador José Benito Churriguera (1666–1725), or at least familiar with his fantastic churrigueresque constructions on the peninsula, Balbás arrived in Mexico City in 1718 to create a new altarscreen for the Mexico City Cathedral. But while the altarscreen project had languished for decades due to a lack of funds, the commission nevertheless angered local criollos, who objected to its foreign artist.

Begun in 1718, the *Altarscreen of the Kings* in the Mexico City Cathedral (Figure 73) introduced a new column to the New Spanish architectural vocabulary. Balbás's altarscreen is dominated by four *estípite* columns, which feature inverted obelisks topped by stacked geometric forms and Composite capitals. Previously reserved for furniture and small architectural ornaments, estípites were monumentalized by Churriguera, whose altarscreens Balbás undoubtedly knew from his time in Spain. He likely also saw the peninsular church façades by Pedro Rivera, who brought the estípite outdoors.[3] Whatever his source of inspiration, Balbás and his colonial viewers admired the ornate columns and their fanciful geometry. They also admired the utter destruction of the reticular grid, as Balbás converted the altarscreen into a single, monumental story that overwhelms and obscures the apse's architecture.

FIGURE 73.
Jerónimo de Balbás.
Altarscreen of the Kings.
1718–37. Mexico City
Cathedral. Mexico City,
Mexico. Photograph
© José Vicente Resino,
photographersdirect.com.

Where once colonial ensambladores constructed fictive architectural structures, Balbás transformed the apse into a dizzying gilded grotto. Balbás drew the four estípite columns away from the altarscreen's concave framework, removing the pretense of architectural purpose, to create an energetic plasticity that envelops the space. Between the columns, the architect introduced a broad pilaster with a niche for sculpture called an *interestípite* in Spanish and a niche-pilaster in English. The sculpted images that fill the niches present the royal saints of the Christian tradition. Female queens and princesses occupy the predella and kings, the middle region. The royal theme ends in the upper tier, which shelters a celestial court consisting of the Holy Family and Saint Teresa of Avila, and God the Father in the pinnacle. The painting in the central zone, Juan Rodríguez Juárez's *Adoration of the Magi*, also contributes to the royalist iconography; his *Assumption of the Virgin* in the upper portion references the cathedral's dedication to Mary as Queen of Heaven. Balbás's reduction of paintings in favor of sculpture was typical of late colonial altarscreens. Other ornamental elements that likewise heralded the new tastes of eighteenth-century architecture and altarscreens include oval niches, rocailles, vegetal scrolls, and simulated hanging textiles known as lambrequins. These forms penetrate the estípite framework and complement the sculpture and painting so that the altarscreen appears as a single, cohesive unit despite its multiple parts.

Balbás's altarscreen took seven years to build and another twelve to gild and paint, but even before it was finished in 1737, its effect was felt in Mexico City's artistic community. Estípite columns appeared in chapel altarscreens in the Mexico City Cathedral by 1729.[4] As much as Balbas's altarscreen heralded a new formal approach, it also spoke of the exuberance of the eighteenth century and the colonists' desire to make visible their bounty. The *Gaceta de México*, New Spain's main gazette, described the "sumptuous altarscreen" with the era's typical hyperbole, lauding the magnificent and famous altarscreen, which "without question, is the most brilliant and costly in America . . . eliciting careful observation and silent admiration."[5] It has been suggested that Balbás's estípite columns received such a warm reception because colonists understood them to reflect Spanish tastes, rather then French. As one scholar explained, "It may not be farfetched to interpret the estípite's unrivaled success in Mexico as an assertion of criollo nationalism. Mexico could now see itself as assuming the mantle of Spanish legitimacy and could justifiably assert that it was more Spanish than Spain itself."[6] Whatever the cause, the effect was that New Spanish architecture was to be filled with the new columns.

More than a decade passed, however, before an architect in New Spain employed monumental estípite columns on a retablo-façade. In 1749, émigré architect Lorenzo Rodríguez (1704–74) began work on the Sagrario Metropolitano, a shrine and parish church attached to the Mexico City Cathedral. The building's Greek cross plan may have been inspired by Sebastiano Serlio's treatise on architecture or, locally, by Arrieta's Basilica of Guadalupe (discussed in Chapter 4). While today the interior of the centrally planned and domed structure no longer

FIGURE 74.
Lorenzo Rodríguez.
Sagrario Metropolitano.
1749–68. Mexico City,
Mexico. Photograph
© Kelly Donahue-Wallace.

retains its original appearance, the exterior remains as Rodríguez designed it.[7] Twin retablo-façades (Figure 74) frame the south and east portals with the first exterior estípite columns in New Spain.

Rodríguez, who worked in Cádiz before crossing the Atlantic, arrived in Mexico by 1731. For the next nine years, he worked as a carpenter and even contributed his labor to Balbás's colossal *Altarscreen of the Kings*. A 1736 architects' guild restriction required foreign masters to submit to local examinations, forcing Rodríguez to delay receiving the title of master architect with the ability to contract jobs until 1740. While Rodríguez, like Balbás, was favored by the ecclesiastical hierarchy, he met great resistance from the criollo architectural establishment in Mexico City. In 1742, local architect Miguel Custodio Durán, whose father José Durán created the original plan of the Basilica of Guadalupe, attacked Rodríguez as a foreigner unfamiliar with New Spanish ways. Local builders, including Custodio Durán and his nephew Ildefonso de Iniesta Bejarano y Durán (see below), nevertheless soon recognized Rodríguez's contribution and skill, and the Spaniard became a respected member of the architecture profession. His designs for the Sagrario came to symbolize New Spanish tastes in the mid- to late-eighteenth century.

The Sagrario's retablo-façades feature two stories of estípite columns and niche pilasters within a rectangular border. The gray chiluca façade, according to local tastes, rests screen-like before the red tezontle building. Not as spatially aggressive as Balbás's altarscreen, Rodríguez's façades are more like heavily populated and wildly ornate tapestries hanging on the Sagrario walls. The columns and niche pilasters are joined by the other leitmotifs of eighteenth-century colonial decoration: lambrequins, rocailles, scrolls, and mixtilinear moldings. One of the latter, lining the mixtilinear pediment atop each façade, is echoed by the chiluca-lined tezontle walls that descend from the pinnacles and give the structure a pyramidal profile. Modern scholars have attributed this pyramidal appearance to a criollo evocation—conscious or not—of Aztec antiquity, which was quite literally right under their feet.[8] Rodríguez may also have been inspired by Arrieta's mixtilinear parapet on the Basilica of Guadalupe. (See Sidebar 15.)

⌒ SIDEBAR 15

Excerpt from an anonymous architectural treatise, circa 1795.

Carved Work and Stone: Frontispieces [Retablo-Façades]

The frontispieces now popular are referred to as *obras de talla* [sculptured or carved work] and, truly, they have come to be nothing more than side altars on the street. The order in which the architect should proceed is the following. The design of the frontispiece should be made by an able painter, but this must be done under the directions given by the maestro to assure, for example, that the proportions correspond to the first and second registers, etc. Better yet, hire a master joiner to draw the plan, or as others say, the front elevation. Joiners are those artisans who make retables. It is said that they are familiar with designing front elevations and using moldings suitable to incorporating *boladas* [spherical elements] and *proyecturas* [other projecting elements]. The architect, before beginning the work, needs to examine and correct [the plan], because if he knows how to design, he envisages the plan which the joiner brings him. He will see if it is agreeable to the eye and if there are any defects to correct—for example, if it is not proportional to the cornice or if the pedestals are not commensurable to the order they are designed for—because it is important that they properly support the Doric shafts, and other things of this tenor. Having corrected the design and having assured himself on all the details, he will call in stone sculptors and, with the overseer of the stonecutters, will confer on whatever is needed to begin the work. Thus they may work following the perspective and iconographic design without exceeding the limits set by the maestro.

—From *Architectural Practice in Mexico City: A Manual for Journeyman Architects of the Eighteenth Century*, translated and with an introduction and annotation by Mardith K. Schuetz. 43–44 (Tucson: University of Arizona Press, 1987).

Despite his initial professional difficulties, Rodríguez's efforts at the Sagrario Metropolitano had a profound impact on local architecture. The retablo-façades displayed the sumptuousness, beauty, proportion, richness, and majesty colonists desired. Critics celebrated the estípite columns as a modern adaptation of the Composite order and one that was particularly appealing to the New Spanish aesthetic of opulence.[9] This new style, frequently called ultra-baroque or estípite baroque in current scholarship, soon found free expression throughout New Spain, especially on the hugely ornate churches of the mining cities of Guanajuato and San Luis Potosí. It is most closely identified, however, with the churches and altarscreens constructed in Mexico City and its environs.

The Society of Jesus

The eighteenth century was the heyday of the Society of Jesus in Latin America. The Jesuit order, as it is also known, was founded in 1540 by Spaniard Ignatius of Loyola. Led by their general in Rome, the order's priests and brothers pursued public lives preaching, educating, and spreading the Gospel. In fact, the Jesuits added a fourth missionary vow to the monastic promises of poverty, humility, and obedience. Hence the order came to the Americas to spread the faith, arriving first in South America in 1567 and later in New Spain in 1572. In addition to establishing missions in territories unclaimed by the mendicants (see below), the Jesuits founded conventos for their membership, primary and secondary schools or *colegios* for Amerindians and Spaniards, and seminaries to train new members. The order's dedication to learning, supported by its well-educated and disciplined clergy, won it the loyalty of the colonial elite who sent their sons to its colegios and seminaries.

The Jesuit seminary in Tepotzotlán outside Mexico City opened in 1585, and enjoyed the patronage of the capital's wealthiest citizens. The powerful Medina Picazo family showered immense wealth on the community in the 1670s and 1680s. The family chose the structure's criollo architect, José Durán, who finished the original structure in 1682;[10] twelve years later Durán accepted another Medina-sponsored project: the Basilica of Guadalupe. It consequently comes as little surprise that when the decision was made to renovate the church façade and interior, the order selected Ildefonso de Iniesta Bejarano y Durán (d. 1781), grandson of José Durán.

The church of San Francisco Xavier at the Jesuit seminary at Tepotzotlán remains one of the most spectacular expressions of the estípite baroque style. Constructed in the seventeenth century, the church underwent renovation of its tower, retablo-façade, and interior between 1760 and 1762. Iniesta apparently designed the retablo-façade in consultation with ensamblador Higinio de Chávez (ac. mid-eighteenth century), author of the interior altarscreens. Both artists applied the lessons of Balbás and Rodríguez with the freedom characteristic of Latin American colonial art, employing new forms according to their unique designs. The results are visually and iconographically harmonious.

The retablo-façade at Tepotzotlán (Figure 75) is more delicate and graceful than the Sagrario Metropolitano; its single, thin tower contributes to the appearance of visual fragility. Iniesta, who was also the nephew of New Spanish architect Miguel Custodio Durán, organized the façade in three levels. His sculpted forms hang like a lacy screen over the rusticated church exterior. Four estípite columns and two niche pilasters occupy the first and second stories; six smaller columns appear in the crowning mixtilinear pediment. Although the retablo-façade, as at the Sagrario, generally respects the division of stories, a central niche bearing a sculpture of the titular saint rises into the upper level, echoing the vertical thrust of the attic story and tower. Four large sculptures of Jesuit saints occupy the flanking niche pilasters—Saints Ignatius of Loyola and Francis Borgia below and Louis of Gonzaga and Stanislaus of Kostka above. Early Christian martyrs and saints also populate the lower tier, while saints of New Spain's evangelical orders inhabit the second story, all in oval and mixtilinear frames. A relief carving of the Virgin and Child crowns the group. The retablo-façade's profuse ornament reprises the decorative vocabulary of Rodríguez's Sagrario, with lambrequins, mixtilinear moldings around the choir and tower windows, rocailles, scrolls, and a profusion of small sculpted figures on virtually every surface. The

FIGURE 75.
Ildefonso de Iniesta Bejarano y Durán. Church of San Francisco Xavier. 1760–62. Tepotzotlán, Mexico. Photograph © Kelly Donahue-Wallace.

iconographic program has been described as a celebration of martyrs, Christ as Savior, and the Virgin Mary.[11]

The exterior of San Francisco Xavier corresponds to the interior altarscreens, both in form and content. In 1753, painter Miguel Cabrera (1695–1768) and ensamblador Chávez designed and constructed the altarscreens (Plate 24) still found inside the church. Cabrera, who had a long-standing relationship with the Jesuits, undoubtedly designed the altarscreens' iconographic program promoting the order; he also painted the vaults and dome. The main altarscreen is dedicated to titular saint Francis Xavier. A sculpture of this Jesuit martyr occupies the central niche accompanied by Saint John the Baptist, Joseph and the Christ Child, Joachim, Anne, and the Virgin of the Immaculate Conception. The altarscreen climbs up into vaults on estípite columns, niche pilasters, and an explosion of ornamental motifs; God the Father looms above the ensemble. The structure makes no pretense of architectural organization and lacks distinct stories and vertical divisions. The transept altarscreens, dedicated respectively to the Virgin of Guadalupe and Saint Ignatius of Loyola with founders of New Spain's evangelical orders, incorporate windows into their design and recall Gian Lorenzo Bernini's theatrical lighting strategies at Saint Peter's and the Cornaro Chapel in Rome. Chávez's windows similarly offer dramatic and mysterious illumination for his gilded constructions. And while colonial architecture may not have offered many spatially dynamic floor plans—with a handful of notable exceptions including the churches of Santa Brígida and Santa María la Redonda in Mexico City—estípite baroque altarscreens rendered projecting and receding walls virtually unnecessary. Reaching up into the vaults and around the viewer, the gilded members of the late colonial altarscreens dramatically transformed the observer's perception of the space he inhabited. Any manipulation of the wall would have been lost behind these retablos.

That said, the shrine of the Virgin of Loreto attached to the church of San Francisco Xavier (Figure 76) has a polygonal *camarín*, or dressing room for the sculpture of the Virgin. The octagonal chamber is visible behind an altarscreen bearing a sculpture of the Virgin of Loreto. The altarscreen is located in a 1733 reconstruction of the Holy House of Loreto, Mary's Nazareth home, which purportedly traveled on angels' wings from Palestine to Italy in the late thirteenth century. The shrine at Tepotzotlán serves as a chapel dedicated to the Virgin of Loreto. The camarín behind the Holy House was also constructed in 1733 when it was covered in polychromed and gilded stucco decoration by Miguel Cabrera.[12] Although few laymen originally had access to the chamber, those who entered experienced a vision of heaven on earth, as the walls, the polygonal telescoping lantern made of translucent alabaster, and the vaulted ceiling are covered by angels, stars, suns, and moons of gilded and polychromed carved and molded stucco. Caryatid figures, a popular motif in South America as well, appear to support the four intersecting ribs of the vault. The devotion was central to the Jesuits and most of the order's churches had a chapel to the Virgin of Loreto, although the appearance of the camarín in Tepotzotlán is unique.

FIGURE 76.
Camarín of the Virgin
of Loreto at the Church
of San Francisco Xavier.
1733. Tepotzotlán,
Mexico. Photograph
© Tomás Muñoz,
photographersdirect.com.

The Church of La Compañía (or The Company, as the Jesuits were popularly known) in Quito similarly embodies the spirit of the order. Begun in 1606, the church is attributed to Father Martín de Aizpitarte.[13] The structure was finished by Father Marcos Guerra thirty years later, although the façade lacked its sculpted portal. The fact that the building's architects were members of the Jesuit order was typical. The Society of Jesus regularly employed its priests and lay brothers as architects and artists, and recruited members skilled in art, design, and construction techniques.

La Compañía, like many larger Jesuit churches, recalls the order's main church, Il Gesú in Rome, and its design was approved by Roman authorities. The cruciform plan includes a three-aisle nave, transept, and crossing dome (Figure 77). A barrel vault tops the nave and saucer domes cap the aisles. The most remarkable feature of the church interior is its profuse ornamentation. Every surface not hidden by a gilded Solomonic altarscreen is covered in gilded and polychrome stucco relief, wood panels, and brickwork executed in the early eighteenth century. The dome, for example, features paintings of Jesuit saints and archangels surrounded by gilded decorations; its pendentives bear reliefs of

FIGURE 77.
Interior of the
Church of La
Compañía with
altarscreen by
Georg Winterer.
Church begun 1606.
Altarscreen finished in
1745. Quito, Ecuador.
Photograph © Hernán
L. Navarrete.

the four Evangelists within similar decorative patterns. The vaults are covered in interlacing low relief strapwork reminiscent of Moorish and Mudéjar ornament. German Jesuit Georg Winterer created the Solomonic main altarscreen, which was gilded in 1745 by renowned quiteño sculptor Bernardo de Legarda (d. 1773).[14] Interestingly, South American architects and ensambladores did not incorporate estípite columns into their architectural repertoires, preferring instead the sinuous qualities of the Solomonic column to accompany their broken pediments and mixtilinear cornices. Although constructed nearly a century after the interior stucco ornamentation was begun, the altarscreen nevertheless matched the spectacle and sumptuousness of the church interior. Multiple side altarscreens repeat the Solomonic ornamental vocabulary. The profuse ornament and the consequent disintegration of the appearance of architectural solidity have been called *cueviforme* or cave-like, and scholars compare it to the dense decoration of Moorish architecture.[15] It also recalls the decorative schemes of New Spain's two Rosary Chapels in Puebla and Oaxaca. Contemporary observer Juan de Velasco described it as the loveliest of all of Quito's churches in his 1789 history of the region.[16] Defending the interior ornamentation from those who criticized its excesses, the chronicler described it as a worthy expression of the veneration of God. (See Sidebar 16.)

La Compañía's retablo-façade (Figure 78) is no less spectacular. Begun by German Jesuits Leonardo Deubler (d. 1769) and Simon Schönherr in 1722, the façade's design was inspired by Jesuit Andrea del Pozzo's architectural treatise *Prospectiva de pittori e architetti* (1700). Italian Brother Venancio Gandolfini finished the façade between 1760 and 1765 after lengthy construction delays. The assembled architectural and sculptural elements explore exaggerated plasticity and dramatic chiaroscuro. The forms project toward the middle, first with stacked Corinthian pilasters, then with thick Solomonic columns; the portal in the center is a gaping void. The upper level, which is linked to the lower by large volutes, features ornately carved pilasters that support a broken rounded pediment. The recessed space over the door contains a shallow broken pediment with a sculpture of the Immaculate Conception, a rounded cornice pushing into the second story, a mixtilinear window, and a large pinnacle. Virtually every surface of the façade bears sculptural ornaments, from the reliefs located on pedestals and friezes, to the carved shafts of the columns and pilasters. The full-round figures in niches across the façade exalt the Jesuit dedication to missionary activity while the relief carvings on the column shafts present symbols of Christ. These forms were widely admired as Velasco's chronicle illustrates.

The beauty of its churches illustrated Jesuit wealth, and their size and centrality in the colonial cities, the order's power. This power, however, troubled

FIGURE 78. Leonardo Deubler and Simon Schönherr. Church of La Compañía. Church begun 1606. Façade begun 1722. Quito, Ecuador. Photograph © Roderick Eime, photographersdirect.com.

Excerpts from Juan de Velasco's 1789 description of Quito.

5. It has been since the earliest days and is without a doubt the greatest and best city in the Territories of Peru, after Lima, and it ranks among the secondary cities of Europe. Its streets are drawn with a cord and divided into regular blocks, with different public squares, except the outskirts, which lack order due to the mountainous terrain and valleys. All the houses within the city have at least two stories or floors, and a few have three. Many are of brick masonry, especially the public buildings and religious houses; some are stonemasonry, and the rest are rough brick, called adobe and mud. . . . All, without exception are roofed with tiles and with large balconies above the streets, comfortable and well appointed and decently ornamented.

6. The Plaza Mayor in the center is square, with a beautiful fountain in the middle, and it is 240 feet on each side. One side is entirely occupied by the Cathedral, a very large and magnificent structure, although without beauty, in the old style, with a stone parapet and niches below running the length of the square. The other side is entirely occupied, with the same type of parapet, by the new Royal Palace of the *Audiencia* and President, a moderately good structure, in the modern style. . . .

7. The city is divided into seven barrios, and a number of other parishes. . . . The churches and convents of the regular Orders are not

the crown. Jesuit presence in the Americas ended abruptly in 1767, when the order was removed by royal decree from Spain and its territories. King Charles III expelled the Jesuits from his lands for many reasons; primary among these was the order's allegiance to the pope. The king also feared the order's power and influence among the educated elite and the indigenous masses to whom they ministered. Finally, the Spanish crown coveted the Jesuits' wealth and landholdings. In the summer of 1767, colonial governments throughout Latin America simultaneously served expulsion notices to several thousand members of the Society of Jesus. With no warning and little time, the order's brothers were taken to coastal ports and expelled from the Spanish territories. Their monasteries, colegios, missions, and seminaries were divided among other orders, and their lands were sold to wealthy colonists. The vast collections of art confiscated after the expulsion were distributed; the Royal Academy of San Carlos received much of the impounded Jesuit art when it was founded in 1783. (See Chapter 8.) Many colonists objected to the preemptory expulsion and viewed the event as yet

only the largest and best in the Territory, but in all of America, as testified to by national and foreign travelers. Standing out among these, in architecture, beauty, and taste are the façades of the great temple that belonged to the Jesuits, the Franciscan church, and the Parish church of the Sagrario, all of lively stonework. . . .

9. On the topic of the Regular convents, all the main and principal churches are very large and magnificent of beautiful architecture; but especially the Franciscan church, which is only comparable to the rarest and best structures in Europe. Among these temples, which are generally large and of beautiful architecture, with domes and tall towers, the best of all is the church that belonged to the Jesuits. Foreign writers describe its magnificence and the ornaments of all its principal altars and the silver plate as excessive and superfluous richness. One could respond that the Spaniards learned this from the Gentiles, and if these people, without the light of faith, employed in their temples for the cults of their idols almost all of the treasures of the [Inca] empire, whose spoils have enriched the world, it is not excessive that Christians and Catholics employ for the cult of the True God a few relics that have remained from these ancient treasures.

—Juan de Velasco, *Historia del Reino de Quito en la América meridional*, edición, prólogo, notas y cronología Alfredo Pareja Diezcanseco, 309–10 (Caracas: Biblioteca Ayacucho, 1981). (Translation mine.)

another insult from a distant central authority that was insensitive to their needs and ignorant of their virtues.

Silver Churches in Late Colonial New Spain and Peru

The eighteenth century saw the rebirth of mining after slumping production in the seventeenth century. Pre-Hispanic societies in both viceroyalties had mined before the Spaniards arrived, as evidenced by the spectacular examples of Pre-Columbian gold such as the gold-sheathed Coricancha in Cuzco and the huge gold Aztec sun that traveled to Europe and left a lasting impression on German artist Albrecht Dürer. After 1521, large-scale mining began in Latin America, even before land surrounding their operations was completely pacified. Silver was particularly abundant in central New Spain and the Andean highlands of Peru. By the seventeenth century, however, mining declined as high taxes and greedy financiers discouraged miners from expanding their business. The demand for silver nevertheless remained high, above all from the Spanish government that relied on American revenue. Bourbon kings consequently dedicated their efforts to reviving the industry. Their reforms reduced the taxes on the mercury required for the refining process, founded a mining guild and academy, and gave financing responsibilities to new silver banks. Improved mining technologies also contributed to the industry's regeneration. As a result, mining generated immense wealth in the eighteenth century, and most of the viceroyalties' richest colonists were directly or indirectly involved in the industry.

The funds generated at mines in northern New Spain and the Andean highlands meant that regional cities, not just the viceregal capitals, could afford spectacular examples of religious architecture. Mining cities did not, however, immediately put their wealth to work building grand churches; grandiose architectural projects lagged nearly two centuries behind the first infusions of mining wealth. For example, when *zacatecanos* were finally ready to build an impressive new church—the Cathedral of Zacatecas was then still a parish church—local mining was in a period of decline.[17] But if the economic conditions were not optimal, social forces were. Newly titled nobles, whose fortunes derived from mining, contributed large sums to the building, and used the church construction to affirm their positions as city leaders.[18] The same may be said of the residents of other colonial mining centers.

The Church of San Lorenzo (Figure 79) in the Villa Rica e Imperial de Potosí in the Viceroyalty of Peru, owes its existence to the nearby mines of the Cerro Rico. As discussed in Chapter 3, silver was discovered in 1545 at the soon-to-be called Cerro Rico (Rich Hill) when llama herder Diego Gualpa accidentally revealed a silver vein. A silver-mining frenzy helped the region to attract a huge population of both criollo and mestizo residents seeking their fortunes and Amerindians sent as *mitayos* to work in the dangerous mines.

The mines of the Cerro Rico in Potosí produced immense wealth, but the city that served them did not reflect these riches for more than a century. Chroniclers bemoaned the city's appearance, calling Potosí ugly and unrefined, and describing streets filled with profligate residents and unattractive huts. The city's reputation as a lawless frontier town was helped by its migrant population of mita laborers. As many as 40,000 mitayos and their families may have passed through Potosí each year.[19] But the nomadic indigenous workers were not the only problem. At least one local criollo complained in circa 1736 about the greedy and corrupt peninsular "wolves" who abused the Amerindians and ran the city poorly.[20] Some of the city's clergy even profited from its corruption, charging fees to the mita laborers for services from baptisms to burials and even hospital admission.[21] More acceptable contributions to the church, especially from rich miners, nevertheless funded a building boom in the late seventeenth and eighteenth centuries during a period when, in fact, the region suffered economic decline. New parish churches, convents, monasteries, palaces, and civic buildings eventually transformed the frontier settlement into a city worthy of the title of *Villa Rica e Imperial*.

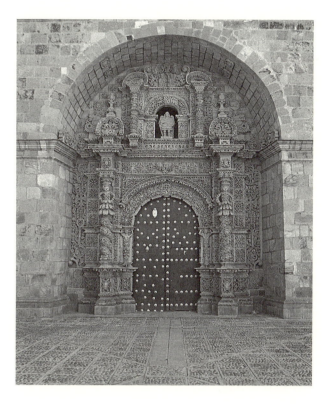

FIGURE 79.
Church of San Lorenzo.
1728–44. Potosí,
Bolivia. Photograph
© James Brunker,
photographersdirect.com.

The Church of San Lorenzo in Potosí was renovated from a provisional state to its current appearance between 1728 and 1744. Although built in 1548 as a parish church for the city's Spanish citizens, in 1572 it became one of the city's fourteen Amerindian parishes, serving the Caranga peoples.[22] The structure, one of only two Amerindian churches located in the city center, reveals the typical Latin American parish church design, with a single nave, cruciform plan, a dome over the crossing, and towers on the façade. The structure's eighteenth-century Mudéjar ceiling is today covered in cloth on the inside and topped on the exterior by the ubiquitous potosino red-tile roofing. Chapels likely filled the transept arms, according to regional traditions.

San Lorenzo's retablo-façade was constructed on top of the original church walls. The work has been attributed to either a Quechua stonemason named Condori or Bernardo de Rojas, a local master architect.[23] The artist's efforts reflect the characteristics of the planiform style discussed in Chapter 4. Potosí was, after all, the southern-most point of this Andean style and the church was constructed at the height of its popularity. The carved portal, which rests under a large arch between the towers, displays the characteristic angular and flat carving technique, tapestry-like and dense ornamentation, and stylized forms. The expression of the planiform style at San Lorenzo nevertheless differs from that found on the retablo-façade at La Compañía in Arequipa constructed half a century earlier and nearly five hundred miles away. San Lorenzo's portal reveals a potosino interest in stark chiaroscural effects, with deeply carved channels and strongly projecting, although similarly cubic, forms. The dramatic lighting effects are exaggerated by the deep arch that casts its shadow over the façade. Potosí's distinct carving style has in fact been likened to woodwork, in which designs are described more by shadow than by light.[24] But as in Arequipa, the potosino planiform style should not be considered a restoration of traditional indigenous styles or a fusion of European and indigenous forms; it was a modern approach that communicated the tastes of the local community.

The retablo-façade's iconography is similarly characteristic of the Andean planiform style. A sculpture of the Archangel Michael appears in a niche above the door. The church's titular saint appears in the small pediment. Every surface is covered in vegetal motifs and small putti. Other sculptural forms include rosettes and double-headed Hapsburg eagles on the breasts of two caryatids, a popular motif in eighteenth-century Latin America. The façade's iconography also consists of two sirens playing musical instruments, a pair of musician angels, and images of the sun, moon, and stars. These relief figures appear as if floating on the wall above the architectural framework. Scholars have interpreted these celestial and musical elements as sophisticated references to Plato's ideas about music and the harmony of the universe, including the eight sirens whose music moves the celestial bodies.[25] The sirens reflect the ecclesiastical strategy of accommodation, as clerics compared these Greco-Roman mythological beings to the fish-women Andeans believed inhabited Lake Titicaca, drawing upon their similarities as temptresses. These malevolent yet appealing characters, symbols of sin in both cultures, are controlled in the façade by the figure of the Archangel Michael, who stands guard over the church door and recalls the militant painted ángeles arcabuceros discussed in Chapter 5.[26]

The church that is now the Cathedral of Zacatecas, located in northern New Spain, (Figure 80) shares some characteristics with Potosí's silver church of San Lorenzo, such as its sculpted caryatids and musicians and its profusely ornamented façade. The two churches also share similar histories. Silver was discovered in this part of northern New Spain in 1546 on a mountain that came to be called La Bufa. The mountain rested in a region that was far from colonized. Workers and settlers traveling to La Bufa and other mines in the area suffered raids by the nomadic Chichimec Indians. Danger notwithstanding, men flocked to the mining camp that became the city of Zacatecas to seek their fortune. By the early seventeenth century, Zacatecas was in fact the third largest city in New Spain, but its reputation, like Potosí's, was as a lawless town filled with a profligate and sinful population of transients.[27] While the mita system did not extend to New Spain, mine work was completed by African slaves and paid indigenous, African, and mixed-race laborers.

During the seventeenth century, however, Zacatecas developed a more stable population anchored by wealthy mine owners. These businessmen used their money to transform the urban setting into a more refined locale. Construction, particularly of churches, boomed as they donated large sums of money both to

FIGURE 80.
Cathedral of Zacatecas.
1718–82. Zacatecas,
Mexico. Photograph
© John Mitchell,
photographersdirect.com.

express their faith through charitable works, and to confirm their own role as city leaders. As noted colonial scholar Clara Bargellini explains, "In the parish church, focus of urban life, the zacatecanos converted into stone their aspirations for a civilized society."[28] The Cathedral of Zacatecas, like other churches in the city, benefited from their aspirations even during periods of economic decline.

The cathedral's construction history recalls the complicated histories of the cathedrals of Mexico City and Lima discussed in Chapter 4. A provisional adobe church occupied the site by 1559.[29] This structure made way in the seventeenth century for a second church, which, in turn, was replaced by the current building constructed between 1718 and 1782. Funds for the new building came not only from the miners and merchants, but also from a tax on corn, alms, and the sale of chapels to local individuals and confraternities. Domingo Francisco de Calera, for example, purchased the chapel of Santa Ana, while the confraternity of Saint John Nepomuk, composed of the city's elite citizens, outfitted its saint's chapel in 1742.[30] The parish church, dedicated to the Virgin Mary, became a cathedral in 1862, more than forty years after the end of the colonial era.

Although many architects assumed the responsibility of maestro mayor at the Zacatecas church, Domingo Ximénez Hernández began construction in earnest in 1729.[31] The three-aisle plan Ximénez built makes it one of the larger of New Spain's parish churches. An unusual feature of the plan is the sacristy located behind, rather than beside, the sanctuary. The dome over the crossing, the groin-vaulted nave, the saucer domes over the aisles, and the twin towers on the façade, on the other hand, were standard for large churches in the eighteenth century.

Scholars attribute the carving of the spectacular retablo-façade at the Cathedral of Zacatecas to mason Marcos de la Cruz. The façade's sophisticated iconographic program is credited to José de Rivera Bernárdez, the Count of Santiago de la Laguna. Rivera, who entered the priesthood after he was widowed, became known as the city's historian.[32] The 1745 façade he designed hangs like a screen in front of the massive stone building. It presents a firm reticular grid organized into three distinct stories with a trapezoidal attic. Six Solomonic columns support the first and second levels, while six smaller and highly ornate columns composed of stacked figural and vegetal elements appear in the top tier. A polygonal doorway surmounted by a mixtilinear choir loft window anchor the central zone. The appearance of geometric clarity and reticular rigidity is undermined, however, by the profuse relief ornamentation that transforms the grid into fragile-looking pink stone lace. It is important to note that while the façade was completed before Lorenzo Rodríguez placed the first estípite columns on the Sagrario's exterior, the Zacatecas sculptors nevertheless incorporated some decorative motifs of the new style into their work. The northern artists adopted the musicians, shells, and rocailles popular in Mexico City, but retained the orderly appearance the capital's architects increasingly rejected. In other words, the artists incorporated those new forms that appealed to local tastes, but rejected those that did not.

Scholarly analysis has revealed that the iconographic program of the Zacatecas retablo-façade can only be appreciated in concert with the church's interior imagery and organization. Thirteen full-round sculptures of Christ and his disciples and a relief image of God the Father appear on the façade; Doctors of the Church surround the window. Christ appears again under the choir loft inside the building, leading the way into a nave filled with the saints and martyrs—most from the secular clergy—who make up the Christian pantheon. Past the crossing dome, with its images of the four evangelists, the main altarscreen bears images of the Virgin Mary and Saint Peter. Seen as a whole, the church's iconography has been interpreted as a celebration of ecclesiastical authority, which was a popular theme in the eighteenth century for clerics witnessing the struggle between Europe's enlightened monarchs and the pope.[33]

Unlike the Cathedral of Zacatecas, which took decades to build and required aggressive fundraising, the Church of Santa Prisca and San Sebastián in Taxco, New Spain (Figure 81), was entirely sponsored by one person, New Spanish miner José de la Borda. It remains today as a spectacular example of baroque rhetoric, whereby a single patron and his artists deployed the media of architecture, sculpture, and paintings to pay homage to God. Like most parish churches, Santa Prisca is a single nave cruciform structure with an octagonal drum for its crossing dome. Financed by Borda, an émigré miner who amassed a spectacular fortune from his mines in the Taxco region of central New Spain, construction lasted from 1751 to 1758. Borda's interest in paying for a new parish church stems from the Catholic requirement of good works. Wealthy Catholics like Borda believed that they improved their chances of salvation by donating large sums to the church. Borda's famous quote on this topic says it all: "God gives to Borda, and Borda gives to God."

Borda engaged architect Cayetano de Sigüenza (1715–78) to build his church and Isidoro Vicente Balbás (d. 1783), adopted son of Jerónimo Balbás, to design the altarscreens inside. Their efforts have been called one of the most important statements of New Spanish *criollismo* thanks to the building's many references to local architectural traditions. The structure displays all of the elements favored by New Spanish architects: poblano polychrome tiles on the dome, mixtilinear arches, niche pilasters, rustication of interior surfaces, tall façade towers, and

FIGURE 81.
Cayetano de Sigüenza.
Church of Santa Prisca
and San Sebastián.
1751–58. Taxco,
Mexico. Photograph
© Archivo Fotográfico
Manuel Toussaint,
IIE/UNAM.

Solomonic columns. Estípite columns only appear on the exterior on the towers, but dominate the interior altarscreens. As with other examples of Latin American colonial architecture, these leitmotifs of the period are nevertheless deployed with great artistic freedom according to local tastes.

Sigüenza's retablo-façade is an elegant expression of those preferences. Organized in two tiers and generally respecting its reticular grid, the architectural framework nevertheless expresses its sculptural plasticity. Each level features two pairs of columns, the lower featuring the Composite order and the upper, Solomonic. Niche pilasters between the columns contain full round sculptures of Saints Peter and Paul below, and titular Saints Prisca and Sebastian above. An oval relief of the Baptism of Christ occupies the second level over the door. A sculpture of the Immaculate Conception flanked by the evangelists Matthew and John crown the retablo-façade. The tall towers have windows with mixtilinear moldings in the bases and a variety of columns, grotesques, and decorative elements framing the bells above.

The interior of Santa Prisca and San Sebastián (Figure 82) looks every bit as tall and elegant as the exterior. Under a high barrel vault, nine altarscreens adorn the single nave and transept. Stacked and rusticated pilasters cover the walls not hidden behind the gilded constructions, making the building seem to quiver as

FIGURE 82.
Interior of the Church of Santa Prisca and San Sebastián with altarscreens by Isidoro Vicente Balbás. 1753–55. Taxco, Mexico. Photograph © Kelly Donahue-Wallace.

if held by an unsteady hand. Balbás's spectacular main altarscreen, carved and gilded between 1753 and 1755, is more free and dynamic than his father's work at the Mexico City Cathedral. The Taxco retablo goes further toward the denial of architectural solidity. Its four colossal estípite columns are dwarfed by the broad and highly ornate niche pilasters they flank. The sculptures of the titular saints and the Virgin Mary are accompanied by a pantheon of other holy figures that appear in full- or bust-length throughout the altarscreen. Seen alongside the nave altarscreens and the ornate treatment of every architectural surface, Balbás's main retablo contributes to the remarkable formal cohesion and overwhelming visual experience of the church's interior. Borda's Church of Santa Prisca and San Sebastián remains a spectacular expression of New Spain's churrigueresque style and testimony to the colonial willingness to spend mining wealth on the celebration of the faith.

Late Colonial Shrines

The eighteenth century experienced the expansion of the cults of miraculous paintings and sculptures. The Virgins of Guadalupe, Copacabana, Guápulo, and los Remedios, and the Christs of Santa Teresa, Esquípulas, and the Earthquakes continued to draw the faithful to their altars. The pilgrims funded construction of new shrines that celebrated these cults in awe-inspiring settings.

The shrine dedicated to the miraculous Christ of Manquirí (Figure 83) is located nine miles from Potosí in the Viceroyalty of Peru. According to legend, the site was venerated as a huaca by local Pre-Columbian peoples, likely due to the thermal steams emitting from underground springs. Like the Virgin of Guadalupe, a sculpture of Christ miraculously appeared on a rock at the site, spawning a cult in its honor.[34] Pilgrims to the 1783 shrine saw the holy figure in his ornate gilded altarscreen, which simultaneously displayed him to the faithful who came to ask his favor and protected him from their zealous adoration. Other interior ornamentation included Cuzco school paintings and at least two works by potosino painter Melchor Pérez Holguín.[35]

The shrine's single-nave temple is built into the natural rock of the adjacent hillside at its apse end. From there, the church continues past two transepts and two crossing domes, one circular and the other elliptical. Twin towers on the façade look out over a great walled atrium with arcades along two sides and posa chapels on the corners.[36] The posa chapel altars, along with the funerary Miserere chapel located in the middle of the atrium, served religious processions and the outdoor services performed to accommodate ever-growing numbers of pilgrims who camped outside the shrine's walls. The church and atrium rest on a tall pyramidal foundation, not unlike those employed at some sixteenth-century missions. The structure may consequently represent a continuing accommodation of indigenous traditions of outdoor worship and veneration of holy sites or huacas nearly two centuries after evangelization.

The retablo-façade of the Manquirí sanctuary, carved in the regional

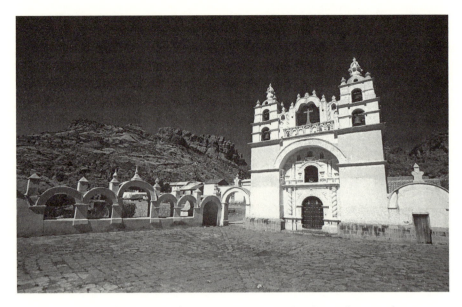

FIGURE 83. Shrine of the Christ of Manquiri. 1783. Potosí, Bolivia. Photograph
© James Brunker, photographersdirect.com.

planiform style, rests under a deep arch between the two towers. It employs
the triumphal arch motif on the lower level; a window flanked by columns and
angelic figures fills the upper story. Saint Peter and two other figures occupy the
area over the door. The surface is covered in low relief vegetal and geometric
designs, including palms carried by angels and cherubs. Sculpted lilies and pomegranates, symbols of the Virgin's purity and of resurrection respectively, also
appear on the façade. The sun, moon, two sirens, and two musicians appear in
the arch's intrados, recalling the façade of San Lorenzo in nearby Potosí.

Inspiration for the portal program as well as the structure itself likely came
from the prophet Ezekiel's descriptions of the ancient Temple of Solomon. Like
the Old Testament structure described in Ezekiel 41:8–26, the shrine at Manquirí
is elevated above the surrounding landscape.[37] The retablo-façade and the interior ornamentation of polychromed and gilded designs feature the angels and
palms Ezekiel described; the six-pointed star of David, father of Solomon, even
appears over the door. But while the elevated structure likely referenced biblical
history, it also recalled local Pre-Columbian platforms and the early colonial
practice of imposing churches atop existing and newly built temple foundations.
In conjunction with the Platonic references to sirens and music, the façade's
program and the structure as a whole comprise a complicated statement of what
art historians José de Mesa and Teresa Gisbert have called, "the union of the
humanistic-pagan and Hebreo-Christian traditions."[38] Hence the pilgrimage
shrine welcomed visitors of diverse beliefs into the Christian fold.

A nearly contemporary New Spanish chapel built between 1777 and 1791
at the location of the Virgin of Guadalupe's miraculous appearance is similarly

innovative in its plan and ornamentation. The Chapel of the Well, known as El Pocito (Figure 84), shelters the well where a spring spontaneously bubbled forth when the Virgin Mary appeared to Juan Diego in 1531. The building, designed and built by criollo architect Francisco de Guerrero y Torres (1727–92), consists of a circular vestibule, an oval sanctuary with four rectangular side chapels, and an octagonal sacristy. A dome surmounted by a lantern and a tall stone cross tops each area. Paired Corinthian columns and pilasters with undulating profiles articulate the interior spaces.

While the plan of the nearby Basilica of Guadalupe, like the shrine at Manquiri, recalled the Temple of Solomon, Guerrero y Torres's structure referenced the circular early Christian baptisteries and their associations with rebirth and regeneration. He was also inspired by the work of Italian seventeenth-century architect Francesco Borromini; the chapel's elliptical plan and spatial manipulation recall Borromini's church of San Carlo alle Quattro Fontane. El Pocito's plan may furthermore have been based on a Roman temple described by Serlio.[39] Whatever its sources of inspiration, El Pocito is nevertheless a unique expression of local culture. Guerrero y Torres, who donated his labor to design and construct the shrine, was simultaneously maestro mayor of the royal palace

FIGURE 84.
Francisco de
Guerrero y Torres.
Chapel of the Well
(El Pocito). 1777–91.
Tepeyac, Mexico.
Photograph © Kelly
Donahue-Wallace.

and the cathedral as well as an engineer interested in fire suppression devices and other machinery.[40] It consequently comes as little surprise that he was familiar with architectural treatises and local building practices.

Guerrero y Torres displayed the increasingly classicizing taste of late colonial New Spanish architecture, known as *neóstilo*, on the exterior of El Pocito. The main portal's ornamental elaboration is relatively restrained compared to its predecessors. Two distinct stories plus attic contain Corinthian columns flanking empty niches. The exterior nevertheless preserves many of the traditions of New Spanish baroque architecture. Geometric forms and intricate linear patterns abound. The door has a mixtilinear arch surmounted by two windows in the shape of six-pointed stars intersecting polylobed forms. Geometric linear moldings cover much of the façade and a tiled diaper pattern spreads across the attic. Guerrero y Torres also employed color contrasts from the local architectural tradition. The gray chiluca stone, for example, contrasts with the red tezontle stone walls and blue and white tile of the domes and attic story. In sum, the colonial architect constructed a shrine that at once respected and exceeded the conventions of local religious architecture, and rewarded visiting pilgrims with a spectacular vision of divinity.

Late Colonial Missions

Up to the moment its priests were expelled from Spanish territories, the Jesuit order dedicated its energies to education and missionary work. Some of the most remarkable Jesuit missions—now in ruins—are found in South America, in the jungle region where Argentina, Paraguay, and Brazil meet today. This mission district, known as El Paraguay, was founded in 1603 to serve the Guaraní and Tupi Indians on the nebulous border between Spanish and Portuguese territories. The Jesuits traveled in pairs into these remote areas of unconverted indigenous peoples who were sometimes hostile to their presence. Upon winning the confidence of the local cacique, the Jesuit priests "reduced" several indigenous communities to a single sedentary mission village consisting of a church, housing, and workshops organized on a grid plan. With the crown's permission, the Jesuits kept Spanish settlers away from their foundations and lived humble existences alongside their native charges, albeit with religious, political, and economic authority over the community. By 1767, Jesuit priests operated thirty reducciones in the region, but had founded over seventy-five separate sites, as many of the reducciones moved due to geography, overpopulation, or to escape raids by the Portuguese *bandeirantes* who searched the countryside for slaves and gold.

The Jesuits created the Guaraní reducciones by assuming the role of the local shaman or *karai* and leading the people to the new settlements, which they called a "land-without-evil" in the local language.[41] Like the sixteenth-century mendicants, the Jesuit missionaries considered the native peoples to be *tabulae rasae*, ready and childlike receptacles for Christian teachings. To achieve this Utopian state of unadulterated Christianity, the natives needed to stay at the mission, which they did. By 1700, nearly 100,000 Guaraní Indians lived in the Jesuit reducciones, spending their days working in the fields and workshops, and worshipping in the mission church. The reducciones' success was helped in large part by the Jesuit policy of cultural accommodation, a technique later called inculturation, meaning "the adaptation of Christian ritual to the traditions of different societies."[42] The Jesuits in El Paraguay adapted Guaraní beliefs and rituals to Christian contexts and meanings, including the local appreciation of oratory and music.

The Church of San Miguel (Figure 85), today just inside Brazilian territory, exemplifies the Jesuit missions of El Paraguay, albeit on a grand scale; at its height in the 1750s, several thousand Guaraní resided at the mission. Its first church, constructed between 1641 and 1643, was likely built of ephemeral local materials: wood, wattle-and-daub, and thatch roofing. When the mission moved to a new site to accommodate a growing population, the priests built the second mission church with adobe walls. The structure was likely topped by a pitched tile roof with broad eaves supported inside the nave by tall wooden pillars according to traditional Guaraní building practices.

The third mission church, a massive stone and brick structure, lies today in ruins. Italian Jesuit Giovanni Battista Primoli (1673–1747) designed and began the ambitious building between 1730 and 1735; the Catalán architect Brother Grimau finished construction in 1747.[43] Like many Jesuit churches, it recalls the plan of Il Gesú, with a three-aisle interior and a transept; two towers were built, but only one remains today.[44] While Primoli may have planned brick vaults

FIGURE 85. Giovanni Battista Primoli. Mission Church of San Miguel. ca. 1730–47. Sao Miguel, Brazil. Photograph © Argosfoto, photographersdirect.com.

and a dome, the roof was made of wood. The façade displays a sober classicism recalling, like many Jesuit mission churches in El Paraguay, Italian late sixteenth-century architecture. The two-story façade features pilasters and niches on the first two levels, and a pediment above. A porch arcade with its own pediment and columns was a late addition to the façade. The porch extended into a broad atrium that may have contained corner chapels recalling the posas found at the missions of central New Spain and later South American sites like Manquirí. The patio served as a space for processions, dances, and other public rituals.

Contemporary drawings reveal that the mission complex may have included more than forty large dormitories organized on a grid plan surrounding the church, cloister, hospital, and workshops. Among the latter was a veritable factory of painters. Jesuits promoted the arts as essential to the practice of Christianity. They based this philosophy on the experiences of sixteenth-century missionaries, the Counter Reformation promotion of didactic art, and Ignatius of Loyola's *Spiritual Exercises*, which promoted images in support prayer. Jesuit missionaries founded art workshops at the reducciones, where they introduced European paintings, sculptures, and prints, but allowed local artists to express the new Christian ideas according to local tastes. Since the Guaraní lacked a history of figural art, the paintings, sculptures, altarscreens, and prints produced at the Paraguay missions resembled contemporary European and colonial urban production; art produced at other Jesuit missions around the globe varied according to indigenous practices. From its foundation, San Miguel's artists were renowned among the Jesuit community for their paintings, but they also made sculptures. In 1735, the mission's storerooms overflowed with sculpture, forcing the community to give its wares away to other churches.[45]

The population at the San Miguel mission was already in decline before the 1767 Jesuit expulsion. The 1750 Guaraní War, when the indigenous peoples protested Spain's concession of several missions to the Portuguese, took a devastating toll on the populations; persistent epidemics killed even more. When the Jesuits left, their expulsion having been partially inspired by the independent empire they created among the native peoples of El Paraguay, their missions were slowly abandoned to the jungle; by the early nineteenth century only a few dozen Guaraní resided at San Miguel. The site today is recently restored and includes a museum containing many examples of Guaraní Christian art.

Eighteenth-century missionary activity was not confined to the Jesuits in South America. The Jesuits and other orders also occupied missions in northern New Spain, in what is today northern Mexico and the southwestern United States. Some of the more famous surviving examples include the Mission of San Antonio de Valero (better known as the Alamo) in San Antonio, Texas; San Xavier del Bac near Tucson, Arizona; and Mission Santa Barbara overlooking the Pacific Ocean. These, like most of the missions on the far northern frontier, belonged to the Franciscans, although San Xavier del Bac and other nearby conventos were constructed by the Jesuits before the 1767 expulsion.

Franciscans were the first missionaries to spread Christianity in the southwestern United States. Franciscan fray Marcos de Niza explored the region in 1538 and accompanied Francisco Vázquez de Coronado on his 1540 expedition through Arizona, New Mexico, Texas, Oklahoma, and Kansas. Franciscans established thirty-three missions among New Mexico's Pueblo peoples between 1598 and 1680; non-Amerindian colonists worshipped at parish churches in Santa Fe, Santa Cruz de la Cañada, and other Spanish settlements. A coordinated uprising of the local indigenous populations in 1680 killed friars and colonists. The uprising destroyed many mission churches and effectively turned back the Spanish presence in New Mexico for the next twelve years. After resettlement in 1693, Franciscans resumed their activities at most of the missions and founded several more over the next century. Missions constructed after the resettlement are uniformly smaller than their seventeenth-century predecessors, suggesting that the friars understood that their presence in New Mexico was at the mercy of the indigenous population.

Franciscan mission architecture in the US Southwest differed by region. Some of the structures look similar to New Spanish parish and convent churches. The mission churches of San José in San Antonio and San Xavier del Bac near Tucson, for example, feature carved stone retablo-façades and even estípite columns and niche pilasters that recall central New Spanish tastes. Ruins of several New Mexican mission churches destroyed in the 1680 rebellion suggest that here, too, the friars constructed grand structures with impressive stone walls. New Mexico's Franciscans nevertheless also adopted building practices that reflected local indigenous traditions, much as they had done at the central New Spanish missions in the sixteenth century. Even the stone walls of the destroyed missions at Abó and Quarai reveal masonry techniques that scholars attribute to local indigenous traditions.

The church of San Esteban at Acoma Pueblo (Figure 86) reveals many of the common features of local seventeenth- and eighteenth-century New Mexican mission architecture. Located alongside a multistoried pueblo on a high mesa, the mission church was constructed after 1629, perhaps under the direction of fray Juan Ramírez; the church was completed by 1664. The structure apparently suffered only minor damage during the 1680 rebellion, though its Franciscan missionary was not as lucky.

When it is recalled that all of the building materials had to be carried up the steep mesa walls, the dimensions of the church at Acoma Pueblo are staggering. The church is a single-nave construction with a polygonal apse and no transept. The convent, with its small cloister and *mirador* balcony, rests to the right side of the temple; an atrium in front is surrounded by a stone wall. Resting on a thick adobe foundation, the sun-dried adobe brick and stone church walls are almost fifty feet tall and ten feet wide. The church façade features only a choir loft window and rests between two low bell towers. This stark face exaggerates the fortress-like appearance of the structure as a whole, which is pierced only by small windows and the projecting ends of the interior ceiling beams known as *vigas*.

The interior, on the other hand, captured the visitor's attention with more

FIGURE 86.
Mission Church of San
Esteban. 1629–64. Acoma
Pueblo, New Mexico,
United States. Photograph
© Kelly Donahue-Wallace.

theatrical effects. Its tamped dirt floor slowly rises toward the altar, which is accessed by stairs. With few windows and no dome, New Mexican builders illuminated the church interior with a transverse clerestory, a rectangular opening where the lower, flat nave roof meets the higher roof over the sanctuary. The resulting shaft of light recalls the mysterious effect of contemporary domes, as the light of God seems to shine on the altar. This beam of light is particularly impressive as the viewer passes out of the darkness under the choir loft and moves toward the sanctuary. Today visitors can only imagine the interior ornamentation the church once housed. Altarscreens, paintings, and sculptures imported from central New Spain lined the nave and filled the apse. The altar was accompanied by an organ and a silver gilt tabernacle.[46] These materials arrived on the tri-annual supply mule train that brought the missionaries the tools, books, and other materials they required.

Local art also adorned this and other mission churches with frescoes painted on the walls, religious paintings executed on animal hides, polychromed wood sculpture, and oil paintings on panel. These works were created by indigenous artists as well as colonists of all ethnicities who arrived from central New Spain. The works' appearances reflected local diversity, ranging from stylized forms inherited from traditional native arts to European-style illusionism. Friars at Acoma and other missions apparently accommodated local preferences as they had elsewhere in the Americas, though visiting authorities from the archbishopric of Durango criticized the "ugly" art. By the end of the eighteenth century, New Mexican artists increasingly favored a stylization and bright coloration still practiced by contemporary *santeros* (saint-makers) in New Mexico.

Even more than the Jesuit mission among the Guaraní, it bears emphasizing how much of the Acoma mission church reflected the traditions and preferences of the local indigenous pueblo. The structure looked, in many ways, like the local pueblo, with adobe plaster covering the walls in a uniform color. It was constructed according to ancestral practices, with men carrying wood from the nearby sacred mountains and women plastering the exterior. While the Christian images were undoubtedly unfamiliar at first, local artists soon made holy Christian images that looked familiar to them; a few mural paintings remain in the convento. Like other indigenous populations, the people of Acoma Pueblo experienced evangelization on their own terms, taking what they liked and incorporating it into their system of beliefs and artistic practices.

Palaces of Late Colonial Latin America

The viceregal capitals of Lima and Mexico City grew during the eighteenth century. In 1750, Lima extended 350 blocks around the plaza mayor and had 50,000 citizens.[47] By 1800, Mexico City sheltered over 130,000 people and was the largest community in the Americas. Both cities constructed or expanded parks and recreational facilities, and continued major civic projects, like the seemingly never-ending desagüe (drainage) project to keep Mexico City above water, and the great defensive wall that tried to keep Lima safe from pirates. The Bourbon reforms likewise left their mark as the viceregal capitals became home to the royal factories that monopolized major industries and the buildings of the royal mints that produced the coins to fuel the economy.

Most urban colonists lived in cramped quarters. Both Mexico City and Lima had neighborhoods of tiny huts built of ephemeral materials to house the poorest residents. Craftsmen slept in the lofts above their ground-floor shops. The more prosperous of this class lived in *casas de vecindad*, two-room apartments opening onto a central patio shared with other tenants. The occupants did not usually own their homes, but rented them, frequently from convents and monasteries, which were the largest landlords in most cities. Wealthy merchants, miners, and nobles lived in *casas solas* or palaces that occupied up to one quarter of a city block. The houses might contain up to eighty rooms organized around one or more interior patios; an 1811 census recorded the occupancy of one particularly well-off Mexico City home at 42 family members and servants.[48] Many of the casas solas were subdivided as families lost their fortunes and sold their homes; only a few of these spectacular residences survive in the historic districts of Mexico City and Lima today.

Building materials varied by family wealth and geography. Poor homes in Mexico City were built of adobe, while well-to-do colonists lived in stone palaces. With little good stone available, Lima's homes were almost entirely constructed with adobe exterior walls, quincha interior partitions, and thatched roofs. Seismic activity kept all but the most opulent limeño homes to one story. Wealthy residences not only had a second story, but also boasted carved stone and plaster portals. They also featured wood balconies known as miradores hanging from their walls. Lima inherited these projecting wood structures from Moorish traditions and used them, like the Moors who occupied southern Spain, to allow women to watch the street without being seen by outsiders. The colonial miradores, like the reconstructed examples found today in Lima, consisted of an armature, eaves, and wood grills known as *celosías* that opened outward at the bottom. Windows without balconies were covered in wood or metal grillwork.[49]

The Torre Tagle Palace in Lima (Figure 87) is a spectacular example of Lima's eighteenth-century domestic architecture. Don José Tagle y Barchino, Marquis of Torre Tagle, began the casa sola in 1733; construction ended in 1738. Tagle spared no expense on the structure, importing the façade's stone from Panama, the mirador's wood from Central America, and the interior's tiles from Sevilla.[50] Resting on a foundation of stone and mortar, the walls of the palace are brick on the first level and quincha above. This combination proved relatively

FIGURE 87.
Torre Tagle Palace.
1733–38. Lima, Peru.
Photograph © Kelly
Donahue-Wallace.

stable and the home survived Lima's devastating 1746 earthquake with little damage. Like a few nearby homes, the palace originally had a tower that allowed its occupants to see the coast;[51] the tower has not survived.

The Torre Tagle Palace's entry portal makes a grand statement about the family's wealth with an ornamental vocabulary shared with contemporary religious architecture. Corinthian columns and stacked pilasters flank the door on the lower level. This portion of the façade is constructed of stone and bears low relief strapwork and vegetal carvings. The strongly projecting entablature supports an ornate upper story made of wood, reeds, and plaster, today painted white.[52] This level repeats the Corinthian columns on a smaller scale but its most spectacular elements are the broken mixtilinear pediments to either side of and above the window. These forms project outward and upward and create strong chiaroscural effects. Another unusual feature is the mixtilinear cornice that departs from the top of the second story pediments and wraps around the building façade. The top of the portal is crowned with a cross surmounting ornate strapwork.

Passing through the portal, visitors enter an equally lavish interior. The *zaguán* (entry foyer for coaches), like the rest of the palace, features an ornate Mudéjar wood ceiling and carved stucco architectural ornaments. The main patio has a second-story arcade of fantastic mixtilinear arches supported by wood columns; a broad staircase provides access to the upper level. The rooms surrounding this main courtyard were occupied by the Torre Tagle family. The Ambassador's Hall, also known as the Balconies Hall, rested over the portal and served as the main reception room. Another second-story chamber was the Salón del Estrado, a sitting room that housed a low platform covered by pillows. This room is where the lady of the house and her guests sat in their large dresses, smoked cigarettes, and enjoyed chocolate and other delicacies. The Salón del Estrado was also frequently the most ornate room in the house, featuring lavish imported and local furnishings and genre scenes, mythological narratives, and other secular works of art. The dining room rested on the back side of the upper level, connected by a narrow passageway to the auxiliary patio. The second courtyard was dedicated to serving the great house with a kitchen, workshops, stables, henhouse, orchard, garden, and well. This area also housed the servants' quarters.

Like most wealthy homes, the Torre Tagle Palace had its own chapel (Plate 25). This small chamber, located on the second story between the main and secondary patios, permitted the family to enjoy private services and personal devotions. While less well-to-do homes had only small, trunk-like shrines, the Torre Tagle Palace's *oratorio* contained a lavish altarscreen that reflected contemporary limeño church retablos, albeit on a smaller scale. The gilded structure features Solomonic columns, mixtilinear cornices and moldings, rocailles, mirrors, scrolls, and the vegetal motifs common to late eighteenth-century altarscreens. Several niches within the structure shelter small sculptures of saints, with Saint Rose of Lima at the top, and other saints of the family's devotions to either side. These small sculptures, many produced by the renowned sculptors of Quito, were popular throughout South America. The family likely also displayed here their sculpted tableau of the Nativity; visiting these domestic installations was an annual Christmas pastime among Lima's elite.

Mexico City's domestic architecture was so grand in the eighteenth century that the viceregal capital was known as the City of the Palaces. By the end of the colonial era, at least forty elite homes occupied the city center, gradually replacing the palaces constructed by the conquistadores with ever more lavish structures. (See Sidebar 3, Chapter 1, and Sidebar 17.) Not all colonists, of course, lived in these casas solas. More humble homes, grouped according to their occupants' profession, were interspersed among the grand domiciles, convents, monasteries, hospitals, seminaries, and colegios surrounding the plaza mayor. Silversmiths, for example, lived and worked on Calle de Plateros between the main square and the Alameda Park. These homes also shared the city streets with the royal buildings, including the new Royal Mint, the renovated Royal and Pontifical University, the granary, the Inquisition Palace, and the Customs House. Since professions were roughly divided by race, so were Mexico City's neighborhoods, with peninsular Spaniards, criollos, and artisan mestizos occupying the central district, and other mixed race peoples, Blacks, Amerindians, and even poor Spaniards on the periphery.

Miguel de Berrio Zaldívar was among the city's wealthiest citizens. Berrio's fortune, built on mining, ranching, wool production and commercial activities, prompted king Charles III to grant him the title of Marquis of Jaral de Berrio in 1774.[53] Soon after, Berrio contracted New Spanish architect Francisco Antonio Guerrero y Torres, builder of El Pocito chapel and maestro mayor of the cathedral and viceregal palace, to construct a new family home. According to legend, Berrio spared no expense on the house in order to tie up the family wealth and keep it away from his profligate future son-in-law. True or not, the legend accounts for the building's immense scale and undoubtedly impressive interior. While today the inside no longer retains its original appearance, it may be assumed that it was not unlike that of the Torre Tagle Palace. One remaining feature is the three-story main patio with its colossal arcade. The façade, on the other hand, still retains its original appearance and presents a potent statement of the Marquis's family wealth and power.

Finished in 1784, the Palace of the Marquis of Jaral de Berrio (Figure 88)—also known by the name of its later occupant, independence hero and emperor Agustín Iturbide—is a monumental, three-story structure that pays homage to its colonial heritage with its architecture and its ornament. The tall main entrance features a carved chiluca portal with undulating, mixtilinear pilasters, Iconic capitals, and grotesque-laden shafts. The geometric designs on these stacked pilasters are emphatic and recall the taste for similar designs in religious buildings. Above the door, two wild men bearing clubs rest on the molding that ends, snail-like, above the entrance; they flank a large lambrequin filled with vegetal motifs and grotesques. These figures recall the wild men on the Casa de Montejo

Excerpts from fray Ilarione da Bergamo's description
of Mexico City, circa 1767.

The city of Mexico is three leagues in circumference and two miles in diameter. The city, with neither walls nor gates, is entered by five *calzadas* or causeways, high and sturdy because of the water . . . The plan of the city is similar to the Bergamo [Italy] market—that is, with straight streets from east to west and from south to north. These streets are moderately wide so that four coaches can comfortably pass side by side . . .

The city of Mexico has more than one hundred and thirty thousand inhabitants . . . There are numerous plazas, and in practically all of them there is a fountain in the middle spurting water. The principal plaza, though, is the one with the cathedral and viceroy's palace, where people primarily gather to carry on their trade . . .

For the quality of the buildings, ornaments, and wealth of its churches, it [the capital] can be said to vie with the finest cities of Italy. It is true that there are no grand palaces, as in Rome and its outskirts, because they cannot erect massive buildings since the foundations are not completely solid. But in their interior, perhaps, they are richer for the sumptuousness of their ornamentation. All the houses of this city are of stone and brick and whitewashed. Viewed in perspective, they are of fine architecture, with well-ordered balconies, windows, and soffits in the Chinese style, magnificent gates, courtyards with marble columns, and spacious and commodious entrance stairways painted between one step and the next in checkered fashion so that, viewed from a certain distance, the entire stairwell looks as though it were covered with cloth. The only defect the houses have is that they are not proportionate in height, though I have seen various ones fives stories high. Most, though, have three. The rooms located on the floor by the door are where the serving people dwell. Above them are the rooms they call *entresuelo*, where there are stores of merchandise, because here practically everyone is a merchant. Finally, there are the masters' quarters.

—From *Daily Life in Colonial Mexico: The Journey of Friar Ilarione da Bergamo, 1761–1768*, ed. Robert Ryal Miller and William J. Orr, trans. William J. Orr, 87–91 (Norman: University of Oklahoma Press, 2000).

FIGURE 88. Francisco Antonio Guerrero y Torres. Palace of the Marquis of Jaral de Berrio (Iturbide Palace). 1784. Mexico City, Mexico. Photograph © Kelly Donahue-Wallace.

in Mérida discussed in Chapter 3. They rest below the balcony where the master of the house stood upon them to represent civility's triumph over barbarity and chaos. The short towers on the third level pay homage to the homes of the conquistadores. Like their predecessors, the Jaral de Berrio towers were united by a loggia and afforded little defense had this been necessary in 1784. More important, of course, was the reference to the conquest and the creation of an elevated space from which to survey the colonial territory.

Unlike the Torre Tagle Palace in Lima, the Jaral de Berrio mansion maintains a visual and psychological distance from the street—that is, it does not project into public spaces with broad balconies and plastic portal sculpture. The façade is planar and, by comparison, severe; other Mexico City palaces offer similarly restrained exteriors of red tezontle, polychrome tile, and gray chiluca. This is not to say, however, that the buildings did not participate in the urban society. Like many colonial mansions, the Jaral de Berrio palace included ground level shops open to the street as sources of revenue. It also featured a mini-story known as the *entresuelo*, between the ground level and second floor; it is unclear whether in this case this area was also open to renters as it was in other colonial palaces.[54] Other homes similarly had a commercial function; the Palace of the Counts of the Valley of Orizaba, for example, better known as the Casa de los Azulejos for its tile-covered exterior, sheltered businesses in its exterior walls.

Even though much of his wealth was generated outside Mexico City at ranches and mines, the Marquis of Jaral de Berrio and other titled nobles understood the need to maintain grand residences in the viceregal capital. Only at the seat of colonial authority could they make profitable business deals, pursue government contracts, secure civic and ecclesiastic positions for their sons, negotiate marriages for their daughters with peninsular husbands, and generally confirm their social status among their peers. The viceregal capital also sheltered the large monasteries and convents that happily accepted their pious donations. The palace played an essential role in this social intercourse and functioned as the setting for formal and informal gatherings that performed essential social rituals. For the Marquis of Jaral de Berrio and the other criollo elite, the furnishings made potent statements along with the architecture. In addition to imported luxury goods from Europe and Asia, home décor provided the opportunity to promote criollo interests, and palaces like Berrio's were filled with the imagery of criollo identity and patriotism discussed in Chapter 7.

At the same time, the elite colonists occupying this and other palaces also extended their social status into the city streets. The elite rode through the city in imported carriages, strolled in the Alameda Park, occupied privileged positions in civic and religious ceremonies and processions, and took leisurely rides along the canals of Iztacalco. They maintained family chapels in—and made huge donations to—local churches. Even the simple act of appearing in public decked in the jewels and rich fabrics that were theirs alone according to colonial sumptuary laws constantly reaffirmed the racial and economic hierarchy. From their palaces, Berrio and his cohorts in the criollo elite exploited the urban context to communicate their wealth and the divine favor they enjoyed, not only to the urban masses but also to the peninsular authorities who the Bourbon reforms placed in the viceroyalties' highest governmental and ecclesiastical positions.

Secular Painting Circa 1600–1800

Religious themes dominated viceregal art. Painters and sculptors spent most of their careers working for the Catholic Church and pious colonists who purchased holy images for houses, chapels, convents, and churches. Yet alongside their sacred subjects, New Spanish and Peruvian artists satisfied the elite's demand for secular images. They painted portraits, genre scenes, mythological narratives, still lives, landscapes, and history paintings to hang in urban palaces and country homes. (See Sidebar 18.) Colonists demanded these objects as reflections of themselves and the society they created. But while their content strayed from matters of faith, the works' formal characteristics reflected the tastes of their era—from mannerist elegance to baroque ostentation and Cuzco school hybridity—with slight adjustments depending upon thematic conventions. This chapter examines three categories of secular painting: portraits, painted screens known as *biombos*, and the ethnographic *pinturas de castas* that pictured the viceroyalties' ethnic diversity. The discussion addresses a breadth of themes within each category and their functional commonalities, particularly as these paintings offered carefully crafted images of viceregal life to local and European audiences.

Portraits

While portraits usually capture a likeness, the paintings also allow patrons to construct their public personae. New Spanish and Peruvian sitters commissioned portraits to record their public service, to bolster their social standing, and to confirm their hereditary privileges. They hung their portraits in public buildings, secular and religious offices, and private homes. Their painters employed iconographic and formal strategies that differed from contemporary European practices and reflected the tastes and interests of the viceregal elite.

Latin American artists made portraits soon after the conquest; the first examples appeared in New Spain and reflect the convergence of Spanish and Mesoamerican artistic traditions; both cultures shared the practice of figural portrait making.[1] Sixteenth-century chronicler Bernal Díaz del Castillo cited perhaps the first example of colonial portraiture, describing portraits made for Moctezuma of Hernán Cortés and his companions as they marched toward Tenochtitlan.[2] Sixteenth-century manuscripts and mural paintings regularly contained images of New Spain's viceroys, friars, and indigenous leaders. The *Codex Mendoza's* circa 1540 image of Moctezuma (Figure 30, Chapter 2), executed by an indigenous tlacuilo, numbers among the earliest colonial examples. Andean indigenous populations, on the other hand, had generally non-illusionistic pictorial traditions when it came to rendering human beings. Pre-Columbian Inca leaders, for example, had an alter ego or *huaqui* carved to commemorate their reign. These sculptures generally represented the rulers in animal forms.[3] Andean artists soon, however, incorporated aspects of European pictorial practice into their works. A 1536 image of the Inca leader Manco Capac II painted on a rock face near Ollantaytambo to warn the approaching Spaniards of his presence employed a stylized human figure. The donor portrait painted on the nave wall at Oropesa (Figure 22, Chapter 2) and Guaman Poma's 1615 self-portrait and likeness of Philip III (Figure 32, Chapter 2) likewise number among the first South American examples.

The early portraits from both viceroyalties, however, privileged their subjects' historical significance rather than their likenesses. The images presented no more than general approximations of the sitters' physical appearance. The individual likenesses understood as portraits in the Western tradition—painted to capture an idiosyncratic facsimile of the subject—were rare in early colonial Latin America. Not until the late sixteenth and seventeenth centuries did urban artists trained in illusionistic pictorial practices paint this type of individual and group portrait for elite patrons.

Official portraits of viceroys and bureaucrats were the first of these "true" portraits to be painted in viceregal New Spain and Peru. Painters in urban guilds made their likenesses to hang alongside royal portraits sent from Spain, but few early examples survive. Their scarcity may be explained as much by contemporary Spanish art theory as by the vagaries of time and events such as the 1692 Mexico City riot that destroyed the portrait collection in the viceregal palace. Peninsular theorist Vicente Carducho (1576–1636) advised that painters only represent kings and princes known for their good government, so early colonial private citizens may have eschewed portraiture for decorum's sake.[4]

Certainly Hernán Cortés's résumé met Carducho's criteria, and the *Portrait of Hernán Cortés* (Figure 89), painted circa 1600, represents the typical characteristics of official portraits. Cortés stands erect in an undefined interior space and gazes into the distance. He wears ornate armor, and holds a baton in his right hand and the hilt of a sword his left. His discarded glove and helmet rest on the nearby table and his heraldic device appears over his shoulder.

Selections from the inventory of the belongings of Antonia de Villareal, Mexico City, 1681

This inventory offers a glimpse of how colonists outfitted their homes. The inventory was compiled after the death of doña Antonia de Villareal, the well-to-do wife of a Mexico City merchant. It was compiled by appraisers from two guilds; painter Juan Correa assessed the value of the paintings and carpenter Diego de Azuaga valued the furniture.

One canvas of *Our Lady of Guadalupe* with its *ayacahuite* wood frame, on a black pedestal . . . 18 pesos

Another canvas of *Our Lady of the Immaculate Conception* with a gilded frame . . . 10 pesos

Another canvas of *Saint Philip of Jesus* with its gilded frame . . . 8 pesos

Another canvas of the archangel *Saint Michael*, without frame, two varas . . . 10 pesos

A painting of *Our Lady of the Column* with gilded frame . . . 8 pesos

Furthermore, five paintings . . . *Our Lady of Mount Carmel, Saint Theresa of Jesus*, and *Saint Helen*, with their gilded frames, and . . . *Saint Joseph* and *Saint Gertrude*, with black frames . . . 20 pesos

Another painting of the glorious *Saint Francis* . . . with its black frame . . . 5 pesos

Seven paintings in their frames of *Saint Augustine*, the *Earthly Trinity* (Holy Family), *Saint Catherine Martyr, Saint Francis, Our Lady of the Rosary, Our Lady of Bethlehem* and *Our Lady of the Assumption* . . . 30 pesos

Another painting of *Our Lady of Popolo* . . . with its black and gold frame . . . 3-1/2 pesos

Another canvas . . . of *Christ Our Father at the Column* and *Saint Peter* . . . 1 peso 4 *tomines* [a unit of currency, with 8 tomines to the peso]

Furthermore, five small paintings, two on copper, one on panel and two on canvas of different saints and faces . . . 3 pesos

Furthermore, three canvases . . . of *Saint Anthony* and *The Earthly Trinity*, and *Our Lady of Bethlehem* with their black frames and tin corners . . . 10 pesos

Another canvas . . . with black frame of *Saint John of God* . . . 2 pesos

Another canvas . . . with gilded frame of a *Sleeping Christ Child* . . . 3 pesos

Three paintings on copper . . . with frames of black *tapincirán* wood . . . of *Christ Crucified* and two of *Our Lady of the Rosary* . . . 27 pesos

Another four . . . copper paintings of *Saint Claire*, *Saint Ignatius*, *Saint Francis*, and *Saint John* with frames of black and gold tapincirán and ebony wood . . . 8 pesos

One ivory panel painting . . . garnished in ebony of *Our Lady of the Immaculate Conception* . . . 12 *reales* [a unit of currency equal to 1/8 peso].

One canopy for a sculpted *Crucifixion* from Michoacán, . . . with its tapincirán wood cross with dark blue velvet backing and a shell with a painting of *Our Lady of Guadalupe* . . . 15 pesos

Another canopy . . . for another wood *Christ* with its ordinary cross, in its baldachin of dark damask, old . . . 1 peso, 4 tomines

Twenty-eight small landscapes of Flowers and Fruits . . . 8 pesos

Furthermore, six landscapes . . . of different stories . . . 12 pesos

A sculpture of *Saint Andrew* without pedestal and another of *Saint John of God* . . . 6 pesos

Two mirrors, one . . . with its pear wood frame and the other . . . with a black frame of ordinary wood . . . 7 pesos 4 tomines

Eight walnut and leather arm chairs from this land, colored, with their gilded brass nails, well treated . . . 32 pesos

Six stools of the same quality . . . 15 pesos

One biombo of ten panels, with two faces, of the painting that imitates Japanese painting, mistreated . . . 16 pesos

A desk from Michoacán . . . worked with gilded shell inlay . . . and a small walnut table . . . 12 pesos

Another desk from Huachinango . . . dark blue and gold with feet of ordinary wood from Xochimilco . . . 9 pesos

One walnut desk with white box and drawers . . . and inlaid tapincirán wood, walnut top . . . 8 pesos

Two desks, . . . inlaid with tapincirán wood and the other . . . inlaid with gilded locks with walnut legs and box . . . 16 pesos.

—From Elisa Vargas Lugo and Gustavo Curiel,
Juan Correa: Su vida y su obra, vol. 3, Cuerpo de Documentos
(Mexico City: UNAM, 1991), 60–63. (Translation mine.)

FIGURE 89.
Attributed to Master
Saldana. *Portrait
of Hernán Cortés.*
Sixteenth century.
Oil on canvas.
Museo Nacional de
Historia, Castillo
de Chapultepec,
Mexico City, Mexico.
Photograph
© Giraudon/
Art Resource.

Like most portraits painted in the colonial era, Cortés's image reflects the sobriety, distant formality, and iconographic clarity found in the portraits by peninsular artists Alonso Sánchez Coello (1531–88) and Juan Pantoja de la Cruz (1553–1608). Like their works, Cortés's portrait privileges symbols of his station over evidence of his personality. The artist assembled a collection of widely understood signs, including the pose and likeness, to construct an image of Cortés's strength. The baton, sword, and armor symbolize political and military might, but the discarded helmet and glove reveal that his warring activities are completed. The stiff pose, reminiscent of Titian's portraits of Charles I and Philip II, not only associates Cortés with his king, but embodies his moral rectitude as well. Viewers also read his handsome, mature face as evidence of his intrinsic heroism, and his high forehead, illuminated as if by God, as proof of his superior intellect.[5] Finally, the coat of arms justifies his position, identifying his nobility through genealogy and his recently awarded title. Later official portraits of viceroys and bureaucrats traded armor and arms for silk suits, books, and writing implements, but sought similar effects.

Cortés's and other colonial portraits present stiff and unnatural bodies compared to contemporary European likenesses and to the graceful elegance and ideal beauty of viceregal religious figures. While the New Spanish painter captured the topography of his subject's face, he gave neither the face nor the body full plasticity. The flat figure seems devoid of life; similar characteristics can be seen in portraits executed throughout the colonial era. Art historians have many explanations for this common feature of colonial portraits. Religious decorum prohibited drawing from the nude, which may have left artists uncomfortable with renderings from life. Portraiture's low status compared to the more esteemed genre of religious and history painting perhaps attracted less-skilled artists. The colonial elite's identification with the sixteenth-century tastes that shaped urban painting schools may have caused them to demand portraits in the formal style of Sánchez Coello and Pantoja de la Cruz. The prevalence of post-mortem portraiture may have resulted in lifeless figures. Finally, the detailed description of costuming, such as Cortés's armor, flattened the bodies painted underneath. Whatever the cause, it stands to reason that colonists saw nothing wrong with their stiff and formal portraits. After all, this approach persisted for two centuries and paintings exhibiting this characteristic remain in family collections today. Surely the colonists would have demanded different characteristics had they found their portraits wanting. It would seem that the opposite was true; patrons believed that the formal and iconographic qualities of their portraits properly embodied their self-image.

Viceregal officials were not the only colonists to have their likenesses painted; society portraits of well-to-do Latin Americans proliferated in the eighteenth century as Carducho's admonition and Hapsburg austerity gave way to Bourbon pomp. Elite portraits immortalized deceased notables, gave visual evidence of noble lineage, and reflected the colonists' participation in a courtly society. The portrait of *Marqués de San Jorge* by Joaquín Gutiérrez (Figure 90) exemplifies the type. Born in Santa Fe de Bogotá, the criollo merchant only recently acquired a title of nobility thanks to his military service, wealth, and the Spanish crown's desperate need for cash.[6] The sitter is surrounded by symbols of his social status, from the new heraldic device hovering to his left to the sash bearing the sign of the Spanish knightly Order of Calatrava on the table beside him. The sword, baton, powdered wig, and fine clothes all testified to the Marquis's wealth and the inscription below chronicled his military credentials. The likeness itself similarly communicates status in the distinctly colonial manner, as the stiff formality and rigidity of the pose and gaze communicated social superiority to colonial viewers.

With some notable exceptions, such as Baltazar Echave Ibía's circa 1630 *Portrait of a Woman* and the 1650 *Portrait of doña Juana Valdés y Llano* by an anonymous Peruvian, Latin American artists painted few portraits of women before 1700. The increase in society portraits after that date, however, also included women's portraits, which were similarly prompted by the desire to illustrate status and wealth. And while male society portraits offered carefully crafted images of manly authority, women's images presented ideal womanly behavior using subtle, yet widely understood, signs to visualize exemplary femininity.

Miguel de Herrera's 1782 *Portrait of a Lady* (Plate 26) does not place his unidentified sitter in the lavish interior some portraitists employed, but no viewer could doubt this woman's fabulous wealth and social standing. Herrera

FIGURE 90.
Joaquín Gutiérrez. *Marqués de San Jorge*. Eighteenth century. Oil on canvas. Photograph © Museo de Arte Colonial, Bogotá, Colombia.

(ac. 1780–1800), one of a handful of Latin American portraiture specialists, pictures a robust family economy. His sitter wears a silk brocade gown with silver-threaded lace reflecting the fashions of contemporary France. Diamonds glisten at her wrists, neck, ears, and even in her immense feathered coiffure, displaying her wealth and the jewelry-making skills of New Spanish silversmiths. Her pale skin testifies to her Spanish heritage while her erect posture, uninviting gaze, and expressionless demeanor illustrate her social superiority. The portrait lacks an inscription, but many women's likenesses included short biographies. The portrait's formality, like others of its era, distinguishes it from its informal and comparatively intimate contemporaries in France and England by François Boucher and Thomas Gainsborough. And while the formality of colonial portraits did not change, its fashions did. New Spanish painter José María Vázquez's *Portrait of doña María Luisa Gonzaga Foncerrada y Labarrieta*, for example, places his sitter in one of the high-waisted and slim-skirted dresses that fashionable viceregal women wore in their early nineteenth-century neoclassical portraits.

Herrera's portrait, like most colonial likenesses, emphasizes costume and ornament, but it also employs an iconographic repertoire that testifies to his sitter's womanly virtues and upstanding character. The fan is not only a fashionable accessory, as elegant ladies frequently owned dozens of imported and local fans, but also communicated its owner's state of mind. Portraits, created to emphasize the chaste modesty of colonial women, invariably present metaphorically closed or mostly closed fans. In this example, the woman's modesty is also communicated by the hand held demurely to her torso. The watch similarly appears here not only as a fashion statement, but as a symbol of mortality in the face of fleeting time. Watches in women's portraits were not the timepieces that represented professional occupation in male portraiture, since women were thought to have no need for keeping a schedule. It was therefore not uncommon for artists to paint women wearing up to four watches, all set to different times.[7] Finally, the cloth in her left hand, held with fingers pointing down, was a widely understood sign of a humble life ruled by faith.[8] By repeating these symbols and conventions, colonial portraits constructed an image of womanhood that was entirely domestic, and governed by social convention, faith, morality, and the need to uphold the principles of criollo life.

Group portraits similarly communicated norms of behavior and belief, either familial or institutional. This portrait category included images of religious organizations, sometimes depicted under the protective mantle of the Virgin Mary or Saint Joseph, but more commonly depicted families. The anonymous portrait of *The del Valle Family at the Feet of the Virgin of Loreto* (ca. 1751–52), featuring the likenesses of don Felipe Antonio del Valle, his wife, and their children, exemplifies the category (Plate 27). As in other colonial portraits, the figures' stiff and inexpressive bodies display impressive wardrobes. Don Felipe and his sons sport fashionable French-inspired brocaded coats open to reveal ornate vests, while the matriarch doña María Anna de Vergara Manrique de Lara wears pearl jewelry and an embroidered gown trimmed with lace. The daughters wear the habit of the Conceptionist order and large painted *escudos de monjas* or nuns' shields on their chests. The biographical inscription at the bottom of the canvas notes that the father and mother had passed away; it also reveals that the painting hung in the family chapel on their hacienda in Apan.[9]

The del Valle family's portrait embodies the ideal of elite colonial life, in which piety came before wealth, status, and all other external concerns. In this case, the kneeling family demonstrates their faith and humility before a sculpted image of the Virgin of Loreto accompanied by Christ and God the Father. The family's postures and gestures mimic the poses of Saints Joseph and Francis, who appear above them. The idealized grace of Saint Joseph and the angels contrasts the family's rigid and lifeless anatomies, distinguishing the earthly family from the heavenly characters above. The daughters' habits, rosaries, and large shields known as escudos bearing images of the Immaculate Conception, similarly testify to the family's exemplary faith. Other group portraits likewise embody wealth and piety with well-dressed families adoring the Virgin of Guadalupe and other Marian cult images.

The del Valles, like other colonial families, clearly took pride in placing their daughters in the exclusive Convent of the Immaculate Conception, an institution open only to Spanish and criolla women. The girls joined the ranks of the nuns who prayed for the viceroyalty's well-being as brides of Christ. Young women who did not marry entered convents where they remained for life, working for God safe from the dangers of secular society. Don Felipe undoubtedly commemorated each daughter's profession with a portrait, which he hung in his home to celebrate their achievement and his wealth, and to embody the family's faith.

Likenesses of nuns number among the countless male and female ecclesiastical portraits found in Latin American private and public collections, nearly all from the eighteenth and early nineteenth centuries. Some present convent administrators standing at their desks while others show exemplary nuns lying on their deathbeds; the latter type was particularly popular in the newly formed Viceroyalty of Nueva Granada, in the region that is today Colombia.[10] A few rare examples, such as likenesses of Sor Juana Inés de la Cruz, picture the nun writing or otherwise engaged in scholarly activity. Most surviving nuns' likenesses are profession portraits commemorating their final vows; this genre was, however, more popular in New Spain than in Peru. And while likenesses of nuns in Discalced Carmelite and other conservative orders are characterized by a general austerity, the profession portraits of the Dominican, Conceptionist, and Hieronymite orders feature the richly dressed crowned nuns, or *monjas coronadas*.

New Spanish painter José de Alcíbar's 1777 *Portrait of María Ignacia de la Sangre de Cristo* (Plate 28) is a technically superior monja coronada portrait. In fact, Alcíbar (d. 1803) is known to have painted more nuns' likenesses than any other New Spanish artist;[11] most portraits however are anonymous. The twenty-two-year-old nun from the Convent of Saint Claire stands in an undescribed interior lavishly dressed to commemorate her vow-taking. Although the figure is rigid and formal, Alcíbar imbued the nun with a plastic liveliness through subtle coloration and chiaroscuro. But the viewer sees little of her body since she wears a richly decorated mantle embroidered with silk thread, and a veil with pearls. She holds a candle ornamented with flowers, a cross, and a crucified pelican piercing his breast. A bouquet in her left hand bears flowers and ribbons, a crucifix, and a painting of John's vision of the Apocalyptic Woman. Her gold crown drips with cut flowers and small figures. In other portraits, professing nuns also wore wedding rings and painted escudos de monjas.

The likenesses of the monjas coronadas are marriage portraits, but these brides marry Christ, not an earthly husband. The groom appears as a small sculpture of the Christ Child (or as the self-sacrificing pelican in this case) to avoid any suggestion of carnal love between the bride and groom. The flowers symbolize beauty and bounty, and represent the nuns' spiritual rather than physical fertility. Their heavy clothes similarly deflect thoughts about their bodies and palm fronds symbolize their virginity. The crown worn by María Ignacia (and by other monjas coronadas) is her reward for triumphing over sin through a life dedicated to God. The crown also identifies her as the bride of the Prince of Peace and the King of Heaven and reminds her of the material world she left behind. Colonial painters may have found inspiration for this iconographic ensemble from Peruvian prints and paintings of Saint Rose of Lima's mystic marriage to the Christ Child.[12]

The final category of viceregal portraits comprises seventeenth- and eighteenth-century likenesses of historical figures. While all portraits have historical value, recording for posterity the sitters' likenesses and attributes, these works represented notable figures, from Inca emperors to Sor Juana Inés de la Cruz, whose praiseworthy lives supported criollo patriotism, indigenous lineages, and the elite colonists' attempt to promote national histories. Therefore, alongside their own images, the elite and their institutions commissioned portraits of figures from Latin America's past. Most of these images reflect the conventions of colonial portraiture, although some painters, freed from painting living or recently deceased sitters, employed a graceful idealization akin to their approach to religious subjects.

The anonymous cuzqueño group portrait known as the *Union of the Descendents of the Inca Empire with the Loyola and Borgia Families* (Figure 91), one of at least seven paintings of the subject, exemplifies the historical portrait type. The painting's inscription elucidates its complicated subject, explaining that don Martín de Loyola, nephew of Saint Ignatius of Loyola, married the Inca ñusta or princess Beatriz. This couple appears in the painting's lower left corner; the bride's family occupies the upper left corner. The couple on the lower right is Martín and Beatriz's daughter, Lorenza, and her husband don Juan de Borgia, son of Jesuit Saint Francis Borgia. Their wedding ceremony appears in the upper right corner of the painting. The two Jesuit saints Ignatius of Loyola and Francis Borgia occupy the center below their order's emblem. Although painted in the eighteenth century, the work represents events that took place two hundred years earlier. In fact, sixteenth-century personalities, especially those associated with the creation of the viceroyalties, were common subjects for this portraiture category.

FIGURE 91.
Cuzco School. *Union of the Descendents of the Inca Empire with the Loyola and Borgia Families.* ca. 1750. Oil on panel. Convent of Nuestra Señora de Copacabana, Lima, Peru. Photograph © The Bridgeman Art Library.

This historical group portrait, painted in the Cuzco school style according to the conventions of viceregal portraiture and offering idealized likenesses based on earlier portraits and the artist's imagination, represents the complicated construction of identity in colonial Latin America. The painting justified and promoted Jesuit involvement in the region by illustrating the familial relationships shared by the order and the Inca imperial dynasty. It likewise embodies the intermarriage of Inca and Spanish political systems through their respective nobilities. The painting consequently represented a Utopian vision of the social and political inextricability of indigenous populations and Spanish political and religious institutions.

Other historical portraits testified to the venerability of Pre-Columbian leaders and the ancient societies they represented, the benevolence of early evangelizers and their importance to the region's introduction of Christianity, and the intellectual prowess of colonial authors, among other themes. The Cuzco school painting *Genealogy of the Inca with the Spanish Monarchs as their Legitimate Imperial Successors* (Figure 92) illustrates the type. The group portrait, one of several of this subject, features the first Inca ruler Manco Capac and his mother Mama Huaco standing above the bust length images of thirteen Inca and nine Spanish monarchs; the genealogy ends with Ferdinand VI (r. 1746–59). Each figure is identified by a lengthy inscription, with Amerindian kings labeled "Inca" and Spanish rulers "Kings of Peru." The sitters each bear the appropriate attributes of rulership. The Inca hold shields and wear tocapu tunics and the Inca crown with its red wool tassel or *maskha paycha*. The Spanish monarchs, dressed in the dark clothes favored by the Iberian court, bear the staff of rule and wear the necklace of the Order of the Golden Fleece around their necks. Only Charles V wears armor and a crown to acknowledge his conquest of Peru. The enthroned figure of Christ above the group offers divine sanction for this imperial lineage.

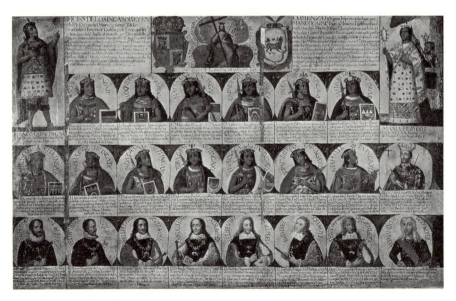

FIGURE 92. Cuzco School. *Genealogy of the Inca with the Spanish Monarchs as Their Legitimate Imperial Successors.* Eighteenth century. Oil on canvas. Convent of Nuestra Señora de Copacabana, Lima, Peru. Photograph © The Bridgeman Art Library.

The painting was commissioned for the Convent of Our Lady of Copacabana in Lima, an institution for noble indigenous women, and clearly promotes the interests of Amerindians before the Spanish crown. It is believed that the papers seen in the hands of Charles II and Philip V are missives the kings authored in defense of native peoples.[13] Unfortunately, whether alone or in groups, many portraits of Pre-Columbian Inca rulers and indigenous post-conquest nobles may have been destroyed by Spanish authorities in the aftermath of the 1780 Tupac Amaru II rebellion. During this bloody uprising, natives decried institutionalized abuses and sought Peru's liberation from Spain. When the insurrection ended, viceregal officials prohibited symbols of indigenous identity, blaming the uprising in part on the government's tolerance of overt signs of Andean heritage and the pernicious influence of the Inca Garcilaso de la Vega's indigenist history, *Royal Commentary on the Inca* (Lisbon 1609).[14] The prohibition offered a tacit acknowledgement of the power of portraits to construct identity and to shape perceptions.

Biombos

Latin American homes contained more than portraits and religious images; many elite interiors included free-standing screens known as *biombos* composed of multiple polychrome canvas panels. The biombos' large size, gilded ornamentation, and complicated narrative and allegorical content brought some of the splendor of viceregal church decoration into private homes. Today the remaining examples offer modern viewers a glimpse of the lavishness of elite palaces. These luxury goods are the most extravagant expression of viceregal secular art and, like portraits, aided the colonial creation of a cultured and sophisticated self-image. Their construction, decoration, sources, and use testify to the hybridity of colonial life, as they conflate Asian, European, and Latin American tastes, materials, and themes.

The biombo's history reflects Latin America's unique position within the Spanish empire. The idea for the painted screens came from Asia via the Philippine Islands and the ships known as the Manila galleons. These Spanish boats began carrying Asian merchandise from Manila to the New Spanish port of Acapulco in 1573. Upon reaching New Spanish shores, the goods were carried by mule to Mexico City and Veracruz, where they embarked for Spain. The Manila galleons carried items collected from all over the Asian continent. Japanese painted screens called *byo-bu* (*byo* meaning protection and *bu* meaning wind) may have appeared among the earliest shipments, since luxury objects appealed to Spanish merchants. The first documented byo-bu (or biombo in Spanish) arrived in 1610 with goods sent to New Spain by the Japanese *shogun* Takugawa Ieyasu; he sent up to ten more to the viceroy of New Spain in 1614.[15] By the seventeenth century, these gifts fueled a fashion for biombos among the viceregal elite; other Japanese screens shipped to Europe during the same period sparked a similar trend. And while it has been suggested that Japanese artists settled in New Spain and taught their art to local painters, it is just as likely that colonial artists simply observed the imported items and used their own ingenuity to build and paint colonial versions.[16]

However they came to practice the art, New Spanish painters produced the majority of known biombos. The genre was apparently not as common among South American artists, although stunning examples, such as the circa 1800 *Hunting Scene in Front of a Palace*, were produced in New Granada. Well-to-do customers in Mexico City purchased imported and local biombos in the Parián market in the city's main square;[17] others undoubtedly commissioned works directly from the artists in the capital, Puebla, Pátzcuaro, Michoacán, and other areas of the viceroyalty. Many Latin American biombos were shipped to Europe as gifts, souvenirs, and merchandise, and Spanish inventories abound with these luxury goods.

Biombos are classified by where they were used in their owners' homes, although the movable objects could be placed anywhere homeowners desired privacy or ornament. Some screens were created for the estrado or parlor, where women entertained their guests seated on pillows—or later, chairs—placed on a low platform. The *biombos rodastrados* framed the sitting area and have been likened to a theatrical backdrop for the elegant reunions.[18] Some biombos rodastrados were merely frames covered in velvet while others offered painted or shell inlay decoration.[19] *Biombos de cama*, as the name suggests, were made for the bedroom. These screens, for obvious reasons, are taller than the biombos rodastrados, measuring up to three meters high compared to the average one to one and a half meter height of the rodastrados. The biombos de cama not only brought color and imagery into the bedroom, but shielded the bed from curious eyes.

FIGURE 93A AND B. Juan Correa. *Meeting of Cortés and Moctezuma.* ca. 1690. Oil on canvas. Photograph © Patrimonio Artístico Banamex/Banco Nacional de México. Mexico City, Mexico.

Colonial biombos adapted Japanese materials and images to the Latin American context. Like the Asian examples, the viceregal screens employed wood frames, but the paintings appeared on wood or canvas panels, not Asian paper or lacquered wood. Latin American biombos comprised four to up to twenty of these panels joined with metal hinges. The screens were painted on one or both sides by the same artists who executed the colony's religious and secular art. Known biombo painters include some of the most renowned artists of the period. And although Juan Correa, Miguel Cabrera, and José Joaquín Magón created beautiful and technically proficient biombos, so too did the anonymous painters responsible for the majority of extant screens. These artists adorned their biombos with molded and gilded stucco and shell inlay, creating glittering frames for the scenes they painted.

Patrons demanded a broad variety of themes for the biombos that decorated their homes. Greco-Roman mythology, allegory, genre, festival scenes, urban views, emblems, and moral lessons appear on remaining examples. The taste for these themes may have derived from contemporary tapestries, which similarly decorated homes and created appropriate settings for elite domestic life.[20] There does not appear to have been any correspondence between a screen's content and its location within the home, however, as battle scenes appeared in bedrooms and amorous mythological couples occupied parlors, and vice versa.[21] Review of four popular themes glimpses the breadth of the imagery with which colonists chose to surround themselves.

The meeting of Cortés and Moctezuma, either with or without scenes of the subsequent battles, appears on several biombos painted in New Spain in the seventeenth century, including Juan Correa's screen in the collection of the Banco Nacional de México (Figures 93a and 93b). Correa (1646–ca. 1716) painted a

single narrative that spans the ten canvas panels. Conquistador Hernán Cortés rides a gray horse on the far right, accompanied by clergymen and well-armed soldiers. Moctezuma, born aloft by Aztec nobles and attended by elegantly dressed courtiers, receives Cortés's gifts on the opposite side. Aztec dancers fill the intervening space on the causeway. A wind-swept Lake Texcoco and the people, wildlife, towns, and mountains of the Valley of Mexico provide the event's backdrop. A gilded flowery border frames the biombo's top and sides, while a trompe l'oeil stone wall above murky brown water appears like the edge of a stage along the bottom.

Correa's decision to frame his narrative like a stage set transformed the meeting of the Aztec and Spanish empires into the historical theater the event had become in the criollo imagination. In late seventeenth- and eighteenth-century New Spain, the criollo elite looked to both their Aztec and European cultural heritages as the twin foundations of their civilization. They identified Cortés as a transitional figure who conquered the great Aztec empire and founded the modern criollo *patria* or nation.[22] By way of comparison, some Peruvian criollos, especially those in Quito, thought likewise of the Pre-Columbian past, albeit to a lesser extent since the persistent visibility and power of indigenous elites made the Inca empire less available for romantic reinvention.[23]

Correa treated Moctezuma, therefore, not as a barbaric tribal leader, but as an ancient ruler and worthy adversary, employing a vocabulary of signs identifiable to criollo and European viewers to embody this role. The Aztec leader wears Roman-style military garb and a European crown. He rests on an ornate throne under an honorific canopy posed like the Roman emperors in contemporary paintings and book illustrations. Moctezuma and his human litter-bearers and attendants, therefore, represent a kind of criollo antiquity. Cortés, on the other hand, appears as a powerful modern leader; his dress, his clerical and military companions, and his mode of transportation identify him as the new political order.

The other side of Correa's biombo presents a similarly theatrical scene. Correa's theme in *The Four Continents* (Figure 94) is allegorical, like many New Spanish biombos. In this case, the allegory represents the known parts of the world, with animals, plants, and royal family groups representing America, Europe, Asia, and Africa. This painting has been associated with prints from Europe, but Juan Correa departed from his sources to fashion the European king into a likeness of Charles II. In fact, the painting may have commemorated the 1683 marriage of the Spanish king and his French bride Marie-Louise d'Orléans.[24] All of the royal families are dressed in opulent, if stereotyped, costumes and their features represent the conventional vision of Africans, Asians, and Native Americans found in contemporary European art. The Amerindian couple, for example, wears feathers and jewels, but careful observation reveals a Roman cuirass and epaulets under the Aztec king's mantle. These additions confirmed the foreign king's nobility for European viewers. Once again, the painting offers an expansive backdrop of idyllic landscapes and hunting vignettes. The arcuated

FIGURE 94. Juan Correa. *The Four Continents*. ca. 1690. Oil on canvas. Photograph © Patrimonio Artístico Banamex/Banco Nacional de México. Mexico City, Mexico.

framing element along the top of the painting and the simulated stone plinth along the bottom repeat the stage-like presentation found on the other side.

The scene of Cortés and Moctezuma on the opposite side of Correa's biombo alters the meaning of *The Four Continents* from the mere reproduction of a popular European theme to a potent statement of criollo patriotism. The allegory locates the modern patria of New Spain, born on the back side of the same painting, within the global stage and, specifically, the Spanish empire. The painting employs the widely recognized vocabulary of European colonialism—stereotyped personifications and exotics plants and animals standing in for non-Western civilizations, and natural bounty available for European exploitation—to claim American participation within a global society. Early modern viewers, accustomed to seeing themselves and their ideas personified by mythological and ancient characters, undoubtedly understood the painting to place America in the great global theater dominated by Charles II and his court.

Biombo imagery also referenced Latin American life and customs directly, and several screens include contemporary genre scenes and views. Some represent colonists engaged in leisure activities and festivals; others offer views of sites such as the New Spanish viceregal palace and the Alameda Park, with colonists of different ethnicities coexisting within the urban domain. Views of the city were particularly popular for screens bearing scenes of the Conquest of Tenochtitlan on the opposite side. The anonymous biombo de estrado in Figure 95 shows Mexico City circa 1700, with the Basilica of Guadalupe at Tepeyac on the left and the *calzadas* or causeways leading to Lake Texcoco's southern shore on the right. The rebuilt Aztec aqueduct from Chapultepec Hill runs along the lower edge of the painting and turns toward the Alameda Park by the Church of San Diego. Although most of the straight thoroughfares are dirt, a few remaining Aztec canals connect the city to the lake. The cathedral and viceregal palace, the latter still showing evidence of a recent attack by rioters, occupy the center of the well-ordered city, and parish churches and convents dot the uniform neighborhoods. An idyllic landscape surrounds the city, and a gilded border filled with flowers and fruits and a simulated stone plinth frame the view.

Paired with the encounter of Cortés and Moctezuma and the battles for the city that followed, the urban view is more than an exercise in civic pride. The screen stands for the creation of New Spain and the civil and orderly life that emerged from the conquest, a theme simultaneously promoted in the writings of criollo patriots. The central position of the cathedral and viceregal palace represents the twin powers that brought clean water, parks, churches, and regulated life to the region. People are notably absent from the city view, omitted so as not to distract from the regularity of the streets and plazas. The Amerindian homes that surrounded central Mexico City are missing as well; these irregular and unseemly huts had no place in the criollo self-image. Despite the greatness of the Aztec warriors who fight bravely on the back of the screen and the widely known descriptions of the Aztec capital and its grid plan, the screen communicates that Mexico City only took shape as an orderly society with the arrival of Spanish secular and canon law. The screen represents another example of the criollo patriots' theatrical self-imagining, in addition to its undeniable value as an idealized record of the city at the turn of the century.

Just as patrons fashioned identity through history paintings and genre scenes, the Latin American elite also surrounded themselves with biombos that communicated their intellectual interests. Themes extracted from ancient mythology and humanist texts decorated wealthy homes; among these, emblem literature was highly fashionable and selections from the moralizing emblems by Flemish scholar Otto van Veen (or Otto Vaenius) appear on at least four

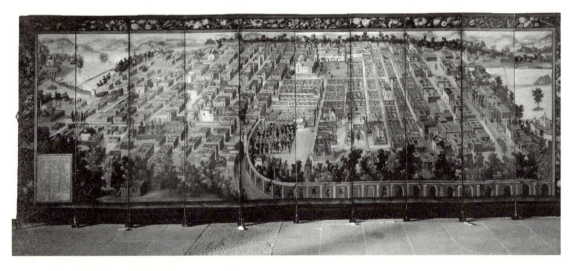

FIGURE 95.
View of Mexico City. Late seventeenth century. Oil on canvas. Photograph © Museo Franz Mayer. Mexico City, Mexico.

eighteenth-century New Spanish biombos. The anonymous screen in the collection of the Dallas Museum of Art (Plate 29) exemplifies the group, although each screen is unique in its composition and selection of emblems.

Each of the eight panels comprising the Dallas biombo bears the motto, image, and poem typical of emblem books, in this case borrowed from Vaenius's text. The images and inscriptions are generally faithful to their sources. For example, one panel bears the motto "Fortune does not hide lineage" and features the crowned monkey and personification of Fortune found in the emblem book. The painter exercised substantial creative freedom in the ornate late-baroque frame he painted around each image, employing the scrolls, asymmetry, and shells employed in contemporary altarscreens and architectural ornamentation. (See Chapter 6.) He was similarly inventive in the areas surrounding the emblematic images; these he painted red and gold and filled with Asiatic-inspired figures to satisfy the growing taste for *chinoiserie* or Chinese-looking objects inspired by the Manila galleon goods.

The paradox of moralizing images painted on luxury goods may have escaped the screen's owners, but this and similar biombos nevertheless present yet another aspect of the elite colonists' carefully cultivated identity. Wealth brought responsibility in colonial Latin America, as society expected elite colonists to embody personal and civic virtue and good behavior. The heirs of ancestral nobilities were widely understood to possess an innate moral rectitude. But Latin America's nouveau riche, whose wealth came from mining or trade, went to great lengths to demonstrate this public role and to justify their right to newly acquired titles and status. Both groups consequently used the biombos bearing moralizing emblems to demonstrate their wealth and their understanding of the responsibilities that came with it.

Casta Paintings

In the early eighteenth century, a type of ethnographic painting emerged in the Latin American viceroyalties. The images presented the colonies' ethnic diversity, which included criollos, Amerindians (often referred to simply as "Indians" or "indios" in these paintings), Black Africans, and myriad racial combinations derived from these three groups. The urge to paint this topic had complex roots, but at its core rested the desire to picture heterogeneous societies, which were largely unknown to Western audiences before Spain's arrival in the Americas. The paintings also represented a society that accorded privileges and rights— such as the right to bear arms or own livestock—by race, and was therefore motivated to identify and maintain racial distinctions.

Voluntary and forced sexual contact with Amerindians began when the first Spaniards arrived in the Americas, despite the crown's desire to maintain separate societies of Spaniards and Amerindians. Miscegenation soon also included Black African slaves brought to the New World to work on large plantations and in wealthy homes. The resulting mixed-race colonists came to be known as the *sociedad de castas* or the society of castes, characterized by a complicated taxonomy containing up to twenty distinct racial combinations, all labeled according to their distinct blood mixtures. For example, a Spaniard and an Amerindian produced a mestizo child; an Amerindian and a Black produced a *Chino Cambujo*. Some of the mixtures combining darker-skinned parents had pejorative and demeaning names, such as the *coyote* child of Amerindian and Mestizo parents. While it should be noted that only the terms Spaniard, Amerindian, Black, mulatto, and mestizo appeared regularly in documents, and even these labels were inconsistently applied, the caste system nevertheless represented an attempt to classify and understand American diversity. In a society that frequently equated race and social status, with the notable exception of indigenous nobility, classifying the sociedad de castas in a hierarchical taxonomy placing Spaniards at the top and Blacks and nomadic Amerindians at the bottom reinforced the notion of Spanish superiority. This imposed social order was similarly articulated in the one hundred known series of casta paintings, all but one of which were made in New Spain.

Casta painters employed a formula exemplified by the circa 1725 series attributed to New Spanish artist Juan Rodríguez Juárez (1675–1746) (Figure 96). Each of the fourteen canvases contains a family group, with parents of different races accompanied by their mixed-blood offspring. The figures are seen to their waists standing before a cloudy sky or, elsewhere in this series, beside buildings. Inscriptions identify the parties' specific ethnic identities. The painter also employed skin color and stereotyped facial features as visual clues to his subjects' ethnicities.

FIGURE 96.
Juan Rodríguez Juárez. *Castas: Español e India, Mestizo.* ca. 1725. Oil on canvas. Photograph © Breamore House, London, England.

Like most casta series, the Rodríguez Juárez painting of the Spanish father and Amerindian mother begins the sequence, not only racially but also economically, and the couple wears garments associated with their ethnicity and social status. Hence the criollo father sports a fashionable French-influenced suit, lace collar, tri-corn hat, and powdered wig. His elite indigenous wife wears a lavishly embroidered huipil or tunic and a head scarf. These garments identify her Amerindian heritage while the pearl jewelry and lace confirm her economic status. And while other castas in Rodríguez Juárez's series do not offer quite the same display of finery, they are nevertheless dressed in the finest clothes available to someone of their station. Hence the paintings suggest that New Spaniards of all races and classes enjoyed comfortable existences within their discrete socio-economic niches.

As in most series, the Rodríguez Juárez casta painting represents a loving family, with the father leading a well-ordered unit. He gazes at the children and offers his infant daughter the paternal caress of a caring head of household. The mother points to her progeny and looks up at her husband, thereby defining her domestic identity. Other mothers in the same series play similar nurturing roles: nursing babies, holding toddlers' hands, serving food, or quieting a tantrum. The fathers engage in more manly behaviors, with an emphasis on work in appropriate trades. Hence the paintings offer an ideal construction of what eighteenth-century viewers considered the natural order of gender relations.[25] And while paintings described below present less harmonious families, the Rodríguez Juárez series and most other casta paintings construct an image of marital stability in accordance with church teachings and social customs, and should therefore recall contemporary religious paintings of the Holy Family or Saint Joseph and the Christ Child (discussed in Chapter 5).

The development of conventions for the new casta painting genre begs the question of why José Rodríguez Juárez and other artists created these series at all. Scholars have offered several theories, all of which point to the paintings as a means of representing Latin America's unique social context and as the fruits of an Enlightenment urge to classify and impose order. Since the mixing of races was virtually unknown in Europe, Spanish colonists and Europeans viewed the practice with suspicion. Many believed that it led to a degraded society and a breakdown of social order. The paintings, reflecting the awkward taxonomy developed to classify the sociedad de castas, presented the opportunity to paint the American people into an orderly socioeconomic hierarchy with criollos firmly in charge, both figuratively and literally as they (and peninsular Spaniards) commissioned the paintings and exercised control over the colony's image found therein.[26] As a result, these series present colonists of all classes in generally harmonious family groups acting according to the behaviors expected of them. The paintings conveyed the message that while Latin America was heterogeneous, its diversity was understood and regulated by colonial authorities. They also allowed European viewers a glimpse of the exotic New World. Notably absent from the series are families of pure Spanish blood, which existed at the pinnacle of colonial society and did not need to be studied or classified since they presented nothing outside the European familial norm.

The Rodríguez Juárez casta paintings also reveal additional information about the role these series played. Between 1711 and 1716, Fernando de Alencastre Noroña y Silva, the viceroy of New Spain, commissioned a series of casta paintings from Rodríguez Juárez to show the Spanish king the viceroyalty's ethnic diversity. While it is not clear whether the series seen here is the result of that commission or another, it nevertheless ended up on European soil like many of the casta series. The New Spanish viceroy was not the only official to send casta paintings across the Atlantic. Documents reveal that several church and crown authorities transported the paintings to Europe, either as souvenirs for themselves or as gifts for others. In 1770 Peruvian Viceroy Manuel Amat y Juniet (1761–76) sent examples of the region's exotic bounty to the Royal Cabinet of Natural History, including twenty casta paintings, coconuts, alpaca wool, and an obsidian-blade sword.[27] The letter accompanying the shipment explained that the viceroy hoped the paintings would enlighten King Charles IV regarding Peru's diverse population. (See Sidebar 19.) Likewise, many casta paintings remain today in private collections in Mexico, suggesting that wealthy families also commissioned the works as evidence of New Spain's unique identity. At least one criollo, however, did not appreciate the image of New Spain the paintings projected. In 1746 Andrés Arce y Miranda wrote to a fellow New Spanish intellectual that the paintings revealed "what harms us, not what benefits us, what dishonors us, not what ennobles us."[28]

Clearly not all elite colonists objected to the casta paintings, since less than two decades after Arce y Miranda's letter, criollo artist Miguel Cabrera (1695–1768) painted one of the most widely admired casta series. The 1763 painting seen here (Plate 30) is the fourteenth image in Cabrera's series and represents the *chamiso* child of mestiza (Spanish and Amerindian) and *castizo* (Spanish and mestizo) parents. The painting employs many of the conventions established by Rodríguez Juárez, including the taxonomic inscription and the intimate family group. The family's threadbare clothing, however, is rustic compared to the garments Cabrera painted for Spaniards, mestizos, and noble Amerindians earlier in the series. This conspicuous poverty appears in three other paintings in Cabrera's series—all similarly low on the racial hierarchy—and was commonly a feature of casta series painted after 1750. Likewise, Cabrera and other painters offered more information about trades in the later casta series, representing Spaniards as members of the leisure class and castas as workers. In this case, the castizo father rolls cigarettes in his humble shop.

The shift in casta painting to represent disadvantaged mixed-race people has been tied to blurred social distinctions in eighteenth-century Latin America and the threat to the colonial social order this represented. Contemporary writers noted that persons of all races dressed in the latest finery as colonists from slaves to nobles wore silks, lace, and jewels. This made it difficult to identify who belonged to which social stratum. Furthermore, skin color could be just as

Letter from the Viceroy of Peru Manuel Amat y Junyent to Crown official Julián de Arriaga accompanying a shipment of casta paintings to the collection of the Royal Cabinet of Natural History (1770).

Your Excellency,

Ardently desiring to contribute to the formation of the Cabinet of Natural History which His Most Serene Prince of Asturias has begun, what I offer will contribute but little to his enlightenment but is one of the principal examples of the rare products found in these parts, the notable mutation of appearance, figure, and color that results from the successive generations of the mixture of Indians and Blacks, which are usually accompanied proportionally by inclinations and properties. With this idea, I ordered copied and sent twenty canvases, described in the accompanying registry; and I will continue urging the completion of these combinations until they are finished, if it is that this humble product of my humility finds some acceptance by Our Prince and Lord by way of Your Excellency's hand. For better understanding, the order of the descendents are graduated by numbers; it should serve as key that the son or daughter of the first couple is, according to his or her sex, father or mother in the next; and that of the next couple in the third, and so on until the end of those which are now copied.

May God preserve Your Excellency for many years.

Lima 13 May 1770 . . . Sr. D. Manuel de Amat

—Pilar Romero de Tejada y Picatoste, "Los cuadros de mestizaje del virrey Amat," in *Los cuadros de mestizaje del Virrey Amat: La representación etnográfica en el Perú colonial* (Lima: Museo de Arte de Lima, 2000), 22. (Translation mine.)

imprecise a measurement as dress, and mixed-race people "passing" for criollos was a constant concern.[29] Consequently, in the fictitious world of casta paintings, artists imposed a visual order on the colonists, clearly articulating the social ranks attached to race and class regardless of the lived realities. If elite patrons could not mandate that castas dress according to their station, they could at least surround themselves with painted castas who did, convincing themselves of the security of the social order upon which they relied for their privileged status.

At the same time, Cabrera and other casta painters active in the later eighteenth century paid greater attention to the manufactured and natural goods accompanying their figures.[30] In the example seen here, Cabrera displays American tobacco products and exotic coconuts; elsewhere in this series he paints armadillos, parrots, tamales, squash, textiles, zapotes, ceramics, and jícamas. Their seemingly superfluous inclusion in the casta paintings can be compared to Viceroy Amat's shipment to the Royal Cabinet of Natural History; now instead of sending exotic American goods along with the casta series to satisfy European curiosity, artists included the natural and man-made items right in the paintings. The practice has also been associated with the criollo patriots' desire to illustrate, as one eighteenth-century author described, "the abundance, wealth, and beauty of this hemisphere."[31] How did they reconcile scenes of human poverty with proof of natural and man-made bounty? It seems that all levels of humanity, even the unfortunate, fit within the natural order of men, manufactured goods, and exotic plants and animals the paintings constructed for the Americas.

The characteristics of late eighteenth-century casta images are most visible in the handful of works, such as Ignacio María Barreda's 1777 example seen here (Plate 31), that employ a single canvas rather than twelve to sixteen separate paintings. Barreda's painting features seventeen casta family groupings contained within painted late-baroque frames; most similar paintings employ similar compartments, although a few works place the subjects in a single continuous space. Barreda began the series with Spanish and Amerindian parents admiring their mestizo child. The Spanish father, as in most casta paintings from the late eighteenth century, shows evidence of his intellectual activity, sitting beside a table bearing writing implements. The mother is once again associated solely with her domestic role. The following six racial groupings, as befit their relatively respectable social standing, engage in leisure activities: picnicking, playing music, or strolling in the fresh air. As the series continues, Barreda's families display less wealth and more manual labor, suggesting that castas work with their bodies, not their minds, and have no time for leisure. Their clothing is correspondingly rustic and their settings more humble. At the same time, they conveniently display examples of local natural and man-made products.

Barreda's painting also displays another characteristic of late eighteenth-century series: misbehavior among the castas. In the thirteenth group, containing a *chino*, *genízaro*, and their *albarazado* child, the painter shows family disharmony. The parents grasp each other by the hair and the father seems about to hit the mother with a rock. In other casta paintings from this era, parents similarly attack each other while their children watch, perhaps the most famous being Andrés de Islas's mulatta mother who raises a mallet to strike her Spanish husband. These violent episodes entered into the series to represent the moral character late eighteenth-century New Spanish society associated with the sociedad de castas, and particularly to the ethnic mixtures including African blood.[32] Another series explained these expected behaviors, noting that mestizos were humble and plainspoken, whereas cambujos were "slow, lazy, and cumbersome."[33]

If we accept that the casta paintings were created to present an image of a well-ordered society, we may ask how misbehaving castas contributed. At one level, the misbehavior was entertainment, as European art since the seventeenth century employed fighting beggars and irate low-class wives as amusement.

The casta paintings merely added a racial dimension to an established tradition. At a more profound level, it has been suggested that the misbehaving castas appeared in the paintings as part of a criollo desire to understand and control the perceived casta nature, to distinguish and classify more completely than earlier paintings that only employed physical features and dress. Misbehaving castas also illustrated the atmosphere that inspired the social reforms initiated by the Bourbon kings in the latter eighteenth century.[34]

The last group in Barreda's casta painting, as in all known series, represents stereotyped nomadic Amerindians, not unlike the couple personifying the Americas in Correa's *The Four Continents*. The figures wear feather skirts and headdresses and carry bows and arrows, despite the fact that Barreda and other casta painters must have known that nomadic Amerindians did not wear this costume. Instead it appears that this stereotype developed as a sign of nomadic lifestyle and distance from civilized urban centers. This unreal image may also have been a strategy to make the un-Christianized nomads, known generically as Chichimecs, seem far away and unthreatening despite the fact that Amerindian raids plagued contemporary northern New Spain.[35] Barreda's painting confirms this identity with the inscription reading, "*[Chichi]mecos* and *[Chichi]mecas*, whose Castas, though many, are all the same." In other words, Barreda's inscription states that while there were many different nomadic tribes in New Spain, they were all alike; his image suggests that they were all keeping to themselves in the wilderness, and far from threatening the colonial social order. As proof, Barreda superimposed the nomads over a landscape containing the renowned recreational areas of Chapultepec, Iztacalco, and Jamaica. Creoles and castas frolic among central New Spain's natural resources and man-made marvels: towns, churches, and the famous Chapultepec aqueduct. Hence the painting, like all casta series, offers an image of an orderly and abundant patria whose diverse populations acted according to their stations. Like the other secular themes examined here, the casta paintings offered Latin America's elite colonists the opportunity to construct their own identity and prove their worth on the global stage. These feelings would, of course, lead to the independence movements soon to transform both American continents.

Art and Architecture
at the End of the Colonial Era

In 1753, New Spanish painter José de Ibarra (1685–1756) and several colleagues petitioned the viceregal government for recognition of their newly formed Academy of Painters. Modeled after the Royal Academy of San Fernando in Madrid, the group met twice a week to "better instruct themselves in [painting] by the correction some [painters] offered others and the order and principles veteran painters offered beginners."[1] The criticism and instruction undoubtedly promoted the classicizing late-baroque painting style Ibarra, Miguel Cabrera, Juan Patricio Morlete Ruiz, and other members practiced. The foundation petition noted that the academy would not only benefit the painters, but would also improve the quality of New Spanish religious art, appealing to the crown's enlightened attitude toward art in the public interest. The members also requested the privileges afforded peninsular academicians, including freedom from guild restrictions. The age of the guilds had waned and these eighteenth-century artists sought the intellectual and social status academic affiliation afforded. Although Ibarra's academy did not attract the royal support it requested, it nevertheless represented the nascent interest in modernizing artistic training and practices in the viceroyalty.

Not long after Ibarra's academy disbanded, engraver José Mariano Navarro (1742–ca. 1809) proved that the academic spirit extended beyond the painting profession. In 1771, Navarro inscribed a message at the foot of an engraved anatomy study that spoke of the printmaker's professional consciousness. Next to a nude male figure adapted from a treatise by Spanish academician Antonio Palomino, Navarro wrote, "This [print] can be found at Navarro's house in front of the Royal Mint where a meeting or pictorial debate is held among some *aficionados*. Those who wish to honor me with their attendance will be well received: some to teach and others to be taught. God grants His gifts and each reaps what He sows."[2] Navarro's message suggests that the engraver's group followed the model of Renaissance academies, where artists met to consider their discipline, not a modern art school with a stable faculty dedicated to teaching youngsters entering the profession. For Navarro, the organization may have seemed particularly useful, since printmakers did not belong to a guild and therefore had no other professional organization advocating for their interests. He likely also hoped to elevate his discipline's social status, as printmaking enjoyed only modest esteem. While we may never know who attended Navarro's gatherings, the inscription confirms a new artistic self-consciousness that would spread throughout Spain's American colonies.

This final chapter considers art and architecture created in the final years of the colonial period. The chapter begins with the foundation of the Royal Academy of San Carlos and the introduction of neoclassical forms to New Spain. It then considers the exploration of the new style in South America by architects and artists, some of whom accompanied scientific expeditions. The chapter ends with several examples of neoclassical painting and architecture in the viceroyalties of Peru, La Plata, and New Granada.

The Royal Academy of San Carlos

The history of Latin America's first art academy began in 1778 when Jerónimo Antonio Gil (1731–98), a member of the Royal Academy of San Fernando in Madrid, traveled to Mexico City to engrave coins and medals at the Royal Mint. Gil also trained the mint's engravers and offered evening drawing classes to all interested students. These sessions became so popular that Gil and mint director Fernando José Mangino petitioned the viceroy for a true art academy in Mexico City. Their request cited the prospective students' enthusiasm and the aid an academy might offer local industries.[3] Their planned institution, like the Spanish academies of San Fernando in Madrid and San Carlos in Valencia, was modeled on the French Académie Royale de Peinture et de Sculpture, a state-sponsored art school and manufacturing center established in 1648, which aimed to improve manufacturing skills, promote an official art, and wrest production away from the guilds.[4] Viceroy Martín de Mayorga granted Gil's request and classes at the so-called Provisional School began in 1781. Spanish King Charles III's approval of the Royal Academy of the Three Noble Arts of San Carlos followed in 1783 and the school inaugurated its governing statutes in 1785. (See Sidebar 20.)

Gil initially staffed the academy with New Spanish artists, but soon replaced the local professors with Spanish academicians. In doing so, he participated in the centralization promoted by King Charles III's reforms discussed in Chapter 6, and ensured that the New Spanish academy reflected peninsular rather than local tastes. The first peninsular faculty, including architect Antonio González Velázquez (ca. 1765–1810) and painters Ginés de Andrés y de Aguirre and Cosme de Acuña y Troncoso, arrived in 1786; engraver José Joaquín Fabregat (1748–1807) followed in 1788. Sculptor Manuel Tolsá (1757–1816) began his long academic

Excerpts of the Statutes of the Royal Academy of San Carlos (1785)

ARTICLE 8. INDIVIDUAL DIRECTORS [OF AREAS OF STUDY]

1. The obligation of the Directors is to help the Academy to direct study in their profession, according to the information given to them by the Secretary selected by the [committee known as the] Junta ordinaria.

. . .

3. It is my will that the Directors and Lieutenants work with and teach the Students, of whatever class or condition they may be, with the greatest love and patience, so that, attracted by this warm and caring environment, they apply themselves with greater fervor . . .

ARTICLE 9. DIRECTORS OF PAINTING AND SCULPTURE

[1.] They will alternate monthly in the Natural or live model [life drawing] room . . .

2. It is their duty to correct the students' drawings and models, teaching them and giving them the appropriate materials.

ARTICLE 10. DIRECTORS OF ARCHITECTURE AND MATHEMATICS

1. So that the study of Architecture may proceed with the perfection I desire, and so that the rest of the Arts and Trades receive the help that Mathematics may provide them, it is my will that they may be taught as much as possible, by two Directors of Mathematics and another two of Architecture.

2. All [of the Directors of Architecture and Mathematics] shall explain the necessary and useful practices in these Sciences, as much for the greater perfection of Architecture as for the perfection of the other arts and trades . . .

3. In the practices that are necessary for the discipline's complete intelligence, the Directors are to assist the Disciples, taking them to exercise on sites or drilling them in the classrooms, as the material requires.

4. One will take special care in the teaching of Architecture with its principal areas of strength, comfort, and beauty, teaching his Disciples, not just in the knowledge and practice of drawing and the rules of good taste, but also principally in the fundamentals that the situation dictates for the solidity and comfort of the Buildings.

. . .

ARTICLE 18. DISCIPLES

1. In the beginners' room shall be admitted without distinction anyone who appears, either with the purpose of completing study in any of the three Arts

[Painting, Sculpture, or Architecture], or Engraving, or with the desire to acquire only the drawing skills necessary to later learn any trade.

2. Drawings shall be presented at the monthly meetings of the Junta ordinaria by those Disciples who have progressed sufficiently to proceed to the next room [stage of study] in the opinion of the Lieutenant Director. Once the drawings are examined by the faculty in whose area the student is inclined, it shall be decided whether he may pass to the Gesso Modeling class . . .

3. Only those who have obtained a passing mark in the Junta ordinaria shall pass from the beginners' class to the Gesso Modeling class . . .

4. The Life Drawing class shall follow the same routine to admit Disciples as described above for the admission to the Gesso Modeling class, so long as the Junta ordinaria agrees that they deserve to pass.

. . .

9. All Spanish Disciples from these Territories and from the Indies may obtain positions as Academicians and other jobs within the Academy.

ARTICLE 19. PENSIONED DISCIPLES.

1. So that we may not lose many talented Youngsters, who abandon their study of the Arts since they do not have any means of subsistence beyond their physical labor, it is my will that the Academy select for now four Disciples of Painting, four of Sculpture, four of Architecture, two in Printmaking, and two in Medal Engraving, with an annual pension sufficient to maintain them, so that they may dedicate all their time to the abovementioned Arts.

2. The essential qualities that these chosen pensioners must have are that they be Spaniards born in those Territories or these, with the necessary and perpetual inclusion of four pure New Spanish Indians who apply themselves to any of the Arts at the Institute of the Academy, being all poor and with the necessary skills: such that being very poor, but not skilled, the student should not receive a pension: and although he be skilled, but not poor, neither shall he receive one.

. . .

6. It is my will that each Pensioner enjoy his pension for a period of twelve years, which is more than sufficient time, with continuous application, to acquire the necessary perfection in his Art, and to support himself with his efforts.

> —From *Proyecto, estatutos y demás documentos relacionados al establecimiento de la Real Academia de pintura, escultura y arquitectura denominada de San Carlos de Nueva España (1781–1802)*, ed. David Marley, xxiii–xl, Colección Documenta Novae Hispaniae (Mexico City: Rolston-Bain, 1984). (Translation mine.)

tenure in Mexico in 1790, and painter Rafael Ximeno y Planes (ca. 1759–1825) arrived in 1796. Other European faculty continued to cross the Atlantic throughout the nineteenth century, even after Mexico's independence from Spain.

The spirit of the academy's foundation is visualized in Andrés López's 1790 portrait of *Viceroy Matías de Gálvez*, who oversaw the academy's royal inauguration in late 1783. The painting features the king's representative, who stands triumphant in the painting's foreground, holding a walking stick as his staff of power. The stiff pose, an attribute-laden table, and a velvet curtain reflect traditional colonial portraiture practices. López (ac. 1763–1811), an academy instructor, imbued his sitter with great personality as Gálvez looks out with an administrator's steely gaze. Standing under the viceroy's paternal hand, two dark-skinned youngsters scurry through the academy halls carrying their drawing papers and portfolios. Their tattered clothes represent the barbaric state the academics ascribed to the local arts professions and to the childlike artists who required retraining in proper academic tastes. This training occurs in the painting's background, where a dark-skinned, semi-nude Amerindian student and his well-dressed criollo classmate study a plaster reproduction of a Greco-Roman sculpture. The painting's message is clear: Gálvez and the Spanish government brought civilization and civility to an uncouth yet grateful New Spanish arts community, trading the chaotic and disorderly baroque for the edifying and ennobling neoclassicism.

As the Gálvez portrait illustrates, training at the New Spanish academy emphasized drawing. Gil promoted drawing as a means to acquire what he called "solid principles," classical values, and a scientific approach to art making—that is, the science of drawing an illusionistic human figure within a perspectival space.[5] This approach was not unknown to New Spanish artists, who were familiar with the classicizing manner of Miguel Cabrera and other mid-eighteenth-century painters. But Gil and the other academy faculty had little regard for local art, writing, "All of the abuses caused by ignorance . . . cause horror . . . in effigies, altarscreens, and public shrines. We see nothing but our own dishonor in the hands of Indians, Spaniards, and Blacks who aspire without rules or fundament to imitate Holy Objects."[6] In other words, the local artists lacked the "rules or fundament" of classical art. To rid New Spain of this unruly baroque style, Gil and his faculty used drawing to impose a new taste. Of course, drawing was not simply useful for artists, but also for engineers, craftsmen, and all other design-based professions. Hence academic principles could extend well beyond the fine arts. The academy, therefore, transformed New Spanish tastes even beyond the noble arts of painting, sculpture, and architecture; its rigorous classicizing spirit soon affected many other aspects of colonial society.

Academy students in all disciplines began by copying imported prints and drawings by the faculty, invariably of religious or mythological themes. With the approval of the governing board, students were then allowed to draw from plaster casts of Greco-Roman and Renaissance sculpture. Another round of approvals permitted students to begin drawing live models.[7] At the same time, the youngsters studied mathematics, anatomy, geometry, and perspective, depending upon their chosen discipline. A 1795 report revealed that by the time students left the academy, they were familiar with the writings of the Roman architect Marcus Vitruvius, Renaissance architectural theorist Giacomo Vignola, German artist Albrecht Dürer, Flemish anatomist Andreas Vesalius, and Spanish academician Antonio Palomino.[8] In other words, the academic training, which lasted twelve years, produced students properly educated in the style, content, and ennobling purpose of classical art. Some of the students who enjoyed prosperous careers following their training included Ximeno y Planes's pupil José María Vázquez (ac. 1790–1822), a respected portraitist; sculptor Pedro Patiño Ixtolinque (1774–1834), who directed the academy after independence; and the engraver José María Montes de Oca, who published a famous illustrated book on the life of Saint Philip of Jesus.

The Spanish faculty reshaped the artistic landscape in New Spain during the viceregal era. The 1796 renovation of Mexico City's main square (Figure 97) and its *Equestrian Portrait of Charles IV* (Figure 98) by sculpture professor Manuel Tolsá (1757–1816), symbolized the transformation. Emulating Michelangelo's redesigned Campidoglio and the Parisian Place Royale, academy architect Antonio González Velázquez designed near the plaza's center an elliptical enclosure with a radiating stone pattern and a gated balustrade. Emerging from the bustling urban center and separated from the plaza mayor's chaotic marketplace, the ellipse was an orderly statement of academic artistic and cultural authority, imposed on the site where Cortés recreated Tenochtitlan as colonial Mexico City nearly three centuries earlier. The 1796 engraving by José Joaquín Fabregat seen here recorded the transformation for posterity; colonists purchased the print to demonstrate their loyalty.

FIGURE 97.
José Joaquín Fabregat. *View of the Zócalo.* 1796. Engraving. Photograph © Nettie Lee Benson Latin American Collection, University of Texas, Austin.

FIGURE 98. Manuel Tolsá. *Equestrian Portrait of Charles IV*. 1796–1803. Bronze. Mexico City, Mexico. Photograph © Kelly Donahue-Wallace.

Tolsá's sculpture occupied the center of the renovated square, although it was not installed until 1803. Like the stonework, the sculpture referenced the Campidoglio and its equestrian portrait of Marcus Aurelius. The Roman bronze sculpture, long thought to represent the Christian emperor Constantine, had inspired similar monuments since antiquity, including François Girardon's 1699 monument to Louis XIV on the Place Royale, and continued to be a favorite means of communicating royal or imperial power. Tolsá's colossal bronze sculpture, popularly known as "El Caballito" or "The Little Horse," employs the standard iconography of this honorific genre. It features the Spanish King Charles IV, dressed as a Roman emperor in breastplate, greaves, and cape. The wreath on his head and the short baton he holds in his right hand similarly identify his imperial status. To balance the king's robust figure, Tolsá sculpted an equally massive horse that both flattered Charles and symbolized his strength. The horse, operating here as in other equestrian monuments, walks forward and strains slightly at his bit, suggesting that his animal power is controlled by Charles's command and authority. His back hoof rests just above an Aztec sword, referring to Spain's authority over the colonized Americas.

Before Tolsá's arrival, lost-wax, hollow-cast bronze sculpture was largely unknown in colonial Latin America, where polychrome wood was the preferred medium for full-round images and stone reliefs adorned architectural façades. The huge sculpture, almost sixteen feet tall, was cast in a single mold and weighed over 6,000 pounds.[9] Difficulties acquiring materials meant that Tolsá's sculpture was not ready for the square's 1796 renovation; a wood and plaster model covered in gold leaf stood in its stead for the inauguration. When finally ready in 1803, the immense sculpture took four days to travel from the academy to the main square—a distance of less than one mile. The sculpture was placed on a tall pedestal from which it proclaimed New Spain's allegiance to Spain and reminded viewers of their position within the Spanish empire.[10]

Today El Caballito faces another of Tolsá's efforts in the New Spanish capital. The Palace of Mining (Figure 99), built between 1797 and 1813, began Tolsá's architectural career. The designs he submitted for the government building led his colleagues to proclaim him Academic of Merit in Architecture despite his training as a sculptor. Of course, academicians believed that drawing was the root of all arts, so even a sculptor possessed sufficient aptitude to pursue other design projects.

Tolsá's structure exhibits a keen understanding of the principles of classical architecture. The symmetrical façade of the massive Palace of Mining is organized like a Renaissance palazzo, with a rusticated lower level, a more refined second story, and an elegant *piano nobile*. A restrained vocabulary of classicizing architectural elements adorns the façade, including a central portico with its pediment topping Ionic-order columns and lateral entries with Doric porticoes. Traces of baroque tastes persist, however, as Tolsá employed broken

FIGURE 99.
Manuel Tolsá.
Palace of Mining.
1797–1813. Mexico
City, Mexico.
Photograph
© Kelly Donahue-
Wallace.

and rounded pediments, spatial and rhythmic dynamism, and a hierarchy of architectural elements; Tolsá applied a similarly eclectic approach to his work on the Mexico City Cathedral and several renovation projects in the capital and beyond.

The Palace of Mining's regular exterior belies a somewhat irregular interior plan, however, perhaps the result of the functional demands of a building that sheltered dormitories, shops, offices, a chapel, and reception halls. The interior ornamentation is generally restrained; some areas have no decoration beyond the simple beauty of their columns, pilasters, arches, and other architectural elements. The chapel, on the other hand, is richly plastic, with Tolsá's sculptural elaboration of the walls' surfaces and paintings by academic painter Rafael Ximeno y Planes. The monumental staircase is similarly ornate, with its vaulted and painted ceiling.

Rafael Ximeno y Planes's tempera paintings for the chapel in Tolsá's Palace of Mining reveal a similarly ornate interpretation of neoclassical art. The academy professor (1759–1825) painted the large canvases in 1809 for the coved chapel ceiling. *The Miracle of the Well*, 1809 (Plate 32), features the Virgin of Guadalupe (the patron saint of mining), Bishop Juan de Zumárraga, and native onlookers on Tepeyac hill. The Virgin Mary hovers above the site of her new shrine, as the assembled group views the natural spring she sent as a sign of her selection. Ximeno's painting is composed according to academic principles. The focal point appears in the center and all framing elements and figures point or gesture toward the miracle. Zumárraga, the spring, and the Virgin of Guadalupe form a clear axis linking New Spain to the heavens. Ximeno also carefully distinguished unconverted Amerindians from the converted Juan Diego, painting the former in the nude and the latter fully dressed in his characteristic tilma. Unlike New Spanish baroque artists, Ximeno restricted his use of angels to a small group hovering around the Virgin Mary. In place of more of these figures, Ximeno filled much of the painting with a brilliant and luminous cloudscape, suggesting God's presence through nature rather than his angelic representatives. Classicism also appears in the idealized figures, especially the Amerindians distinguished by their hairstyles and dark skin tones; each figure's pose and gesture pantomimes his or her role in the narrative.

Like the renovation of Mexico City's main square, the Palace of Mining, which was home to the Royal Mining Office and its engineering school, made a potent political statement about New Spain at the end of the colonial era. Mining was essential to the colony's wealth, and minerals extracted from New Spanish mines supported the dismal Spanish economy. The engineering education the government offered mining students led to improvements in mining technologies, including better extraction and refining methods developed by local engineers, thereby bolstering New Spain's economy with peninsular help. The chapel's painting of the Virgin of Guadalupe spoke to this nationalism and the criollo promotion of the Virgin of Guadalupe as proof of God's love for the New Spanish nation. Hence, like the Royal Academy of San Carlos, the Palace of Mining stood simultaneously for New Spain's industrial modernization, its fealty to Spain, and its self-promotion.

Academic principles were not confined to the academy. As academic credentials replaced guild affiliation, local artists sought the title of Academic of Merit granted by the institution's faculty. At the same time, the academy ensured that major building and other commissions conformed to neoclassical principles.[11] Academy statutes required that "before beginning any work, whether church, convent, or other considerable building they [the architects] must present their plans to the Junta Superior de Gobierno [the governing body of the academy] and submit, without objection or excuse whatsoever, to the corrections made in them, and with the warning that in case of resistance they will be severely chastised."[12] Hence all major building projects in New Spain were to adopt the neoclassical style. Renovations of many colonial church interiors soon traded gilded baroque altarscreens and polychrome sculpture for gold-trimmed white retables with a decidedly more architectural appearance. It should be noted, however, that some architects, notably Francisco Antonio Guerrero y Torres (1727–92), the architect of El Pocito discussed in Chapter 6, avoided academy involvement in their endeavors.[13]

Francisco Eduardo Tresguerras's Church of Nuestra Señora del Carmen in Celaya, Guanajuato (1802–7) represents the spread of neoclassicism beyond Mexico City. Tresguerras (1759–1833) may have spent only a year at the Royal

FIGURE 100. Francisco Eduardo Tresguerras. Church of Nuestra Señora del Carmen. 1802–7. Celaya, Mexico. Photograph © Ron Savage, photographersdirect.com.

Academy of San Carlos when he was already in his thirties, but his architecture, paintings, and engravings demonstrate his self-taught neoclassicism and the Latin American eclectic approach. While the church's cruciform plan differs little from the parish church type discussed in Chapter 4, its exterior and its interior surface elaboration reveal a radical formal shift. The façade (Figure 100), for example, features a Doric-order portico. Resting above the attic story, however, a colossal tower violates the principles of classical scale and proportion, dwarfing the portico as it rises nearly one hundred feet into the air. Tiny volutes that awkwardly join the lower story and the tower represent a further departure from classical norms. Tresguerras defended his eclectic approach, writing in a local newspaper, "[T]he architect cannot be satisfied with an insipid monotony and better to be condemned for excessive license . . . because variety produces beauty, harmony, and an orderly disorder."[14] Eclectic or not, the neoclassical approach would dominate New Spanish architecture for most of the following century.

Neoclassical Art in the Viceroyalties of Peru, New Granada, and La Plata

Art in the South American viceroyalties of Peru, New Granada, and La Plata in the decades leading up to independence from Spain shared in the neoclassical approach. As in New Spain, the new direction was promoted by foreign artists, but in South America these European artists did not arrive to inaugurate a royal art academy. In fact, South America did not have an official art academy to rival Mexico City's Academy of San Carlos during the colonial era; a proposed art school for the Viceroyalty of New Granada never opened. The Academy of San Ildefonso in Lima reached the point of developing statutes, but the institution never materialized.[15] Another limeño drawing and painting school directed by quiteño painter Javier Cortés opened at the very end of the colonial era, but too close to the independence struggles to have much impact.[16]

South America did offer private drawing schools and academies of industrial arts, such as the Academy of San Luis in Santiago de Chile in the Viceroyalty of La Plata, which opened its doors in 1797 under the direction of Manuel de Salas y Corbalán.[17] The Society of Jesus also operated a private art and craft school outside Santiago de Chile from 1748 to 1767.[18] Drawing schools were also attached to research expeditions conducted by the Spanish government to explore the new lands. In 1786, the School of Drawing opened in Mariquita, Ecuador, to prepare artists for a botanical expedition led by José Celestino Mutis; the school moved to Santa Fe de Bogotá in 1791, where it trained up to thirty-two students.[19] In the next two decades, Mutis's artists produced thousands of watercolor renderings of American flora.

Sevillan José Joaquín del Pozo (ca. 1757–1821), a painter from the Royal Academy of the Three Noble Arts in Sevilla, joined the Alejandro Malaspina expedition when it departed from Cádiz in 1789.[20] His purpose was to draw the flora, fauna, and geography encountered during Malaspina's global circumnavigation, making scientific study of the lands and peoples he encountered. The five-year journey only reached the South Pacific before turning back. It nevertheless embodied the Spanish crown's promotion of Enlightenment principles of systematic exploration and scientific study, as well as Spain's desire to match expeditions undertaken under English and French flags. Pozo and the five artists accompanying the expedition were essential to the mission's success, since they provided the visual record of Spain's engagement with enlightened global exploration. Among the other expedition artists were the talented autodidact cabin boy José Cardero, who provided the most images, and Tomás de Suria, an engraver at the Royal Mint in Mexico City and Jerónimo Antonio Gil's protégé, who joined the expedition in Acapulco in 1791. Suria's journal and drawings of the American Pacific coast are the earliest pictorial record of this part of the world and remain a valuable source for the study of US Northwest coast native peoples.

Pozo's 1789 *Encounter with the Patagonians* (Figure 101) numbers among the Malaspina expedition's narrative vignettes rather than scientific studies. The pencil and charcoal drawing depicts a casual shoreline meeting between Spanish sailors and the never-before-drawn Patagonian peoples. The Amerindians are dressed in fur wraps and boots, and ride horses; the expedition's officers and crew appear in naval uniforms. The interaction between the two cultures is amiable, and several Patagonians chat with the Spaniards, who are armed but clearly not concerned for their safety. Dogs and children mingle with the group to confirm the pacific scene.

Pozo's drawing may appear casual, as if the artist captured a lived moment, but the image is far from documentary. Like other drawings, this one was sketched on site and "finished" later. The final preparation altered the observed

Concurrencia con los Patagones en el Puerto Deseado.

FIGURE 101. José del Pozo. *Encounter with the Patagonians*. 1789. Pencil and charcoal on paper. Photograph © Museo Naval. Madrid, Spain.

action and figures to create a composition with greater artistic merit—that is, Pozo applied artistic criteria to his rendering of the historical moment.[21] He gave the Patagonians classically proportioned figures and composed the scene according to eighteenth-century academic genre strategies, including the children and dogs.[22] Likewise, there is little ethnic specificity in the Patagonians' likenesses; they appear instead simply as non-Europeans, slightly darker and with rounder faces than the Spaniards. Hence, it is clear that even tasked with recording nature, Pozo could not shed his academic training and the "good taste" he acquired by studying classical models as a youth. For the finished drawing, Pozo subjected the events he witnessed to the filter of his artistry to translate the event into a legible allegory of Spanish enlightened curiosity and good will.

When Malaspina's ships reached Lima's port of Callao in 1790, Pozo abandoned the expedition, either due to poor health or, according to Malaspina's journal, because the artist was insufficiently prepared for the rigors of naval life; the cabin boy Cardero assumed his duties.[23] Pozo remained in Lima, where his academic credentials mattered more to the limeño elite than his disaffection for military rigor. Hence, Pozo established a private drawing and painting school in 1791, which became Peru's first art school to receive viceregal approval.[24] The painter subsequently received many commissions for portraits and religious paintings; his most famous surviving work from this period is the *Annunciation*, a Murillo-inspired painting in the Rosary Chapel at the Church of Santo Domingo in Lima.

The academic principles Pozo brought to the Peruvian capital were not unfamiliar to limeño art patrons. Spanish painter and architect Matías Maestro (1776–1835) arrived in the late eighteenth century and introduced neoclassicism to Lima. Almost immediately upon arrival, Maestro embarked on a campaign to impose the new style, replacing baroque altarscreens and renovating many of the city's churches that had been damaged in a devastating 1746 earthquake. Between 1803 and 1805, Maestro replaced several altarscreens in the Church of San Francisco (discussed in Chapter 4), including the main retablo at a cost of 30,000 pesos.[25] Maestro and other classicizing painters working in Lima produced portraits, religious works, and even casta paintings, but they had little influence beyond the court; Cuzco school painting still found wide approval and saw broad distribution.

Peruvian painter José Gil de Castro (1785–1841), known as "El Mulatto," may have trained with Pozo or learned to draw as part of his military training.[26] Whatever the source of his education, Gil de Castro put his talents to work as a portraitist in late colonial Lima. Between 1810 and 1825, he worked in Santiago de Chile in the Viceroyalty of La Plata, achieving the status of Maestro Mayor in the Santiago painters' guild in 1816. The painter also continued his military service in the corps of engineers, and worked on behalf of liberation from Spain. Gil de Castro's military career undoubtedly provided him access to the criollo elite in both his homeland and in Chile. The local heroes of independence from Spain numbered among the artist's sitters; Gil de Castro painted six likenesses of Simón Bolívar, nine portraits of Argentine hero José de San Martín, and four of Chilean liberator Bernardo O'Higgins.

Gil de Castro's 1820 portrait of *Capitan General Bernardo O'Higgins* (Figure 102), painted two years after Chile's liberation from Spain, illustrates South American independence-era portraiture strategies. The painting features the figure of independent Chile's first leader gazing directly at the viewer. His large body, clad in military garb, fills the picture plane. No longer fighting for liberation, O'Higgins holds his plumed hat under his left arm and his sword rests at his side. He holds a paper in his right hand; this is presumably Chile's Act of Independence, which O'Higgins signed in 1817. The inscription at the bottom of the painting identifies the sitter. The background, which may have been embellished after Gil de Castro finished the painting, portrays the 1817 Battle of Chacabuco, following which O'Higgins was declared Director Supreme of the Nation. Gil de Castro's painting preserves the formality and rigidity of traditional colonial portraiture; his painting privileges his sitter's facial topography and the details of his symbolically potent wardrobe. Evidence of neoclassical tastes includes O'Higgins's fashionable hairstyle and military uniform, and

FIGURE 102.
José Gil de Castro.
*Capitan General
Bernardo O'Higgins.*
1820. Oil on canvas.
Photograph © Museo
Histórico Nacional.
Santiago, Chile.

the absence of ornament and overt heraldry. The figure's flatness and awkward proportions—features seen in many period portraits—likely testify as much to his patrons' preference for formality and tradition as to the painter's limited technical proficiency.

Neoclassical architecture arrived in South America with Europeans as well. Builders from the Royal Corps of Military Engineers constructed fortifications and other civic monuments according to classical principles; the new palace of the viceroy of New Granada in Bogotá numbers among their more famous works.[27] The Captaincy General of Chile in the Viceroyalty of La Plata, which had previously enjoyed the German Baroque influence of the Jesuits who staffed the order's art and craft academy until their 1767 expulsion, also built several neoclassical projects. Sometime after taking office in 1775, Chile's Governor Agustín de Jáuregui y Aldecoa requested an architect from Madrid to execute several major civic projects, including the Royal Mint and the Santiago Cathedral.[28] Like the new buildings and renovations made by the academics in Mexico City, this building program promoted a modern and enlightened image of the centralized government.

Joaquín Toesca y Ricci (ac. 1754–99), an Italian architect who had worked for Charles III in Naples and followed the monarch to Madrid for his 1760 coronation, reached Santiago in 1780. His first project in the Chilean city was to complete the cathedral, which he encased in a classicizing shell. Toesca's cathedral façade employs a classicizing vocabulary of pilasters, porticoes and pediments imaginatively combined for decorative effect. But the Royal Mint commission permitted the architect to exercise more completely his neoclassical vision.

Soon after his arrival, Toesca submitted drawings for the new mint. Construction began two years later and lasted beyond the architect's 1799 death. The immense façade (Figure 103), which runs the length of a city block, employs a severe classical vocabulary. It is symmetrical and unornamented, with colossal paired pilasters spanning its two stories and a balustrade along the roofline. The central doorway is reminiscent of Roman triumphal arches, with paired engaged columns flanking an arched opening topped by a triangular pediment. The deep recessions between the strongly projecting pilasters and columns create a dramatic chiaroscuro. The façade's regularity is echoed in the plan, which locates offices, living quarters, and workshops around a series of orderly patios and passageways.

Like Manuel Tolsá's Palace of Mining in Mexico City, Toesca's mint embodied the state's authority. Manufacturing coins bearing the likeness of the king, the building reinforced Santiago's colonial relationship to the metropolis. Its currency guaranteed an economic lingua franca, as all Spanish subjects employed identical weights and measures in the marketplace. Hence the building stood as a monument to the unity of the vast Spanish empire. Its neoclassical style evoked the same aura of governmental authority inherited from Roman antiquity that informed contemporary monuments in Europe and the Americas. The classical forms and their associated meaning undoubtedly inspired Chilean politicians to

FIGURE 103. Joaquín Toesca. Royal Mint. 1782. Santiago de Chile. Photograph © Kelly Donahue-Wallace.

use Toesca's structure as a mint, government office building, and, now, presidential palace.[29]

Another European, Spanish Capuchin friar and architect Domingo Petrés (1759–1811), helped establish neoclassicism as the official style in the Viceroyalty of New Granada. Soon after his 1792 arrival, Petrés engaged religious and civic projects, including the first observatory in the Americas, constructed for José Celestino Mutis in the Garden of the Botanical Expedition. His work on the Bogotá Cathedral, however, remains his most enduring legacy.

The Cathedral of Santa Fe de Bogotá, like most colonial cathedrals, has a long and complicated history. By the time fray Domingo Petrés began his work in 1807, the structure had undergone at least three major construction phases. The last effort, by military engineer Domingo Esquaqui, suffered damage in an 1805 earthquake, which Petrés had predicted after viewing the structure.[30] Upon finally receiving the commission to reconstruct the church in 1807, Petrés rebuilt and enlarged the building's broad, three-aisled nave with a dome over the crossing according to the traditional Spanish and Latin American cathedral plan. (See Chapter 4.) Petrés died before the façade (Figure 104) was completed, but it generally reveals his design.

The façade employs a classical vocabulary reminiscent of Juan de Herrera's sixteenth-century monastery and palace of El Escorial near Madrid. The lower story is broad and low, with paired pilasters projecting slightly from the

FIGURE 104.
Fray Domingo
Petrés. Cathedral of
Bogotá, Colombia.
1807. Photograph
© Nicolás Osorio,
photographersdirect.com.

smooth stone wall. The central portal's broken pediment, escutcheon, and niches over the flanking doors are its only ornamental elements. Paired dentils, stacked pilasters, and emphasis on the central doorway nevertheless offer a subtle rhythm. The second story, which may depart from Petrés's designs, is more ornate with a pedimented portico, paired pilasters, and a central niche. Geometric designs in the central pediment reflect Petrés's desire to derive visual pleasure from firm lines and clear architectural description, an effect violated only by the small volutes linking the second story to the first. The towers' third story and cupolas are treated more sculpturally, although renovations have altered their original appearance.

While crown administrators may have viewed the neoclassical style as evidence of American loyalty to Spain, many Latin Americans, particularly the elite criollo populations, may not have agreed. Independence-minded colonists may have associated neoclassicism with the art of France and the United States of America, whose late eighteenth-century revolutions soon inspired Latin Americans to pursue freedom. The style that arrived to draw the viceroyalties into the centralized fold of the Spanish state became instead the art of independence and of new republics. This was probably not the intention of Academy of

San Carlos founder Jerónimo Antonio Gil or of Governor Agustín de Jáuregui y Aldecoa, who requested artists from Europe to transform his city.

As New Spain, Peru, New Granada, and La Plata fought for independence between 1810 and 1824, artistic production suffered from a lack of funding. Some of the artists contributed their efforts to anti-monarchy or loyalist forces. New Spanish academic Manuel Tolsá designed and cast cannons for the Spanish army while academy student José María Montes de Oca fought for Mexico's freedom. José Gil de Castro continued his military service throughout the conflict and is best known for his portraits of South America's heroes of the independence movement. But major commissions and building programs would have to wait until well after 1820–24, when José de San Martín freed Chile, Argentina, and Upper Peru; Simón Bolivar liberated Venezuela, Colombia, and Lima; and Agustín Iturbide and others achieved Mexican independence.

# NOTES

Chapter One

1. The 1494 Treaty of Tordesillas, authored by Pope Alexander VI, divided the non-European world between Spain and Portugal. Most of the Americas went to Spain, but today's Brazil became Portuguese territory.

2. George Kubler, *Mexican Architecture of the Sixteenth Century* (New Haven: Yale University Press, 1948), 329.

3. Cited in Kubler, *Mexican Architecture*, 466.

4. The term Mudéjar refers to objects and monuments created in Spain after the *reconquista* from the Moors, and reveals the influence of Islamic art and architecture.

5. Kubler, *Mexican Architecture*, 332.

6. Jaime Lara, *City, Temple, Stage: Eschatological Architecture and Liturgical Theatrics in New Spain* (New Haven: Yale University Press, 2004), 146.

7. Gloria Espinosa Spinola, *Arquitectura de la Conversión y Evangelización en la Nueva España durante el Siglo XVI* (Almería: Universidad de Almería, 1999), 96.

8. Ibid., 185.

9. Kubler, *Mexican Architecture*, 459.

10. Ibid., 88.

11. Mario Córdova Tello, *El convento de San Miguel de Huejotzingo, Pue.* (Mexico City: INAH, 1992), 63.

12. Espinosa Spinola, *Arquitectura de la Conversión*, 106–7.

13. Lara, *City, Temple, Stage*, 152.

14. Serge Gruzinski, *El águila y la sibila: Frescos indios de México* (Barcelona: Moleiro Editor, 1994), 65.

15. Constantino Reyes Valerio, *Arte indocristiano* (Mexico City: Instituto Nacional de Antropología e Historia [INAH], 2000), 328.

16. *Tequitqui* is Nahuatl for "tributary," and was designated by twentieth-century art historian José Moreno Villa to mean art made by indigenous artists working under Spanish rule.

17. Kubler, *Mexican Architecture*, 180.

18. Rafael García Granados and Luis MacGregor, *Huejotzingo: La ciudad y el convento Franciscano* (Mexico City: Talleres Gráficos de la Nación, 1934), 163.

19. Marcela Salas Cuesta, *La iglesia y el convento de Huejotzingo* (Mexico City: Universidad Nacional Autónoma de México [UNAM], 1982), 82.

20. Santiago Sebastián, Mariano Moterrosa, and José Antonio Terán, *Iconografía del arte del siglo XVI en México* (Mexico City: Gobierno del Estado de Zacatecas/ Ayuntamiento de Zacatecas/Universidad Autónoma de Zacatecas, 1995), 95.

21. Ibid., 94.

22. Lara, *City, Temple, Stage*, 135.

23. Salas Cuesta, *La iglesia y el convento de Huejotzingo*, 88.

24. See Reyes Valerio, *Arte indocristiano*, 120–23.

25. José G. Montes de Oca, *San Agustín de Acolman, Estado de México* (Mexico City: Biblioteca Enciclopédica del Estado de México, 1975), 22.

26. Reyes Valerio, *Arte indocristiano*, 246.

27. Salas Cuesta, *La iglesia y el convento de Huejotzingo*, 68 and 87.

28. Kubler, *Mexican Architecture*, 20.

29. Joseph M. Barnadas, "The Catholic Church in Colonial Spanish America," in *The Cambridge History of Spanish America*, vol. 1, Colonial Spanish America, ed. Leslie Bethell, 516 (Cambridge: Cambridge University Press, 1984).

30. Garcilaso de la Vega, *Royal Commentaries of the Incas and General History of Peru*, translated and with an introduction by Harold V. Livermore (Austin and London: University of Texas Press, 1966), 43 and 93.

31. Ibid., 189–90.

32. Norman Meikeljohn, *La iglesia y los Lupacas de Chuchito durante la colonia* (Cusco: Centro de Estudios Rurales Andinos "Bartolomé de las Casa"/Instituto de Estudios Aymaras, 1988), 26.

33. Valerie Fraser, *The Architecture of Conquest: Building in the Viceroyalty of Peru 1535–1635*, Cambridge Iberian and Spanish American Studies, ed. P. E. Russell, 88 (Cambridge: Cambridge University Press, 1989).

34. Ibid., 90.

35. Gauvin Alexander Bailey, *Art on the Jesuit Missions in Asia and Spanish America 1542–1773* (Toronto: University of Toronto Press, 1999), 155.

36. Ramón Gutiérrez, Carlos Pernaut, Graciela Viñuales, Hernán Rodríguez Villegas, Rodolfo Vallin Magaña, Bertha Estela Benavides, Elizabeth Kuon Arce, and Jesús Lambarri, *Arquitectura del altiplano peruano*, 2nd edition (Buenos Aires: Libros de Hispanoamérica, 1986), 97.

37. Ibid., 72.

38. Santiago Sebastián, José de Mesa Figueroa, and Teresa Gisbert de Mesa, *Arte Iberoamericano desde la colonización a la Independencia*, Summa Artis Historia General del Arte, vol. XXVIII, primera parte, 3rd edition (Madrid: Espasa-Calpe, 1989), 379.

39. Gutiérrez et al., *Arquitectura del altiplano peruano*, 313.

40. Teresa Gisbert and José de Mesa, *Arquitectura andina 1530–1830*, 2nd edition (La Paz: Embajada de España en Bolivia, 1997), 381.

41. Cited in Sebastián, Mesa, and Gisbert, *Arte Iberoamericano*, 326.

42. Gutiérrez et al., *Arquitectura del altiplano peruano*, 72.

43. Ibid., 71.

44. Sebastián, Mesa, and Gisbert, *Arte Iberoamericano*, 337–38.

45. Gisbert and Mesa, *Arquitectura andina*, 124.

46. José de Mesa, *Expresión de fe: Templos en Bolivia* (La Paz: Editorial Quipus y Entel, 1998), n.p.

47. Gutiérrez et al., *Arquitectura del altiplano peruano*, 315 and 317.

48. On the style of Andean church façades, see Fraser, *The Architecture of Conquest*.

49. Harold Wethey, *Colonial Architecture and Sculpture in Peru* (Cambridge: Harvard University Press, 1949), 35.

50. George Kubler and Martin Soria, *Art and Architecture in Spain and Portugal and their American Dominions 1500–1800*, The Pelican History of Art (Baltimore: Penguin Books, 1959), 87.

51. Fraser, *The Architecture of Conquest*, 153.

52. Gisbert and Mesa, *Arquitectura andina*, 151.

53. Gutiérrez et al., *Arquitectura del altiplano peruano*, 78.

54. Sebastián, Mesa, and Gisbert, *Arte Iberoamericano*, 333.

55. Gisbert and Mesa, *Arquitectura andina*, 176.

56. Gutiérrez et al., *Arquitectura del altiplano peruano*, 69.

Chapter Two

1. Pablo Joseph de Arriaga, *The Extirpation of Idolatry in Peru*, trans. and ed. L. Clark Keating, 130–31 (Louisville: University of Kentucky Press, 1968).

2. Cited in Samuel Y. Edgerton, *Theaters of Conversion: Religious Architecture and Indian Artisans in Colonial Mexico* (Albuquerque: University of New Mexico Press, 2001), 116.

3. Constantino Reyes Valerio, *Arte indocristiano*, 445. Translation mine.

4. Cited in Thomas B. F. Cummins, *Toasts with the Inca: Andean Abstraction and Colonial Images on Quero Vessels* (Ann Arbor: University of Michigan Press, 2002), 176–77.

5. Cited in Reyes Valerio, *Arte indocristiano*, 415. Translation mine.

6. Jeanette Favrot Peterson, *The Paradise Garden Murals of Malinalco: Utopia and Empire in Sixteenth-Century Mexico* (Austin: University of Texas Press, 1993), 50.

7. Cited in Alexandra Kennedy Troya, "La pinturas en el Nuevo Reino de Granada," in *Pintura, escultura y artes útiles en Iberoamérica, 1500–1825*, coordinator Ramón Gutiérrez, 140 (Madrid: Ediciones Cedra, 1995). Translation mine.

8. Teresa Gisbert, "The Artistic World of Guaman Poma," in *Guaman Poma de Ayala: The Colonial Art of an Andean Author* (New York: Americas Society, 1992), 79.

9. Thomas B. F. Cummins, "The Madonna and the Horse: Becoming Colonial in New Spain and Peru," in *Native Artists and Patrons in Colonial Spanish America*, ed. Emily Umberger and Tom Cummins, *Phoebus: A Journal of Art History* (Phoenix: Arizona State University, 1995), 68.

10. Cited in Valerie Fraser, *The Architecture of Conquest*, 97.

11. Cummins, "Madonna and the Horse," 52.

12. Teresa Gisbert, *Iconografía y mitos indígenas en el arte* (La Paz: Editorial Gisbert, 1980), 11.

13. Reyes Valerio, *Arte indocristiano*, 386.

14. Peterson, *Paradise Garden Murals*, 52.

15. Jorge A. Flores Ochoa, Elizabeth Kuon Arce, and Roberto Samanez Argumedo, *Pintura mural en el sur andino*, Colección Arte y Tesoros del Perú (Lima: Banco de Crédito de Perú, 1993), 38.

16. Serge Gruzinski, *Águila y la sibila*, 104 and 122.

17. José de Mesa and Teresa Gisbert, *Historia de la pintura cuzqueña* (Lima: Fundación Augusto N. Wiese, 1982), 237.

18. Gisbert, *Iconografía y mitos*, 32.

19. Teresa Gisbert, "La pintura mural andina," in *Catastro, evaluación y estudio de la pintura mural en el area centro sur andina* (La Paz: Organización de los Estados Americanos, 1998), 20.

20. Gisbert, *Iconografía y mitos*, 31.

21. Gisbert, "Pintura mural," 22.

22. Peterson, *Paradise Garden Murals*, 163.

23. Ibid., 63.

24. Edgerton, *Theaters of Conversion*, 125.

25. Flores Ochoa, Kuon Arce, and Samanez Argumedo, *Pintura mural*, 80.

26. See Gisbert, *Iconografía y mitos*, 17.

27. Pablo Macera, *La pintura mural andina siglos XVI–XIX* (Lima: Editorial Milla Batres, 1993), 26.

28. Teresa Gisbert, *El paraíso de los pájaros parlantes: La imagen del otro en la cultura andina* (La Paz: Plural Editores, 2001), 149.

29. Ibid., 150.

30. Peterson, *Paradise Garden Murals*, 87.

31. Ibid., 104.

32. Ibid., 133.

33. Jeanette Favrot Peterson, "Synthesis and Survival: The Native Presence in Sixteenth-Century Murals of New Spain," in *Native Artists*, 31.

34. Gisbert, *Iconografía y mitos*, 12.

35. Reyes Valerio, *Arte indocristiano*, 282.

36. Alicia Albornoz Bueno, *La memoria del olvido. El lenguaje del tlacuilo. Glifos y murales de la Iglesia de San Miguel Arcángel Ixmiquilpan, Hidalgo* (Pachuca, Hidalgo: Universidad Autónoma del Estado de Hidalgo, 1994), 43.

37. Edgerton, *Theaters of Conversion*, 133.

38. Gruzinski, *Águila y la sibila*, 38.

39. Ibid., 35.

40. John B. Glass, "A Census of Middle American Testerian Manuscripts," in *Handbook of Middle American Indians*, vol. 14, General Editor Robert Wauchope, *Guide to Ethnohistorical Sources*, part 3, Volume Editor Howard F. Cline (Austin: University of Texas Press, 1975), 282.

41. Ibid., 281.

42. Elizabeth Hill Boone, *Stories in Red and Black: Pictorial Histories of the Aztecs and Mixtecs* (Austin: University of Texas Press, 2000), 24 and 26.

43. For a detailed discussion of the style of colonial manuscripts, see Donald Robertson, *Mexican Manuscript Painting of the Early Colonial Period: The Metropolitan Schools* (Norman: University of Oklahoma Press, 1994).

44. Boone, *Stories*, 254.

45. Ibid., 245.

46. Ibid., 202.

47. Ibid., 247.

48. Xavier Noguez, *Tira de Tepechpan: Códice colonial procedente del valle de México* (Mexico City: Biblioteca Enciclopédica del Estado de México, 1978), 64.

49. Ibid., 58.

50. Boone, *Stories*, 199.

51. Eloise Quiñones Keber, *Codex Telleriano-Remensis: Ritual, Divination, and History in a Pictorial Aztec Manuscript* (Austin: University of Texas Press, 1995), 111.

52. Ibid., 170.

53. H. B. Nichols, "Fray Bernardino de Sahagún: A Spanish Missionary in New Spain, 1529–1590," in *Representing Aztec Ritual: Performance, Text, and Image in the Work of Sahún*, ed. Eloise Quiñones Keber, 25 (Boulder: University Press of Colorado, 2002).

54. Peterson, *Paradise Garden Murals*, 53–55.

55. Eloise Quiñones Keber, "Representing Aztec Ritual in the Work of Sahagún," in *Representing Aztec Ritual*, 5.

56. Cited in Ellen T. Baird, "Adaptation and Accommodation: The Transformation of the Visual Text in Sahagún's Manuscripts," in *Native Artists*, 44.

57. Boone, *Stories*, 246.

58. Frances F. Berdan and Patricia Rieff Anawalt, *The Essential Codex Mendoza* (Berkeley: University of California Press, 1997), 79.

59. Ibid., xii.

60. Ibid., 224.

61. Ibid., 222.

62. Kenneth J. Andrien, *Andean Worlds: Indigenous History, Culture, and Consciousness under Spanish Rule, 1532–1825* (Albuquerque: University of New Mexico Press, 2001), 149; and Barbara E. Mundy, *The Mapping of New Spain: Indigenous Cartography and the Maps of the Relaciones Geográficas* (Chicago: University of Chicago Press, 1996), 29.

63. Dana Leibsohn, "Colony and Cartography: Shifting Signs on Indigenous Maps of New Spain," in *Reframing the Renaissance: Visual Culture in Europe and Spanish America 1450–1650*, ed. Claire Farago, 273 (New Haven: Yale University Press, 1995).

64. Mundy, *Mapping of New Spain*, 159.

65. Ibid., 116.

66. *Los siglos de oro en los Virreinatos de América: 1550–1700* (Madrid: Sociedad Estatal para la Conmemoración de los Centenarios de Felipe II y Carlos V, 1999), 216.

67. Rolena Adorno, *Guaman Poma: Writing and Resistance in Colonial Peru*, second edition (Austin: University of Texas Press, 2000), 83.

68. Ibid., 100.

69. Ibid., 114.

70. Ibid., 5.

71. María Concepción García Sáiz, "Nuevos materiales para nuevas expresiones," in *Siglos de oro*, 133.

72. Ibid., 128.

73. Cited in García Sáiz, "Nuevos materiales," 132.

74. Donna Pierce, Rogelio Ruiz Gomar, and Clara Bargellini, *Painting a New World: Mexican Art and Life 1521–1821* (Denver, CO: Denver Art Museum, 2004), 102.

75. Ibid., 96.

76. Ibid., 97.

77. Cummins, *Toasts with the Inca*, 26.

78. Thomas B. F. Cummins, "Representation in the Sixteenth Century and the Colonial Image of the Inca," in *Writing Without Words: Alternative Literacies in*

Mesoamerica and the Andes, ed. Elizabeth Hill Boone and Walter D. Mignolo, 206 (Durham and London: Duke University Press, 1996).

79. Cummins, *Toasts with the Inca*, 152.

80. Cited in Cummins, *Toasts with the Inca*, 153.

81. Cited in Gisbert, "Pintura mural andina," 20.

82. Cummins, "Representation in the Sixteenth Century," 207.

83. Cummins, *Toasts with the Inca*, 155.

84. Elena J. Phipps, "Textiles as Cultural Memory: Andean Garments in the Colonial Period," in *Converging Cultures: Art and Identity in Spanish America*, ed. Diana Fane, 151 (New York: The Brooklyn Museum in association with Harry N. Abrams, 1996).

85. *Converging Cultures*, 184.

86. Phipps, "Textiles," 154.

Chapter Three

1. Guillermo Tovar de Teresa, "La Utopia del Virrey Mendoza," in *La Utopia mexicana del siglo XVI: Lo bello, lo verdadero, y lo bueno* (Mexico City: Grupo Azabache, 1992), 23–24.

2. Lara, *City, Temple, Stage*, 102.

3. Hernán Cortés, *Letters from Mexico*, trans. and ed. Anthony Pagden, intro. J. H. Elliott (New Haven and London: Yale University Press, 1986), 270.

4. Fray Toribio de Benavente Motolinía, *Memoriales de fray Toribio de Motolonía*, ed. Luis García Pimentel (Mexico City: [En casa de Luis García Pimentel], 1903). Cited in Kubler, *Mexican Architecture of the Sixteenth Century*, 71.

5. Francisco Cervantes de Salazar, *Life of the Imperial and Loyal City of Mexico in New Spain* (1554), translation by Minnie Lee Barrett Shephard with Introduction and Notes by Carlos Eduardo Castañeda, reprint of University of Texas Press, 1953 edition (Westport, CT: Greenwood Press, 1970), 43.

6. Silvio Zavala, *Una etapa en la construcción de la catedral de México alrededor de 1585*, Jornadas 96 (Mexico City: El Colegio de México, 1995), 3.

7. James Early, *The Colonial Architecture of Mexico* (Albuquerque: University of New Mexico Press, 1994), 121.

8. Gruzinski, *Águila y la sibila*, 143.

9. This section draws from Tom Cummins's inspired study of the two cities in "A Tale of Two Cities: Cuzco, Lima, and the Construction of Colonial Representation," in *Converging Cultures: Art and Identity in Spanish America*, ed. Diana Fane, 157–70 (New York: Harry N. Abrams, 1996).

10. Ibid., 160.

11. Gian Battista Ramusio, *Navigationi et viaggi*, vol. 3, ed. R. A. Skelton and G. B. Parks (Amsterdam: Theatrum Orbis Terrarum, 1967–70), cited in Fraser, *Architecture of Conquest*, 27.

12. Fraser, *Architecture of Conquest*, 59.

13. For a full description of this complicated ornamental program, see Santiago Sebastián, *El barroco iberoamericano. Mensaje iconográfico* (Madrid: Ediciones Encuentro, 1990), 251–54.

14. Cummins, "Tale of Two Cities," 160–61.

15. Fraser, *Architecture of Conquest*, 69.

16. Richard Kagan, *Urban Images of the Hispanic World 1493–1793* (New Haven and London: Yale University Press, 2000), 176.

17. Cummins, "Tale of Two Cities," 159.

18. Fraser, *Architecture of Conquest*, 76.

19. Bernabé Cobo, *Obras del P. Bernabé Cobo* (Biblioteca de Autores Españoles. Madrid: Ediciones Atlas, 1956), 308.

20. Cummins, "Tale of Two Cities," 164.

21. Kagan, *Urban Images*, 162.

22. On colonial festivals, see Linda Curcio-Nagy, *The Great Festivals of Colonial Mexico City: Performing Power and Identity*, Diálogos Series (Albuquerque: University of New Mexico Press, 2004).

23. Kagan, *Urban Images*, 101 and 193–95.

24. See Víctor Mínguez Cornelles, "Efímero mestizo," in *Iberoamérica mestiza. Encuentro de pueblos y culturas* (Madrid: Fundación Santillana, 2003), 62.

Chapter Four

1. *Siglos de oro*, 163–64.

2. Ibid., 245n6. Translation mine.

3. Martha Fernández, *Arquitectura y gobierno virreinal. Los maestros mayores de la Ciudad de México siglo XVII* (Mexico City: UNAM/IIE, 1985), 50.

4. Martha Fernández, *Cristóbal de Medina Vargas y la arquitectura salomónica en la Nueva España durante el siglo XVII* (Mexico City: UNAM/IIE, 2002), 25 and 40.

5. Ibid., 40.

6. Ibid., 37.

7. Manuel Toussaint, *La Catedral de México y el Sagrario Metropolitano. Su historia, su tesoro, su arte*, 3rd edition (Mexico City: Porrua, 1992), 79.

8. Sebastián, Mesa, and Gisbert, *Arte Iberoamericano*, 367.

9. Alfredo Benavides Rodríguez, *La arquitectura en el Virreinato del Perú y en la Capitanía General de Chile*, 3rd edition (Santiago de Chile: Andrés Bello, 1988), 25–26.

10. Antonio San Cristóbal Sebastián, *Arquitectura virreynal religiosa de Lima* (Lima: Studium, 1988), 59.

11. Cited in San Cristóbal Sebastián, *Arquitectura virreynal religiosa*, 61.

12. Roberto Ramírez del Villar, "Un monumento de la Lima virreinal," in *San Francisco de Lima*, Tesoros del Arte Colonial Peruano (Lima: Auge, 1974), 11.

13. María Antonia Durán Montero, *Lima en el siglo XVII. Arquitectura, urbanismo y vida cotidiana* (Sevilla: Diputación Provincial de Sevilla, 1994), 120.

14. Ibid., 57.

15. Diego Angulo Íñiguez and Enrique Marco Dorta, *Historia del arte hispano americano*, vol. 1, 2nd edition (Mexico City: Instituto de Estudios y Documentos Históricos, 1982), 615.

16. Kubler and Soria, *Art and Architecture*, 87.

17. Rafael López Guzmán, Lázaro Gila Medina, Ignacio Henares Cuellar, and Guillermo Tovar de Teresa, *Arquitectura y carpintería mudéjar en Nueva España*, Arte Novohispano (Mexico City: Azabache, 1992), 27.

18. Juan de Velasco, *Historia del Reino de Quito en la América meridional*, edición, prólogo, notas y cronología Alfredo Pareja Diezcanseco (Caracas: Biblioteca Ayacucho, 1981), 310.

19. Cobo, *Obras*, 421.

20. Durán Montero, *Lima en el siglo XVII*, 119.

21. Ramírez del Villar, "Un monumento," 25.

22. Ibid., 73.

23. Ibid., 77.

24. Gisbert, *Paraíso de los pájaros parlantes*, 162.

25. Antonio de San Cristóbal, "Reinterpretación de la arquitectura planiforme," in *Territorio, espacio, y arte. Arte barroco iberoamericano* (Sevilla: Universidad Pablo Olavide, 2002), 969.

26. Joaquín Bérchez, *Arquitectura mexicana de los siglos XVII y XVIII*, Arte Novohispano (Mexico City: Azabache, 1992), 57.

27. Manuel Toussaint, *Arte colonial en México*, 5th edition (Mexico City: UNAM/IIE, 1990), 108.

28. Durán Montero, *Lima en el siglo XVII*, 123.

29. Damián Bayon and Murillo Marx, *History of South American Colonial Art and Architecture* (New York: Rizzoli, 1989), 159.

30. Ricardo Mariátegui Oliva, *La ciudad de Arequipa del siglo XVII en el Monasterio de Santa Catalina* (Lima: n.p., 1952), 10.

31. Ibid., 18.

32. Fernández, *Cristóbal de Medina Vargas*, 215.

33. Josefina Muriel, *Los conventos de monjas en la Nueva España* (Mexico City: Editorial Santiago, 1946), 375.

34. D. A. Brading, *Mexican Phoenix. Our Lady of Guadalupe: Image and Tradition Across Five Centuries* (Cambridge: Cambridge University Press, 2001), 2.

35. D. A. Brading, *The First America: The Spanish Monarchy, Creole Patriots, and the Liberal State, 1492–1867* (Cambridge: Cambridge University Press, 1998), 110.

36. Fernández, *Cristóbal de Medina Vargas*, 392.

37. Bérchez, *Arquitectura mexicana*, 25.

38. Sebastián, *Barroco iberoamericano*, 54.

39. Brading, *Mexican Phoenix*, 147.

40. *El Santuario de Copacabana de La Paz a Tiahuanaco*, Documentos de Arte Colonial Sudamericano, Cuaderno VII (Buenos Aires: Academia Nacional de Bellas Artes de la República Argentina, 1950), xxxiii.

41. Ibid., xvii.

42. Scholars differ in their attribution of this monument. This attribution is from José de Mesa and Teresa Gisbert, *Bolivia: Monumentos históricos y arqueológicos*, Comisión de Historia 122, Monumentos Históricos y Arqueológicos XV (Mexico City: Instituto Panamericano de Geografía e Historia, 1970), 20. Cited in *Santuario de Copacabana*, xix).

Chapter Five

1. Gabrielle Palmer, *Sculpture in the Kingdom of Quito* (Albuquerque: University of New Mexico Press, 1987), 67.

2. Mario Chacón Torres, *Arte virreinal en Potosí* (Sevilla: Escuela de Estudios Hispanoamericanos, 1973), 234.

3. Mesa and Gisbert, *Historia de la pintura cuzqueña*, 310.

4. Jorge Bernales Ballesteros, "La pinturas en Lima durante el Virreinato," In *Pintura en el Virreinato del Perú* (Lima: El Libro de Arte del Centenario, 1989), n.p.

5. Carolyn Dean, "The Renewal of Old World Images and the Creation of Colonial Peruvian Visual Culture," in *Converging Cultures: Art and Identity in Spanish America*, ed. Diana Fane, 172–73 (New York: The Brooklyn Museum/Harry N. Abrams, 1996).

6. Brading, *Mexican Phoenix*, 172.

7. Ibid., 75.

8. Gisbert, *Iconografía y mitos indígenas*, 20–21.

9. Gisbert, *Paraíso de los pájaros parlantes*, 227.

10. Verónica Salles-Reese, *From Viracocha to the Virgin of Copacabana: Representation of the Sacred at Lake Titicaca* (Austin: University of Texas Press, 1997), 27.

11. Ibid., 25.

12. Dean, "Renewal of Old World Images," 173.

13. Alfonso Rodríguez G. de Ceballos, "Usos y funciones de la imagen religiosa en los virreinatos americanos," in *Los siglos de oro en los Virreinatos de América 1550–1700* (Madrid: Sociedad Estatal para la Conmemoración de los Centenarios de Felipe II y Carlos V, 1999), 94. For a more detailed discussion, see Barbara Duncan, "Statue Paintings of the Virgin," in *Gloria in Excelsis: The Virgin and Angels in Viceregal Painting of Peru and Bolivia* (New York: Center for Inter-American Relations, 1986), 32–57.

14. Mesa and Gisbert, *Historia de la pintura cuzqueña*, 302.

15. Duncan, "Statue Paintings," 49.

16. The painting bears the signature of Potosí artist Melchor Pérez Holguín (ca. 1660–1733), but it does not appear to be Pérez's work. Mesa and Gisbert, *Historia de la pintura cuzqueña*, 305.

17. Holguín's paintings are discussed in José de Mesa, "Painting in Potosí," in *Potosí: Colonial Treasures and the Bolivian City of Silver* (New York: Americas Society Art Gallery, 1997), 45.

18. Carol Damian, *The Virgin of the Andes: Art and Ritual of Colonial Cuzco* (Miami Beach: Grassfield Press, 1995), 79.

19. Ibid., 79.

20. Clara Bargellini, "Cristo en el arte barroco," in *Arte y mística del barroco* (Mexico City: Consejo Nacional para la Cultura y las Artes, 1994), 45.

21. Elisa Vargaslugo, *Arte y mística del barroco*, 150.

22. See Kelly Donahue-Wallace, "Publishing Prints in Eighteenth-Century Mexico City," *Print Quarterly* 26, no. 2 (2006): 134–54.

23. Jaime Cuadriello, "Tierra de prodigios: La ventura como destino," in *Los pinceles de la historia: El origen del Reino de la Nueva España 1680–1750* (Mexico City: Museo Nacional de Arte, 1999), 220.

24. Palmer, *Sculpture*, 114.

25. Luisa Elena Alcalá in *Siglos de oro*, 326.

26. Charlene Villaseñor Black, "Love and Marriage in the Spanish Empire: Depictions of Holy Matrimony and Gender Discourses in the Seventeenth Century," *Sixteenth Century Studies Journal* 32, no. 3 (2001): 664. See also Villaseñor Black's fuller

treatment of this theme in *Creating the Cult of St. Joseph: Art and Gender in the Spanish Empire* (Princeton: Princeton University Press, 2006).

27. Barbara von Barghahn, "Imaging the Holy Family of Nazareth in the Viceregal Andes: An Alloy of European and Inca Cultures," in *The Holy Family as Prototype of the Civilization of Love: Images from the Viceregal Americas*, ed. Joseph F. Chorpenning, 68–69 (Philadelphia: Saint Joseph's University Press, 1996).

28. Archivo General de la Nación (Mexico City), Inquisición 1790, vol. 1306, exp. 4, fol. 256–58.

29. Sebastián, *El barroco iberoamericano*, 200.

30. Villaseñor Black, "Love and Marriage," 664.

31. Ibid., 650–51.

32. Mitchell A. Codding, "The Decorative Arts in Latin America, 1492–1820," in *The Arts in Latin America 1492–1807*, exhib. cat. (Philadelphia: Philadelphia Museum of Art, 2006), 107.

33. Guillermo Tovar de Teresa, *Miguel Cabrera: Pintor de cámara de la reina celestial* (Mexico City: Inver Mexico Grupo Financiero, 1995), 168.

34. Ibid., 177.

35. Suzanne Stratton-Pruitt, *The Virgin, Saints, and Angels: South American Paintings 1600–1825 from the Thoma Collection* (Stanford, California: Skira in association with the Iris and B. Gerald Cantor Centor for Visual Arts at Stanford University, 2006), 114.

36. Gustavo Navarro Castro, "Latin American Iconography of Saint James the Killer of Moors," in *America: Bride of the Sun: 500 Years Latin America and the Low Countries* (Antwerp: Imschoot Books, 1992), 190.

37. Gisbert, "Andean Painting," in *Gloria in Excelsis*, 62; and Gisbert, *Paraíso de los pájaros parlantes*, 78.

38. Dean, "Renewal of Old World Images," 172.

39. Elisa Vargaslugo, *Estudios de pintura colonial hispanoamericana* (Mexico City: UNAM, 1992), 108–9.

40. On New Spain's multiethnic angels, see Elisa Vargaslugo, *Estudios de pintura colonial*, 55–63.

41. Rodríguez, "Usos y funciones," 104.

42. Gisbert, "Andean Painting," 63. This accommodating strategy may likewise have led to Cuzco painter Diego Quispe Tito's beautiful, yet unusual zodiac series, in which the Christ and his Holy Family are dwarfed by nature and the heavens.

43. Gisbert, *Paraíso de los pájaros parlantes*, 124.

44. Julia P. Herzberg, "Angels with Guns: Image and Interpretation," in *Gloria in Excelsis*, 65.

45. Gisbert, *Paraíso de los pájaros parlantes*, 251.

46. Carolyn Dean, *Inka Bodies and the Body of Christ: Corpus Christi in Colonial Cuzco, Peru* (Durham and London: Duke University Press, 1999), 184–85.

47. Gisbert, *Paraíso de los pájaros parlantes*, 250.

48. Dean, *Inka Bodies*, 3.

Chapter Six

1. Fernández, *Arquitectura y gobierno virreinal*, 295.

2. Ibid., 304. Translation mine.

3. Bernales Ballesteros, "La pintura en Lima," 85.

4. Ibid., 87.

5. Justino Fernández, *Estética del arte mexicano* (Mexico City: UNAM/IIE, 1972), 202–3.

6. Johanna Hecht, "Eighteenth-Century Mexico: Tradition and Transformation (1715–1785)," in *Mexico: Splendors of Thirty Centuries* (New York: The Metropolitan Museum of Art, 1990), 358.

7. Bernales Ballesteros, "La pintura en Lima," 89.

8. Bérchez, *Arquitectura mexicana*, 262.

9. Fernández, *Estética del arte mexicano*, 206–7.

10. Guillermo Tovar de Teresa, "La Iglesia de San Francisco Xavier de Tepotzotlán: Eco de la vida artística de la ciudad de México en los siglos XVII y XVIII," *Archivo Español de Arte* 61, no. 244 (1988): 360.

11. Ibid., 368.

12. Marco Díaz, "Arquitectura en Tepotzotlán," in *Museo Nacional del Virreinato. Tepotzotlán. La vida y la obra en la Nueva España*, 2nd edition (Mexico City: Consejo Nacional Para la Cultura y las Artes [CONACULTA]/INAH, 2003), 149.

13. Bailey, *Art on the Jesuit Missions*, 50.

14. Ibid., 48.

15. Sebastián, *El barroco iberoamericano*, 60.

16. Velasco, *Historia del Reino de Quito*, 310.

17. Clara Bargellini, *La arquitectura de la plata. Iglesias monumentales del centro-norte de México 1640–1750*, (Mexico City: UNAM/IIE, 1991), 92–93.

18. Ibid., 96.

19. Gisbert and Mesa, *Arquitectura andina 1530–1830*, 228.

20. Cited in Kagan, *Urban Images*, 187.

21. Enrique Tandeter, *Coercion and Market: Silver Mining in Colonial Potosí, 1692–1826* (Albuquerque: University of New Mexico Press, 1993), 57.

22. Gisbert and Mesa, *Arquitectura andina 1530–1830*, 229.

23. Sebastián, *El barroco iberoamericano*, 60.

24. Kubler and Soria, *Art and Architecture in Spain and Portugal*, 97.

25. Gisbert, *Iconografía y mitos indígenas*, 49.

26. Gisbert and Mesa, *Arquitectura andina 1530–1830*, 334.

27. Bargellini, *La arquitectura de la plata*, 97.

28. Ibid., 101.

29. Ibid., 226.

30. Ibid., 272 and 277.

31. Ibid., 86.

32. Ibid., 102.

33. Ibid., 84–85.

34. Mesa and Gisbert, *Bolivia*, 62.

35. Ibid., 63.

36. Gisbert and Mesa, *Arquitectura andina 1530–1830*, 151. Posa chapels constructed in the eighteenth century were not uncommon in South America, particularly in Bolivia.

37. Ibid., 23.

38. Ibid., 25.

39. Bérchez, *Arquitectura mexicana*, 281.

40. Manuel Toussaint, *Arte colonial en México*, 5th edition, 151.

41. Bailey, *Art on the Jesuit Missions*, 152.

42. Ibid., 7.

43. Ramón Gutiérrez, *The Jesuit Guaraní Missions/Les missions jesuitas des Guaranies* (Rio de Janeiro: UNESCO, 1987), 62.

44. C. J. McNaspy, *Lost Cities of Paraguay: Art and Architecture of the Jesuit Reductions 1607–1767* (Chicago: Loyola University Press, 1982), 113.

45. Bailey, *Art on the Jesuit Missions*, 162.

46. James Early, *Presidio, Mission, and Pueblo: Spanish Architecture and Urbanism in the United States* (Dallas: Southern Methodist University Press, 2004), 73.

47. Luis Enrique Tord and Pedro Gjurinovic, *El palacio de Torre Tagle y las casonas de Lima/The Torre Tagle Palace and the Old Mansions of Lima* (Lima: Asociación de Funcionarios del Servicio Diplomático del Perú, 2001), 21.

48. Early, *Colonial Architecture of Mexico*, 139.

49. Durán Montero, *Lima en el siglo XVII*, 162.

50. Benavides Rodríguez, *La arquitectura en el Virreinato del Perú*, 71.

51. Tord and Gjurinovic, *El palacio de Torre Tagle*, 36.

52. Ibid., 46.

53. Early, *Colonial Architecture of Mexico*, 151.

54. Toussaint, *Arte colonial*, 162.

Chapter Seven

1. Elena Isabel Estrada de Gerlero, "El retrato en la Nueva España en el siglo XVI," in *El retrato civil en la Nueva España*, exhib. cat. ([Mexico City]: Consejo Nacional Para la Cultura y las Artes/Instituto Nacional de Bellas Artes [INBA], 1991), 16.

2. Cited in Elizabeth Hill Boone and Thomas B. F. Cummins, "Colonial Foundations: Points of Contact and Compatibility," in *The Arts in Latin America 1492–1820*, exhib. cat. (Philadelphia: Philadelphia Museum of Art, 2006), 13.

3. Cummins, *Toasts with the Inca*, 124.

4. Marita Martínez del Río de Redo, "El retrato novohispano en los siglos XVII y XVIII," in *Retrato civil*, 24.

5. Jaime Moreno Villarreal, "In Praise of Heat and Fan," in *El retrato novohispano en el siglo XVIII*, exhib. cat. (Puebla: Museo Poblano de Arte Virreinal, 1999), 148.

6. *The Arts in Latin America 1492–1820*, exhib. cat. (Philadelphia: Philadelphia Museum of Art, 2006), 456.

7. Martínez, "Retrato novohispano," 34.

8. Moreno Villareal, "In Praise of Heat and Fan," 152.

9. *El retrato novohispano en el siglo XVIII*, exhib. cat. (Puebla: Museo Poblano de Arte Virreinal, 1999), 175.

10. Alma Montero Alarcón, *Monjas coronadas* (Mexico City: Consejo Nacional Para la Cultura y las Artes, 1999), 15.

11. Ibid., 12–13.

12. Ibid., 16.

13. Luis Eduardo Wuffarden, "Effigies of the Incas or Kings of Peru," in *The Arts in Latin America 1492–1820*, exhib. cat. (Philadelphia: Philadelphia Museum of Art, 2006), 465.

14. Brading, *The First America*, 491.

15. Gustavo Curiel, "Los biombos novohispanos: escenografías de poder y transculturación en el ámbito doméstico," in *Viento detenido: Mitologías e historias en el arte del biombo. Colección de biombos de los siglos XVII al XIX de Museo Soumaya* (Mexico City: Museo Soumaya, 1999), 14.

16. Marita Martínez del Río de Redo, "Los biombos en el ámbito doméstico: Sus programas moralizadores y didácticos," in *Juegos de ingenio y agudeza: La pintura emblemática de la Nueva España*, exhib. cat. (Mexico City: Patronato del Museo Nacional de Arte, 1994), 133.

17. Teresa Castelló Yturbide and Marita Martínez del Río de Redo, *Biombos novohispanos* (Mexico City: INAH, 1970), 13.

18. Curiel, "Biombos," 19.

19. Castelló and Martínez del Rio de Redo, *Biombos novohispanos*, 23.

20. Martínez del Rio de Redo, "Biombos," 134.

21. Curiel "Biombos," 21.

22. Brading, *First America*, 368.

23. Ibid., 342 and 420.

24. *Mexico: Splendors of Thirty Centuries*, exhib. cat. (New York: Metropolitan Museum of Art, 1999), 427.

25. Ilona Katzew, "Casta Painting: Identity and Social Stratification in Colonial Mexico," in *New World Orders: Casta Painting and Colonial Latin America*, exhib. cat. (New York: Americas Society Art Gallery, 1996), 23. See also Ilona Katzew, *Casta Painting: Images of Race in Eighteenth-Century Mexico* (New Haven and London: Yale University Press, 2004), 93.

26. Katzew, *Casta Painting*, 109.

27. Pilar Romero de Tejada y Picatoste, "Los cuadros de mestizaje del Virrey Amat," in *Los cuadros de mestizaje del Virrey Amat: La representación etnográfica en el Perú colonial*, exhib. cat. (Lima: Museo de Arte de Lima, 2000), 22.

28. Cited in Katzew "Casta Painting," 14.

29. Magali M. Carrera, *Imaging Identity in New Spain: Race, Lineage, and the Colonial Body in Portraiture and Casta Paintings* (Austin: University of Texas Press, 2003), 14.

30. Katzew, *Casta Painting*, 111–61, associates the characteristics of late colonial casta paintings with the Bourbon reforms, among other historical and social factors.

31. Juan de Viera quoted in Katzew, *Casta Painting*, 197.

32. Katzew, *Casta Painting*, 115.

33. María Concepción García Sáiz, *Las castas novohispanas: Un género pictórico americano*, ([Madrid]: Olivetti, 1989), 108.

34. Carrera, *Imaging Identity*, 133–35.

35. Elena Isabel Estrada de Gerlero, "The Representation of 'Heathen Indians' in New Spanish Casta Painting," in *New World Orders*, 46.

Chapter Eight

1. Xavier Moyssen, "La primera academia de pintura en México," *Anales del Instituto de Investigaciones Estéticas* 35 (1965): 23–24. Translation mine.

2. Efraín Castro Morales, "Un grabado neoclásico," *Anales del Instituto de Investigaciones Estéticas* 33 (1964): 108. Translation mine.

3. "Proyecto para el establecimiento en México de una academia de las tres nobles artes de Pintura, Escultura, y Arquitectura," in *Proyecto, estatutos, y demás documentos relacionados al establecimiento de la Real Academia de pintura, escultura, y arquitectura de Nueva España (1781–1802)*, facsimile edition, Colección Documenta Novae Hispaniae, editor David Marley, n.p. (Mexico City: Rolston-Bain, 1984).

4. Eduardo Báez Macías, "La Academia de San Carlos en la Nueva España como instrumento de cambio," in *Las academias de arte*, VII Coloquio Internacional en Guanajuato (Mexico City: UNAM, 1985), 37–38; and Mejanes, *Academias: Francia y México*, 26.

5. Baez Macias, "Academia," 43.

6. Cited in Abelardo Carrillo y Gariel, *Datos sobre la Academia de San Carlos de Nueva España: El arte en México de 1781 a 1863* (Mexico City: Academia de San Carlos, 1939), 30. Translation mine.

7. Jean Charlot, *Mexican Art and the Academy of San Carlos, 1785–1915* (Austin: University of Texas Press, 1962), 25–26.

8. "Plan de Estudios," Archivo de la Antigua Academia de San Carlos, Document 910, 1795.

9. Thomas Brown, *La Academia de San Carlos de la Nueva España*, vol. 2 (Mexico City: Secretaría de Educación Pública, 1976), 30.

10. Clara Bargellini, "La lealtad americana: el significado de la estatua ecuestre de Carlos IV," in *Iconología y sociedad: Arte colonial hispanoamericano*, XLIV Congreso Internacional de Americanistas (Mexico City: UNAM, 1987), 216.

11. Ignacio González-Polo, "Barroco vs. Neoclásico en la arquitectura novohispana," *Revista de la Universidad de México* XLIV, no. 467 (1989): 15.

12. Cited in Early, *Colonial Architecture of Mexico*, 193.

13. Ignacio González-Polo, "La posición de los criollos en la Academia de San Carlos (1785–1800)," *Revista de la Universidad de México* XLVI, no. 480–81 (1991): 70.

14. Francisco Eduardo Tresguerras, "El templo del Carmen de Celaya," *Diario de México* (December 15, 1808): 691, cited in González-Polo, "Posición," 68.

15. Bernales Ballesteros, "La pintura en Lima," 64.

16. Ibid., 68.

17. Isabel Cruz de Amenabar and Graciela Vinuales, "La pintura en Chile y en el Virreinato del Río de la Plata," in *Pintura, escultura y artes útiles en Iberoamérica, 1500–1821*, ed. Ramón Gutiérrez, 181 (Madrid: Ediciones Cátedra, 1995).

18. Bailey, *Art on the Jesuit Missions*, 49.

19. Marcelo Frías Núñez, *Tras El Dorado vegetal: José Celestino Mutis y la Real Expedición Botánica del Nuevo Reino de Granada (1783–1808)* (Sevilla: Diputación de Sevilla, 1994), 267 and 281.

20. Ricardo Mariátegui Oliva, *José Gil de Castro ("El Mulato Gil"): Vida y obra del gran pintor peruano de los libertadores* (Lima: Año Bicentenario de la rebelión emancipadora de Tupac Amaru y Micaela Bastidas, 1981), 38; and Carmen Sotos Serrano, *Los pintores de la expedición de Alejandro Malaspina*, vol. 1 (Madrid: Real Academia de la Historia, 1982), 68.

21. *The Malaspina Expedition 1789–1794: Journal of the Voyage by Alejandro Malaspina*, vol. 1, ed. Andrew David, Felipe Fernández-Armesto, Carlos Novi, and Glyndwr Williams, introduction by Donald Cutter, lx (London: The Hakluyt Society and the Museo Naval, 2001).

22. Ibid., 88n2.

23. Ibid., 231; Soto Serrano, *Pintores*, 72–73; *Malaspina Expedition*, xlvi.

24. Mariategui Oliva, *Gil de Castro*, 38.

25. Ramírez del Villar, "Un monumento de la Lima virreinal," 73.

26. Patricia Díaz Silva, "Reactivando la memoria: el pintor retratista José Gil de Castro (1785–1841)," in *José Gil de Castro en Chile*, exhib. cat. (Santiago de Chile: Museo Nacional de Bellas Artes, 1994), 18.

27. Ramón Gutiérrez, Rodolfo Vallín and Verónica Perfetti, *Fray Domingo Petrés y su obra arquitectónica en Colombia* (Bogotá: Banco de la República/ Ancora Editores, 1999), 60.

28. Benavides Rodríguez, *Arquitectura*, 251.

29. Ibid., 255.

30. Gutiérrez, Vallín, and Perfetti, *Fray Domingo Petrés*, 180.

# GLOSSARY

ac.: Used to indicate the active period of an artist when his life-span dates are unknown

alarife: In architecture, a builder, usually a stonemason

alfiz: From Islamic architectural ornamentation, a square or rectangular framing element around the decoration surrounding a door or other opening

altarscreen: Also known as an altarpiece; an ornamental construction behind the altar, usually bearing painted or sculpted images of religious themes

apse: The semicircular or polygonal recess containing the main altar at the end of a church nave

arcade: A sequence of arches

archivolt: Small architectural ornament in the shape of an arch, usually surrounding a door or other opening

ashlar masonry: Construction executed with courses of finely hewn stones

atlantid: In architecture, a supporting member in the shape of a male body

atrial cross: A cross, usually stone, placed in the atrium of a monastic compound

atrium (pl. atria): An open area within a walled enclosure, frequently before a church

balustered column: A column with a shaft that tapers and swells recalling the shape of a baluster

barrel vault: A roofing system consisting of a single, semicircular form spanning the opening below

basilica (adj. basilican): An architectural structure with a long axis flanked by lower aisles

bay: In church architecture, the internal division of space usually corresponding to the size of the crossing where the nave and transept meet

biombo: From the Japanese *byo-* meaning wind and *bu* meaning break, a painted screen

brocateado: In painting, the use of gold on the surface of the canvas to simulate the appearance of brocade cloth

broken pediment: A pediment with a discontinuous cornice, creating a break or opening in the pediment's triangular or semicircular form

cartouche: A shield or escutcheon

casta painting: A genre of images featuring the ethnic diversity of Latin America, usually featuring parents of different races and their mixed-race child(ren)

cathedral: In Catholic architecture, the church where the bishop officiates

chiaroscuro: From Italian for light and dark; in painting refers to the dramatic play of light and shadow to create the illusion of volume

choir loft: In architecture, a balcony for the choir

Classical orders: From ancient Greek and Roman architecture and subsequent periods employing their forms, Doric, Ionic, Corinthian, and Composite styles of columns, capitals, and entablatures

classicizing: Based on the formal principles of Classical (ancient Greek and Roman) art and architecture

clerestory: A bank of windows

codex (pl. codices): A book

colonnade: A row of columns

convento: In viceregal architecture, the monastic compound consisting of atrium, church, monastery, and sometimes an open chapel and posas chapels

cornice: In architecture, an ornamental molding, usually horizontal, that tops the entablature

crossing: In architecture, the location within the church where nave and transept meet

cruciform: In the shape of a cross

cult image: In Catholic art, a painted or sculpted image of a holy figure that is the focus of fervent devotion

dado: Ornamental painting, woodwork, or tile covering the lower portion of a wall

domical vault: A roofing system with a semicircular dome rising over each bay without pendentives or squinches

dressed masonry: Coursed construction executed with cut stones

eared frame: Rectangular decorative molding that projects out at the four corners or along the vertical sides

emblem: A symbolic image alluding to an idea or concept, usually accompanied by explanatory text and/or motto

encarnación: Technique of lifelike painting for wood sculpture using flesh-tone pigments and varnish

ensamblador: Assembler of altarscreens

entablature: In Classical or classicizing architecture, the area above the column, consisting of architrave (or epistyle), frieze, and cornice

estípite: In architecture, a column consisting of stacked geometric forms resting on an inverted obelisk

estofado: Technique of painting wood sculpture to resemble brocade fabric consisting of pigment and gilding

gilding: To apply gold leaf to architecture, sculpture, or painting

grotesque: In painting and sculpture, an ornamental element recalling decorative motifs employed in ancient Roman architecture

guild: A professional organization governing the practice of a trade

hall church: An architectural structure in which the nave and flanking aisles are the same height

horror vacui: Latin for "fear of emptiness," used in art and architecture to refer to the use of profuse ornamentation in dense arrangements

hypostyle hall: A structure employing row upon row of columns or arches to support the roof

maestro mayor: The principal architect or builder

mestizo baroque: Stylistic label applied to painting and sculpture that appears to combine naturalism and stylization, perhaps caused by native artists reconciling ancestral traditions and European approaches to image-making

mirador: An overlook, usually a balcony

monjas coronadas: In viceregal painting, a genre of portraiture featuring nuns in ornate accessories including flowery crowns

Mudéjar: Stylistic label referring to Spanish and Latin American art and architecture that employs forms of Moorish origin

nave: The central aisle of a church

ogee arch: An arch with a profile that has several changes of direction or an s-shaped curve

open chapel: An outdoor chapel

par y nudillo: A wood ceiling form with sloping sides and a flat central area

passionary: referring to Christ's final days or his Passion

pendentive: In architecture, a triangular form that directs the forces of a round dome down into its four supporting piers

pediment: In an entablature, a projecting form, usually triangular, created when the cornice rises above a horizontal level

pictograph: A form of writing in which pictures represent ideas and objects

pilaster: In Classical and classicizing architecture, a flat vertical support that projects from the wall

planiform baroque: Stylistic label applied to architectural ornamentation that appears to combine naturalism and stylization and is characterized by low relief forms

portería: In architecture, the threshold of the monastery entrance

polychromy: In painting, the use of multiple colors

portico: A doorway

posa: In Latin American monastic architecture, a small outdoor chapel employed in religious processions

predella: The lowest portion of an altarscreen, usually bearing painted or sculpted images

putto (pl. putti): From Classical art and architecture, a cherub

quero (or qero, kero): An ornamented cup employed by Andean societies, given in pairs

quincha: In South American architecture, a material mixing reeds and plaster used to construct light-weight roofing systems

quipu (or qipu, khipu): An Andean device for recording information consisting of colored and knotted strings

quoins: From Classical architecture, rusticated stones located at the corner of a building

retablo-façade: In Latin American architecture, facade ornamentation that recalls the forms and images found on an altarscreen

rib vaults: From European Gothic architecture, a roofing system that uses ribs to direct thrust into supporting piers and buttresses

roundel: From Classical architecture, circular relief generally used as a framing device

rosette: An ornamental flower

rustication: In architecture, the treatment of masonry to appear rough and not completely finished

sail vault (also known as handkerchief vault): A roofing system organized by bays with a high central area on a continuous curve with the pendentives, recalling the appearance of a billowing sail or handkerchief

Solomonic column: A column that twists around its axis, believed to recall the columns found at the Temple of Solomon

tequitquí: Stylistic label applied to painting and sculpture that appears to combine naturalism and stylization, perhaps caused by native artists reconciling ancestral traditions and European approaches to image-making

transept: In architecture, the aisle that runs perpendicular to the nave and intersects it at the crossing

traza moderada: A plan developed in the mid-sixteenth century to correlate the size of a monastic complex, the number of resident clergy, and the population of the indigenous community

BIBLIOGRAPHY

Abbreviations

CONACULTA: Consejo Nacional Para la Cultura y las Artes (Mexico)

IIE: Instituto de Investigaciones Estéticas (Mexico)

INAH: Instituto Nacional de Antropología e Historia (Mexico)

INBA: Instituto Nacional de Bellas Artes (Mexico)

UNAM: Universidad Nacional Autónoma de México

Adorno, Rolena. *Guaman Poma: Writing and Resistance in Colonial Peru*. 2nd edition. Austin: University of Texas Press, 2000.

Albornoz Bueno, Alicia. *La memoria del olvido. El lenguaje del tlacuilo. Glifos y murales de la Iglesia de San Miguel Arcángel Ixmiquilpan, Hidalgo*. Pachuca, Hidalgo: Universidad Autónoma del Estado de Hidalgo, 1994.

Andrien, Kenneth J. *Andean Worlds: Indigenous History, Culture, and Consciousness under Spanish Rule, 1532–1825*. Albuquerque: University of New Mexico Press, 2001.

Angulo Íñiguez, Diego, and Enrique Marco Dorta. *Historia del arte hispanoamericano*. Vol. 1. 2nd edition. Mexico City: Instituto de Estudios y Documentos Históricos, 1982.

Arbalaez Camacho, Carlos, and F. Gil Tovar. *El arte colonial en Colombia*. Bogotá: Ediciones Sol y Luna, 1968.

Archivo de la Antigua Academia de San Carlos. "Plan de Estudios." 1795.

Archivo General de la Nación (Mexico City), Inquisición 1790, vol. 1306, exp. 4, fol. 256–58.

De arquitectura, pintura y otras artes: Homenaje a Elisa Vargaslugo. Editors Cecilia Gutiérrez Arriola and María del Consuelo Maquívar. Mexico City: UNAM/IIE, 2004.

de Arriaga, Pablo Joseph. *The Extirpation of Idolatry in Peru*. Translated and edited by L. Clark Keating. Louisville: University of Kentucky Press, 1968.

Arte de las academias: Francia y México, siglos XVII–XIX. Exhibition catalog. Mexico City: Antiguo Colegio de San Ildefonso, 1999.

Arte y mística del barroco. Exhibition catalog. Mexico City: CONACULTA, 1994.

The Arts in Latin America 1492–1820. Exhibition catalog. Philadelphia: Philadelphia Museum of Art, 2006.

Báez Macías, Eduardo. "La Academia de San Carlos en la Nueva España como instrumento de cambio." In *Las academias de arte*. VII Coloquio Internacional en Guanajuato. Mexico City: UNAM, 1985.

Bailey, Gauvin Alexander. *Art on the Jesuit Missions in Asia and Spanish America 1542–1773*. Toronto: University of Toronto Press, 1999.

Baird, Ellen T. "Adaptation and Accommodation: The Transformation of the Visual Text in Sahagún's Manuscripts." In *Native Artists and Patrons in Colonial Spanish America*, edited by Emily Umberger and Tom Cummins. Series: *Phoebus: A Journal of Art History*, vol. 7. Phoenix: Arizona State University, 1995.

Bantel, Linda, and Marcus Burke. *Spain and New Spain: Mexican Colonial Arts in their European Context*. Exhibition catalog. Corpus Christi, TX: Art Museum of South Texas, 1979.

Bargellini, Clara. "La lealtad americana: El significado de la estatua ecuestre de Carlos IV." In *Iconología y sociedad: Arte colonial hispanoamericano*. XLIV Congreso Internacional de Americanistas. Mexico City: UNAM, 1987.

———. *La arquitectura de la plata. Iglesias monumentales del centro-norte de México 1640–1750*. Mexico City: UNAM/IIE, 1991.

———. "Cristo en el arte barroco." In *Arte y mística del barroco*. Exhibition catalog. Mexico City: CONACULTA, 1994.

Barnadas, Joseph M. "The Catholic Church in Colonial Spanish America." In *The Cambridge History of Spanish America*. Vol. 1. Colonial Spanish America. Edited by Leslie Bethell. Cambridge: Cambridge University Press, 1984.

Bayon, Damián, and Murillo Marx. *History of South American Colonial Art and Architecture*. New York: Rizzoli, 1989.

Benavides Rodríguez, Alfredo. *La arquitectura en el Virreinato del Perú y en la Capitanía General de Chile*. 3rd edition. Santiago de Chile: Andrés Bello, 1988.

Bérchez, Joaquín. *Arquitectura mexicana de los siglos XVII y XVIII*. Arte Novohispano. Mexico City: Azabache, 1992.

Berdan, Frances F., and Patricia Rieff Anawalt. *The Essential Codex Mendoza*. Berkeley: University of California Press, 1997.

Bernales Ballesteros, Jorge. "La pintura en Lima durante el Virreinato." In *Pintura en el Virreinato del Perú*. Lima: El Libro de Arte del Centenario, 1989.

Black, Charlene Villaseñor. "Love and Marriage in the Spanish Empire: Depictions of Holy Matrimony and Gender Discourses in the Seventeenth Century." *Sixteenth Century Studies Journal* 32, no. 3 (2001): 637–68.

———. *Creating the Cult of St. Joseph: Art and Gender in the Spanish Empire*. Princeton: Princeton University Press, 2006.

Bonet Correa, Antonio. "Tratados de arquitectura y el arte en Colombia: Fray Domingo de Petrés." *Archivo Español de Arte* 44 (1991): 126–36.

Boone, Elizabeth Hill. *Stories in Red and Black: Pictorial Histories of the Aztecs and Mixtecs*. Austin: University of Texas Press, 2000.

———, and Thomas B. F. Cummins, "Colonial Foundations: Points of Contact and Compatibility." In *The Arts in Latin America 1492–1820*. Exhibition catalog. Philadelphia: Philadelphia Museum of Art, 2006.

Brading, D. A. *The First America: The Spanish Monarchy, Creole Patriots, and the Liberal State, 1492–1867*. Cambridge: Cambridge University Press, 1998.

———. *Mexican Phoenix. Our Lady of Guadalupe: Image and Tradition Across Five Centuries*. Cambridge: Cambridge University Press, 2001.

Brown, Thomas. *La Academia de San Carlos de la Nueva España*. Vol. 2. Mexico City: Secretaría de Educación Pública, 1976.

Burke, Marcus. *Treasures of Mexican Colonial Painting*. Davenport, IA: The Davenport Museum of Art, 1998.

Buschiazzo, Mario J. *Historia de la arquitectura colonial en Iberoamérica*. Buenos Aires: Emecé Editores, 1961.

Carrera, Magali M. *Imaging Identity in New Spain: Race, Lineage, and the Colonial Body in Portraiture and Casta Paintings*. Austin: University of Texas Press, 2003.

Carrillo y Gariel, Abelardo. *Datos soble la Academia de San Carlos de Nueva España: El arte en México de 1781 a 1863*. Mexico City: Academia de San Carlos, 1939.

Castelló Yturbide, Teresa, and Marita Martínez del Río de Redo. *Biombos novohispanos*. Mexico City: INAH, 1970.

Castro Morales, Efraín. "Un grabado neoclásico." *Anales del Instituto de Investigaciones Estéticas* 33 (1964): 107–10.

Catálogo comentado del acervo del Museo Nacional de Arte: Nueva España. Vols. I–II. Mexico City: Museo Nacional de Arte, 2004.

Cervantes de Salazar, Francisco. *Life of the Imperial and Loyal City of Mexico in New Spain* (1554). Translation by Minnie Lee Barrett Shephard with Introduction and Notes by Carlos Eduardo Castañeda. Reprint of University of Texas Press, 1953 edition. Westport, CT.: Greenwood Press, 1970.

Chacón Torres, Mario. *Arte virreinal en Potosí*. Sevilla: Escuela de Estudios Hispanoamericanos, 1973.

Chara Zereceda, Oscar, and Viviana Caparó Gil. *Iglesias del Cusco. Historia y arquitectura*. Cuzco: Editorial Universitaria UNSAAC, 1998.

Charlot, Jean. *Mexican Art and the Academy of San Carlos, 1785–1915*. Austin: University of Texas Press, 1962.

Cobo, Bernabé. *Obras del P. Bernabé Cobo*. Biblioteca de Autores Españoles. Madrid: Ediciones Atlas, 1956.

Codding, Mitchell A. "The Decorative Arts in Latin America, 1492–1820." In *The Arts in Latin America 1492–1807*. Exhibition catalog. Philadelphia: Philadelphia Museum of Art, 2006.

Converging Cultures: Art and Identity in Spanish America. Exhibition catalog. Editor Diana Fane. New York: The Brooklyn Museum in association with Harry N. Abrams, 1996.

Córdova Tello, Mario. *El convento de San Miguel de Huejotzingo, Pue*. Mexico City: INAH, 1992.

Cortés, Hernán. *Letters from Mexico*. Translated and edited by Anthony Pagden. Introduction by J. H. Elliott. New Haven and London: Yale University Press, 1986.

Cruz de Amenabar, Isabel, and Graciela Viñuales. "La pintura en Chile y en el Virreinato del Río de la Plata." In *Pintura, escultura y artes útiles en Iberoamérica, 1500–1821*, edited by Ramón Gutiérrez. Madrid: Ediciones Cátedra, 1995.

Cuadriello, Jaime. "Tierra de prodigios: La ventura como destino." In *Los pinceles de la historia: El origen del Reino de la Nueva España 1680–1750*. Mexico City: Museo Nacional de Arte, 1999.

Los cuadros de mestizaje del Virrey Amat: La representación etnográfica en el Perú colonial. Exhibition catalog. Lima: Museo de Arte de Lima, 2000.

Cummins, Thomas B. F. "The Madonna and the Horse: Becoming Colonial in New Spain and Peru." In *Native Artists and Patrons in Colonial Spanish America*, edited by Emily Umberger and Tom Cummins. *Phoebus: A Journal of Art History*. Phoenix: Arizona State University, 1995.

———. "Representation in the Sixteenth Century and the Colonial Image of the Inca." In *Writing Without Words: Alternative Literacies in Mesoamerica and the Andes*, edited by Elizabeth Hill Boone and Walter D. Mignolo. Durham and London: Duke University Press, 1996.

————. "A Tale of Two Cities: Cuzco, Lima and the Construction of Colonial Representation." In *Converging Cultures: Art and Identity in Spanish America*. Exhibition catalog. Edited by Diana Fane. New York: Harry N. Abrams, 1996.

————. *Toasts with the Inca: Andean Abstraction and Colonial Images on Quero Vessels*. Ann Arbor: University of Michigan Press, 2002.

Curcio-Nagy, Linda. *The Great Festivals of Colonial Mexico City: Performing Power and Identity*. Diálogos Series. Albuquerque: University of New Mexico Press, 2004.

Curiel, Gustavo. "Los biombos novohispanos: Escenografías de poder y transculturación en el ámbito doméstico." In *Viento detenido: Mitologías e historias en el arte del biombo. Colección de biombos de los siglos XVII al XIX del Museo Soumaya*. Mexico City: Museo Soumaya, 1999.

Curiel, Gustavo, Fausto Ramírez, Antonio Rubial, and Angélica Velázquez. *Pintura y vida cotidiana en México 1650–1950*. Mexico City: Fomento Cultural Banamex/CONACULTA, 1999.

Damian, Carol. *The Virgin of the Andes: Art and Ritual of Colonial Cuzco*. Miami Beach: Grassfield Press, 1995.

Dean, Carolyn. "The Renewal of Old World Images and the Creation of Colonial Peruvian Visual Culture." In *Converging Cultures: Art and Identity in Spanish America*. Exhibition catalog. Edited by Diana Fane. New York: The Brooklyn Museum/Harry N. Abrams, 1996.

————. *Inka Bodies and the Body of Christ: Corpus Christi in Colonial Cuzco, Peru*. Durham and London: Duke University Press, 1999.

Díaz, Marco. "Arquitectura en Tepotzotlán." In *Museo Nacional del Virreinato. Tepotzotlán la vida y la obra en la Nueva España*. 2nd edition. Mexico City: CONACULTA/INAH, 2003.

Díaz Silva, Patricia. "Reactivando la memoria: El pintor retratista José Gil de Castro (1785–1841)." In *José Gil de Castro en Chile*. Exhibition catalog. Santiago de Chile: Museo Nacional de Bellas Artes, 1994.

Duncan, Barbara. "Statue Paintings of the Virgin." In *Gloria in excelsis: The Virgin and Angels in Viceregal Painting of Peru and Bolivia*. New York: Center for Inter-American Relations, 1986.

Durán Montero, María Antonia. *Lima en el siglo XVII. Arquitectura, urbanismo y vida cotidiana*. Sevilla: Diputación Provincial de Sevilla, 1994.

Early, James. *The Colonial Architecture of Mexico*. Albuquerque: University of New Mexico Press, 1994.

————. *Presidio, Mission, and Pueblo: Spanish Architecture and Urbanism in the United States*. Dallas: Southern Methodist University Press, 2004.

Edgerton, Samuel Y. *Theaters of Conversion: Religious Architecture and Indian Artisans in Colonial Mexico*. Albuquerque: University of New Mexico Press, 2001.

Espinosa Spinola, Gloria. *Arquitectura de la conversión y evangelización en la Nueva España durante el siglo XVI*. Almería: Universidad de Almería, 1999.

Estrada de Gerlero, Elena Isabel. "The Representation of 'Heathen Indians' in New Spanish Casta Painting." In *New World Orders: Casta Painting and Colonial Latin America*. Exhibition catalog. New York: Americas Society Art Gallery, 1996.

————. "El retrato en la Nueva España en el siglo XVI." In *El retrato civil en la Nueva España*. Exhibition catalog. [Mexico City]: CONACULTA/INBA, 1991.

Fernández, Justino. *Estética del arte mexicano*. Mexico City: UNAM/IIE, 1972.

Fernández, Martha. *Arquitectura y gobierno virreinal. Los maestros mayores de la Ciudad de México siglo XVII*. Mexico City: UNAM/IIE, 1985.

———. *Cristóbal de Medina Vargas y la arquitectura salomónica en la Nueva España durante el siglo XVII*. Mexico City: UNAM/IIE, 2002.

Flores Ochoa, Jorge A., Elizabeth Kuon Arce, and Roberto Samanez Argumedo. *Pintura mural en el sur andino*. Colección Arte y Tesoros del Perú. Lima: Banco de Crédito de Perú, 1993.

Fraser, Valerie. *The Architecture of Conquest: Building in the Viceroyalty of Peru 1535–1635*. Cambridge Iberian and Spanish American Studies. Edited by P. E. Russell. Cambridge: Cambridge University Press, 1989.

Frías Núñez, Marcelo. *Tras El Dorado vegetal: José Celestino Mutis y la Real Expedición Botánica del Nuevo Reino de Granada (1783–1808)*. Sevilla: Diputación de Sevilla, 1994.

García Granados, Rafael, and Luis MacGregor. *Huejotzingo: La ciudad y el convento franciscano*. Mexico City: Talleres Gráficos de la Nación, 1934.

García Sáiz, María Concepción. *Las castas novohispanas: Un género pictórico americano*. Madrid: Olivetti, 1989.

———. "Nuevos materiales para nuevas expresiones." In *Los siglos de oro en los Virreinatos de América: 1550–1700*. Exhibition catalog. Madrid: Sociedad Estatal para la Conmemoración de los Centenarios de Felipe II y Carlos V, 1999.

Garcilaso de la Vega. *Royal Commentaries of the Incas and General History of Peru*. Translated and with an introduction by Harold V. Livermore. Austin and London: University of Texas Press, 1966.

Gisbert, Teresa. *Iconografía y mitos indígenas en el arte*. La Paz: Editorial Gisbert, 1980.

———. "Andean Painting." In *Gloria in excelsis: The Virgin and Angels in Viceregal Painting of Peru and Bolivia*. Exhibition catalog. New York: Center for Inter-American Relations, 1986.

———. "The Artistic World of Guaman Poma." In *Guaman Poma de Ayala: The Colonial Art of an Andean Author*. New York: Americas Society, 1992.

———. "La pintura mural andina." In *Catastro, evaluación y estudio de la pintura mural en el area centro sur andina*. La Paz: Organización de los Estados Americanos, 1998.

———. *El paraíso de los pájaros parlantes: La imagen del otro en la cultura andina*. La Paz: Plural Editores, 2001.

———, and José de Mesa. *Arquitectura andina 1530–1830*. 2nd edition. La Paz: Embajada de España en Bolivia, 1997.

Glass, John B. "A Census of Middle American Testerian Manuscripts." In *Handbook of Middle American Indians*. Vol. 14. General Editor Robert Wauchope. *Guide to Ethnohistorical Sources*. Part 3. Volume Editor Howard F. Cline. Austin: University of Texas Press, 1975.

González-Polo, Ignacio. "Barroco vs. Neoclásico en la arquitectura novohispana." *Revista de la Universidad de México* XLIV, no. 467 (1989): 11–18.

———. "La posición de los criollos en la Academia de San Carlos (1785–1800)." *Revista de la Universidad de México* XLVI, no. 480–81 (1991): 67–70.

Gruzinski, Serge. *El águila y la sibila: Frescos indios de México*. Barcelona: Moleiro Editor, 1994.

———. *Images at War: Mexico from Columbus to Blade Runner (1492–2019)*. Translated by Heather MacLean. Durham and London: Duke University Press, 2001.

Gutiérrez, Ramón. *The Jesuit Guaraní Missions/Les missions jésuites des Guaranies*. Rio de Janeiro: UNESCO, 1987.

Gutiérrez, Ramón, Rodolfo Vallín, and Verónica Perfetti. *Fray Domingo Petrés y su obra arquitectónica en Colombia*. Bogotá: Banco de la República/Ancora Editores, 1999.

Gutiérrez, Ramón, Carlos Pernaut, Graciela Viñuales, Hernán Rodríguez Villegas, Rodolfo Vallin Magaña, Bertha Estela Benavides, Elizabeth Kuon Arce, and Jesús Lambarri. *Arquitectura del altiplano peruano*. 2nd edition. Buenos Aires: Libros de Hispanoamérica, 1986.

Hecht, Johanna. "Eighteenth-Century Mexico: Tradition and Transformation (1715–1785)." In *Mexico: Splendors of Thirty Centuries*. Exhibition catalog. New York: The Metropolitan Museum of Art, 1990.

Herzberg, Julia P. "Angels with Guns: Image and Interpretation." In *Gloria in excelsis: The Virgin and Angels in Viceregal Painting of Peru and Bolivia*. New York: Center for Inter-American Relations, 1986.

Iberoamérica mestiza. Encuentro de pueblos y culturas. Exhibition catalog. Madrid: Fundación Santillana, 2003.

José Gil de Castro en Chile. Exhibition catalog. Santiago de Chile: Museo Nacional de Bellas Artes, 1994.

Juegos de ingenio y agudeza: La pintura emblemática de la Nueva España. Exhibition catalog. Mexico City: Patronato del Museo Nacional de Arte, 1994.

Kagan, Richard. *Urban Images of the Hispanic World 1493–1793*. New Haven and London: Yale University Press, 2000.

Katzew, Ilona. "Casta Painting: Identity and Social Stratification in Colonial Mexico." In *New World Orders: Casta Painting and Colonial Latin America*. Exhibition catalog. New York: Americas Society Art Gallery, 1996.

————. *Casta Painting: Images of Race in Eighteenth-Century Mexico*. New Haven and London: Yale University Press, 2004.

Kennedy Troya, Alexandra. "La pinturas en el Nuevo Reino de Granada." In *Pintura, escultura y artes útiles en Iberoamérica, 1500–1825*, coordinator Ramón Gutiérrez. Madrid: Ediciones Cedra, 1995.

Kubler, George. *Mexican Architecture of the Sixteenth Century*. New Haven: Yale University Press, 1948.

————, and Martin Soria. *Art and Architecture in Spain and Portugal and their American Dominions 1500–1800*. The Pelican History of Art. Baltimore: Penguin Books, 1959.

Lara, Jaime. *City, Temple, Stage: Eschatological Architecture and Liturgical Theatrics in New Spain*. New Haven: Yale University Press, 2004.

Leibsohn, Dana. "Colony and Cartography: Shifting Signs on Indigenous Maps of New Spain." In *Reframing the Renaissance: Visual Culture in Europe and Spanish America 1450–1650*, edited by Claire Farago. New Haven: Yale University Press, 1995.

López Guzmán, Rafael, Lázaro Gila Medina, Ignacio Henares Cuellar, and Guillermo Tovar de Teresa. *Arquitectura y carpintería mudéjar en Nueva España*. Arte Novohispano #7. Mexico City: Azabache, 1992.

Macera, Pablo. *La pintura mural andina siglos XVI–XIX*. Lima: Editorial Milla Batres, 1993.

The Malaspina Expedition 1789–1794: Journal of the Voyage by Alejandro Malaspina. Vol. 1. Edited by Andrew David, Felipe Fernández-Armesto, Carlos Novi, and Glyndwr Williams. Introduction by Donald Cutter. London: The Hakluyt Society and the Museo Naval, 2001.

Manuel Tolsá: Nostalgia de la "antiguo" y arte ilustrado México-Valencia. Exhibition catalog. Mexico City: Generalitat Valenciana/Consorci de Museus de la Comunitat Valenciana/UNAM, 1998.

Mariátegui Oliva, Ricardo. *La ciudad de Arequipa del siglo XVII en el Monasterio de Santa Catalina*. Lima: n.p., 1952.

————. *José Gil de Castro ("El Mulato Gil"): Vida y obra del gran pintor peruano de los libertadores*. Lima: Año Bicentenario de la rebelión emancipadora de Tupac Amaru y Micaela Bastidas, 1981.

Martínez del Río de Redo, Marita. "El retrato novohispano en los siglos XVII y XVIII." In *El retrato civil en la Nueva España*. Exhibition catalog. [Mexico City]: CONACULTA/INBA, 1991.

————. "Los biombos en el ámbito doméstico: Sus programas moralizadores y didácticos." In *Juegos de ingenio y agudeza: La pintura emblemática de la Nueva España*. Exhibition catalog. Mexico City: Patronato del Museo Nacional de Arte, 1994.

McNaspy, C. J. *Lost Cities of Paraguay: Art and Architecture of the Jesuit Reductions 1607–1767*. Chicago: Loyola University Press, 1982.

Meikeljohn, Norman. *La iglesia y los Lupacas de Chuchito durante la colonia*. Cuzco: Centro de Estudios Rurales Andinos "Bartolomé de las Casa"/Instituto de Estudios Aymaras, 1988.

Mesa, José de. "Painting in Potosí." In *Potosí: Colonial Treasures and the Bolivian City of Silver*. Exhibition catalog. New York: Americas Society Art Gallery, 1997.

————. *Expresión de fe: Templos en Bolivia*. La Paz: Editorial Quipus y Entel, 1998.

————, and Teresa Gisbert. *Bolivia: Monumentos históricos y arqueológicos*. Comisión de Historia 122. Monumentos Históricos y Arqueológicos XV. Mexico City: Instituto Panamericano de Geografía e Historia, 1970.

————. *Historia de la pintura cuzqueña*. Lima: Fundación Augusto N. Wiese, 1982.

Mexico: Splendors of Thirty Centuries. Exhibition catalog. New York: The Metropolitan Museum of Art, 1990.

México en el mudo de las colecciones de arte: Nueva España. Mexico City: Secretaría de Relaciones Exteriores/UNAM/IIE/CONACULTA, 1994.

Mínguez Cornelles, Víctor. "Efímero mestizo." In *Iberoamérica mestiza. Encuentro de pueblos y culturas*. Madrid: Fundación Santillana, 2003.

Montero Alarcón, Alma. *Monjas coronadas*. Mexico City: CONACULTA, 1999.

Montes de Oca, José G. *San Agustín de Acolman, Estado de México*. Mexico City: Biblioteca Enciclopédica del Estado de México, 1975.

Moreno Villarreal, Jaime. "In Praise of Heat and Fan." In *El retrato novohispano en el siglo XVIII*. Exhibition catalog. Puebla: Museo Poblano de Arte Virreinal, 1999.

Moyssen, Xavier. "La primera academia de pintura en México." *Anales del Instituto de Investigaciones Estéticas* 35 (1965): 15–30.

Mundy, Barbara E. *The Mapping of New Spain: Indigenous Cartography and the Maps of the Relaciones Geográficas*. Chicago: University of Chicago Press, 1996.

Muriel, Josefina. *Los conventos de monjas en la Nueva España*. Mexico City: Editorial Santiago, 1946.

Navarro Castro, Gustavo. "Latin American Iconography of Saint James the Killer of Moors." In *America: Bride of the Sun: 500 Years Latin America and the Low Countries*. Exhibition catalog. Antwerp: Imschoot Books, 1992.

Nichols, H. B. "Fray Bernardino de Sahagún: A Spanish Missionary in New Spain, 1529–1590." In *Representing Aztec Ritual: Performance, Text, and Image in the Work of Sahagún*, edited by Eloise Quiñones Keber. Boulder: University Press of Colorado, 2002.

Noguez, Xavier. *Tira de Tepechpan: Códice colonial procedente del valle de México*. Mexico City: Biblioteca Enciclopédica del Estado de México, 1978.

Palmer, Gabrielle. *Sculpture in the Kingdom of Quito*. Albuquerque: University of New Mexico Press, 1987.

Palmer, Gabrielle, and Donna Pierce. *Cambios: The Spirit of Transformation in Spanish Colonial Art*. Albuquerque: University of New Mexico Press, 1992.

Perú: Fe y arte en el virreinato. Exhibition catalog. Córdoba: Publicaciones obra Social y Cultural Cajasur, 1999.

Peterson, Jeanette Favrot. *The Paradise Garden Murals of Malinalco: Utopía and Empire in Sixteenth-Century Mexico*. Austin: University of Texas Press, 1993.

———. "Synthesis and Survival: The Native Presence in Sixteenth-Century Murals of New Spain." In *Native Artists and Patrons in Colonial Spanish America*, edited by Emily Umberger and Tom Cummins. *Phoebus: A Journal of Art History*. Phoenix: Arizona State University, 1995.

Phipps, Elena J. "Textiles as Cultural Memory: Andean Garments in the Colonial Period." In *Converging Cultures: Art and Identity in Spanish America*. Exhibition catalog. Edited by Diana Fane. New York: The Brooklyn Museum in association with Harry N. Abrams, 1996.

Pierce, Donna, Rogelio Ruiz Gomar, and Clara Bargellini. *Painting a New World: Mexican Art and Life 1521–1821*. Exhibition catalog. Denver: Denver Art Museum, 2004.

Los pinceles de la historia. El origen del reino de la Nueva España, 1680–1750. Exhibition catalog. Mexico City: Museo Nacional de Arte/Banamex/IIE/CONACULTA, INBA, 1999.

Los pinceles de la historia. De la patria criolla a la nación mexicana. Exhibition catalog. Mexico City: Museo Nacional de Arte/Banamex/IIE/CONACULTA, INBA, 2000.

Pintura en el Virreinato del Perú. Lima: El Libro de Arte del Centenario, 1989.

Proyecto, estatutos, y demás documentos relacionados al establecimiento de la Real Academia de pintura, escultura, y arquitectura de Nueva España (1781–1802). Facsímile edition. Colección Documenta Novae Hispaniae. Editor David Marley. Mexico City: Rolston-Bain, 1984.

Quiñones Keber, Eloise. *Codex Telleriano-Remensis: Ritual, Divination, and History in a Pictorial Aztec Manuscript*. Austin: University of Texas Press, 1995.

———. "Representing Aztec Ritual in the Work of Sahagún." In *Representing Aztec Ritual: Performance, Text, and Image in the Work of Sahagún*, edited by Eloise Quiñones Keber. Boulder: University Press of Colorado, 2002.

Ramírez del Villar, Roberto. "Un monumento de la Lima virreinal." In *San Francisco de Lima*. Tesoros del Arte Colonial Peruano. Lima: Auge, 1974.

El retrato novohispano en el siglo XVIII. Exhibition catalog. Puebla: Museo Poblano de Arte Virreinal, 1999.

Reyes Valerio, Constantino. *Arte indocristiano*. Mexico City: INAH, 2000.

Robertson, Donald. *Mexican Manuscript Painting of the Early Colonial Period: The Metropolitan Schools*. Norman: University of Oklahoma Press, 1994.

Rodríguez G. de Ceballos, Alfonso. "Usos y funciones de la imagen religiosa en los virreinatos americanos." In *Los siglos de oro en los Virreinatos de América 1550–1700*. Exhibition catalog. Madrid: Sociedad Estatal para la Conmemoración de los Centenarios de Felipe II y Carlos V, 1999.

Romero de Tejada y Picatoste, Pilar. "Los cuadros de mestizaje del virrey Amat." In *Los cuadros de mestizaje del Virrey Amat: La representación etnográfica en el Perú colonial*. Exhibition catalog. Lima: Museo de Arte de Lima, 2000.

Salas Cuesta, Marcela. *La iglesia y el convento de Huejotzingo*. Mexico City: UNAM, 1982.

Salles-Reese, Verónica. *From Viracocha to the Virgin of Copacabana: Representation of the Sacred at Lake Titicaca*. Austin: University of Texas Press, 1997.

San Cristóbal Sebastián, Antonio de. *Arquitectura virreynal religiosa de Lima*. Lima: Studium, 1988.

———. *Lima: Estudios de la arquitectura virreinal*. Lima: Epígrafe Editores, 1992.

———. *Arquitectura planiforme y textilográfica virreinal de Arequipa*. Arequipa: Universidad Nacional de San Agustín de Arequipa, 1997.

———. "Reinterpretación de la arquitectura planiforme." In *Territorio, espacio, y arte. Arte barroco iberoamericano*. Sevilla: Universidad Pablo Olavide, 2002.

El Santuario de Copacabana de La Paz a Tiahuanaco. Documentos de Arte Colonial Sudamericano. Cuaderno VII. Buenos Aires: Academia Nacional de Bellas Artes de la República Argentina, 1950.

Sebastián, Santiago. *El barroco iberoamericano. Mensaje iconográfico*. Madrid: Ediciones Encuentro, 1990.

———, José de Mesa Figueroa, and Teresa Gisbert de Mesa. *Arte iberoamericano desde la colonización a la independencia*. Summa Artis Historia General del Arte. Vol. XXVIII, primera parte. 3rd edition. Madrid: Espasa-Calpe, 1989.

———, Mariano Moterrosa, and José Antonio Terán. *Iconografía del arte del siglo XVI en México*. Mexico City: Gobierno del Estado de Zacatecas/Ayuntamiento de Zacatecas/Universidad Autónoma de Zacatecas, 1995.

Los siglos de oro en los Virreinatos de América: 1550–1700. Exhibition catalog. Madrid: Sociedad Estatal para la Conmemoración de los Centenarios de Felipe II y Carlos V, 1999.

Sotos Serrano, Carmen. *Los pintores de la expedición de Alejandro Malaspina*. Vol. 1. Madrid: Real Academia de la Historia, 1982.

Stratton-Pruitt, Suzanne. *The Virgin, Saints, and Angels: South American Paintings 1600–1825 from the Thoma Collection*. Stanford: Skira in association with the Iris and B. Gerald Cantor Centor for Visual Arts at Stanford University, 2006.

Tandeter, Enrique. *Coercion and Market: Silver Mining in Colonial Potosí, 1692–1826*. Albuquerque: University of New Mexico Press, 1993.

Tord, Luis Enrique, and Pedro Gjurinovic. *El palacio de Torre Tagle y las casonas de Lima/The Torre Tagle Palace and the Old Mansions of Lima*. Lima: Asociación de Funcionarios del Servicio Diplomático del Perú, 2001.

Toussaint, Manuel. *Arte colonial en México*. 5th edition. Mexico City: UNAM/IIE, 1990.

———. *Pintura colonial en México*. 3rd edition. Mexico City: UNAM/IIE, 1990.

———. *La Catedral de México y el Sagrario Metropolitano. Su historia, su tesoro, su arte*. 3rd edition. Mexico City: Porrúa, 1992.

Tovar de Teresa, Guillermo. "La Iglesia de San Francisco Xavier de Tepotzotlán: Eco de la vida artística de la ciudad de México en los siglos XVII y XVIII." *Archivo Español de Arte* 61, no. 244 (1988): 31–41.

———. *Jerónimo de Balbás en la Catedral de México*. Mexico City: Asociación Amigos de la Catedral Metropolitana, 1990.

———. "La Utopia del Virrey Mendoza." In *La Utopia mexicana del siglo XVI: Lo bello, lo verdadero, y lo bueno*. Mexico City: Grupo Azabache, 1992.

———. *Miguel Cabrera: Pintor de cámara de la reina celestial*. Mexico City: Inver Mexico Grupo Financiero, 1995.

Uribe, Eloisa. "El dibujo, la Real Academia de San Carlos de Nueva España y las polémicas culturales del siglo XVIII." In *Arte de las academias: Francia y México, siglos XVII–XIX*. Exhibition catalog. Mexico City: Antiguo Colegio de San Ildefonso, 1999.

Vargaslugo, Elisa. *Estudios de pintura colonial hispanoamericana*. Mexico City: UNAM, 1992.

————, José Guadalupe Victoria, et. al. *Juan Correa: Su vida y su obra*. Mexico City: UNAM/IIE, 1985.

Velasco, Juan de. *Historia del Reino de Quito en la América meridional*. Edición, prólogo, notas y cronología Alfredo Pareja Diezcanseco. Caracas: Biblioteca Ayacucho, 1981.

Viento detenido: Mitologías e historias en el arte del biombo. Colección de biombos de los siglos XVII al XIX del Museo Soumaya. Mexico City: Museo Soumaya, 1999.

von Barghahn, Barbara. "Imaging the Holy Family of Nazareth in the Viceregal Andes: An Alloy of European and Inca Cultures." In *The Holy Family as Prototype of the Civilization of Love: Images from the Viceregal Americas*, edited by Joseph F. Chorpenning. Philadelphia: Saint Joseph's University Press, 1996.

Webster, Susan Verdi. *Arquitectura y empresa en el Quito colonial: José Jaime Ortiz, Alarife Mayor*. Quito: Abya Yala, 2002.

Wethey, Harold. *Colonial Architecture and Sculpture in Peru*. Cambridge: Harvard University Press, 1949.

Wuffarden, Luis Eduardo. "Effigies of the Incas or Kings of Peru." In *The Arts in Latin America 1492–1820*. Exhibition catalog. Philadelphia: Philadelphia Museum of Art, 2006.

Zavala, Silvio. *Una etapa en la construcción de la catedral de México alrededor de 1585*. Jornadas 96. Mexico City: El Colegio de México, 1995.

INDEX

Note: Page numbers set in italics indicate illustrations. Plates (PL.) are located between pages 132 and 133.